ALSO BY T. M. LUHRMANN

Persuasions of the Witch's Craft

The Good Parsi

OF TWO MINDS

OF TWO MINDS

THE GROWING DISORDER IN AMERICAN PSYCHIATRY

T. M. LUHRMANN

ALFRED A. KNOPF   NEW YORK   2000

THIS IS A BORZOI BOOK
PUBLISHED BY ALFRED A. KNOPF

Copyright © 2000 by T. M. Luhrmann
All rights reserved under International and Pan-American Copyright Conventions.
Published in the United States by Alfred A. Knopf, a division of Random House, Inc., New York,
and simultaneously in Canada by Random House of Canada Limited, Toronto.
Distributed by Random House, Inc., New York.

www.aaknopf.com

Knopf, Borzoi Books, and the colophon are registered trademarks of Random House, Inc.

Library of Congress Cataloging-in-Publication Data
Luhrmann, T. M. (Tanya M.), [date]
Of two minds : the growing disorder in American psychiatry / T. M. Luhrmann.
        p.   cm.
Includes bibliographical references and index.
ISBN 0-679-42191-2
1. Psychiatry—Study and teaching.   2. Psychiatry.
I. Title.
RC336.L78   2000
616.89'0071'173—dc21
99-40732
CIP

Manufactured in the United States of America

First Edition

For my father

I would like to thank my wife, Sally. . . . Along those lines—Thanks respectively to Wyeth/Ayerst Laboratories and Stuart Pharmaceuticals for further expanding that narrow channel of joy by manufacturing Effexor and Elavil; drugs so good they feel illegal.

—Thom Jones, *Cold Snap*

Trying to understand experiences that are at once personal and cultural calls for a kind of passionate detachment that is, I think, almost impossible to sustain alone. Susan Robertson, my psychotherapist, has been a constant source of emotional support and thoughtful analysis.

—Kathryn Dudley, *The End of the Line*

CONTENTS

AUTHOR'S NOTE

This ethnographic material has been taken from hundreds of hours of tape recording, note taking, and more casual conversation. In the interest of anonymity, the names of people interviewed have been changed (except for some whose work, by its visible nature, removes their anonymity). In the interests of coherence, some quotations have been edited for flow, although content has been preserved. And in the interests of both narration and anonymity, some individuals, while loosely based on real people, are intended to be composite figures, and some quotations by other people have been attributed to them. The story of "Gertrude," for example, is a composite of events in the lives of three different women. All the events, it should be said, happened in the manner described, and all the details and quotations are accurate within the limits of anthropological note taking, although identifying details have been omitted or changed. Some quotations are based on taped conversations. Others are based on field notes taken after the encounter and often recorded in the third person.

OF TWO MINDS

INTRODUCTION

In the autumn of 1989, I arrived as a new assistant professor in an anthropology department known for its long tradition of psychological anthropology. I was already an experienced ethnographer, with a book on modern witchcraft behind me and another on Zoroastrianism under way. But I was a relative newcomer to psychological anthropology, at least in its American form (I had done my training in England), and my colleagues suggested that it might be helpful for me to attend the lectures to the new psychiatrists in training.

American psychological anthropology grew out of a tradition of using psychoanalytic ideas to make sense of cultural practices. (My background was more cognitive.) Margaret Mead was one of its founding mothers. She used a loosely Freudian understanding of childhood experience in different societies to explain their adult behavior. So for years, graduate students in my department had been sent to learn a clinical perspective on Freud and psychoanalysis from the lectures given to young psychiatrists. As it happened, they had long been complaining that the lectures had nothing to do with anthropology, but I didn't know that at the time. I just showed up, with a mixture of excitement and trepidation, in a year when no graduate students came along.

I told myself that the lectures would not be entirely unfamiliar territory: my father is a psychiatrist, and I myself had seriously considered becoming one, settling on anthropology because I saw myself more as a writer of books than as a healer of patients. As one of my colleagues points out, this makes me a "halfie" anthropologist, someone who grew up half in the world she writes about professionally, like an anthropologist with an Egyptian father who goes off to live with the Bedouin. There are a number of halfie anthropologists these days. Being one gives you a little edge, because you grew up speaking the language of the world you later describe.

So when I began to go to the Thursday-morning classes for the new psychiatrists in training, I was not thinking of writing an ethnography. I wanted to learn about psychosis and depression, how psychoanalysis works, and whether the psychiatric illnesses I saw in San Diego would look the same in Tibet and Borneo, places where virtually no one had heard of Freud. For six months I went to two classes every Thursday morning, fascinated by this complicated, contradictory, confusing world. Then one of the young psychiatrists turned around one morning and asked, "Why don't you write about us? Isn't that what anthropologists do?"

He was, of course, right. (He was also somewhat alarmed that I took him seriously.) I had found the process of psychiatric training—at least, what I could see of it then—disturbing and perplexing but also deeply intriguing. I knew I was beginning to see people in a different way, to search for the marks of darker moods in the way they held themselves and glanced and gestured. In part that was because I was literally beginning to see different people. In the everyday world, you don't see the patients who end up in psychiatric inpatient units, or at least you don't see them sick. The odds are that in a lecture hall of a hundred students, several have something seriously amiss psychiatrically, but I rarely saw it; nonpsychiatrists rarely do. When people were a little too impulsive, a little too sad, a little too thin, it was easy to read them as having a bad week. They were still normal, still like "us." (There was, of course, the student who took exception to Émile Durkheim and on the morning of the final exam presented me with the charred remains of *The Elementary Forms of the Religious Life.* She was unusual.)

In these psychiatry classes, I saw a man brought in for treatment because he had been found in his kitchen, holding his wife's bloody heart in his hands, a carving knife beside him on the floor. I remember a woman, a graduate student in comparative literature at one of the best schools in the country, with long, golden *Baywatch* hair. But she hunched over with her hair across her face and her misery was so palpable that my throat choked up as if I would cry. I remember a man so anxious that I wanted to jump from my chair and run, but the room was full of watching students and the man's eyes scanned us forward and back. Nobody dared to move. I began to be afraid of the highway, because two patients said they had thought of committing suicide by shutting their eyes at seventy miles per hour. A little later I met an undergraduate who was sophisticated, chic, articulate, slender—when I had been an undergraduate, I had yearned to be someone like that, an Audrey Hepburn from Central Park West—and she was checking into the hospital because she was anorexic and her mother was divorcing her father and sending her money from Europe but not answering the phone.

After a few months, it was impossible to doubt that there was a "there"

there of psychiatric illness. Grand sociological theories that claimed that psychiatry punished those who were merely eccentric and unconventional seemed absurd to me. I began to see in students, friends, and supermarket baggers little flickers of the craziness I saw in case conferences. Then I began to worry that I was seeing more than was there. I became fascinated by what psychiatrists saw, how they knew what they knew, whether they were right, and what that even meant.

Psychiatry is unquenchably compelling because it forever changes the way you understand human experience. It lets you into the back bedroom of conventional behavior, so that you glimpse behind the polite interfaces of everyday life the true weirdness of human feeling. It shows you despair harsher than you had imagined and exhilarating, terrifying ecstasy and strange irrationality. Most of us are charitable interpreters of other people's behavior, to use the philosopher Donald Davidson's phrase. We assume that other people are just like us—normal—until it becomes apparent that they are not. Psychiatry forces upon you, more abruptly and with an in-your-face confrontation, the lessons anthropology is meant to teach: that the landscape of human thought and feeling is more gaunt and jagged but also more breathtaking than most of us, Horatio-like, have dreamed of in our little local worlds. I thought that if I could describe the way I was learning to see, which is the way psychiatrists are taught how to see, I would be doing what every anthropologist is supposed to do, but by traveling into the familiar, not away to the exotic.

But psychiatrists do not see in one single manner. The Thursday-morning lectures were remarkably diverse. Some mornings, men would come in wearing white medical coats. They would talk about neurotransmitters and catecholamines and draw diagrams of biochemical interactions on the board. They spoke a language I hadn't heard since high school science. Other mornings, men (almost always men) would arrive in tweed jackets, wearing spectacles. They would sit, hands folded, and talk with us about loss, mourning, and the nadir point in psychotherapy. They spoke as if life happened inside the mind. There was someone who drew graphs that explained when schizophrenics were born (he thought the Christmas drinking season might be partly to blame), someone else who practiced therapy but didn't believe in the unconscious, and yet another who carefully wrote Erik Erikson's life stages on the board and then never discussed them. I heard lectures on alcohol, combat, sexual abuse, sleep disorders, epilepsy, and the whole range of psychopharmacological treatments. Behind all this, behind the advice, the biochemical diagrams, and the commentary about psychotherapeutic transference, lay at least two profoundly different notions of what it is to be a person: to feel, to choose, to do good, to have meaning. No one mentioned those deep issues explicitly. They talked about what you should do with a particular patient. But surrounding the practice issues around, say, a late-night suicidal phone call were some of our oldest philosophical dilemmas.

Why do we suffer? In the dramas of classical antiquity, we watch great individuals suffer, and we feel pity and terror for them because in the inexorable doom of the unfolding story, we see that they are caught up in circumstances they have not chosen but in which they have made choices that will destroy them. Antigone does not choose the conflict between blood rights and state rights: her greatness is that she sees but does not flinch from the moral need to bury her brother, despite her king's command that she must not. Being the person she is, she chooses to honor family over king, and so she dies whereas another person might have lived. The flaws in her character are also the unwavering commitments that make her great. Today we use the word "tragedy" in a more pedestrian sense, to refer to personal circumstances over which we genuinely have no control: an aircraft exploding in midflight, a flood wiping out a summer's crops, a senseless, arbitrary murder. I say pedestrian, but life is really made up of small circumstances that hem us in so tightly that we can scarcely move. To understand that these circumstances are more important than the choices we make within them is to see a very different staging of human experience. That difference is the major tension in the way psychiatrists are taught to look at the world.

Psychiatrists have inherited the Cartesian dualism that is so marked a feature of our spiritual and moral landscape. Sometimes they talk about mental anguish as if it were cardiac disease: you treat it with medication, rest, and advice about the right way to eat and live. A person who has had a heart attack will never be the same—he will be always a person who has been very seriously ill—but he is not his heart attack. His heart attack is in the body, not the mind. When psychiatrists talk in this manner, psychosis and depression become likewise written on the body. This style of speaking has gained preeminence in the last two decades. It is usually called "biomedical" psychiatry, an approach to mental illness that treats it as an illness of the body that is more or less comparable to other physical illnesses. Sometimes, though, psychiatrists talk about distress as something much more complicated, something that involves the kind of person you are: your intentions, your loves and hates, your messy, complicated past. This style is associated with psychoanalysis and psychoanalytic psychotherapy, usually called "psychodynamic," which dominated psychiatry in the middle decades of this century and which remains the fountainhead of all psychotherapies. From this vantage point, mental illness is in your mind and in your emotional reactions to other people. It is your "you."

Of course, this is a false dichotomy, as most psychiatrists would agree.

But it is the way that psychiatrists are taught. It seemed clear to me that there were, broadly speaking, two main areas of skill that psychiatrists in training are expected to acquire: on the one hand, diagnosis and psycho-pharmacology, which are usually the dominant focus of inpatient psychiatry, and, on the other, psychodynamic psychotherapy, which tends to be taught as an outpatient specialization distinct from the skills of hospital psychiatry. The psychiatrists and the staff I spent time with spoke comfortably about the differences between psychotherapy and biomedical psychiatry. They argued about psychiatry in ways that took the dichotomy for granted. Their training schedule (at least two lectures a week, usually one on psychopharmacology and diagnosis, another on psychotherapy) clearly indicated that their seniors thought that those were the two major and different areas of skill. They learned two different ways to identify, understand, and respond to mental anguish. Young psychiatrists are supposed to learn to be equally good at both talk therapy and drug therapy, psychotherapy and biomedical psychiatry, and the American Psychiatric Association thinks that this integration is what training programs in psychiatry teach. Psychiatrists are supposed to understand these approaches as different tools in a common toolbox. Yet they are taught as different tools, based on different models, and used for different purposes. Some psychiatrists do integrate them to some extent. But those who do have to integrate two approaches that are different from the outset that carry with them different models of the person, different models of causation, and different expectations of how a person might change over time.

The actual practice of psychiatry is, of course, greatly complex. Psycho-analysts, although they dominated psychiatry for many years, never had an exclusive hold on psychotherapy inside or outside the psychiatric profession: milieu therapy, group therapy, cognitive behavioral therapy, interpersonal therapies—talk therapies are as various as the country is wide. Nor are biomedical psychiatrists a single kind of doctor. Different psychopharmacologists have very different styles, and the gap between a clinician's view of an illness and the view of a laboratory-based psychiatric scientist can be a ravine. There are psychiatric specialties in community psychiatry, geriatric psychiatry, cultural psychiatry, the psychiatry of substance abuse, and many others that are not primarily oriented toward psychotherapy but certainly could not be classified as "biological." Nevertheless, the psychiatry of the last half century has been formed around the psychoanalytic rise to power and the new psychiatric science, followed by the health care revolution, which has brought psychoanalytic dominance to its knees.

These two approaches now exist in uneasy alliance with each other. They are a kind of contradiction to each other because their models of how suffering works are so opposed. Young psychiatrists are socialized into this contradiction, so that they learn to believe and to say that these different models should be integrated in the practice of psychiatry. But no one really knows where truth lies, although periodically brilliant new syntheses are published in the leading journals. As an anthropologist, I was interested not in answering the question of which approach was more correct but in understanding how the approaches worked as "culture" for the psychiatrists and thus for their patients. I wanted to know the way these different approaches changed the way the psychiatrist perceived, felt, thought, the way he became excited and challenged, the way he became bored. After all, these two approaches, the psychodynamic and the biomedical, have their roots in the more fundamental Western division between mind and body that our society, for all its sophisticated caveats, still endorses. We still think of the body as something unintentional, something given, something for which any individual is not responsible. That is why we are so interested in metabolic set points, inborn temperaments, learning disabilities, and the genetic roots of attention deficit disorder. If something is in the body, an individual cannot be blamed; the body is always morally innocent. If something is in the mind, however, it can be controlled and mastered, and a person who fails to do so is morally at fault. If someone is fat because he gives in to craving, we can laugh at him, we think; certainly for years, during the height of the fat-conscious decades, those who were fat were perceived by many, not least themselves, as morally weak. But if someone is fat because his metabolism is unalterably askew, we must admire his courage. If a child gets poor grades because of a learning disability, she should not be punished for not studying but should be given special help, the way we help those with other special physical needs. If I am lazy because I was born that way, I don't need to be guilty and embarrassed by the slope of my career. Biology is the great moral loophole of our age. This is not to say that I think this to be entirely inappropriate. As a good American, I believe that it is wrong to hold people responsible for something they cannot control. Nevertheless, a moral vision that treats the body as choiceless and nonresponsible and the mind as choice-making and responsible has significant consequences for a view of mental illness precariously perched between the two.

Understanding the way a set of ideas and practices can change a person is what anthropologists are trained to do, and as an anthropologist, I was better positioned to observe these changes than a member of the tribe. I went through much of the formal learning process. But I didn't need to commit myself professionally as a member of the field. My professional job was to watch myself learning, to watch others learning, to sketch out a kind of anatomy of the way learning took place, and to understand what was learned that was not necessarily intentionally taught. My job was to understand how a nonpsychiatrist (an ex–medical student) can enter the culture of psychiatry and become a fluent speaker of the local tongue. This informal learning is manifestly not the kind of thing that people talk about in interviews, because it happens so accidentally and changes you so incrementally that people often do not even notice that they have become profoundly different. Like the rest of medicine, psychiatry is a craft. It involves a kind of hands-on knowledge that is as much doing as knowing, something that invokes the philosopher's distinction between "knowing that" and "knowing how" (this is also known as declarative and procedural knowledge). A young psychiatrist—skilled, competent, articulate—learns to *do* psychiatry, not so much to describe what she does. She learns her psychiatry the way a young violinist learns to play the violin: to listen for the notes of a scale, to hear pitch and know when a string is in tune, to feel pride in the calluses that develop on the tips of the fingering hand, to know how to hold a bow by the feel of its weight. For someone who is good at her task, those ways of perceiving settle in so deeply that they become the way the person moves, hears, and observes when at that task. To understand what psychoanalysts and psychopharmacologists see, you must follow what young psychiatrists are taught and how they learn it. You must understand what they begin to do naturally as they carry out their tasks. You must understand how they come to think, how they feel, to what they aspire, and from what they flinch. You must understand how they handle their own anxiety about being any good at their profession. You cannot understand this just by asking people about it, any more than you can learn to canoe in an armchair with a reading lamp.

Since 1989, I have done more than four years of fieldwork, including more than sixteen months of full-time, intensive immersion. (I should say that I did all the work within the constraints of the willingness of the participants. Patients were always asked if they were comfortable having me sit in on a clinical interview, and if they declined, as they sometimes did, I left; I also left when psychiatrists were not comfortable with my presence.) The work began in a local hospital, where I attended lectures, hung out with residents (residency is the three-year specialty training in psychiatry after medical school and a one-year internship), and participated in medical meetings. I also spent four months at an elite private psychiatric hospital; three months in a community service hospital; and stretches of a week or two each in a psychoanalytic hospital, a scientific research unit, a state hospital, and a nonacademic community hospital's psychiatric unit. I traveled around the country (to Kansas, Louisiana, New York, Massachusetts, California) speaking with hospital administrators, psychiatry residency program directors, and young psychiatrists. I watched hundreds of lectures to residents through three years of training; I attended well over a hundred rounds or team meetings in which patients are presented and sometimes interviewed with the aim of establishing a diagnosis and treatment plan; I have "shadowed" residents during the day on the inpatient unit and during on-call evenings, and I have spent substantial periods of time on psychodynamic, eclectic, and biological units; I have watched countless admissions interviews; I have interviewed most residents in every class at one program annually for three years and many others elsewhere; I have followed eight individual patients for psychotherapy under the supervision of a senior psychoanalyst, one once a week and three twice a week for more than a year; I was in twice-a-week psychotherapy with a senior psychoanalyst for more than three years; I jointly led a group for indigent patients for a year; I attended fifteen major psychiatric conferences; I had so many meals with psychiatrists that for a time there was a standing joke among my friends that my entire social life was tax-deductible.

Let me say quickly that my role as an anthropologist is compromised (or liberated, depending on your point of view) by the fact that I believe both the biomedical and psychodynamic approaches to psychiatric illness to be substantially correct and equally effective, although not always for the same person. It seems clear to me that people have motivations that are not apparent to them, and that the way they experience the world is profoundly shaped by their personal history, often in ways they do not grasp; it also seems clear that there is something organically wrong with most people who are sick enough that they are admitted, these days, into a psychiatric hospital. I don't think that either approach mirrors the reality of mental illness, but then I don't think that any domain of knowledge "mirrors" the world as it is. The real issue for me is how one learns to look at mental illness through different lenses and the consequences of those ways of seeing.

The lenses are terribly important, and understanding how psychiatrists see is also terribly important, because madness is both frighteningly, palpably present, and yet elusive. There are no diagnostic tests in psychiatry (at least, none for genuinely psychiatric disorders: there are some conditions, such as brain tumors, that at first appear to be classic psychiatric disorders but are not). You cannot draw someone's blood, stick someone into a magnetic resonance imager, or take any medical reading that will tell you definitively whether that person is depressed or not. So it matters a great deal how a psychiatrist is taught to look at mental illness, because the "how" cannot be clearly separated from the "what" of the disease. To understand psychiatric ways of seeing, we have to proceed knowing that what counts as "fact" is a tinted window onto a world you cannot step outside to see.

It used to be fashionable in intellectual circles to say that madness didn't really exist at all, that it had been created when society's quest for order defined some people as deviant. This was done with crudeness by the antipsychiatry movement of the 1960s and 1970s and with finesse by Michel Foucault. Foucault did presume that madness had always existed, but he romanticized it in a way that, despite all his insights, did a terrible disservice to its pain. He argued that asylums had emerged in the eighteenth century as embodiments of middle-class morality and were like a kind of "gigantic moral imprisonment"; they dampened the free intensity of madness into "the stifling anguish of responsibility."[1] He wrote movingly about the way that after the asylum, the true genius of madness could be seen only in the writings of philosophers and poets. Others made similar arguments out of a naive yearning for a past when those we now call psychotic would have been esteemed as religious experts. (Some of these arguers come to my office wanting to write papers on how today's schizophrenics would have been yesteryear's shamans.) George Devereux, a psychiatric anthropologist who was not so much romantic as persuaded that the shamans in the society he worked in were pretty odd, wrote a famous paper arguing that shamanism provided a social role for the mentally ill that our society conspicuously lacked. "Briefly stated, my position is that the shaman is mentally deranged."[2] He suggested that the difference between the publicly recognized shaman and the "private" psychotic is that the shaman is able to use ritualized conventions in his society to manage his distress. This is a complicated and important issue, because it is clear that the way a culture interprets symptoms may affect an ill person's prognosis. However, in the 1960s and 1970s, people used popular versions of this notion to suggest that our society was too fearful and uptight to tolerate vivid passions and so condemned these people as sick. Peter Shaffer's very successful play *Equus,* for instance, dramatized a young boy whose therapist comes to see the attempt at therapy as the destruction of his passion and a kind of moral hubris. "The Normal is the indispensable, murderous God of Health, and I am his Priest," the therapist says. "I have talked away terrors and relieved many agonies. But also—beyond question—I have cut from them parts of individuality repugnant to this God."[3] R. D. Laing argued, with the style of a social prophet, that the schizophrenic was just someone who was too creative, too insightful, too existentially aware for our society. We normals were afraid, he implied, to be so bold.[4]

More recently, Susanna Kaysen wrote *Girl, Interrupted,* an account of her psychiatric hospitalization as a teenager. She was admitted when she was an adolescent, when she was angry at her parents. It was 1967, and she wore black and slept around and was deeply unhappy. When she went for a doctor's appointment, he put her in a taxi and sent her to McLean, a lovely, graceful hospital, where she remained for nearly two years. When the book was published, the reviewers condemned psychiatry for characterizing

emotional women as mentally unstable and for treating teenage unhappiness as a scapegoat for a dysfunctional family. "How thin the line is," Susan
Cheever fumed in the *New York Times Book Review*, "between those society
deems mad and those it deems sane."[5] Yet despite Cheever's understandable indignation, it is clear that something was wrong. Kaysen had tried to
kill herself before she was admitted. She was suicidal. She wrote, "I was
having a problem with patterns. Oriental rugs, tile floors, printed curtains,
things like that. Supermarkets were especially bad, because of the long,
hypnotic checkerboard aisles. When I looked at these things, I saw other
things within them. . . . Reality was getting too dense."[6] She describes the
experience of what she calls insanity, which she says comes in two forms, a
viscosity so sluggish you cannot breathe and a velocity so frenetic you cannot cope.[7]

Madness is real, and it is an act of moral cowardice to treat it as a
romantic freedom. Most people who end up in a psychiatric hospital are
deeply unhappy and seriously disturbed, and many of them lead lives of
humiliation and great pain. To try to protect the chronic mentally ill by saying that they are not ill, just different, is a misplaced liberalism of appalling
insensitivity to the patients and to the families who struggle so valiantly
with the difficulties of their ill family members. Most people who are really
schizophrenic are far too ill to serve as religious experts.

Moreover, the fantasy that innocent victims are imprisoned in asylums
where they go slowly mad under the weight of the psychiatrist's expectation and society's rejection is exactly that, a fantasy. These days, with the
pressure of insurance companies eager to deny psychiatric care if at all
possible, the only people admitted to psychiatric services are usually so ill
that there is no other option. Patients' rights are in general well protected,
although this varies from state to state, and a patient who is able to explain
where he lives, perhaps has some money—maybe $20—or at least some
place to go, and claims to have no intent to kill himself or anyone else goes
free if he wants. Given that one of the common characteristics of psychosis
is that the person does not experience himself as ill, people just barely able
to function often reject psychiatric help. ("Psychosis" describes an unmis-
takable distortion of reality, such as believing that the CIA has implanted a
microchip radio broadcaster in your mind. It is not a psychiatric disorder
per se but a symptom of psychiatric illness, the way a sore throat is a symptom of a cold.) I never saw anyone held against his or her will in a hospital
whom I felt was there unjustly. On the contrary, my experience was that
people were denied clinical care when they should have been treated. At
one point during my study, my liberal friends would lecture me on the evils
of psychiatric incarceration while one of my psychiatrist friends was being
stalked by a psychotic man refusing psychiatric care.

It is hard to describe, to someone who has never seen it, how terrible and intractable madness often is. Even firsthand narratives do not always help, either because the author (now recovered) seems either too sane to have been ill (as in Kaysen's case) or because the story seems too storied and bizarre (as in *I Never Promised You a Rose Garden*). The way we perceive madness does affect the madness experienced, but still there is an obdurate, unignorable presence to these illnesses. Over the years, at least for the last few centuries (some people argue that schizophrenia is a product of the last few centuries[8]), certain strange miseries have recurred in the history and literature of madness. Psychiatrists have classified them somewhat differently over the past few decades, but the symptoms and their severity have remained consistent. These days, they are classified as depression, manic depression (also known as bipolar disorder), and schizophrenia. Residents call them the "big three" because they dominate inpatient services and psychiatric emergency rooms. They have a kind of irrefutable reality.

William Styron was able to capture some of the gravitas of major depression in *Darkness Visible* by recounting, in blunt detail, the forced steps taken by his mind as the depression came upon him like a darkness with talons:

> I was on Martha's Vineyard, where I've spent a good part of each year since the 1960s, during that exceptionally beautiful summer. But I had begun to respond indifferently to the island's pleasures. I felt a kind of numbness, an enervation, but more particularly an odd fragility. . . . [T]he overall effect was immensely disturbing, augmenting the anxiety that was by now never quite absent from my waking hours. . . . [Then] it was October, and one of the unforgettable features of this stage of my disorder was the way in which my old farmhouse, my beloved home for thirty years, took on for me at that point when my spirits regularly sank to their nadir an almost palpable quality of ominousness. . . . One bright day on a walk through the woods with my dog I heard a flock of Canada geese honking high above the trees ablaze with foliage; ordinarily a sight and sound that would have exhilarated me, the flight of birds caused me to stop, riveted with fear, and I stood stranded there, helpless, shivering, aware for the first time that I had been stricken by no mere pangs of withdrawal but by a serious illness whose name and actuality I was able finally to acknowledge. . . . [F]ood . . . was utterly without savor . . . my few hours of sleep were usually terminated at three or four in the morning. . . . Death . . . was now a daily presence, blowing over me in cold gusts.[9]

Those who suffer from major depression cannot sleep, do not eat, and are obsessed by the thought of their own death. Their depression feels to them like a physical pain. They cannot concentrate. They cannot function. Many of them cannot leave their beds. One in every six will kill themselves.[10] Styron was lucky, even though he did not respond to medication. He came very close to suicide. He destroyed his personal notebook (emblem of a writer's self), rewrote his will, plotted his death. (He couldn't write a suicide note; this Pulitzer Prize–winning author could not find the words.) He felt, he wrote, that he had made an irreversible decision. Then, late at night, brooding, he heard some music that somehow pierced his desolate chill. He roused his wife. She made some phone calls. He soon found himself in the safety of the hospital, protected from the domestic goods that seem harmless to most of us but are deadly invitations to the suicidal: razors, staircases, knives, plastic bags, ropes, vodka, medicine cabinets. Time slowly healed him.

Depression, psychiatrists say, strikes one in five to ten people.[11] Schizophrenia strikes one in one hundred. Recent research suggests that there may be more than one disease process involved in schizophrenia (in other words, more than one bodily abnormality), but patients bearing this diagnosis have similar traits. They have seriously abnormal thoughts: that Peter Jennings is speaking specifically to them, that their bodies have died and been replaced by plastic. Psychiatrists call this divorce from reality "psychosis." In addition, their faces seem curiously flat and blunted, and their lives fall apart. One in ten will commit suicide.[12] Their illness tends to have a chronic, debilitating course, although as many as a third of schizophrenic patients may ultimately recover or at least lead somewhat normal lives.[13] One of the most famous literary schizophrenics was a real woman known as Sylvia Frumkin whose life was chronicled by Susan Sheehan in *The New Yorker* and later in *Is There No Place on Earth for Me?* It is a painstaking account of the life of a young, brilliant woman whose illness was basically unaltered by either medication or psychotherapy, who went into and out of psychiatric institutions of varying quality, and whose life was chaotic and painful for herself and her family. This remarkable book opens with this paragraph:

> Shortly after midnight on Friday, June 16, 1978, Sylvia Frumkin decided to take a bath. Miss Frumkin, a heavy, ungainly young woman who lived in a two-story yellow brick building in Queens Village, New York, walked from her bedroom on the second floor to the bathroom next door and filled the tub with warm water. A few days earlier, she had had her hair cut and shaped in a bowl style, which she found especially becoming, and her spirits were high. She washed her brown hair with shampoo and also with red mouthwash. Some years earlier, she had

tinted her hair red and had liked the way it looked. She had given up wearing her hair red only because she had found coloring it every six weeks too much of a bother. She imagined that the red mouthwash would somehow be absorbed into her scalp and make her hair red permanently. Miss Frumkin felt so cheerful about her new haircut that she suddenly thought she was Lori Lemaris, the mermaid whom Clark Kent had met in college and had fallen in love with in the old "Superman" comics. She blew bubbles into the water.[14]

Sylvia Frumkin was articulate, engaging, and bizarre. When she was tested in grade school, her IQ was 138. She was not well liked then, although her teacher thought her sensitive and eager. Other girls her own age said she was uncouth. Sylvia went to one of New York's best public high schools, but in tenth grade things began to go wrong. The psychiatrist she saw at that point described her as unattractive, untidy, restless, overtalkative; she switched too readily from tearfulness to giggles; she interpreted people poorly and in odd ways. She was diagnosed as paranoid schizophrenic. Sylvia seemed to do well in therapy and to become more like a normal adolescent: she acquired a best friend, she listened to popular music, she liked the Beatles, she cut her hair and bought attractive clothes. Then she was hit by a car, by a teenager driving alone on a learner's permit. She briefly lost consciousness and suffered a concussion. Soon she became more anxious than before (she had always been nervous). She would stay up all night; each day she smoked three packs of cigarettes and took three showers. Her casual comments sounded more and more crazy. Her therapist began to give her small doses of Stelazine, an antipsychotic. Two months later, Sylvia became highly agitated and began asking people to adopt her. She was hospitalized for the first time. She insisted, as she drove to the hospital, that Paul McCartney was going to come and take her away to England. From then on she went into and out of psychotic delusions and psychiatric hospitals.

Manic depression, or bipolar disorder, is the third of the trio. It is, like depression but unlike schizophrenia, classified as a "mood" disorder, which means that the most salient problem lies with the patient's emotional tone, not his or her thought process, although a bipolar patient in the grip of mania can seem crazy in the same way as an acutely psychotic schizophrenic patient. People with manic-depressive disorder experience periods when they are profoundly depressed and other periods when they are manic, a state of erratic, disinhibited euphoria: they don't sleep, they talk wildly, they are grandiose and sometimes psychotic. Kay Jamison's memoir of manic-depressive disorder, *An Unquiet Mind* (1995), describes her years before she allowed herself to manage the illness with lithium:

I was a senior in high school when I had my first attack of manic-depressive illness; once the siege began, I lost my mind rather rapidly. At first everything seemed so easy. I raced about like a crazed weasel, bubbling with plans and enthusiasms, immersed in sports, and staying up all night, night after night, out with friends, reading everything that wasn't nailed down, filling manuscript books with poems and fragments of plays, and making expansive, completely unrealistic, plans for my future. . . . Not only did everything make perfect sense, but it all began to fit into a marvelous kind of cosmic relatedness. . . . I did, finally, slow down. In fact I came to a grinding halt. Unlike the very severe manic episodes that came a few years later and escalated wildly and psychotically out of control, this first sustained wave of mania was like a light, lovely tincture. . . . Then the bottom began to fall out of my life and mind. . . . Nothing made sense. . . . [My mind] was incapable of concentrated thought and turned time and again to the subject of death.[15]

Many people who are manic-depressive, or who experience bouts of depression, function quite well when not ill, but some never manage to live a normal life. Like those who have a "unipolar" depression (they are never manic), one in six will kill themselves. "He reminded me," Jamison writes of a patient who was not among the lucky ones, "of films I had seen of horses trapped in fires with their eyes wild with fear and their bodies paralyzed in terror."[16] Her own life after high school became a riveting story of voyaging between extremes. In her first job, as assistant professor of psychiatry at UCLA, she found herself exuberant and brilliant at a professional party and went higher; she bought a fantastic array of stuff, among it three expensive watches, twelve snakebite kits, and, most horrifying later on, a stuffed, preserved fox; higher still, she wrote a poem, inspired by her spice collection and archived in the refrigerator, entitled "God Is a Herbivore." Then she crashed, with a bloodred vision of a splattered test tube. Over the years she swung high, then low. She bought a gun, confessed she owned it, gave it away. She fought with lithium and the need to take it, then overdosed on a massive amount of it. She was saved by sheer luck. She wrote of that time, "I can't calm this murderous cauldron, my grand ideas of an hour ago seem absurd and pathetic, my life is in ruins and—worse still—ruinous. . . . In the mirror I see a creature I do not know but must live and share my mind with."[17]

These are not romantic illnesses. Nor are they creativity and insight in another form. Every culture recognizes certain people at certain times as mad, and treats them as being different.[18] (The diagnoses that are generally accepted to be valid worldwide are schizophrenia, manic-depressive disorder, major depression, substance abuse, and certain anxiety disorders, although, as we will see, the local experience of illness may vary widely.) These people do not become shamans and priestesses and artists because they are mad, although artists may possibly be more successful if they are (mildly) manic-depressive. (This is an important distinction. Being mad probably does not make you creative, but if you are creative, glimpsing the depths of human despair and then reaching the heights of confidence with infinite energy probably enhances your ability to use your gift.[19]) Crazy people cannot fend for themselves when they are sick. They struggle to survive with the generosity and protection of others. There is no reasonable doubt that madness is an intrinsic feature of human life, not a by-product of asylum building or of a shift in religious practice.

At the same time, it is true that madness is involved with our social fabric. To return to the sociological point, the way illness is socially conceived does seem to alter the way it is individually expressed and experienced. It is true, as Sue Estroff wrote in her classic ethnography of psychiatric clients, that "being a full-time crazy person is becoming an occupation among a certain population in our midst."[20] Our psychiatric professionals, as well as the rest of us, have expectations of the psychiatrically ill, and we institutionalize those expectations in subtle and unsubtle ways that can lead people to mimic the symptoms we think that they should have. If a homeless veteran wants a warm bed for the night, he can learn what words and gestures will persuade the psychiatrist on call to admit him to the hospital. If a woman receives a disability check each month for her psychiatric diagnosis, she will learn how to avoid having the support curtailed. When Erving Goffman wrote in *Asylums* of an institution's "direct assault on the self," he was describing the reality that, both inside the hospital and without, the psychiatrically ill learn to play roles our society has designed for them.[21] One of the unintended consequences of social assistance is that we reward people for becoming and remaining ill. Sometimes we trap them in their illness.

This is where much of the good psychiatric anthropology has been focused. These anthropologists have shown us that there is a complex dance between what a clinician learns to treat and how a patient learns to be treated. For example, Allan Young describes the gradual construction of "posttraumatic stress disorder" out of the lives of traumatized Vietnam veterans, the way the clinicians used the diagnostic criteria to include people they felt ought to be seen as sick, and the way patients began to present themselves in order to fit into that diagnostic structure.[22] It has now become apparent that not all women diagnosed with multiple personality disorder had that disorder before they walked into the psychiatric consulting room. That many of them had major emotional and behavioral problems seems clear. Many seem to have struggled with dissociation, a long-term consequence of a childhood escape mechanism used when a child confronts bullying or abuse she cannot physically flee. Such a child learned to "check out" when the distress began. She would no longer be there, in the same way you can "check out" when the dentist's drill begins to whir. As adults, these women had difficulties with concentrating, keeping track of time, being effective and reliable in human relationships. Some learned—from popular best-sellers such as *The Courage to Heal*, from support groups, from Internet chat groups, and from therapists sensitized by feminism to the dangers of male sexual authority—to understand their pain as caused by male transgression and to experience their disconnectedness as the result of a fragmented self. Dissociation is a skill, and the use of that skill can be learned. Some learn involuntarily, and their dissociation is pathological: unwanted, intrusive, uncontrollable. Some learn willingly to go into trance, possession, out-of-body states, and, for that matter, channeling. And the content is manipulable. Someone can dissociate by zoning out and then learn to experience that sensation as possession. In the 1980s, many women learned to handle their dissociation and general distress by learning to experience multiple personalities that switched on and off in disturbing ways.[23] By that point, a therapist who helped a woman to gain control over a disturbing, unwanted dissociation by teaching her how to "call" her "alters" (alternative personalities) was acting appropriately and effectively to help her. But the therapist may not have been doing what she thought she was.

History shapes the kind of madness people experience and the frequency with which it occurs. Poverty, war, and dislocation are bad for people—an obvious point, but important if you are tempted to think of psychiatric illness as purely hereditary. A recent survey on world mental health observed that in all different age, gender, and cultural categories everywhere, the most important risk factor for mental health is social disruption.[24] Social isolation also seems to exact a high cost. Depression, and mood disorders in general, may be more common in the twentieth century than ever before, because in no other time of human history have so many people been so isolated.[25] (It is, however, extremely difficult to figure out what would count as evidence here—it is very difficult to judge the rate of mental illness in earlier centuries.) More people live alone in America than ever before—a quarter of all Americans, compared to less than 10 percent in 1940 and probably almost none in our ancestral past. Mothers who work hand their children over to strangers for long periods of time. Mothers who don't work are at home alone with small children. From a human evolutionary perspective, this is bizarre. In hunter-gatherer societies, child rearing is extensively social, as are work and life in general. In modern societies, isolation is a leading risk factor for suicide.[26]

Historical and cultural conditions also seem to affect significantly the way mental anguish is internally experienced and socially expressed. For instance, people in non-Western societies are likely to report somatic symptoms—aches, pains, problems of the body—as the primary difficulty of being abnormally sad, while Westerners are more likely to report psychological symptoms—feeling down, guilty, suicidal, having difficulty concentrating. Are they suffering from the same psychiatric difficulty? When Arthur Kleinman went to China as an American psychiatrist in the 1970s, he thought that the Chinese who came to the clinic complaining of aches and anxieties often looked depressed. Moreover, most of them met the American psychiatric criteria for major depression. But they called their difficulties neurasthenia, the major symptoms were not those of depression, and the meaning and explanation of the difficulties were quite distinct. Neurasthenia was (conceived as) a physical problem having to do with nerves, not an emotional problem with sadness. And it became apparent that neurasthenia was also a role for people whose lives had been crippled by the Cultural Revolution, which had left a generation terrorized and humiliated and then stranded them without any way to compete professionally with the next generation. This is not to say that people pretended to have neurasthenia: they experienced neurasthenia, and not all victims of the Cultural Revolution had it. But Kleinman, whose 1986 study has become a classic, came to believe that to understand these patients, you had to understand their difficulties as part of a social suffering, as part of a culture's history, not as a series of unrelated personal complaints.

Anthropologists have learned to address these ambiguities by distinguishing between "illness" and "disease."[27] "Disease" refers to abnormalities in the structure and function of bodily organs and systems. Physicians, for example, refer to "disease pathways" when describing the physical causes of the symptoms that bring someone to a clinic. "Illness," by contrast, refers to the patient's experience. A person can experience illness without having a disease (Kleinman points out that 50 percent of doctor visits may be for complaints without a curable biological base).[28] The same disease can underlie different illness experiences, depending on the cultural, historical, and personal circumstances of the people involved. The distinction is helpful when the distinction is clear—when looking at the difference between the way a local population and the World Health Organization manage a cholera outbreak, for instance. Often, however, the distinction is more ambiguous. Japanese women, for example, do not experience menopause in the same way as American women. They do not feel the same demoralization and passing of youth; this may be because Japanese women may have more respect and power in their maturity than in their youth. They also do not have hot flashes. Is their lack of hot flashes their culture's impact on the same bodily process (one hesitates to call menopause a "disease"), or does their diet of soy and fish alter their biology? Or is their biology different to begin with?[29] The distinction between disease and illness is deeply ambiguous in psychiatry, because while psychiatric problems often clearly have an organic element, they are also enmeshed with the social context. Nor is it usually clear what the psychiatric "disease process" is—unlike the case with, for instance, cholera.

There is no medical test for a specific disease pathology for any major psychiatric illness. You cannot know whether there really is an underlying "disease" in psychiatric illness. There is no way to determine, once and for all, whether someone has depression or not, and there is no reason to suppose—despite occasional claims to the contrary—that we will have any way to do so anytime soon. No one can say whether Chinese neurasthenia is "really" the same as American depression. It *is* clear that, no matter how you slice the research, psychiatric problems involve genetic vulnerability, bodily stress, social milieu, cultural interpretation, family history, and individual temperament. (The unwieldy term that was supposed to sum this up was "biopsychosocial," but even that refers to too few factors.[30]) As a result, it is particularly important to understand how psychiatrists look at these illnesses and thus how we in turn understand them (psychiatric knowledge seeps into popular culture like the dye from a red shirt in hot water). The way we understand these illnesses affects not only the way they are treated but the way they are experienced, their outcomes, and our sense of responsibility toward those who suffer.

This is what an anthropologist can observe. I was, after all, watching people learn. They came into psychiatric residency as nonpsychiatrists, and they left as qualified psychiatric professionals. I could see what they were taught explicitly, by those appointed to teach them; I could also see what everyday experience with psychiatric patients confronted them with and how they learned from one another to defend themselves against its assaults. I saw how they learned to find significance and meaning in behavior other people might not even notice and how they learned to communicate their sense of that behavior in an ordinary language other people might not grasp, even when understanding each individual word. And so I was able to observe what anthropologists now call the "transformation of subjectivity." You cannot observe a man think and feel, but if there is a group of men, you can see what a man needs to do to be a member of that group. You can see what he learns to react to, how he learns to react, how he comes to joke about it, what he comes to fear. The anthropologist Clifford Geertz pointed out that what the anthropologist can find out through fieldwork is what is public in the exchanges people have with one another. This doesn't mean that the psyche remains closed to observation. It means that what you can observe is how the psyche is shaped by practical and mundane things.

For example, Hugh Gusterson, another anthropologist of science, described the way politically liberal young men at Lawrence Livermore Laboratory turned into weapons scientists. They graduated with doctorates in physics from elite universities. Not all of them were politically liberal, but many were, and many were hesitant about contributing to the nuclear arms race. But they didn't believe in unilateral disarmament, and these jobs paid well and were more secure than the precarious world of up-or-out university tenure decisions. So the men took these jobs and years later found themselves committed to the importance of nuclear weapons with a passion that matched that of the antinuclear protestors. Why? This anthropologist argued that through the process of living in their skins at work, coming to terms with their fear of radiation and annihilation, and feeling pride in their skill, they came to feel powerfully and deeply that their work was morally important and necessary to human survival. He saw three features of their everyday environment that were crucial to that unintended transformation. First, there was the thrill of being in a secret group, with the sense of specialness but also of constant panopticon surveillance, and the slow corrosive impact of that separate, secret world on the intimacies of private life, as a result of which the laboratory loomed ever larger in the scientists' sense of self. Then there was the way the men handled their fears by jokes in which they identified with the machines and not with fleshly corpses—they were powerful, like the bombs, not weak, like the bodies burned by them. He described the way they learned from laboratory culture to experience excitement and not desperation at the violence of explosion. (At least, those who stayed in the lab did. The others left.) Finally, they felt a sense of mastery when the nuclear tests actually worked, and in the joy of a job well done, those tests became fun for the scientists and seemed reasonable, ordinary, and intrinsic to the proper functioning of the lab.[31] And so these Berkeley doctoral students grew into the men the Berkeley radicals came to protest.

I will describe here an anatomy of the way psychiatrists come to see the people who come to them as patients. It is an anatomy of how a psychiatrist empathizes with a patient because it became clear to me that these different tasks—biomedical and psychodynamic—teach young doctors to empathize with their patients in different ways. Both are empathic, but they are not empathic in the same way. Empathy is a process—*not* a squashy, feel-good emotion nor, as the colloquial use would have it, the state of being warm and fuzzy. It is a process in which you, the empathizer, imagine what it is to be someone else, the person you are empathizing with. Empathy can never be completely accurate. The density of one person's experience exceeds what an observer can grasp, and so in empathy as in life, there are many truths, each one springing from a specific conjunction of the empathizer and the empathized with. You can be more empathic or less, but the way you are empathic and with what in a person's life you empathize and how, has a great deal to do with who you are and how you conceive of your task at that moment, in that place.[32] And empathy has components that an observer can observe when a student is taught to perform an empathic task: how to perceive the person being empathized with, how to relate to him, how to behave appropriately with him, and whom to aspire to be with him. We know that all these are present in the way we hear and respond to one another: the person we see, as the person we hope we are, with feelings and behaviors we have been encouraged to adopt.

No person is simple. We hear their sorrows through the din of our occluding pasts, and we can grasp only the sounds to which we are attuned. Psychiatrists are taught to listen to people in particular ways: they listen for signals most of us cannot hear, and they look for patterns most of us cannot see. Their two primary tasks, however—diagnosis and psychopharmacology, on the one hand, and psychodynamic psychotherapy, on the other—teach them to listen and look in different ways. As an anthropologist, I could see what young psychiatrists had to achieve in diagnosis and in psychotherapy, and I could see what they learned to do in order to achieve it. I could see how they learned to perceive the patient in order to do their task, and I could see that what they had learned was inherent in the tasks themselves, not due to the style or personality of the doctor. I could also see how they learned to anticipate patients in the settings of their different tasks, how they learned to fear or hate or love them, and I could see what counted as appropriate behavior on the units dominated by either biomedical or psychodynamic concerns. Again, these differences were part of the tasks, not the result of the doctor's personality, although certainly different tasks did seem to draw different kinds of people for keeps. And I could see who was admired in these different domains, so that one could ask, when a young doctor was with a patient, not only what he saw in the patient but whom he should aspire to be in response. All this is part of the way young psychiatrists learn to be doctors with patients, focused on two different tasks. That is the anatomy this book sets out to describe.

This book also reaches a more disturbing conclusion. However we understand the possible causes of mental illness, the available evidence we have suggests that for most patients and for most disorders, psychophar-macology and psychotherapy work best in combination. Patients improve more quickly and stay out of the hospital for longer when the two approaches are used in tandem. Both are important; both are necessary, as most psychiatrists—regardless of their orientations—agree. But a combi-nation of socio-economic forces and ideology is driving psychotherapy out of psychiatry. It is harder than ever before for residents to learn psychotherapy or to see its relevance in a hospital setting, harder than before for a patient or doctor to be reimbursed for it. If psychotherapy is axed from psychiatry by the bottom-line focus of managed care companies, psychiatrists will be taught to see, think, and respond only as the biomed-ical task would teach them. That would be a terrible mistake. It would be bad for psychiatrists, who are more perceptive about patients, even when diagnosing and prescribing medication, when they have some psychothera-peutic background. It would be bad for our society, for biomedicine encourages a way of thinking about mental illness that can strip humanity from its sufferers. And above all it would be bad for patients, who will be treated less well and less effectively if treated from a purely biomedical perspective.

➡ There is also a more subtle risk. Psychiatry is inevitably entangled with our deepest moral concerns: what makes a person human, what it means to suffer, what it means to be a good and caring person. By the word "moral" here I do not mean a code of right behavior so much as our instinc-tive sense of what it is to be responsible, when to assign blame, how we come to see our ambitions as fundamentally right and good. The biomed-ical and psychodynamic approaches nurture two very different moral instincts by shaping differently the fundamental categories that are the tools of the way we reason about our responsibilities in caring for those in pain: who is a person (not an obvious question), what constitutes that person's pain, who are we to intervene, what intervention is good. These two approaches teach their practitioners to look at people differently. They have different contradictions and different bottom lines. Both have their strengths and their weaknesses. Each changes the way doctors perceive patients, the way society perceives patients, and the way patients perceive themselves. The irony is that while Freud perhaps saw himself as demon-strating that human nature was shackled by its own design, his legacy has been to create a moral expectation of human agency and self-determination that we do ill to jettison.

What I wanted to do that morning when the resident turned around and suggested I write about what he was being taught to do was just to understand how these ways of knowing differ. I wanted to know what these young psychiatrists learn to notice and how they come to notice it. Lenses are important; they enable us to see. But when we use this metaphor to describe how we come to understand one another, we must remember that lenses, while necessary, are a distortion, for humans always slip away from the clarity we impose on them. Now, as we risk the loss of one of the lenses entirely, there is a possibility that our psychiatrists, and perhaps our society, will learn to see even less complexity than before.

CHAPTER ONE

❧❧

WHAT'S WRONG WITH
THE PATIENT?

What's wrong with the patient? That is the most basic question in medicine. And when new psychiatrists begin to act as psychiatrists, what they learn to see as the patient's problem is shaped not only by what they are taught explicitly about psychiatric illness but also by how they learn to act like a psychiatrist in that setting. In the hospital, the way psychiatrists learn to admit patients and present them to supervisors encourages them to think of psychiatric illness as an organic disease, a "thing" underlying and generating the symptoms. Doing the same things in the outpatient clinic encourages that same psychiatrist to think in terms of interaction, about the way the patient has learned to be with people. And so complex, inchoate misery is crystallized into two different kinds of clarity. Because psychiatrists start their training in the hospital, we begin the story there. Then we turn to the experience of outpatient psychiatry.

IN THE HOSPITAL

Gertrude was one of nine new residents I met on July 1, 1992, in the oak-paneled room the hospital reserved for its occasional formal events, such as board meetings and residency orientation. She seemed young and wary, determined not to look nervous. This was her first day of psychiatric training (the medical year runs from July to July). She had graduated from medical school one year previously. Her first year after graduation from medical school had been spent in internship, an intensive, lived-in-the-guts, all-consuming apprenticeship in a general hospital. Some psychiatrists-to-be take a rotating internship, with several months on a psychiatric or neurological service. But the more elite internships are a rigorous, focused, sleep-deprived, and thoroughly medical experience. Gertrude had been such an elite intern. Her only experience of psychiatry had been as a medical student, as an insubstantial presence on a psychiatry unit for some weeks, assigned to residents only marginally less naive than she, whom she and her fellow students had followed around like abandoned puppies. She had good reason to be anxious.

Medicine trains its students by having them act as if they are competent doctors from their first days on the job. Although psychiatric residents are "in training," they are also acting—from the day they arrive—as psychiatrists. Gertrude was assigned to a hospital unit as one of its psychiatrists. She was immediately assigned patients to care for. As the year progressed, she needed less supervision, but she was still doing the same tasks. As is common in medicine, she learned by doing. She was expected to be able to manage the hospital's entire psychiatric service after hours by herself in a matter of weeks: doing emergency admissions, signing orders that only doctors can authorize, prescribing emergency medications to calm unexpectedly agitated patients. During that summer I sat through two months of orientation, the "summer seminar," some analogue of which is held at every psychiatric residency in the country. It taught the basic survival skills of psychiatry. In the summer seminar, Gertrude and her peers were taught by residents one or two years older—psychiatric residency is a three-year training in which senior residents train junior ones—with a kind of in-group coaching meant to get them up to speed rapidly so that they could pull their own weight in caring for patients and dispense with step-by-step supervision. There were lectures for a few hours a day. The rest of the time the residents spent doing their jobs with patients. "These are basic lectures," the chief resident said during the first class on psychopharmacology. (The chief resident is the young doctor in charge of all the other residents.) "When it gets down to gamma-2 level receptors, then it's religion, not science." He meant that the psychiatrist's basic skill is knowing how to use medications, that only the overzealous care exactly how they work. The new psychiatrists were expected to understand this, to come prepared with the pragmatic expectation that they must avoid disaster but not strive for perfection. "I can tell who the weak residents are already," the chief resident said to me after a week. "They're the people who are taking this too seriously. Those are the ones who will have trouble."

The summer seminar series aimed to teach Gertrude and her fellow students how to avoid egregious errors, not how to become excellent psychiatrists. What it taught, then, teaches us what counts as basic adequacy. The lecture list went as follows:

Week one: On call in the hospital; psychiatric emergencies; introduction to psychopharmacology; process notes and supervision.

Week two: Antipsychotics; the dangerous patient; mental status examination; diagnosis.

Week three: Antipsychotics; beginning psychotherapy (1); beginning
psychotherapy (2); medical issues in psychiatric care.

Week four: Sedatives, hypnotics, and stimulants; overview of substance
abuse; introduction to interviewing; violent patients.

Week five: Tricyclic antidepressants, overview of sleep disorders; legal
issues in psychiatry; suicidal patients.

Week six: MAOIs [monoamine oxidase inhibitors, a kind of antidepressant medication] and novel antidepressants; overview of
cognitive/behavioral treatment; psychological testing; rating scales.

Week seven: Mood stabilizers; neurologic emergencies; sexual issues in
psychiatry; case presentations.

Week eight: ECT [electroconvulsive therapy]; history of psychiatry;
case formulation; case presentation.

Week nine: Psychopharmacology of Axis II disorders; wrap-up.

The first lectures were on psychiatric emergencies and the dangerous
patient, then the admissions process and an overview of various medications. Eventually they moved to psychotherapy but really focused on
hospital psychiatry. What the young psychiatrist has to know—and
immediately—is how to handle psychiatric emergencies and admissions.
New apprentices must know how to cope with people who may be violent
or intensely suicidal, people who are brought in by the police or by a dis-
traught family, people who have intentionally sliced their wrists or necks,
spent seven hours in surgery, and been transferred by ambulance to the
psychiatric hospital. It is the resident's job formally to admit the patients
and to make the first decisions about treatment—whether to prescribe
medications and the kind and dose, whether the patient should be on a
locked or unlocked unit, and so forth.

The most unnerving time for the new residents was when they were "on
call." Then they were the psychiatrist in charge of the entire psychiatric
service in the evening and throughout the night, when the senior psychiatrists had departed and only the night staff—some nurses, some mental
health workers—stayed on. After only a month of experience in psychiatry,
the on-call doctor might be the only doctor in a hospital with more than a
hundred patients (other doctors were available by phone, but it is hard to
call a senior in the middle of the night to ask him a question he thinks you
ought to be able to answer yourself). If a patient went out of control, the
nurses needed the doctor to prescribe a tranquilizer or sign an order to use

physical restraints. If a patient arrived—that is, had showed up in some urban hospital's emergency room and a transfer had been arranged—the doctor admitted the patient and signed the orders. If a person showed up crazy, on grounds, the doctor had to decide whether to commit him. If a patient suddenly developed an acute allergic reaction to antipsychotic medication, that doctor had to know what to do. Depending on the level of anticipated work, there might be other residents on call as well, to help with admissions or to advise the nervous newcomer. Often in those first few months, a somewhat more senior resident would also stay on to help out. But not always. The resident had to act like a knowledgeable doctor despite the newness of the patients, the circumstances, and his task. "So you're on call," the chief resident said, "and some guy has come into the entrance [a lonely house, set far back from the main admissions building] and he's punched the emergency number into the hospital phone. You and Sergeant Carter go over [all forays to distant buildings at night are accompanied by the security guard], and you ask this guy why he rang in an emergency. He says he thought he might want to be admitted, but now he's not sure. Sergeant Carter is getting bored. You ask the guy why he wanted to come in, and he says, 'Just . . .' and trails off. Sergeant Carter says that you seem to have this under control and can he leave? You say 'No.' Why? Because you don't know. You don't know. When the guy trails off into silence, he might just be hearing a voice that says, 'Eliminate this fool.'"

In August, I went on call with Gertrude. She was noticeably uneasy. This was her first night as DOC, "doctor on call." She was one month into her training, and she was legally liable (although covered by the hospital's malpractice plan) for every decision she made. Although she had some help—another resident, one year her senior, joined her for part of the evening—she was alone (apart from the watchful anthropologist) for much of the night, running back and forth from building to building, holding the walkie-talkie that enabled the switchboard operator to reach her, assigning admissions to the one or two other residents who remained in the hospital, covering orders for psychopharmacological and physical restraints, doing admissions herself, trying to get enough time to eat and, if possible, change into the casual clothes that a doctor is allowed to wear on call but never during the day.

At night the hospital was an eerie place. Located as it was in the suburbs, this hospital had many "scheduled" admissions, patients whose doctors called up to arrange for hospitalization and who then arrived on the subdued afternoons of the regular workweek. But often the patients arrived unexpectedly and after hours, brought in by police or despairing relatives to a city emergency room and shipped out to the suburban hospital because the city hospitals were full. Even a large urban hospital is strange after midnight, as the acoustics of the long, empty corridors change markedly when there are no people in them. This hospital, with its strung-out buildings, each containing different units, was so much like a small liberal arts college that in the day I would have to stop myself from referring to the patients as students. At night it became forbidding. The grounds felt deserted, and the distances between the buildings were dark fields broken by inadequate pools of light. No matter how many residents there were in the early part of the evening, spread out in the great stretches of the hospital grounds, the night was still desolate. The security guard told me that the most dangerous creatures at the hospital at night were the raccoons. But it is nerve-racking to be alone at midnight by the dark woods of an asylum. When I was there I found myself repeating the guard's words sternly to myself.

Gertrude made it through the night without mishap, but her personality style, like that of many doctors, did not sit comfortably with the sudden demand to care for people in ways she did not understand. She seemed as if she had always been competent, that she was a responsible older sister who had baby-sat her younger brother and washed the dishes. She did not like the model of good-enough adequacy; she was not laissez-faire; she worried that if she pretended to be competent without having full knowledge, one of her patients would develop a strange undiagnosed disease and die. She had been a solid, successful undergraduate—the kind who'd been accepted by many medical schools—and had done it by working until she became one of the best in her class. Like many psychiatrists, she was shy and had always been reserved. She loved parties but was vaguely embarrassed when standing around in a chattering group. She seemed to manage well, but that was because she did what other people told her to do, and it left her cynical and distrustful. It bothered her intensely to cut so many corners and to have to depend on other people to give her a sheen of adequacy in doing a job she had not yet been taught to do well.

"It's all politics," she said bitterly. "That's what you learn—how to talk on rounds, how to talk to patients, how to talk to nurses. You're taught by mistakes and by apprenticeship coaching, not all of which are consistent. Sometimes people give completely different advice. You start out so idealistic. Then you begin to cut your losses.

"Because the nurses will call and say, 'We've put so-and-so in restraints [leather cuffs for ankles and wrists], please write the order,' or 'We've just given so-and-so Ativan [a minor tranquilizer used to calm agitated patients], please write the order.' And in three months it won't matter, I'll know people, know whether I can trust their judgment. Still, I'm the one who takes the legal responsibility now. And where's my legitimacy? What is it like to be the nurse who's worked here for twenty years and calls up a new resident in July and has to persuade him to do something? They *have* to push me into agreeing with them, but the whole mess seems kind of inappropriate. Like, as DOC I need to be a protective watchdog on the phone. I need to protect the nurses by not taking patients that will make them feel uncomfortable. But I need to protect the hospital from bankruptcy. There's no way of doing it well."

This practical, rapid apprenticeship remains the primary teaching method throughout the residency period (as is typical in medicine). During the three-year training period, residents usually spend their first year in inpatient care, their second in outpatient, and their final year either in administrative positions (as "chief resident" for various services in the hospital) or in some other elective pursuit: research or in further specialized training. Often, what the resident does in the third year tends to mimic her first, the difference being that in her third she tends to have supervisory responsibilities. The second year, the outpatient year, is unusual because the resident is working not in the hospital but in a clinic, sometimes some distance from the hospital to which it is attached. That is when residents commonly have the greatest exposure to psychotherapy.

Gertrude's program was in a large psychiatric hospital. At the time I was visiting, there were nine units, each oriented to a different patient population: patients who were depressed or traumatized or had eating disorders and so forth. Gertrude and her peers would rotate through three units for four months apiece. While in the rotation, they would be assigned one or more patients on the unit as their primary responsibility. Gertrude would attend most meetings concerning her patients—meetings to discuss the patient's treatment, meetings with family members—and most meetings of the unit. In addition, she was expected to work in the admissions building, admitting patients, one afternoon a week, to be on call one or two evenings a week, to attend four hours of lectures a week, to participate in a group therapy session for the entire class of residents, and to begin to follow at least one outpatient for psychotherapy. In fact, residents often attended lectures sporadically after the first few months. In one residency, faculty resorted to attendance sheets and still the residents refused to show up; they pointed out irritably that their responsibility was to care for their current patients, not to sit dutifully in a class. What residents actually learn is to do what they have to do: admit, diagnose, and medicate patients, and— less pressing these days—see them in psychotherapy.

Of all the skills that Gertrude had to master, the most important, most tested, and most public was her ability to admit patients to a hospital service. An "admission" is a ritual-filled process that identifies an ill person as a patient and produces a few pages that are the single most consistently read document about the person as a patient throughout the hospitalization and beyond. As the hospitalization goes on, more and more pages are added: nursing notes, psychiatrists' notes, notes from the occupational therapist and the social worker and so forth. Each subsequent admission adds more paper. Soon the patient's chart—the folder with his name on it—bulges out to one inch, then to three; patients from the old psychiatric units, where stays were long and note taking was extensive, have charts that are literally feet in width. You see residents carrying these older charts out of Medical Records with hunched, strained shoulders. Every time a hospital staff member sees a patient, every time a doctor consults or a nurse takes over a shift or an occupational therapist drops by, a note is added to the chart. To read such a massive dog-eared volume, you turn first and foremost to the admission notes: clean, typed summaries that explain why the patient came into the hospital and what the doctor thought about that person at that time. To write that note, the doctor interviews the patient and dictates several paragraphs, which are the medical and legal justification for the patient's presence in the hospital and which provide the evidence and argument for the identification of the illness.

During my summer at the oak-paneled hospital, I saw Gertrude prepare her first psychiatric admission note. It took four hours. By the end of the year, it would take her no more than an hour to interview the patient and dictate the admission note to the chart, but the afternoon I sat with her she was paralyzed. She had been a highly effective intern at her prestigious internship. She knew, she said, what to do about chest pain. At the end of her internship she knew which patient would "code" that night—who would slip into cardiac or respiratory arrest and need to be resuscitated. But now she was panicked.

What I found fascinating about her panic was that she had all the intellectual knowledge she needed. She had interviewed her first patient with a senior resident, and they had concluded that the patient had obsessive-compulsive disorder. She had the official diagnostic handbook for psychiatry, which she'd opened to the page on obsessive-compulsive disorder. She had a copy of another admission note for a patient with obsessive-compulsive disorder. She had a mass of notes on the patient she'd just interviewed. But after the patient had gone she stood behind the desk, her body tight and clenched, swaying slightly, desperate and terrified in her neat suit.

She understood that she had to provide, for the section marked "History of the Present Illness," a chronological account of the illness, with generalizations backed up by specifics that provided evidence for one or more diagnoses. The admission note, she said, was not an account of what the patient had said; it was what the doctor, who supposedly excludes irrelevant details, interpreted the patient to have been saying. The note was supposed to demonstrate that the patient met the criteria for the diagnosis of obsessive-compulsive disorder. (There might later be a longer note detailing the entire course of the patient's history.) These criteria basically are the following:

1. *The patient must have* obsessions *(recurrent thoughts or impulses that are intrusive and distressing; they are not simply excessive worries about real-life problems; the person attempts to suppress them; the person knows the thoughts are a product of his own mind; e.g., he is not psychotic)* or compulsions *(repetitive behaviors such as hand washing, door checking, and so on, or mental acts such as praying, that the person feels driven to perform; these acts are aimed at preventing some dreaded event but are not realistically connected to its prevention).*
2. *The person has recognized at some point that these obsessions or compulsions are unreasonable.*
3. *The obsessions or compulsions cause marked distress, are time-consuming (requiring more than an hour a day), or significantly interfere with the person's life.*
4. *The obsessions or compulsions are not due to another psychiatric illness (such as obsessing about food in anorexia nervosa).*
5. *Nor are they due to some other medical or drug-related condition.* [1]

An appropriate admissions note would probably have looked like this example from a psychiatric textbook:

The patient is a 24-year-old white single man who comes to the clinic, referred by and accompanied by his mother, for consultation about compulsions and obsessions. He presents with a history of rituals starting in childhood and becoming more disabling over time. He reports that after college he began checking the locks on his house repeatedly and checking his car for break-ins, then checking household appliances repetitively for safety. He developed excessive grooming rituals and became so obsessive at his work as an accountant that he was forced to quit. He then became fearful of losing control and of public aggression, fearful of acquiring AIDS, and concerned about the symmetry of objects. He has recently moved back into his parents' home, where his rituals have become so extensive that they consume the entire day, and he is no longer able to bathe or groom himself in consequence. The patient is aware that these behaviors are excessive and unreasonable, but when he attempts to stop them he becomes so overwhelmed with anxiety that he ends up redoubling his ritual efforts. There appears to be no precipitating cause for these behaviors in medical illness or any other psychiatric illness. There also appears to be no family history of this condition. The patient presents as an unkempt, poorly groomed man who is intellectually intact and without symptoms of psychosis.[2]

diagnosis: obsessive-compulsive disorder 300.3

But Gertrude's patient hadn't produced a story much like that: organized, abstract, distant from the minutiae of the facts. Patients never do, unless they have been through many, many admissions, and then only if they want to cooperate with the doctor. In psychiatry, patients don't produce information as easily as they do in other medical settings. Most patients with physical disorders are frightened by their pain and eager to give information about it. Psychiatric patients have a very different relationship to their symptoms and don't always want to answer questions. Gertrude's patient probably found his rituals deeply embarrassing. He probably wanted the help, but he also probably wanted to tell this stranger as little as possible to get it. The paranoid patient, who has an unrealistic fixed belief that people are out to get him, may not feel, at the time, that it is of any relevance to the doctor that there is a conspiracy of aliens against him. The manic-depressive patient, whose judgment is usually quite poor during periods of illness, may take a dislike to the doctor and say that she has been behaving perfectly normally. Interviewing a psychiatric patient can be like trying to catch fish with your hands.

Moreover, while Gertrude had a clear, abstract idea about obsessive-compulsive disorder (all those notes), she had no "intuition." The diagnosis didn't feel ingrained, at her fingertips. "In internship," she said, "at the beginning of the year, I remember the senior resident rotating around the floors checking out how things were going for the intern who was there all night. What would happen would be that the nurses would pull him aside and say, 'You know, this patient in room 114 doesn't look too good to me.' So the senior resident would, in a very nonchalant way, saunter over and say, 'How's it going, how is that patient in 114 doing?' and the intern might say, 'Oh, not so bad,' and the senior would say, 'Oh, let me look at the vital signs [blood pressure, temperature, etc.]. Oh, that looks kind of funny, let's go take a look at him together.' As a beginner, you miss a lot of things, because you haven't seen the volume of patients. As the year progresses, you find that by even walking into the room and just *looking*, you can tell, this patient does not look good. That's intuition."

Clinical intuition is what doctors develop when they become what other doctors call "good." It is their expertise. Intuition is the capacity to recognize patterns in body and behavior that are relevant to clinical problems, to see what is wrong with a patient, to judge the severity of the problem, and to choose an intervention that leads as quickly as possible to the patient's recovery. When the average person walks through fields with a birder, he or she sees flowers and grass; the birder sees twenty species of birds and a complex range of their habitats. In bird-watching as in medicine, intuition means being able to pick up little, unobvious details, such as a type of grass or a smell or a little phrase, that helps you to know what you are seeing. But in medicine, the field guides to disease have an oblique relationship to sick people. It is rarely the case that a particular symptom (dizziness, for example) is produced by one and only one disease. Physicians learn how to diagnose from clusters of related symptoms so that they recognize patterns even when many of the pieces aren't manifest. Part of their skill involves making helpful guesses about which disease the pattern of symptoms suggests. A "good" or "classic" case of hypothyroidism is a depressed-looking, overweight woman with a thick tongue and dry, scaly arms. If you were a senior doctor, you might teach "hypothyroidism" to your medical students with such a case, but the hypothyroidism you diagnose in your office might have very few of those classic features. Luckily, for some illnesses, there is a simple test—a "pathognomonic test"—that confirms the diagnosis, such as a brain scan that reveals a tumor that has been causing headaches. Even in medicine this is often not true: Alzheimer's disease, for example, can be diagnosed definitively only by autopsy. In psychiatry, of course, there are no such tests—no blood tests, no X rays, no urine samples apart from those used to detect alcohol or drugs.

Because none of the psychiatric categories (at least, none of the ones that count as truly psychiatric) can be diagnosed by a test or a telltale symptom, most of the diagnoses are presented as a checklist of criteria, in which the patient has to have some but not all of the items on the list to qualify for the diagnosis. This, for example, is the diagnostic checklist for major depression:

> Five or more of the following symptoms have been present during the same two-week period, and at least one of them is depressed mood or loss of interest and pleasure:

1. *Depressed mood*
2. *Markedly diminished interest or pleasure*
3. *Significant weight loss or gain*
4. *Insomnia or hypersomnia*
5. *Psychomotor agitation or retardation (being agitated or moving leadenly)*

6. *Fatigue or loss of energy*
7. *Feelings of worthlessness or guilt*
8. *Diminished concentration*
9. *Recurrent thoughts of suicide*[3]

The obsessive-compulsive disorder checklist is more straightforward, but there is still a gulf between what a patient says and the abstract itemized diagnosis. The reason the admissions process for Gertrude's first admission took so long was that Gertrude kept trying to match up what the patient had said with what the diagnostic criteria stated. She had difficulty remembering the details in the patient's account because they didn't really yet seem like part of a story. Washing one's hands a hundred times a day seems frankly incomprehensible to most of us, a weird Borgesian exaggeration, not evidence of "excessive grooming." Ditto for checking the house lock thirty times before leaving for work or not taking out the garbage for six months. The young psychiatrist's pen hesitates at that thought: What does the place really look like? What makes it an illness, not a Hollywood fantasy? Admissions notes seem so calm and measured. Those first interviews are alien.

To new psychiatrists, fresh from treating cardiovascular disorders and lung cancer, diagnoses for which you need five of nine symptoms seem strange, despite the fact that certain medical diseases, such as lupus, are also diagnosed by checklist. These diagnoses become particularly suspect when the criteria include items such as "feelings of detachment or estrangement from others" or "feelings of worthlessness or guilt." These complaints do not seem like "real" diseases; they do not feel "organic." They suggest that a committee sat down one afternoon and voted on what "depression" should include. Which, of course, some committee did. To a young psychiatrist like Gertrude, this committee work initially has the look of whim. It is not clear to her that she is dealing with distinctly different physical processes in the body. "It was very different being an intern," she said in her first summer. "As an intern you had an agenda. You knew much more precisely what to ask. And there was always something *organically wrong,* even if it presented with a variety of symptoms. There was none of this five of nine of this or that."

Through the process of psychiatric training, those doubts disappear in practice, even among those who remain vociferously skeptical to the end. By the time young psychiatrists have finished training they can recognize the disorders immediately, the way plane spotters can spot Boeing 747s, the way bird-watchers can spot great snowy owls, the way dog lovers know the difference between a Jack Russell terrier and a beagle. Often, they talk and act as if the diagnoses pick out diseases that are as clear and distinct from one another as Jack Russells and beagles. That first year, when Gertrude learned to diagnose quickly and accurately, she began to behave as if there were psychiatric diseases that people came down with, just as they came down with meningitis. "You're sizing up the patient right away," Gertrude told me some months later, "just like in medicine. After a year of seeing people and doing countless admissions, two to five or more a week, you walk into a room, you see how they address you, and you're already thinking the diagnosis."

That summer I watched the new residents do admissions. Each was assigned one case at one o'clock and another at three. The resident would walk over to the Admissions Building after lunch, pick up any previous medical chart in the main office, thumb through it, go out to meet the patient in the waiting room, and take him or her to an interview room. Usually, the resident spent an hour interviewing the patient, and then, after a quick physical exam, the patient would be sent out to wait for an escort to the unit. One resident said to me after her first admission interview, "My job, in the admission interview, is first that I'm the primary contact with the hospital, and I want that to be a good and healing experience for the patient, and I want to convey interest in her life. But what I *have* to do is to collect information. *That's* what goes into the admission note. The art is to produce the information in a seamless way, as if you were naturally having a conversation. But that's hard. I haven't learned it, and so I fire streams of questions at the poor patient." As the doctor you want to behave "normally" in an initial interview, in a trustworthy and compassionate way, both because you want to be helpful and because the patient won't talk unless he trusts you. At the same time, your real job is to probe with specific questions into areas the patient may find embarrassing, humiliating, or distressing.

There are two distinct kinds of questions. First, there are direct questions about illness, like those medical doctors ask about medical diseases. A psychiatrist "probes" for obsessive-compulsive illness by asking questions such as "Do you wash your hands very often?" He probes for psychosis with questions such as "Do you feel that the television has special messages for you?" He probes for depression with questions such as "Have you thought recently about killing yourself?" The younger the clinician, the more likely he is to pursue the full range of possible questions with the medical student's studious anxiety, regardless of what the patient thought he came in to talk about. I once saw a second-year resident interview a nineteen-year-old man who had made the appointment because he'd decided to tell his mother that he was gay and it happened to be the one-year anniversary of his father's death from AIDS. People who lose someone close to them often feel a return of acute grief on the anniversary of the

death. It was very likely that the young man had come in for psychotherapeutic counseling. He probably wanted to talk about his grief, his anxiety,
and his need to be honest but not to hurt his mother. The young psychiatrist asked him all the diagnostic questions for psychosis (Do you think that
you can read my mind? Do you have special thoughts about the cosmos?),
for depression (Have you lost weight recently? Do you have difficulty concentrating?), and for antisocial personality disorder (Did you ever set fires
before you were sixteen?). The adolescent, who had clearly cinched up his
courage to come talk about his decision, sat in baffled astonishment. More
often the clinician will ask a series of targeted questions around the diagnosis the psychiatrist thinks will fit the patient, and those questions will
focus on the defining characteristics of that category. If a psychiatrist sus-
pects that the patient became manic, she will ask: Were you talking very
quickly? Did you spend a lot of money? Was it a great weekend for sex?

Then there are questions that are essentially indirect ways of getting
information the patient may not want to, or cannot, give. Often the psychiatrist asks some everyday questions and gives small tests to judge whether
there is anything bizarrely amiss in the patient's thinking. A patient may, for
example, be asked to count backward from one hundred by sevens; to
remember the words "car," "book," and "umbrella" and repeat them a few
minutes later; who the president is; what day it is; what "A stitch in time
saves nine" means; what he would do if he saw a stamped, addressed enve-
lope lying on the sidewalk. There are at least two versions of this last
test of common sense, the other being "What would you do if you saw a
fire?" In the summer seminar session on the mental status exam, one of the
senior residents described a patient, bored at the end of his admission
interview, who when asked what he would do if he saw a fire said that he
would put it in the mailbox. That, said the resident, was a patient of many
admissions.

Sample Admissions Protocol

Patient name:
Identifying data: Age, ethnic group, sex, marital status, employment
    status, referral source.
Chief complaint: Complaint in patient's own words.
History of present illness: Use problem-oriented format. For each symp-
    tom/problem include age of onset, severity and duration of symp-
    toms, precipitating and maintaining factors, presence or absence of
    neurovegetative signs, response to medications. Use back of page if
    necessary.
Past psychiatric history:

Substance abuse: Number of drinks/day, last drink. History of DWIs, etc.

Medications: Current psychotropic and nonpsychotropic medications.

Allergies:

Family history: List current and past family psychiatric disorders (including substance abuse) and medical disorders. List treatment received and effectiveness. Also include suicides in the family.

Medical history: Include history of head trauma, major illnesses, hospitalizations, and operations.

Current functioning: Indicate living arrangements, occupation, economic status, social and leisure activities, sexual orientation and functioning.

Past development: Describe sibling rank, relationships with family members and peers. Describe key relationships and dating, marital and sexual history (including sexual abuse). Describe educational history, highest grade completed, and work history.

MENTAL STATUS EXAM

1. *General appearance and behavior*
   Examples: Appearance: in relation to age, grooming, clothing, eye contact; behavior: agitated, retarded, bizarre, abnormal movements, restlessness; attitude: cooperative, defensive, guarded, hostile.
2. *Speech*
   Examples: Rate, rhythm, pitch, intensity, fluency.
3. *Mood and affect* (Mood: patient's subjective description of feeling tone over time. Affect: the outward manifestation of the patient's emotional state at the moment.)
   Examples: Mood: happy, sad, depressed, irritable, angry; affect: appropriate, flat, constricted, depressed, euphoric, anxious, elated, angry.
4. *Thought process and content*
   Examples: Tangential, circumstantial, loose associations, flight of ideas, thought blocking, delusions, paranoia, ideas of reference, intrusive thoughts, obsessions, compulsions, phobias, hallucinations, illusions, suicidal/homicidal ideation.
5. *Cognitive functions*
   Examples: Orientation, attention, memory, serial 7s, presidents, proverbs.
6. *Insight and judgment* (Insight: awareness of being ill; judgment: ability to compare and assess facts and alternatives in deciding on a course of action).

What's Wrong with the Patient?

DSM *diagnosis and code (five axes):*
Psychosocial assessment:
Goals:
Treatment plan:

From Gertrude's earliest days on the ward, as she prepared to take call and to do her first admissions, she memorized lists of diagnostic criteria, sometimes with mnemonic aids, such as SIGECAPS for depression (depressed mood plus four of these eight: sleep, interest, guilt, energy, concentration, appetite, psychomotor retardation or agitation, suicidality). Medical students attend lectures on the differences between depression and psychotic depression, or between organic delusional disorder and schizophrenia, in which the resident who is teaching the class writes the criteria out on the board and explains them. During the first months of doing admissions, new residents will pick up the small *DSM (Diagnostic and Statistical Manual)* handbook while talking to a patient and turn to a specific diagnosis to make sure they've asked about all the criteria. And often the lore passed on to new residents about the admission process circles around the symptoms and the criteria. In the summer seminar series the chief resident advised Gertrude's class, "Try to memorize the topic you always forget; I always used to forget about obsessive symptoms." And the daily structure of hospital life creates a learning environment that is highly effective in persuading residents to memorize these complex categories by criteria, because the failure to be "good enough" becomes a public humiliation.

Medical rounds, for instance, often amount to a junior resident's public performance of diagnostic knowledge. In a hospital, most of the important decisions are made or discussed in team meetings, or rounds, where all ward staff members—junior and senior psychiatric residents, psychiatric attendings, psychologists, nurses, social workers, and so forth—meet to discuss each patient assigned to their team. These meetings take place usually twice a week, although "sign-in rounds," when the on-call doctors hand off responsibility to the day staff, meet every morning. Newly admitted patients are presented and discussed in detail, in discussions that may take more than half an hour each. Other patients are more briefly presented, and their progress is assessed. In most cases the presentations are done by a junior resident (or his or her medical student) who has been assigned as the responsible doctor on the case. When this is so, the job of the assembled ten people is to check the work of the most junior doctor. If the junior doctor gets the diagnosis or medication wrong, he is made to feel not only stupid but culpable. There is, after all, a patient's life involved, and most residents and students feel guilty and embarrassed when they make mistakes. Sometimes the senior doctors deliberately humiliate them. I remember this happening most commonly over prescription errors. In one hospital, the resident did not want to place her patient on an antipsychotic. Her senior psychiatrist disagreed. When they got to her patient in the team meeting, he announced that she had made a mistake and insisted that she write the order in the chart during the meeting, so that everyone could see that she had done it. Shame is a common teaching tool in medical education.

In one hospital, each inpatient team had two junior residents, and each semiweekly team meeting ran through all of one resident's eight to twelve patients. The resident would pull out his patient identification cards from his shirt pocket and begin to recite in a tired voice, "Mr. Jones is our fifty-one-year-old depressed divorced white male. He presented in the ER last Thursday with suicidal ideation, sleep disturbance, and appetite loss. We've started him on imipramine, and he's now up to fifty milligrams t.i.d. [three times a day]." These are, of course, the criteria: depressed mood for at least two weeks and at least four out of eight further criteria, of which—and this is the clinical knowledge that accompanies the memorization of diagnostic criteria—suicidality, weight loss, and changed sleep patterns are really the most distinctive and important. When a patient has been admitted and is being presented for the first time, the resident develops the account more fully and presents the diagnosis as a conclusion. New presentations are an argument for a diagnosis: "Mr. Jones is a fifty-one-year-old divorced white male with the chief complaint 'I don't want to live anymore.' He presented in the ER last night with intense suicidal ideation. He described feelings of hopelessness and guilt and reported a weight loss of ten pounds in the last three weeks. He reports extremely poor sleep with early-morning awakening. . . ."

By their second year, residents begin to talk about the "feel" of the disorders. They say that they "sense" or "intuit" psychosis. In her second year, Gertrude remarked, "There's something to be said for having seen a thousand schizophrenics and a thousand bipolars. You begin to get a 'feel.' It's kind of the art of medicine." A classmate remarked around the same time that "if you're doing your medical clerkship, your admission note is eight pages long and you have every detail under the sun. Then the intern comes along and writes a two-page note and the resident comes along and writes a one-page paragraph. Somehow that paragraph is able to distill what is important, pick it out much more clearly than the eight pages by the clinical students. Now, for me, diagnosis is more of a feel. You kind of have a feel for a patient. Someone just comes across to you as a schizophrenic or bipolar patient. I've come to appreciate what clinicians gain with time, that these people fifty and sixty years old have this wealth of experience and they

observing Dr. Newport

really get to the heart of the problem in a way that I'm only beginning to understand."

At some point in the first year, then, the resident moves from memorizing criteria to recognizing prototypes. By "prototype," I mean a cluster of characteristics that constitute a "good example" of a class. When you use prototypes in your thinking, you ask whether the item in question resembles the best example of that class, not whether it meets specified rules or criteria of that category. Is an ostrich a bird or a grazing animal? A prototype user asks himself whether the ostrich is more like a sparrow or more like a cow, relying both on what he can see and on an array of background theory and assumptions. An impressive battery of work in cognitive science argues that for most of our everyday categories—particularly our "basic-level" categories such as "table, chair," and "dog"—we reason by prototype. When you look at a piece of furniture to decide whether it is a table or a chair, you do not list the rules of membership in the "table" and "chair" categories in your mind. That takes time. It also often does not work, since many category members do not have all the apparent criteria of the class. (A bird that cannot fly, like the penguin, is still a bird.) Instead, the evidence suggests, you call to mind the best examples of each category, and you decide which one the questionable object most resembles.[4] You don't ask yourself whether this chair meets the criteria for chairship. You look at it, and you know it's a chair.

The great advantage of prototype use is that it is fast and efficient. You recognize rather than remember a list of membership rules. The cost is that the boundaries between categories become starker. Cognitive scientists use the phrase "prototype effects" to describe this phenomenon. People process information about prototypes more quickly than about nonprototypes, but they also tend to clump information around prototypes, so they are more likely to overinterpret similarity to a prototype.[5] If a very new resident is asked whether a patient meets *DSM* criteria for, say, schizophrenia or paranoia, that resident will pick up *DSM* and read the criteria for each. She may find that the patient meets some for both and that the difference between the two categories is not that straightforward, at least in this case. If you ask that same resident about such a patient one year later, when she has developed prototypes for the illnesses, she will probably not reach for the diagnostic handbook, and she will probably not feel that the difference between the categories is inherently uncertain. She is more likely to believe that there are clear differences between illness categories and more likely to pick up data in a case presentation that correspond to the prototype and ignore information that does not. As this happens, it becomes difficult for the psychiatrist to remember that initial skepticism about the diagnostic criteria. A patient's illness seems less like a sorting problem—is it like this or like that?—and more like a simple identification task. Diagnoses begin to feel like real, distinct objects in the body.

Certainly young psychiatrists talk about the diagnostic manual as if they use it casually and as if the disorders are there in the person's body regardless of what the manual says. As a second-year resident said, "I'm fairly sloppy about [DSM]. I use it to diagnose several broad categories, and I don't worry much about the nuances." Another, at the end of his first year, remarked, "PTSD [posttraumatic stress disorder]. . . . I couldn't give you every little ABCD, but I know what PTSD is. You have to experience one of these four things, ABCD. Category B, you have to have two of these seven things. I don't know what these things are precisely, but I kind of know what it feels like. For generalized anxiety disorder you have to worry about things, and then you have to have, like, six out of the eighteen somatic symptoms—I have no idea of what those eighteen things are, but I know when someone's anxious." Sometimes the residents seem more interested in treating people who need help than finding out whether, strictly speaking, those patients meet the printed criteria. One second-year resident remarked, "There's a lot of gray. They're sad, they're not sleeping too well, their wife just left them. Or they're anxious and it sounds like a panic attack but it just doesn't meet the criteria. If someone had to meet the diagnosis strictly before getting treated, a lot of people wouldn't be treated." Sometimes they think about the social impact of the diagnosis they choose, mostly preferring to give a diagnosis with a better prognosis for the long term (such as manic-depressive disorder) than one with a less good prognosis (such as schizophrenia) if there's any ambiguity. And they will sometimes mention diagnostic characteristics not listed in the diagnostic handbook, such as clothing or makeup. "I once diagnosed someone as hypomanic by the way they listed their name in the phone book, with *all* their names," someone told me. Or "If you ask a depressed woman whether she's ever tried to kill herself and she says, 'Fifty times,' you've got a diagnosis [borderline personality disorder]."

Young psychiatrists also act with the speed that suggests that diagnosis is more like recognizing chairs and tables than it is like pulling out a manual and carefully double-checking the printed criteria. When I began this study, an anthropologist told me that University of Kentucky residents took thirty seconds to make a diagnosis.[6] I thought at the time that he was pulling my leg. Then I spent an evening with a resident at her night job. To entertain me, she would diagnose the patient after glancing at him through the plate-glass window that separated the staff room from the waiting area. We sat in the staff room; we looked at the patient as he or she walked in the door, and my friend would say, this one's depressed, that one's manic, that one's high. Then we walked out together and she interviewed the patient, often in the presence of the police. The man she said was depressed had been picked up on a bridge, threatening to jump because he wanted to die. The man she said was manic had been running down the street half naked and was, when he began talking, clearly on a drugless high. The one she said was on drugs obviously was. That is, it was obvious to me when he began to speak; it was obvious to my psychiatric friend when she glanced at him. Shortly after I had seen Gertrude struggle through her four-hour marathon to admit *one* patient, I had lunch with a senior resident who merrily announced that he'd admitted seven patients the previous evening (in other words, after 5 p.m.) and been in bed by 1 a.m. That is less than an hour each to meet a patient, interview him or her, do a physical exam, and dictate the admission note for the chart. When I began to canvass people on the anthropologist's provocative comment the senior faculty were alarmed and defensive—they took pains to explain how carefully diagnoses were made—but residents chuckled and wondered why those Kentucky residents were so slow. Of course, few patients who appear in the hospital are totally new to psychiatry, so in most cases the patient carries a prior diagnosis, but even so the quick assessment occurs. "It's pattern recognition," Gertrude explained. "Does this seem like somebody who as you sit with them seems psychotic? Do they seem depressed? Like a trauma patient? I kind of ask myself what are they making me feel, what sense am I getting, and then once I feel confident about what direction they're heading, I'll kind of go through a list more confirming what I already sense. Just in case I'm missing something, I'll also ask about hallucinations even if they don't seem psychotic, suicide even if they don't seem suicidal. Things like that. But first I get this general gist, and then I confirm it." Psychiatrists do treat these initial diagnoses like hypotheses that their interviews will support or overturn, but the point is that they are fast. I once stood in an elevator with a psychiatrist known for his work on the diagnostic categories, and I asked him how long it took him to make a diagnosis. He looked thoughtful and slightly troubled, and then he said, "Quickly. Very quickly."

It doesn't always work like this, of course. Once a week, a hospital (or a hospital unit) will hold a case conference, and usually the point of that conference is to have a senior clinician diagnose a "diagnostic difficulty," a patient who doesn't seem to fit any category well, as if he were part table, part chair, or both at once. For example, I attended one about a patient admitted to the hospital because of a dangerous suicide attempt. He didn't really seem depressed. He "felt" psychotic to some of the doctors. When he talked about his life, it sounded schizophrenic to them. "He's very isolated," one psychiatrist said. "He has a lot of crazy ideas about the Internet, and when you talk to him, he comes across as disconnected and sort of affectless." But the patient said he was bipolar, and he talked about being "manic" and "depressed" with accomplished ease. He'd been hospitalized several times, but the medical charts from the other hospitals probably wouldn't arrive until after he'd been discharged, so it was impossible to know what he had looked like to other doctors then. He said he didn't "like" lithium or the other mood stabilizers. He said they didn't help. Was he a schizophrenic who had once been told he was bipolar and had since worked that up into a near delusion? Was he bipolar? Did he have a psychotic depression? When I saw him interviewed, the senior clinician was sure he was bipolar. But then, this senior clinician specialized in the treatment of bipolar patients. He more or less thought that most patients were bipolar. This is not that uncommon. One hospital has a PTSD (posttraumatic distress disorder) research unit with a charismatic leader, and in an admission interview the residents probe more deeply about abuse than they might elsewhere and diagnose PTSD more often. Another program is known for its schizophrenia research. There the eager residents are more likely to suspect schizophrenia than bipolar disorder in patients. In this case, the other two mature clinicians in the room thought the patient was schizophrenic.

Still, the cumulative effect of the learning process is to imply that for each diagnosis there is an underlying disease, a "stuff" the diagnosis names, and that the stuff trumps the diagnosis. That is, through the process of memorizing the criteria and learning to prototype the categories, psychiatrists learn to talk and act as if the disorders are there in the world, that they are instantly recognizable, and that the printed diagnostic criteria may only partially describe the real disorders. Young psychiatrists behave as if these categories are "natural kinds." A "natural kind" is something real in the world, such as a zebra or a horse (but not a table). We know that there is a "natural" difference between a zebra and a horse, even if an albino zebra has no stripes and a troublesome philosopher has painted black stripes on a white horse. The difference between zebras and horses is genuine. It is not a matter of social convention, we didn't invent it, and whatever makes the difference is intrinsically, even causally, related to the difference between categories. Gold is not the same as fool's gold, even though both are golden, because it is made from a different chemical compound.[7] We know that experts know the difference between the two, and we know that there is a real, underlying difference, even though we may not know what it is.

Doing a lot of diagnoses, using prototypes, and writing those admission notes tends to give one the sense that there *are* underlying essences that can be seen, named, and possibly controlled, even when the actual problem seems elusive and perplexing. One of the oldest ideas in human thought is that when you name something mysterious and out of control, you gain mastery over it. In magic and religion in cultures throughout history, to know the name for a tree or a person or a malicious spirit was to grasp its essence and so control it (unless you were too weak or impure, in which case uttering the sacred name might kill you). In medicine, of course, diagnosis gives a doctor control because it tells him how he might be able to help a patient. But something of the old magical echoes linger. To produce a name makes you feel that you have begun to master the reality of the problem and that there is, in fact, something there to master. And medical training has already persuaded the resident that diseases are natural kinds existing in the body. A viral infection is not the same as a bacterial infection, even if they sometimes produce similar symptoms and even if the difference between them is not easily explained, and the doctor's job is to figure out which disease it is.

The practical demands of psychiatric training lead young psychiatrists to speak and act as if the illnesses they diagnose in the hospital are diseases of inherently different kinds. As a result of the demands placed on them in this situation, they are told that the patient has an illness that they must identify. They are told as well by this situation that they can get the identification wrong, and if so they will be humiliated; the identification, in other words, is not trivial but meaningful. They are told that identifying a patient as having both bipolar disorder and schizophrenia, for example, is a mistake, whereas suggesting that a patient has either bipolar disorder or schizophrenia (or even schizoaffective disorder) can be understood as a reasonable identification.[8] They learn to identify a category by clumping available information around good examples. They know that although the diagnostic handbooks are composed by committees, there are experts, revered within psychiatric culture, who believe that the basic diagnoses are diseases. They have already been deeply schooled in the disease model of medicine by their training in medicine. Psychiatric illness is probably more complicated than many medical diseases and certainly in many cases less well understood. The difference between the diagnostic categories is genuinely more ambiguous because there are no clear-cut medical tests that distinguish them unambiguously and there are genuine questions about whether there really are distinct underlying diseases or not. Yet because the disease model of illness is reinforced by the cognitive experience of psychiatric training in the hospital, the inherent ambiguity of psychiatric diagnosis can rapidly disappear from the young psychiatrist's experience.

Gertrude started out skeptical and uncomfortable with the categories and their lists. By the end of the year she saw the illnesses as clearly as when we suddenly catch on to an optical trick and can no longer see the feature that makes it a puzzle for everyone else. And with that she became confident. She could do admissions quickly, manage night call easily, and she no longer looked fraught and tense at lectures. "The more you see," she said over lunch one day, "the more you develop a sense for a problem. You do work with prototypes, you see a number of patients with OCD, you know what questions to ask, what's important, you learn to ask for the HPI [history of the present illness], you learn what the clinician on the other end will be interested in knowing about the person's presentation. That knowledge only comes from seeing people over and over again. With a patient with bipolar disorder, you know what to ask for: sleep is a *major* marker for what's going on with this person. You'll ask them why they are in the hospital. With bipolar disorder, they often exhibit no insight or judgment [i.e., they don't perceive themselves as ill]. That helps you. You just learn certain—formulas, in a way. Okay, this is a person with bipolar disorder, these are the things I have to look at. But I also try, in my formulation, to raise a differential diagnosis [list other possible diagnoses for the condition]. The problem with prototypes is that you forget what other things might be happening. The person I admitted last night has only a three-year history of bipolar disorder and she's forty-eight, so she got it when she was forty-five. So she's presenting manic, but I'm not totally convinced, because it doesn't really jive with what we know about bipolar disorder [which usually manifests itself before thirty-five]. It makes me think there might be something else. Does she have a tumor in her head? Does she have an occult cancer that's metastasized to her brain and is causing this funny behavior? It makes you suspicious that something else could be going on, and that's what we mean by differential diagnosis. Clinicians put a lot of emphasis on that."

There are two important caveats here. The training experience that tends to encourage young psychiatrists to treat diagnoses like different underlying diseases is relevant, these days, only to some diagnoses. The organizing committee for the first postpsychoanalytic diagnostic manual (*DSM III*, in 1980) wanted the manual to bridge the field's differences, to be accepted by everyone in the field, even while knowing that they were creating a revolutionary document. So they made an effort to be deferential to the psychoanalysts, and they created two kinds of diagnostic categories, Axis I and Axis II. (There were and are other axes as well: one for medical conditions, one for stressors such as divorce or moving, one for general level of functioning. The authors of *DSM III* seem to have envisioned a set of continua that located a patient precisely in some multidimensional descriptive world. For the most part, psychiatrists worry only about the first two axes.) Axis I, the first group of diagnoses, is thought of as being more "biological." It was the product of the new psychiatric scientists who began to emerge in the 1970s and 1980s. In this group one finds schizophrenia, bipolar disorder, major depression, obsessive-compulsive disorder, panic disorders, posttraumatic stress disorder, dissociative disorder, and a great many other categories. These are supposed to be "clinical syndromes." The thinking behind this was that one has such a disorder more or less for life but there are certain times when it becomes more "active." Axis II, the second group, was developed by the psychodynamically oriented members of the committee. Here one finds "personality disorders" of various types: narcissistic, schizoid, obsessive-compulsive (as distinguished from the Axis I clinical syndrome), borderline, antisocial, and so forth. These are supposed to be long-standing problems of character. They are not supposed to become more active at one time than at another (although clinicians in fact treat them as if they do). They just are, like being a nervous person or an intense one. Sometimes psychiatrists say that Axis I disorders are like "states"—you go into and out of them—while Axis II disorders are like "traits," such as having brown hair.

These days psychiatric researchers have heated debates about whether these clusters are fundamentally distinct. Certainly some of the personality disorders can be as deadly as Axis I disorders, in that people with personality disorders can be at significant risk for suicide. But—and here enters a social force—only Axis I diagnoses are learned with bird-watching acuity as distinct, clear-cut objects. Because the character disorders are supposed to imply long-standing, constant problems, most hospitals (or at least their insurers) insist on limiting psychiatric hospital admissions to patients who can be described as having an Axis I category in an acute phase. Hospital admissions are meant to be limited to those who are a danger to themselves or others or incapable of self-care. In the admission note, those states are usually attributed to an Axis I disorder, the patient is treated for the Axis I disorder, and the personality disorder becomes something that makes him more or less difficult to treat (he is dramatic, irritable, entitled, and so forth) and not the cause of his illness. Whether or not these Axis I disorders (or for that matter the Axis II disorders) turn out to have underlying diseases, they are already powerfully institutionalized as if they did and as if the personality disorders did not.

The second caveat is that there is a major contradiction in the learning process that challenges the naturalness of these distinctions. Psychopharmacology is the great, silent dominatrix of contemporary psychiatry. It is what psychiatrists do that other mental health professionals cannot do; and as mental health jobs become defined more by their professional specificity, more and more psychiatrists spend more of their time prescribing medication. This is where the weight of most psychiatric research is placed. More money is spent developing, testing, and analyzing psychopharmacological drugs than in any other area of psychiatry; more people are involved in the research; more patients (these days) are probably touched by these agents than by anything else the psychiatric profession does. And when a doctor medicates in psychiatry, he or she is thinking in a way that can cut across diagnostic categories and undermine the notion that there are separate underlying diseases that correlate with those categories.

Psychiatric medications treat symptoms, not diseases. They touch the way people act, not the underlying mechanisms. So when psychiatrists focus on medications, they sometimes behave as if the symptoms are the things in the world and the diagnostic categories have been invented by committees and reified by insurance companies. They say things such as "First you sort of break things down into gross categories. Are you dealing with a mood disorder? Is there more an anxiety component or an affective component? The bulk of what you treat, the question is psychotic spectrum versus biochemical depression or anxiety versus neurotic issues." At the end of her first year, Gertrude said, "The first thing I'm trying to get a handle on is whether they will need medication. I'm kind of thinking *DSM,* and, based on their chief complaint, they're either going to go down a depression road, a psychotic road, or an anxiety road." There are only a small number of symptoms that make up a wide variety of psychiatric illnesses, and even these symptoms are not straightforward. You can't see them directly like a runny nose or test them objectively like a fever. There is the lead-dragging soul weariness of depression; the hallucinatory disconnectedness of psychosis; mood swings; and anxiety. There are, of course, many more particular symptoms—obsessiveness, impulsivity, addiction, and more—but depression, psychosis, mood swings, and anxiety are the most important. They are, however, inferred from behavior. Depression is inferred from lethargy, insomnia, poor appetite, suicidal thoughts, and other behaviors; psychosis is inferred from hallucinations, bizarre beliefs, and the like. You call someone "psychotic" when you *interpret* him as having a seriously and significantly distorted view of reality. You call someone depressed when you *interpret* her as having a seriously and significantly lower mood than is normal. Psychiatric disorders are inferred, in turn, from different combinations of these symptoms. Psychosis is a symptom of schizophrenia, bipolar disorder, delusional disorder, psychotic depression, and other disorders. Someone can be interpreted as being psychotic (he has told a doctor that she is the president's sister), but that in itself is not enough to diagnose him as schizophrenic. Depression is a symptom of depressive illness but is also found in bipolar disorder, schizoaffective disorder, and others. And medication treats the symptom, not the disease.

Because of the way she has been trained, Gertrude acts as if she believes that psychiatric illnesses pick out real and discrete disease processes in the body. She talks about figuring out what is going on with a patient the way an ophthalmologist talks about figuring out if a patient has a corneal erosion. At the same time, her primary practical concern is with what medication to prescribe, and the medications target symptoms found across many diagnostic categories. So she also behaves as if the symptoms are the "real" physical processes and the diagnoses are just some labels some committee dreamed up. That ambiguity arises from the intersection of diagnosis and medication. It is a messy, complicated intersection.

It is true that medication can help a doctor to specify a diagnosis. If a patient doesn't seem to need medication for a particular symptom, he shouldn't be diagnosed with a disorder in which that symptom is prominent. For example, mood swings are necessary (but not sufficient) for the diagnosis of bipolar disorder. If the supposed manic-depressive does not respond to lithium or to another of the mood stabilizers, a psychiatrist will wonder whether after all he's schizophrenic. If a supposed schizophrenic is managed effectively on antianxiety agents or even without medication, a psychiatrist will question whether she is, in fact, schizophrenic. For instance, a first-year resident remarked, "This guy, I'm not convinced he is schizophrenic although he probably meets criteria; in ways he's a sort of classic description of it. But there are some things in his background that make me wonder about whether he really is a paranoid schizophrenic. Because he's been treated with a lot of different medications, and none of them are antipsychotic, and it makes me wonder. And then he was off meds for four or five years, and before that he was on Valium. *Valium* [i.e., not a very strong medication and certainly not one that targeted psychotic symptoms]." Another psychiatrist said about a different patient, "I don't know about this label [schizophrenia]. She's had a partner, she's actually got this guy interested in marrying her and he's apparently perfectly reasonable, she's managed without meds. I just don't think that the label makes sense." Or a second-year resident: "You try to give them the benefit of the doubt, you call them manic-depressive, and you put them on lithium and see what happens. I like to give the better diagnoses, the ones with better prognoses, unless there's no choice."

The psychiatrist's willingness to diagnose post facto on the basis of medication is not unlike the rest of medicine. ("Take the antibiotics, and if the rash doesn't go away, we'll know it wasn't Lyme disease.")[9] But at least in medicine, some problems can be diagnosed through tests and scans. Combine the fact that in psychiatry you cannot test for the disease with the fact that the medications often don't work, and the psychiatric picture begins to look murkier than the medical. To make matters even more complicated, most patients are on more than one medication. They may be on Stelazine or Risperdal for psychotic symptoms, as well as on Prozac or Elavil for their depression; maybe Cogentin to counteract the others' side effects; trazodone, another antidepressant, for sleep; occasionally Ativan for agitation; Tegretol because someone wondered whether mood instability was involved. The patient may enter the hospital with an arm's-length list of different medications, the cumulative result of multiple "doctors' attempts to be both conservative and effective. Occasionally a scientific paper is published arguing that patients should be taken off their multiple medications to create "baseline" conditions, but more often the study fails because some patients who have been medicated for years cannot function without their pills and the doctor is sued for his negligence. Hospitals used to admit patients for long inpatient stays for precisely this reason. Some were famous for taking their patients off all medications and then adding them back slowly one by one to see which ones were helpful and which not. Most psychiatric medications take several weeks to take effect, and even those that create behavioral changes immediately—such as the antipsychotics—need time in order to determine the most effective dosage. But in a five-day admission, which is fairly standard these days, there is no time to take a patient off medications to see what works or doesn't. Most patients, then, tend to be continued on whatever they are on.

Moreover, while the major psychiatric symptoms are targeted by clusters of medications—antipsychotics, antidepressants, antianxiety agents (or anxiolytics), and mood stabilizers—not all medications of a cluster will help a patient with a particular symptom. Different bodies respond differently to medications in the same chemical family, and there are many subtleties in the common interactions between different medications. In fact, there is no reason to be confident that any medication will work. Sometimes depression doesn't respond to anything. All of the symptoms are associated with more than one illness. As a result, a medication response really alters diagnosis in psychiatry only when a medication works when you would not expect it to, or when a patient does well without a medication the diagnosis would seem to demand. A medicine's failure to work reveals nothing.

Thinking in terms of medication can leave a psychiatrist skeptical and hesitant about diagnosis itself because ultimately the medication is more important than the diagnosis, and because prescribing medication is what the doctor actually does. For all the uncertainty, psychopharmacology makes young residents feel like doctors. Prescribing medication makes them feel as if they are doing something to relieve the body's pain, to act against the venom of disease within the body. They borrow the verb "use" to describe what they do when they prescribe. Psychiatrists say, "With an older patient I'll use half or a third what I'd use with an adult." Or "I use trazodone at lower levels during the day if the patient is still anxious and depressed." It is a striking verb: doctors, of course, never touch the medication. They merely write a few words on a piece of paper and hand it to the patient, or perhaps make a note in the chart. But this action serves metaphorically as their incising surgical knife in an act to remove the tumorous illness, and so well established is this metaphorical sensibility that some insurance companies will not cover a psychiatric inpatient stay unless the psychiatrist prescribes psychiatric medication and the patient takes it. (I remember standing at the door in rounds once, listening to a doctor plead with his patient to take his medications, because the insurance company would not cover his stay if he did not.) As young psychiatrists inhabit this metaphor, they come to feel convinced that they are dealing with organic disease.

Then they can turn around and question the diagnostic categories because in a sense they no longer need them. At this point, challenging the categories does not challenge the existence of organic disease. For instance, by the end of their residency, young psychiatrists will say that the people "just don't fit the categories" and will not infrequently describe themselves as focusing on symptoms rather than on categories. They'll talk of being "phenomenologically" minded. They'll talk about the "lore" of psychiatry, rule-of-thumb generalizations that have arisen from their own experience and that they will teach their students but that rarely appear in the official teaching texts of the profession. As one psychiatrist said, "Mine is a very experiential diagnosis. When I have to bill for services or write something down in the chart, I'll follow the basic guidelines of *DSM*, but with regard to treatment [sometimes] you have to use other rules." Another said, "You know, you've been asking me about *DSM* and it's funny. . . . Now, I see three patients an hour, about three hundred a month, and I love it. . . . I do the diagnosis, the treatment plan, the med management and you know, I don't find slapping *DSM* labels on patients all that useful. I find, at these clinics, that it's a lot more useful to use a symptom-oriented approach, keeping in mind that it's a whole syndrome, because a psychotic agitated schizophrenic can look a lot like a psychotic manic and someone who's suicidal because they're depressed can end up killing himself just like someone who kills himself because he's psychotic. Sometimes," this resident continued, "I think there's too much time and energy wasted on trying to redefine everything. There's this idea, the great medical model, that if we get the chronic paranoid schizophrenic nailed exactly right, then we'll have our diagnostic category, we'll have everyone fit into this category, you'll have the treatment, but I don't think so. And the patients are more compliant if they feel that you're working with their symptoms rather than putting some proclamation down."

One of the results of this complexity is that an anthropologist can see a two-tier level of expertise among psychiatrists. There is what I call "basic competence." After a year, a young psychiatrist can usually diagnose very rapidly, and he knows a fair amount about some medications associated with the major disorders. "Learn three medications well," the chief residents advised in the summer seminar. An adequate young psychiatrist can sound knowledgeable, prescribe adequate doses, and expect to see behavioral change if he is familiar with one antipsychotic, one or two antidepressants, one mood stabilizer, and perhaps one or two antianxiety agents for good measure. At this level of expertise, sometimes a psychiatrist behaves as if the underlying "stuff" is the disease and sometimes as if the "stuff" is symptoms picked out by medication. In team meetings and case conferences, he talks about schizophrenia, psychotic depression, and so forth. When he worries about what to do for the patient, he talks about anxiety, psychosis, and despair.

Ten years later (in any field, it seems to take about ten years to acquire deep expertise), some psychiatrists seem to reach what I call a level of "connoisseurship" in diagnosis and psychopharmacology. In some ways, this is what physicians call the "art" of medicine. Older psychiatrists who work in a hospital describe themselves as being faster and sharper in diagnosis than they were when they were younger. They say that they move more economically down a decision tree; that they rarely ask all the questions they used to; that they rely more heavily on questions that discriminate between categories; that they interpret with cues arising out of clinical experience in addition to those in *DSM*. "Compared to the residents, my hypotheses are faster, there's better intuition, an interview that's shorter but obtains more information. There's more economy of effort. I can be more conversational. More relaxed. I can spend the first fifteen minutes on *DSM* and the rest on psychodynamics." They become very sophisticated in their views on drugs and their interactions. The resident says that she doesn't think that Mr. X is responding well to drug Y; the senior psychiatrist responds, "Someone who comes in agitated like him rarely does; if you supplement with drug Z, you'll find that drug Y is more effective." On one unit, a woman admitted after a car accident had become so depressed that she couldn't formulate sentences. The resident said to the senior doctor that she thought Prozac would be a good drug for the patient, because it was stimulating. He replied, "No. People think that Prozac's stimulating because it's not sedating, but I think that she has dopaminergic problems. If you want to stimulate her, you'd use something that would hit that neurotransmitter, like Wellbutrin. Or maybe try an

MAOI. You can try Prozac, but I think you'll fail." The cynical take on this "art" is that psychiatrists prescribe medications according to simple inductive rules. As one resident remarked sardonically, "I had five patients and each had one brown eye and one blue eye, and each responded well to Wellbutrin [an atypical antidepressant]." The less cynical take is that after a physician has seen a thousand depressed patients, he may have a good "nose" for the issues. Of course, people often act as if they know what they are talking about even when they do not. When I was spending time with psychiatrists, there were some whose inferences I'd have trusted absolutely and others who I thought were selling snake oil.

At this level, the distinctions between the categories break down, and the contradiction between the thinglike diseases that the diagnoses pick out (in which the symptoms are merely surface features) and the thinglike symptoms that the medications treat (in which the diagnoses are merely convenient labels) tends to be replaced by more tentative subcategories generated by knowledge of the brain, of psychopharmacological process, and by sheer clinical experience of illness behavior. And as at other levels of high expertise (in cardiology, oncology, or, for that matter, stamp collecting), consensus breaks down. Different senior psychiatric experts have widely diverging ideas about what they are treating and how to treat it. One expert sees mood disorders where another sees personality disorders. One expert sees dissociative disorder where another sees histrionics. More generally, connoisseurship in the biomedical domain involves complicated knowledge of biological pathways. An adequate resident can recognize depression and know which drugs to prescribe and at what dose without knowing anything about what happens to the brain in depression or anything about how the drugs might work. That ignorance makes depression seem particularly thinglike because it makes the depression-disease relationship seem simple. The more sophisticated the psychiatrist the more depression appears to be the behavioral endpoint of an array of neural pathways shaped by genes, environment, life events, psychodynamic habits, temperament, diet, and luck.

This becomes particularly evident when you realize how poorly we understand the way the drugs actually work. Neurotransmitters are the chemicals that communicate at the synapse of two neurons. Generally speaking (according to the experts), there are at least three neurotransmitter systems that are thought to be involved with psychiatric illness: the dopamine system, the norepinephrine system, and the serotonin system. For years, schizophrenia was explained by the "dopamine hypothesis," which supposed that psychosis (and other symptoms) resulted from a functional excess of dopamine; mood disorders were explained by the "catecholamine hypothesis," which supposed that depression was the result of too little norepinephrine and mania the result of too much; then, because the Prozac family blocks serotonin reuptake, the new depression hypothesis held that depression had to do with serotonin. But none of those theories appears to be accepted anymore, because research and the new medications that treat these various symptoms suggest more complicated stories. The new antipsychotics, for example, also seem to be involved with serotonin, and the dopamine receptors that are blocked by the old antipsychotics are not very common in the areas of the brain associated with cognition, which one would think would be associated with schizophrenic deficits. In fact, the more that is learned about neurotransmitters and psychopharmacology, the more complex the picture grows: there are more kinds of neurotransmitters, more kinds of receptors, more interdependence. There are, as a recent textbook explains, no simple neurotransmitter-illness relationships.[10] On the other hand, enough is now known about these various systems that it is an enormously exciting time to be a psychiatric scientist, because there are so many puzzles to solve.

Many psychiatric publications attempt to bridge the gap between complex knowledge and basic competency. One example is Stephen Stahl's *Essential Psychopharmacology*. Its pages bristle with detailed information about what is currently known and hypothesized about the neural pathways of the major psychiatric disorders. It is full of incomprehensible sentences like these (in the depression chapter): "Receptor subtyping for the serotonergic neuron has proceeded at a very rapid pace, with at least four major categories of 5-HT receptors, each further subtyped depending upon pharmacological or molecular properties. 5-HT receptors are a good example of how the description of neurotransmitter receptors is in constant flux, and is constantly being revised."[11] Most psychiatrists have last encountered such sentences in medical school, and the words have no relationship to what they do day to day as clinicians. Thus, accompanying the prose are delightful cartoons of the synapses and the activity around them. Enzymes are drawn as little ghosts that pump and kill and otherwise bat the neurotransmitters around. Stahl explains the various competing biological theories of depression and the evidence for and against each; he then explains how the drugs affect each pathway involved in the different viable hypotheses (to the extent that this is understood). He points out the differences between these treatments and the biochemical logic of how they might be combined. The book can be read and used effectively by people with varying degrees of knowledge (thus the cartoons), but one point shines clearly: the deeper your knowledge, the less you are convinced that there is a simple disease process and the more you are convinced that medications affect particular pathways that are often, but not always, involved in the behavioral manifestation of a very complex illness.

Psychopharmacology is a remarkable enterprise, full of hope and greed and also spectacle. In 1994, a pharmaceutical company launched a new anti-depressant at the annual meeting of the American Psychiatric Association, a professional convention attended by more than a quarter of the practicing psychiatrists in the country. The annual meeting's air of carnival is much enhanced by the exhibition area, a vast gymnasium space subdivided into small display areas usually occupied by pharmaceutical companies. There are other occupants, residential treatment centers or new health care services, but their small booths have a lonely, fretful feel. The large pharmaceutical companies—Upjohn, Sandoz, Dista—rent areas the size of large houses and install in them classical temples to their drugs, with "Paxil," "Xanax," "Risperdal" in the tympana. Some of them devise complex strategies to attract passersby. That year, Sandoz had a high-tech video display of Freud's life and its neighbor mounted a show of art by the mentally ill. Most booths gave out pens and occasionally more expensive items. Over several years I acquired an umbrella, William Styron's memoir of depression, and varied mugs, one of them a heat-sensitive cup with a blue stripe that faded, when the cup was filled with hot water, into the phrase "panic comes out of the blue." If the marketing works, the reward is considerable: with 20 million people on Prozac, there are still millions more who may need but are not given treatment. One reputable estimate states that the lifetime prevalence for psychiatric illness is 22 percent of all Americans, more if alcoholism and substance abuse are included. Most of these illnesses strike young and are chronic or recurring, and 20 to 30 percent of those affected are never treated.[12] The needs of this market are a manufacturer's dream.

In 1994, the largest, most dramatic, and by far the most memorable exhibit on the floor was the "brain booth," Wyeth-Ayerst's marketing device for Effexor. It was a sort of converted Volkswagen minibus. Above it hung huge flat brains with drooping brain stems. Red lightning shot through the brains at intervals. Somewhere discreetly to the side was the name "Effexor." You could line up to enter the brain booth, for a voyage to the interior of the brain. I did so and found myself in a small, dark cavity with eleven other people. The door shut, and in the darkness a screen lit up with a picture meant to represent the inside of the brain stem. To add a sense of drama, the minibus now began pitching and heaving, so as to evoke the rough, uncharted terrain through which we were passing. I stopped focusing on not being claustrophic and began to concentrate on not having motion sickness. We stopped the voyage at various points, mostly at neuronal synaptic clefts, where geometric shapes of different colors floated around to demonstrate neurotransmitter activity. There were also opportunities for interactive learning, with a little board in front of us with buttons to push in response to questions posed by bearded, knowledgeable scientists in the video. (I noticed at these points that my fellow travelers seemed also to be more intent on their lack of motion sickness than on the little boards.) Which neurotransmitter was commonly associated with depression? Which did new research suggest might also be involved? Which neurotransmitters, now that we were on the topic, did Effexor target? Exactly those. "You should see the brain booth," a psychoanalyst told me before I entered the exhibit area. "If you can explain the brain booth, you can explain contemporary psychiatry."

IN OUTPATIENT PSYCHOTHERAPY

"Beginning to get decent at psychotherapy is like discovering an extra limb and finding it incredibly useful. Once you discover it, it's a little difficult to go back to doing things with two hands. When I'm in a social interaction, I get a little embarrassed with myself. You see people who have boundary problems, and they're seductive and alluring and you can get sucked in. It would be hard, now, to let myself go with the flow with someone like that. Part of me would be noticing what was going on, what was happening. I can't turn it off completely."

Earle is a tall, slim New Yorker, quite elegant, rather sardonic. He had, as most psychiatrists used to, a background in the humanities. He was thought to be one of the better psychotherapists in his residency program. He was considering analytic training. "The way I think now," he said, "is very different from the way I thought in medicine. There is so much less that is explained by rules that apply to more than one person. When I first started, I wanted there to be some unifying theory. Rules and so on. Actually, what's important is knowing the particular person. All people have their own system, their own way of how things work, with particular fears, particular wishes. Getting to know that instance is much more important than the rule it may test or not. One thing I've noticed is that I'm much less judgmental of my patients than they imagine me to be. I really am. It's not interesting to me anymore to make a judgment; it's interesting to understand. The more I know my patients, the less I diagnose them. The closer you get, the less helpful it is to classify and the more you doubt the classifications. I think my process has been that of coming at the patients with some vague and cherished theories and hoping that they won't disprove them. And they did. They always do."

Psychodynamic thinking is a curious and highly distinctive manner of thought: between those who think psychodynamically and those who do not, there is a gulf as wide and alienating as between those who think logically and those who do not. It is notoriously difficult to characterize. Psychotherapists produce an array of metaphors to describe the therapeutic encounter—it is a dance, a duel, a drama, an attempt to listen with a different ear, to listen for what is under the surface or behind the words; it is peeling the onion, unraveling the psyche, piercing the armor of the character; it is an attempt to see the translation of motive into action in which every action serves the self.

If achieving basic competence in diagnosis and psychopharmacology is like becoming a master bird-watcher, learning the skill of psychotherapy is more like learning to be a storyteller. One might describe Freud's central contribution to psychotherapy by saying that he "discovered" the unconscious, or at least that more than any of its other discoverers he demonstrated that we are all motivated in ways we do not grasp for reasons we cannot give.[13] But his more fundamental legacy was to suggest that we can decode our behavior and our history to discover the grammar of a particular person's emotions, the implicit rules that explain why a remark offends one person but makes another laugh, why one person enjoys aggression and another finds it terrifying. Analysts listen for the stories that emerge from the way people talk about other people, the way they experience those people, the way they experience the therapist, and the way they experience themselves, although what the analyst hears is not just what the patient says. As diagnosticians listen for clues to a diagnosis, therapists too listen for clues to a model. They listen, however, in a very different way.

At some point in their first year, young psychiatrists are assigned their first psychotherapy outpatient. In their second year, which is their outpatient year, residents can take on more cases, but only an ambitious resident—ambitious, that is, as a psychotherapist—will take on as many as ten. (That year, their other patients are outpatient psychopharmacology patients. A resident may carry a monthly caseload of more than one hundred psychopharmacology patients, whom he sees for fifteen or twenty minutes apiece, and three psychotherapy patients.) In the past, residents were encouraged to see their psychotherapy patients twice or even three times weekly, but these days many factors militate against doing so. Usually a resident meets with each patient once a week for forty-five or fifty minutes, although occasionally a patient will arrange to come in less frequently (usually for financial reasons) or more frequently (maybe twice a week). For each patient, or for every two patients, the resident has a supervisor, usually an analyst who volunteers his time in exchange for an affiliation with the medical school. The resident meets in private with the supervisor once a week to discuss the case. During the outpatient year, each resident also runs a therapy group for patients, usually with two residents per group, and as a class residents participate in a once-a-week session that is described as their own group therapy. At least one hour of lecture time each week (usually out of two to four hours) is devoted to psychotherapy throughout the residency, in all residency programs I have seen. Most residents also enter psychotherapy, some even psychoanalysis, at some point during residency, in part for their own training and in part because they feel they need it. A great deal of time, then, is designated for learning psychotherapy, or at least was when I was doing fieldwork. This training, however, is more optional than the training in diagnosis and psychopharmacology. As a psychiatric resident, you *must* admit patients and diagnose them. That is your job. Psychotherapy training involves more choice, more willingness to go along with what is offered or seek out what is not.

The specific kind of therapy taught to psychiatric residents is called "psychodynamic psychotherapy," and its theories and practice derive from psychoanalysis. Psychiatrists use the term to refer to therapy that is guided by psychoanalytic thinking but in which a patient may come anywhere from five times a week to once a month and may use a couch but usually sits in a chair and talks with the therapist face-to-face. The term "psychoanalysis" is reserved for a specific kind of practice: the patient has very frequent sessions, the patient lies on a couch and cannot see the analyst, the therapist is in or has completed training at a psychoanalytic institute. The term "psychodynamic" is used more broadly to include not only psychoanalysis per se but a way of thinking and practicing that is psychoanalytic in feel and style. Psychoanalysts serve as the primary psychotherapy teachers for young psychiatrists, and psychoanalytic writings serve as the primary texts. Residents are supposed to learn the theory and practice of other kinds of psychotherapy as well—cognitive-behavioral therapy, couples therapy, family therapy—but in general these approaches have low visibility and low prestige in psychiatric training programs. When I refer to psychotherapy, then, my prototype is psychodynamic psychotherapy.

The learning process itself is more practical than this description suggests. In American culture, psychoanalysis is often associated with intellectuals. People who read Freud are often fairly highbrow. What is taught to young psychiatrists about psychodynamic psychotherapy is not intellectual at all. The expertise they acquire has to do with Freud only obliquely. It develops beneath the surface of texts and lectures.

In the first place, the lectures on psychotherapy, for the most part, do not present general theories of human experience. They do not discuss the extensive scientific literature on emotion and human development. They do not explore the difficult psychoanalytic writings of W. R. D. Fairbairn, D. W. Winnicott, Otto Fenichel, Heinz Kohut, Harry Stack Sullivan, Otto Kernberg, and others. Discussion of Sigmund Freud and human development is extremely cursory. No young psychiatrist is seriously expected to read much; even when reading is assigned, there is no sanction against a resident who does not read, and it is widely understood that the clinical needs of the hospital take precedence over a resident's lectures. The primary method of training is apprenticeship. I sat through an eight-week seminar on child development in which Jean Piaget's stages were presented but never fully explained, never critiqued—despite an enormous psychological literature on the topic—and never mentioned by any resident again. I have listened to hundreds of lectures to psychiatric residents. Few of them presented as much material as an average professor's lecture to undergraduates. Very few of them gave evidence of even an hour's preparation for an hour's lecture. Virtually none was attended by all of the residency class.

Nor, for that matter, does the institution treat the lectures as very important. In the first year the first psychotherapy patient is often assigned before residents have been told much, formally, about the actual process of psychotherapy, as if to imply that the resident can't do much harm, even though the gist of the teaching is that in fact the resident is a lumbering bear in the patient's porcelain psyche. One first-year resident was incensed by this: "Well, there was a lot of anxiety because you don't know what you're doing, and I was very angry at the department for thrusting us into that situation before we had had any lectures at all. What is psychotherapy? How does it work? What are some basic principles? I knew a little bit by reading and by three months of therapy I had had, but that wasn't much, and I just really didn't know. My role was very ill defined, and I just felt a lot of anger."

The point of the lectures is not to teach facts or a science but to teach a practical skill. The lectures talk about what to do in therapy rather than why the therapy works. (This is also true for the lectures on psychopharmacology and diagnosis.) In the summer seminar series I attended, the lectures on psychotherapy were so down-to-earth as to seem brutally naive to the outsider. Where do you put the clock in your office? If you must meet a patient a hundred feet from your office, do you talk on the way there? About what? Do you shake hands? These turn out, as it happens, to be matters of great concern, but they do have a fugitive air of teaching etiquette to someone about to host a dinner party with neither food nor drink.

When a seminar does focus on a text, as did one that I attended with advanced psychiatric residents, the discussion tends to circle around the ways that the ideas can be borrowed to understand one's current patients. Even in this class, where the text—Melanie Klein's *Envy and Gratitude*— was treated with greater historical and textual sensitivity than I had ever

59

encountered in a psychiatric setting, the young psychiatrists took the ideas loosely to interpret their patients' behavior. When the class looked at a sentence in which Klein talked about "incorporating the breast," for example, one of the psychiatrists exclaimed that this was exactly what her patient was doing with her now. Klein, of course, was being somewhat metaphorical about infant thought, but whereas a psychology graduate student might have struggled to understand the specific meaning of the metaphor for Klein, the clinically oriented resident ignored that question and instead stretched the metaphor further.

The primary teaching of psychotherapy takes place in the one-on-one "supervision" for an hour a week, often days after the actual therapy has taken place. Unlike the rest of medicine, the teacher sees the student perform very rarely. In surgery, there may be a see-one, do-one, teach-one approach to cutting, but a senior surgeon hovers by a student's elbow. In most cases, a psychotherapy supervisor never sees a patient in person. In many cases, the supervisor never sees a video of the session or listens to a tape recording of it. Instead, the resident and supervisor meet at a pre-arranged time, the resident tells the supervisor what went on in the session, and the supervisor advises the resident on what to do next. Periodically the supervisor sends an evaluation of the resident to the director of residency education. The belief that residents learn anything more than the fine art of deception from this process springs directly out of the psychodynamic way of looking at the world.

In psychodynamic psychotherapy, one person pays a second person a significant sum—$50 to $150, occasionally more—for the privilege of talking to him for less than an hour. He may repeat the exercise once or more each week for many years. The second person, the "expert," comments on what the first person has said. What makes the relationship strange is that the goal of the second person is not to understand and say what is true about the first person's remarks or even what he thinks. The psychotherapist is explicitly taught not to give advice, not to counsel, not to act as a kindly friend. The psychotherapy relationship is deliberately not modeled on teaching, though there is often more coaching in it than is acknowledged.

Psychodynamic psychotherapy has developed out of the belief that our deepest motivations are occult, for the expert as well as for the seeker of help. Thus, therapy cannot provide a one-way window into the patient's soul. The patient cannot see the real source of his unhappiness—we cannot see our sunglasses when we are wearing them, but everything we see is darkened by them—and the therapist knows that he too is limited by his own personality, though because of his training less so than the patient. Instead, therapy is conceived of as a relationship between two people from which the nature of the patient's hidden psyche must be inferred. Freud's metaphor was that the psychoanalyst and the patient were like passengers on a train. The patient sits by the window, describing the scenery as it passes by, but she does not know what is important. The psychoanalyst knows what is important, but he sits beside her blindfolded. He must infer from the way she talks to him what the landscape really looks like. The therapist's job is also to interpret the relationship between therapist and patient as a means of understanding the patient, despite the full awareness that neither party has full access to the thoughts and feelings of either.

Psychodynamic supervisors assume that because we are all shrouded from ourselves, young residents cannot but reveal their implicit assumptions about their relationships with a patient. Particularly in residency—that is, at the earliest stage of training in psychotherapy—supervisors tend to treat supervision as being focused on residents' insecurities and blind spots, for our inability to understand other people owes much to the hard shell of our emotional defenses. In other words, supervision is really about the resident. That's why handwritten notes—"process notes," scribbled dialogue written on scrap paper at the end of the session—are understood (in this culture) to be as helpful as video recordings.

A supervisor listens primarily to the way in which a resident thinks and responds. He is trying to understand the way a resident presents herself and what she presumes in a conversation that might be interpreted by someone else in a way the resident might not expect. One supervisor told me that he treated the supervision as couples' counseling with half the couple present. There is also more than this. A supervisor tries to interpret, through a resident's account, what a patient is actually like. But the focus tends to be upon the resident even when the discussion centers on the patient. In 1992, I sat through a summer's worth of one resident's supervisions with two different supervisors. Paula spent hours writing up the notes from each session (she was very conscientious), and at each supervision she would arrive with the sheaf of paper and read it through, with the supervisor commenting on what was said and whether it should have been said another way.

The transcript of one such supervision ran in part as follows. In the therapy hour, the patient and therapist (the resident) were discussing the patient's anger at seeing the therapist in the supermarket, because the patient claimed that the therapist had seen her and turned away, while the therapist said she had not seen her. The resident read these notes to her supervisor:

PT: You've misunderstood me.
TH: No, you've been saying a lot of hurtful things.
PT: No.

TH: It's hard to see that you can be hurtful. When you hurt, perhaps it helps to put people down.

PT: No, I never put anyone down.

[The supervisor remarks to her, "You are young, and you have everything you want." Paula continues to read without comment:]

TH: In a relationship, you feel that no one should get hurt.

PT: Yes, that's right.

TH: That's why you're so isolated. It'll be a long wait for a relationship that doesn't hurt.

PT: I'm isolated?

TH: Yes.

PT: You have something there—but the issue here is chemistry.

[Paula says in an aside to the supervisor, "Every time it gets heated, it goes into chemistry."]

PT: Like Sam.

TH: Were there specific things that bothered you about Sam?

PT: Yes [she lists them].

TH: And with me?

PT: No, it's just chemistry.

TH: Baloney. I think you call it chemistry because you're uncomfortable.

PT: It just reminds me, when I come here, that I see someone younger, who has done something with her life. I haven't.

[Supervisor doesn't say anything here, even though it confirms his earlier comment.]

PT: I don't mean to change the subject, but I was thinking about how you think I've tried to hurt you. People always misunderstand me. They used to call me a snob. I'm shy.

SUPERVISOR: The subtext here is that she was shy in the supermarket, that's why she didn't come over. She's not a snob, not aggressive—just avoidant. If you were feeling less embattled and more warmly, you could have interpreted that to her and said, "I wish I *had* seen you, so that you wouldn't have had to feel as rejected as you did. I hope that if I had seen you, I would have had the wherewithal to introduce you to my husband."

PAULA: She never says things directly, never owns things. I had to do this for me.

SUPERVISOR: She said pretty directly that you bothered her, and that you've succeeded at things she's failed at. She hints at this, as if you could be two girls chatting together.

PAULA: She asked me if we could do therapy outside.

SUPERVISOR: Talking about it is more important than doing it.

PAULA: With her, in therapy, doing is key.

SUPERVISOR: The issue is doing it with you. You embody so much she's not. She's on a slippery slope, got a late start, blew it with the first attempt. You come along, dressed in *pink,* even, she's seen you smile—think of her fantasy life. You're lucky, and you don't deserve it. How can she justify this? She's been unfairly treated, and it will come so easy for you and you don't even make attempts to be nice the way she does.

PAULA: How would you make her feel more comfortable?

SUPERVISOR: Well, you could apologize for what happened in the supermarket.

PAULA: But I've *done* that. I truly think she needs me to go to lunch with her or walk around the campus. All I was trying to get her to do was to own her own aggressiveness.

SUPERVISOR: Good, but you would have done it differently if you'd realized that this issue was jealousy, not the comparison with her previous therapist. You are acting here as if you don't think enough of yourself to believe that someone could be jealous of you.

What the supervisor said quite clearly is that this resident could not hear the patient envy her. To become a better therapist, she would have to learn to listen to all the ways a patient might perceive her. But now she cannot hear the patient clearly because her own personality muffles her ears. For the supervisor to see this, it didn't really matter that the session had been written down from memory. As Freud remarked about dreams, recollection is as useful as exact recall because what was unconscious then will not be consciously removed in the retelling. We reveal ourselves as vividly when we lie as when we are trying to be honest.

Supervisors tend to be supportive. This supervisor was consistently so. Supervision can nevertheless be exquisitely painful. Paula was just shy of thirty during these sessions, and at the time she was lonely and depressed. (There was something going on at home.) I am struck, looking back over my notebooks several years later, that I knew she felt bad about herself when we met. I wrote about her bad feelings in my notebooks. Yet somehow, as we spoke over the course of the summer, as I talked to her about psychotherapy and what it was like to do it, as I went from supervision to supervision with her, I could no longer see her as someone who might be stiff and awkward with patients because she was depressed. I think that it was so painful to see her expose herself week after week despite her determination to present herself as a good therapist that I could not bear to see her as clearly as her supervisor did, although I sat there recording the supervision in my notes; I think that may be a clue to the level of shame residents can experience in the kindest supervision. Certainly Paula experienced the supervisions like a switch on sunburnt skin. Shortly after this exchange, the patient left therapy.

If a therapist is not helpful, whatever that means to a patient, the patient usually goes away. The force of this experience as a training exercise, that the outpatient is not like some graduate school paper assignment but an independent person who votes on your skills by choosing to see you or not (which the inpatient, of course, cannot) did not become clear to me until my own bout of doing psychotherapy. To get some sense of this skill, I had signed up as a volunteer at a local outpatient clinic. I had eight patients, one once a week and three twice a week for more than a year. I was supervised by the same people who supervised the residents.

My second patient was a rude, miserable man who didn't think much of women to start with—his girlfriend had just thrown him out—and when he called up the outpatient clinic for an appointment, he protested at the standard price and asked for someone cheaper. He was passed on to me, the anthropologist in training who because she was not training for a degree could accept reduced fees ($10 per session; it went to the clinic). Although he no doubt felt that he had been offered cut-rate goods, he decided to see me. During our first hour, he remarked aloud that I probably wasn't smart enough to have gone to medical school, suggested that I was too young to be of any use to him, told me that when I grew up I'd have some business cards, and then, after railing about my inability to get his girlfriend back, left after several sessions and did not return for months. He was not, as they say, an ideal candidate for psychotherapy. Yet I felt terrible when he dropped out of therapy and tremendously reassured when, eight months later, he decided to reconnect. (I referred him elsewhere because of my teaching schedule.)

Very few of the patients whom residents see for psychotherapy are ideal candidates for psychotherapy, and so the feeling of being abandoned by a patient is quite common. Student therapists enter the clinic hoping to do long-term therapy with people like themselves and instead find themselves speaking in rounds about the self-esteem issues of drug addicts and felons. (At clinics where trainees are allowed to take patients for very low fees, there are more noncriminal, job-holding, well-put-together patients who are willing to see a student therapist if it costs them virtually nothing.) Even so, what students learn is that keeping patients is more important than understanding theory. In private practice, a psychiatrist has an income only if he keeps his patients. That is why there are two Freuds, the Freud who is read by scholars and intellectuals, who take the abstract portrait of the psyche seriously and who debate the epistemological issues he raises, and the Freud of the clinicians, sometimes unread but inspiring, who helps clinicians think in a way that is helpful to patients.

One way to characterize the Freud of the clinicians is by saying that training in psychodynamic psychotherapy teaches student therapists to be more conscious of the way they empathize. Empathy is a natural human process. You see someone crying; you feel sad. You see someone smile; your day brightens. It is also true that when you become more self-conscious about empathy, you see how constrained it is by who you are—the way you perceive someone, the way you feel about that person as a certain sort of person, the form of your own past and of your own anxieties, hopes, fears, ambivalences. The psychoanalyst Roy Schafer places a dissection of the therapist's empathy at the center of his book *The Analytic Attitude,* a taut exegesis of the way analysts do their work. Schafer does not pretend that analysts have an uncluttered, transparent view of patients, nor that analytic theory—the intellectual's Freud—always provides accurate and reliable insight. He sees that a patient tries to describe himself to an analyst and that the analyst experiences empathy for the patient. That is, the analyst genuinely tries to understand what the patient is feeling and thinking, and in that process vicariously experiences some of what the patient thinks and feels. Schafer points out that what the analyst feels empathically is not exactly what the patient feels. For a start, an analyst may build many models in his mind of who the patient is, all of which might be consistent with the "data," with what the patient has said. The analyst has his own sense of who he is in the analytic setting; so too does the patient. Each has a kind of "second self": the patient presents himself as more miserable than most of his colleagues think he is; the analyst presents himself as more competent than most of his colleagues think *he* is. In fact, Schafer says, the relationship between analyst and analysand—between their second selves—is "fictive." The two create it together. It is their own narrative, and it is a story about who they are to each other. That, Schafer says, is what makes analysis work as therapy. The analyst does not feel exactly what the patient is feeling, because his perceptions of the patient, drawing as they do from his prior analytic experience and his idiosyncratic understandings, are always subtly different from the patient's own, particularly because the patient is slightly different in the consulting room and in his life outside the analytic encounter. When a patient looks into the mirror of his analysis, then, he sees not a direct reflection of who he thinks he is but something different.[14] This gives him possibility, Schafer argues. It makes him feel free.

That awareness of the difference between what a patient thinks and feels, what a therapist thinks and feels, and how each thinks and feels about the other, is one of the first major lessons of the resident's psychotherapy training. Suzanne, for instance, started out shocked that psychiatric patients were not always grateful for her help but would actually see her as the enemy. She was the classic "nice girl," always friendly, always helpful, a June Cleaver in a brash late-twentieth-century world. By the end of her first year, she had decided that "sensitivity" was her main problem. She called it "overinvolvement": "Working with these disturbed patients, they can pick up things and they can read things that normal patients cannot, and they zero in on your insecurities. I had one patient whom we committed to the hospital. Every day she would say to me, 'I hate you, I hate you because you keep me here.' For me it was a devastating thing to be told. I care about people a lot, more than they care about themselves sometimes, more than I should."

By the end of her second year, Suzanne felt far more competent as a therapist. She ridiculed herself for thinking that she had known what she was doing before: "This year has been an incredible year for personal growth. I laugh sometimes because at the end of last year, my first year, we had what we called 'therapy patients.' What a joke! I had no idea of what I was doing at all. I remember this one young woman, a young married woman who had a new baby and was having sexual problems. I would sit there week after week not knowing what to say, just feeling totally overwhelmed. [Suzanne, never married, had at that point just broken up with her boyfriend.] She came back week after week; it was just beyond me. Hearing all these intimate things and not knowing what to say or do, what my role was, I felt that I wasn't prepared for this, the lecture course we had just wasn't enough to prepare me to sit in a room with another person who was suffering and feel like I can work with them in some way to help them gain insight and make changes.

"I started to understand more and more. I could see why the patients were coming back, that if a patient feels understood he's going to come back, he is getting something. I learned to lower my expectations, to meet people where they are and they will feel understood. Sometimes they feel like maybe you're the only person on earth that they can come and sit in a room with.

"Sometimes I feel like I'm engaged in a dance with the patient—they're doing some steps around me and I'm trying to follow them on the dance floor in a sort of figurative way. Sometimes we're moving in the same direction, and other times we're just falling over each other. One week a patient all of a sudden turned on me. It felt like a bucket of anger just thrown over me. At first I was shocked. Then I said to myself, wait a minute. This has got to be transference ["transferred" from another context] because I know realistically I've done nothing to offend him. Sure enough, it had to do with feelings from his mom that were projected in the anger and the hurt. I didn't confront him at the time because he was too upset to appreciate the interpretation, plus he was mad. Weeks later we did. But I'll tell you, even more critical to me was the fact that during the session, I had stepped back. I had recognized this. It feels like I now have a view of the world that is very special and is kind of neat."

Recognizing the patient's distortion of the therapist is the psychotherapeutic equivalent of getting a driver's license. The story implies that the young therapist is beginning to do real therapy because she is able to distinguish what the patient is experiencing from what she has experienced. All of us know that sometimes someone is angry at us because he's really furious at the boss, but most of us still get angry in response. Therapists try to live in a double-entry bookkeeping state at all times. They try to be deeply, emotionally engaged with the patient and yet not to respond out of their own needs, not to hit back after being hit, not to express pain after being hurt. They try not to respond in kind. That is the "special, neat" way of perceiving the world in psychodynamics: that we each create the world we live in; that we always see through molded glass; and that much of the time, when people are angry at us, we are not the cause of their anger but merely the vehicle for their self-generated, self-inflicted, wounding rage.

After the end of residency, Suzanne explained that what she had learned in residency was to understand the patient without interrupting with her own needs (getting angry at an insult), yet still to be able to use her own sense of self in the service of understanding someone else: "What psychiatry did for me was to take away my insulation. I found myself face-to-face with a lot of ugliness, and I had to learn to tolerate it, to let it be real. There was no way to close my own pain out, and if you're careful it becomes really useful. For example, I don't think I ever really learned how to deal with anger or process anger myself, and I see that in a lot of my female patients.

It's real useful for me because I know where they're coming from. I know what the problem is. At first you think, what do I bring to them, I haven't solved this one. But I'm not in the same boat. I don't walk in their shoes. I may have gone through similar things but not the same thing, and I can keep the distance. You can say, 'When he said that to you, I bet you were furious,' and the look of relief on their face! 'How did you know? I could have stabbed him.' So you use your experiences, and you help the patient."

Young psychiatrists say repeatedly that what they learn to do in psychotherapy is to interpret someone else by factoring out their own participation, by overriding their need to see a good, just world, their need to maintain their honor, or their need to have other people see them as kind. That is, they become increasingly capable of understanding a relationship as the outcome of two complex interacting individuals and to interpret the behaviors of the other person more intricately through the contours of their own selves, as if they were predicting the speed and height of waves by the features of the shore on which they break. They say that they learn to bring their experience to bear on understanding someone else and yet to act on none of their own reactions, which are merely tools for further understanding.

In order to do this, young psychiatrists (or student therapists) need to construct self-conscious models of patients and themselves: "I know realistically I've done nothing to offend him. . . . [The anger] had to do with feelings from his mom." The way they develop those models is by talking endlessly about people and what makes them tick: their secret fears, their wants, their dreams, their embarrassments, their confusions. They learn to talk about an event by explaining it from the perspective of all the different actors, and their tales get funnier because they develop a sharper sense of the parallel universes people sometimes seem to inhabit. This is not like the process of learning to diagnose. The person diagnosing learns to distill a diagnosis out of a patient's narrative and to see that many different lives can share a common label. In psychodynamics, the models are rarely taught and memorized abstractly (although some models are, such as the Oedipus complex, in which a male child separates from his mother and identifies with his father). For the most part, the models remain specific, as something some patient did at some time that is kind of like what she did some months later. Mostly, the models are about motivation, and because of the cleaner attention to motivation, the young psychiatrist becomes an increasingly better spinner of tales.

Tom, for example, entered residency later than most of his peers, first working for years in internal medicine. He is a bluff man, pragmatic and to the point. He spends Saturday playing ball with his kids, rarely reads novels, and thinks he ought to follow the research in his field but doesn't. In the first months of his residency, he felt demoralized about doing psycho-therapy: "I'm frankly terrible still at any kind of real psychotherapy. I mean, basically I'm comfortable with trying to make a diagnosis and prescribe the right medicines for these guys. If it's just me sitting there trying to help someone in psychotherapy, I just don't know enough. Actually, I don't know anything." He was reassured to discover that he liked the patients. He had had dreams, before residency, about being locked up with crazy people. "But the real surprise here has been that I've really enjoyed the patients. No matter how crazy some of these guys are, I can really empathize with them. It's made me feel real good to feel that kind of a bond with the patients."

At the end of that year, Tom said that one of his greatest problems was empathizing too well. Understanding his patient's misery made him miserable: "It's terribly difficult. People come to you day after day, just pour out all this misery and open up to you. It's gut-wrenching. When someone's not psychotic but they live with so much pain, you really feel it. Psychiatry just pulls down all these horrors. You feel so drained." At the same time, he was clear that he felt that he had become better at understanding his therapy patients: "It's hard to say how you arrive at some kind of idea of what kind of person you're talking to. It's not any one question or one physical or emo-tional characteristic of that person. It's the combination of a lot of little things. I think I've become a much more feeling and sensitive person this year." In his last year, Tom said he didn't believe in classical technique. He thought that a good therapist is more helpful when he does not try to help. He said that psychotherapy worked because he had seen it work for him; but he said that it worked in spite of and not because of grand theory. He said that what was important about the process was that a patient was will-ing to give up the "big secret" that he had been holding inside, namely that things had not been working right. He said that he didn't think it mattered so much what you did at that point as a therapist as long as you were "there to help guide them in this exploration of themselves."

And as his sense of what he was doing seemed to become more simple and concrete, his account of motivation grew more acute: "I had this one patient, this huge woman who came in last year. She's a really good person, funny, witty, would never miss an appointment. We have a great time. Her whole story is kind of indicative of how loose my psychotherapy can be. Once her depression had cleared [this is a very medical phrase], I was try-ing to explore her childhood [first the medical necessities, then the psycho-therapy]. She picked up that I felt uneasy about what I was doing.

"Well, I moved offices after we'd started meeting, and when she saw how desolate this room is, she brought in a plant. It was pretty much a sick plant. I said, 'You're not supposed to bring gifts, and I can't take care of plants. These things die. I don't even water them. I'm incapable of watering plants.' She said, 'No problem.' She just left it there. Unconsciously, I guess I wanted to torture her by letting this plant die in front of her. Every week we would joke because I never watered it. I honestly completely forgot about it consciously when she wasn't there, and she would accuse me of being sadistic.

"Now, I have this other patient who is young and attractive. I didn't think she was that seductive, but I had her on videotape, and my supervisor certainly thought she was. He said that there was all this transference. In fact what he said was 'Oh, boy.' Well, she starts to comment on the plant, week after week. I never told her somebody gave it to me, I just said, 'I never water it. I don't take care of it.' She said, 'Well, I'll take it home. I'll bring it to life.' I said, 'No, you can't do that.' At the end of one session she just picked it up and left with it. So one of these weeks she's going to come in with the plant she brought back to life for her psychotherapist, whom she loves, which is okay except that now I have to explain this to the other patient who thinks I'm a sadist. I never should have taken the thing to begin with."

"We're really storytellers," one resident remarked. One of the more remarkable qualities of psychotherapeutically oriented psychiatrists is how capable they are of remembering the story. This becomes obvious in a case presentation or a seminar with psychodynamic clinicians. Like any academic presentations, a presentation has a great deal of data and some theoretical framing. In an academic setting, however, the audience tends to focus on the theory. The listeners remember the theoretical claim being advanced, and they tend to pursue it with questions, often quite forgetful about the actual data mentioned by the speaker. In the psychodynamic setting, the listening clinicians tend not to pursue the theoretical argument (the speaker disagreed with So-and-so's reformulation of such-and-such an argument). Instead, they talk about patients, and they remember what seems to an outsider to be a stunning amount of detail: where a forty-year-old patient attended school, how her mother behaved at graduation, what her father said about it. A first-year resident said, "I used to find it very difficult to remember what was going on with a patient. Then the guy who ran the psychiatric emergency room said, 'Remember the story. Everyone's got a story.' And then I began to remember."

What they remember has a certain form. Master chess players can be distinguished from nonplayers because they hold thousands upon thousands of chessboard positions in their memory. When master chess players are shown, in an experimental setting, a chessboard pattern that could be arrived at by play, they can remember it far more accurately than non-chess-playing subjects—and probably associate with it moves that would take advantage of the position or even specific games. But they are no better than non–chess players at remembering random images or randomly rearranged chessboards that could not be arrived at by normal play.[15] Academic psychologists have argued that expertise depends in large part on the amount and organization of knowledge around the area of expertise— what they call the "domain": chess, ballet, Aztecs, psychiatry, whatever the expert is an expert in. Many argue that the highest level of expertise is indeed (as therapists argue) reached after ten years in the domain. Experts' memories seem to depend on their capacity for perceiving meaningful patterns (cognitive scientists would call them "schemas"), and the immense storage in their domain of expertise seems to enable them to plan strategically in that domain and anticipate potential sequences of moves in the future.[16]

What a psychotherapist remembers is a lexicon of narrative patterns that she uses to understand what is going on with a patient, moment to moment, in a particular session and over a long analysis. The complexity of this memory is not unlike the complexity of a chess player's memory. Like the psychodynamic understanding of a life, a chess game consists of a series of patterns each of which has some causal relationship to the past but is not entirely determined by it. Like a life, each chess game is unique, but, also like a life, the chess game moves from pattern to pattern (board position to board position, event to event) that appear in many other games and many other lives. And like the skilled therapist's, the skilled chess player's expertise lies in part in being able to remember and recognize these patterns far more readily than the untrained person and to anticipate strategy on the basis of those patterns.

These patterns are best described as "emotion-motivation-behavior bundles." By that I mean an emotion (such as anger) that interacts with a motivation (she is a nice person and does not see herself as hating her patient) that causes some piece of behavior (she was furious at her patient but didn't allow herself to recognize the anger, and during the session for some reason she was unable to hear her patient). Young psychiatrists tell stories by chunking details around such patterns, which can then be combined in many different ways, or which may emerge in new form in new patients. (The word "chunk" is used by cognitive scientists to evoke the way people remember details by pulling them into a central concept, like iron filings to a magnet.) Identifying these bundles is complicated by the inherent oddity of separating out an expert's own emotional responses from the relationship the expert is trying to interpret. That is why it takes so long to become a psychotherapist and why it is easier to be a competent diagnostician (but not a psychopharmacological connoisseur). In psychotherapy, there are many more patterns related to one another in more complicated ways. In some important sense, you are not a competent psychotherapist until you are a connoisseur-level expert. There is no public and clear-cut threshold of adequacy, no basic competence, as there are in diagnosis and psychopharmacology.

When psychotherapists tell stories, they are learning to figure out the emotion-motivation-behavior bundles that (as they would see it) explain the way people in the story relate. Telling the story well (convincingly) demonstrates their mastery. For example, for many months I met with a psychotherapeutically oriented resident every Friday and chatted with her while the tape recorder was running. When I met her, she was the chief resident of the outpatient clinic. The strain of this responsibility on someone naturally shy and prone to identify even with people she didn't like made her so nervous that she lost ten pounds in the course of the year and began to smoke. Over that year we talked about psychotherapy, how she had learned to do it, what it was like to go into analysis—she had just started analysis at the time of our conversations—and how she understood what she was doing. These excerpts from our conversations give a flavor of the way she told stories about how people were with people, why they acted, and what they felt.

She's a very troubled lady. She was incredibly depressed, chronically suicidal. She would come to my office and—"sob" is not the word for it, the building would empty. Everyone in the annex knew my Friday 3:00 patient was there. Through all this she kept telling me in a semiconvincing way how she loved me, in a maternal way. She suddenly partially got it together, decided to get a job, went from no Prozac to three pills a day, and started doing wonderfully. We went from doing crisis management to talking about how she felt about things and how she reacted to people and what hurt her. How she felt about being in therapy as opposed to how suicidal she was this week. Then I went on vacation. I came back and tried to talk to her about what she felt like. She says, yes, she missed me, but you know she understands I have to go on vacation. By the way, she says, I flushed my Prozac down the toilet and there's nothing to talk about because I can't help her and life is hopeless. Then she canceled her appointment the next week. I tried to bring it up, but she was absolutely not angry at me, I was important to her, all this positive stuff. What happened to me is that I sat there and I started to get furious at her. At some point I realized how angry I was, I realized it was probably coming across to her, and I felt I had to make some acknowledgment of that. But then she canceled the next appointment. What my anger was telling me was how incredibly angry and hurt she was but she's not able to express that to me. So what she did was not conscious, obviously, but basically she made me feel it and one of us was conscious of it and could do something with it. The initial reaction is, no, I'm not really feeling this because it wouldn't be right to feel that, how can I get angry at my wonderful poor sick kind patient who obviously needs help and is in such distress. I couldn't be having thoughts of strangling her right now, could I? So first you try to pretend it's going to go away or it's not really there. When denial doesn't work, you hopefully start to become aware of it, and if you're comfortable enough with yourself and your emotions, you can pick it up and look at it.

I think [a second-year resident] has learned to be out there, to really let his emotions out with the patient, to really react however you react and be able to feed that back. Because he doesn't feel threatened anymore. I think I'm more engaged now than I was a year or two ago because I know I can shut it off. I know that I have control over myself and my life, and I'm not going to lose it in a session with a patient if I let myself get angry, if I let myself feel close to them. I used to have a lot of reluctance to doing that. Supervisors would say, what are you afraid of? The more I let myself be comfortable looking at that, then I could use the information. I could drift into a fantasy about this patient and wonder, what's the character of the fantasy? That tells me where the patient is. But the threat is that your emotions are out. It's safer to say, no matter what this patient says or does it will not affect my life I'm not going to get upset or angry.

I got this intake, there was this couple that had come in basically because the wife was having so much trouble with her workaholic husband and she really felt like he was putting in too many hours and working too hard, he wasn't home for her, he wasn't emotionally available, he wasn't this, that, and the other thing, and I sat through the interview going, this is my life, I don't know how to help myself, I don't know how to help them, and I presented in team. I went with the facts, but basically my presentation to the team leader was, I can't take this case, first of all, I relate too much, and second, I haven't figured out how to deal with it and maybe someone older and wiser could figure out how to deal with it. I haven't been able to figure out how to do it in my own life. And the team leader just thought it was charming and wonderful and he said, "Well that's great I think that's exactly why you have to take the case. Because you have so much common experience, you can really use that to help them." I said, "I've been struggling with this at home for a year and a half and all we do is scream at each other."

He said, "Trust me." They had five sessions of couples therapy and sent me a postcard six months later saying that their marriage had never been better. I have no idea what I did.

Analysis—I'm now in the second week—truly is regressive. I've gotten back in touch with feelings that I had as a child, which I never had access to. In face-to-face therapy, I was making some effort to dredge up all this stuff, and it wasn't working. Now, it seems like all this stuff is accessible that wasn't accessible before. The whole experience has been rather like being in the dark and having the lights turned on. They're not all turned on at once, but you can now start to make out shapes where all you could see before was black. You have a little more access to yourself. But also, as you find the light switch for yourself, you go back to your office and show someone else where it is so they can turn their own on.

I think as I get more experienced, I have a better cognitive understanding of what I'm doing. I feel more like, you know, when someone asks you how to get to the restaurant and you can't really draw the map. I want to say, I know how to get there, I know that when I see this house I turn, but I can't say, well it's on this street. That's kind of how I feel.

Here feelings are causes. They become entangled with a motivation, with someone's complicated set of hopes, fears, and dreams, and through that entanglement they cause a particular behavior. Mostly, the feelings the therapist talks about are negative. That makes sense because the negative ones are those that trouble people most. ("I didn't realize that I was upset with her, but I put the oatmeal on the burner for breakfast, and you know, I just forgot about it and her pot was destroyed.") What the therapist often does in a story is to follow a feeling through a range of emotion-motivation-behavior bundles. For instance, in the discussion of the "very troubled lady," the resident talks about the good-girl patient who is so miserable (and, one later infers, angry) that she lets the entire building know but also loves the therapist, wants to please the therapist, and so pulls her life together. The therapist goes on to say that the patient is furious at the therapist when she takes a vacation but does not want to acknowledge the anger, and the conflict leads her to flush away the medication that she was taking to please her therapist. Then the therapist segues into an account of how the patient's unacknowledged anger made her, the therapist, angry, and how she sort of recognized it and tried to "catch" it but didn't entirely succeed, and the patient felt hurt and mad and canceled the next session. This then led into a discussion of communicating anger without being able to express it and ultimately into the therapist's anxiety about her difficulty in acknowledging her own anger. A major theme of "powerful feelings that you are afraid to acknowledge" dominates the account, but there are multiple smaller patterns that the therapist infers and patches together into a coherent narrative of a portion of someone's life. In listening to this story, it becomes clear that the therapist has met many people who have difficulty recognizing their own anger. They are all different from this woman—each person is unique—yet, listening to this therapist talk was like watching a chess player recognize board positions and know instinctively what is going on and what to do next.

There are several other features of this therapist's discourse that are not uncommon. First, while good psychodynamic residents use a language marked as a specialist's language, with words such as "regressive," "transference," "internalized," and so forth, the language rarely—at least in my experience—dominates the discourse, which tends to be couched in commonplace words. Second, they use abundant metaphors to indicate the thinking and feeling process. This woman uses spatial metaphors to indicate emotionally powerful events—"shaping" events—and she uses contact metaphors to indicate her capacity to understand her own emotions: she "is in touch with" or "has access to" herself.[17] All people do this, but this discourse is so much more feeling-focused than average that the metaphorical quality seems very marked. The metaphors are particularly striking when this resident talks about what she does *as* a therapist. Again and again, this therapist resorts to spatial and contact metaphors to point to what she does, and she feels inadequate to put the details of her practice into words. This feeling of inadequacy is quite common among even the most skilled and senior therapists. They have, in general, a remarkably difficult time verbalizing what it is that they do. Third, many therapists tell stories against themselves and use patients' stories to make sense of their own experience. This is what this woman does, for instance, in the supervision anecdote and the couples therapy anecdote: the resident who cannot listen when he is threatened, the workaholic husband who frustrates his wife because he is unavailable. The stories are funny because they suggest that the doctor must remember that the patient is the one with the illness. Finally, this therapist, like many others, thinks that what she has learned to do requires courage and is inherently good.

For young psychiatrists—particularly psychotherapeutically oriented ones—this language of feeling pervades their lives. "Two visitors? Oh no, that brings up all my childhood anxieties." They are encouraged to talk about their feelings about their patients, their teachers, and one another. They are told that the most important feature of relationships is talking about feelings. They are told—and they experience—that psychotherapy is full of intense feelings. They are told—probably correctly—that emotion is at the center of psychotherapy, that the therapy will "take" only if a patient is emotionally involved in it, that a patient can hear something fifty different times but will understand it only if he hears it when he is emotionally vulnerable. They are told that understanding people is understanding emotions. They use a language that is so feeling-rich that to outsiders it seems a little strange.

Residents become deeply immersed in one another's lives. Despite the striking and increasing emphasis on biomedicine, young psychiatrists are enculturated by their institution into the expectation of intense involvement with one another. My field notes are full of this intensity, of April's feelings about Bambi, of Bambi's interpretation of Chris's anxiety about April's feelings about Bambi, of David's understanding of the role of Dr. Edwards's supervision of Bambi on April's feelings about Bambi, of a constant over-interpreted interdependence with peers. With psychiatrists, particularly young psychiatrists testing the waters of their psychodynamic knowledge, standard expectations of social distance disappear. If you do not talk about your feelings and their personal sources in one-on-one social interaction, you are substandard. This is heightened by an intensified observational alertness, which means that psychiatrists notice anxiety or distress more quickly than nonpsychiatrists and are much more likely to ask about its meaning (this livens up dinner parties attended by both psychiatrists and nonpsychiatrists).

A resident breaks up with her boyfriend and says, "But it's really good to go through this with a group of psychiatrists, they really understand." Chances are that she will speak about the breakup in detail with many, if not most, members of her class. Young psychiatrists will talk and talk about their experiences and one another's with them, with others. They are, with respect to private matters, the singularly most talkative people I have ever met. They talk about private matters to the point that they may feel abused. "We were very, very close," Suzanne said when she was talking about another resident. "We started out last year in the same location, even on the same team. He trusted me, I trusted him. We were both going through a bad time, he's having trouble with his girlfriend, I'm having trouble with my boyfriend. We're very supportive of each other. What happened was that I started going to a therapist so I had someone to unload on, but he didn't, he kept coming to me. Boy, did he need to go to a therapist, but he didn't, he kept coming to me. I had to sort of withdraw. I love this person, I care about him a lot. It felt like his problems were starting to overwhelm me, and I started to feel used."

The rest of the class talked about whether she had a crush on him or he on her; why had he talked to her so much; why had she put up with what had become an asymmetrical exchange; could she tell, once he went into therapy, that he was changing; what about her; what did that say about their therapists? their capacity for therapy?

One could argue that these young adults have chosen a career in psychiatry because they enjoy talking about feelings, and for many of them this might be true. But it is not true for all, and whatever an individual's motivations may be, the culture created by psychotherapy training is so powerful that the social demands are hard to avoid. Residents get to know one another extremely well. They work with one another, hang out with one another, are enculturated side by side. They also participate in group therapy together. Most residencies have what is known as a therapy "T-group," or training group, which is run by a professional expert in group therapy and meets every week for an hour. In the residencies I visited, participation was explicitly required only for a year, but most groups continued to meet throughout the residency period. I was never allowed to attend these groups, on the grounds that they were too private. But I frequently heard about what had happened in them. During these sessions, people who worked together daily were expected to talk about their private vulnerabilities and fantasies about one another. Sessions not infrequently ended up in tears or rage. They were promptly followed by working interactions with the same people.

In the T-group, discourse was actively psychodynamic. "There is a lot that goes on in the group," remarked one resident, "and it's weird because we're aware of it. I've had kind of transferential feelings towards Fred because I consider him to be like a father. I project feelings onto him. I've told him so. I caught myself doing it. I described to him that I felt that way, and fifteen seconds later I was doing it again." This discussion must have been particularly memorable in the group—I heard about it from several people—because the two men involved were at that time competing, at the end of their second year, for a chief residency position, an administrative post with a fair amount of prestige. The resident continued, "For me to drop my guard and admit my weaknesses to someone that I'm openly competing with is a concern to me because I'm showing weakness when I'm supposed to be in competition and looking strong. Also, thoughts come to your head, like you realize that you just admitted some degree of psychopathology to everyone you work with. What will people think?" Yet to be open is to be competitive, because it is to assert psychodynamic competence, as if to say, "I know myself, while you fear yourself, you refuse to acknowledge your weaknesses." Another resident said irritably about the first meeting of one T-group that Agnes—the resident who was soon labeled the most psychodynamically astute in the group—had asked to be the first person to tell the story of her life (they went around the group in turn, in the beginning), and, by choosing to be very personal, she had upped the ante and taken control of the group.

When young psychiatrists gossip, they are learning how to work. They are at least as nosy and curious as the rest of us. Unlike the rest of us, what they get from their gossip is professional expertise, little narrative packets of behaviors, motivations, and emotions. And the gossip is probably as important to their development as their supervision is. I found the informal focus on how people are emotionally put together particularly remarkable in the discussions about residents who were disliked. Those residents the other residents dissected. They knew that they should not really pass judgment on these people, who they thought might be much like themselves, yet they couldn't stand them. They really tried to figure out what drove them nuts about these people. The following are excerpts from my conversations.

I don't really know, all I know is that he apparently has a much harder time. When he was growing up, he didn't have any parents, or maybe a stepmother or something like that, and Florida was kind of a drug capital in that period, and I think he probably had a lot of problems. I know he had a lot of therapy, but trying to give him the benefit of the doubt, I just hope this is an improvement over the way it used to be. I hope he's going in the right direction. I think there are a lot of times when he shows that he has a conscience and he's genuinely sorry for what he does. It doesn't seem like it prevents him from doing a similar thing again. I will say this, though, he has definitely added a lot of life, a lot of spark to our otherwise kind of boring social life that we had last year. There's a certain neediness about it.

I've had conflicts with Anne, for example. I've definitely used my understanding of her dynamics. I've understood that the only way to resolve problems is to be very frank and honest rather than harbor resentments. I haven't told her why I feel that she's done what she's done. Very often, my understanding of her is that she's rather narcissistic and that she really tends to walk over people sometimes, and so when she goes to walk over me, I've called her on it and I've told her that this is where I stand and these are my concerns and this I why I would appreciate it if she wouldn't do what she's doing, and she's responded to that. I haven't told her, well, you're narcissistic and just don't think about other people. Obviously that wouldn't go over too well.

Diane is what I would call a group deviant. She's flamboyant, she's hysterical, by that I mean very dramatic, everything's extreme in her descriptions of things. People looked at that as peculiar and odd. So she got set on the outside fringe of the group, not yet labeled the group deviant. Then she engaged in some behaviors that irritated and angered, alienated her from certain charismatic members of the group, and these charismatic members spread the word. So everyone became sympathetic to the charismatic members and further alienated from the outlier, and that was when she became the group deviant. To fit in now, she would have to dump the odd behavior, I mean that's like telling someone to grow two right arms. It's just not possible for her to change her behavior like that. She would have to go through five years of analysis to be able to change her defense patterns and behaviors. When people get together and talk about the difficulties of residency, it's Diane. All their concerns were legitimate, but they weren't talking about anything more important, like how hard it is to take care of people who don't want to become better. How hard it is to take care of people who will never be functional. That's hard. So we use Diane as a way of expressing anxieties and frustrations and ventilating.

These accounts display many features of a young therapist's discourse: the technical language, the spatial metaphor (although in the absence of personal reflections, there are no contact metaphors), the identification of feelings, and sequences of emotion-motivation-behavior patterns. What they add is the sense of relentless determination in trying to figure out why, despite all their training and all their rationality, some of their peers behaved so badly (on the one hand) and the other residents weren't mature enough to cope (on the other).

Psychologically minded people create such models (large and specific) all the time. Psychiatric residents (and others in training) have two additional sources of help in building these models. The first is psychodynamic theory, which provides a great abundance of partially abstract models to interpret human behavior. The residents learn this theory from teachers, from peers, and occasionally from books. The theoretical model suggests that if someone exhibits a certain set of behaviors, the behavioral pattern is this and the motivating emotions are that. For example, in a well-known book entitled *The Drama of the Gifted Child*, the analyst Alice Miller describes highly successful people who do not have the secure self-assurance you would imagine. Their success seems hollow to them, their failures monumental; although they are envied and admired by many, they feel empty, abandoned, and depressed. They strive for more success to quench these feelings, but to no avail. Miller calls these patients "narcissistic." She describes a narcissistic person as someone who learned to be and to do in order to please someone else and to be loved by them in return. That is why they are so successful and why their success is so meaningless to them. Such a model explains what motivates these patients and, ultimately, how therapy should be focused so as to help them understand and reshape their motivations. Young psychiatrists read such a book and make sense of it by using the model to explain people they know or indeed to explain themselves. (Miller remarks that many insightful, intuitive children who grow up taking care of their parents by being good, responsible children become psychotherapists as adults. That is how they make use of their earlier intense interest in what their parents felt and needed.) The models offered in various texts do not all complement one another. Sometimes they flatly contradict one another. (A famous example is penis envy. Some psychoanalytic writers believe that women are motivated by penis envy; others do not.) In general, psychiatric residents (or psychiatric clinicians) are not worried by the contradictions, and in general they do not see their task as one of arbitrating them. These models are tools they can use to help them understand their patients. They are like spades and garden shears, useful or not useful, rather than like equations, true or false.

The second source of models is a privileged access not only to a greater-than-average range of human experience (including serious depression and psychosis, which laypeople rarely see and recognize) but also to feelings and stories usually kept private. By the time they graduate, psychiatric residents not only have seen hundreds of severely disturbed patients, they have heard hundreds of detailed accounts of fantasies, actions, desires, frustrations, and so forth, the likes of which most people encounter only in novels and in a handful of living people. These are not abstract models. They are stories of how one patient spoke about commonplaces for three months in therapy and suddenly began to cry or another abruptly quit therapy and called back four months later, or how the son of an entrepreneur was crippled by his father's great success, yet had to take care of him as he sank into senility. These are like chess games a young psychiatrist plays again and again, seeing lives unfold, looking for the ways different strategies play out in different settings. They help a psychiatrist say to herself, "Ah, that is the way *you* reacted to your brother's death, but it is not the way all people would react. It is a unique reaction, and it tells me something about you, because I have seen similar reactions to different problems and I have seen people react differently to similar problems."

This learning process probably helps most young psychiatrists to sense other people's emotions more accurately.[18] At least the process helps residents to make fine distinctions between emotions and their roles in different settings. I think it also enables residents to sense emotions more keenly. My evidence is simple and observational. I believe, having spent years in this world, that good, psychodynamically oriented residents become more intuitive over time. They seem to be able to meet a person for a short time and to summarize that person's experience in a manner that rings true. Some residents become identified as "wizards" who are able to interview a patient and dazzle a crowd with their skill in understanding, who give people in their office a sense that they have understood them deeply. Even so, the understanding is undoubtedly shaped in an idiosyncratic fashion: out of the many possible valid interpretations of one person's behavior, a therapist settles on one, and, because no person has a single interpretation of his own life, a patient's sense of being understood arises in what is essentially a negotiation between his perspective and that of his therapist. It must also be said that some psychiatrists never learn. Some residents are clumsy in the psychodynamic china shop at the beginning of their residency and remain so at the end.

"It's an anxious profession," another resident remarked at the end of his first year. It seemed to me, in sorting through my transcripts and notes, that there were different modes of and stages in coming to terms with psychotherapy. First and most common was rejection and a sense of inadequacy, coupled with an appreciation that psychopharmacology is easier to master. All psychiatry residents feel this inadequacy to some degree throughout most of their residency. How could they not? A second-year resident, skeptical of psychotherapy but caught by his own expectation that to be a good psychiatrist was to be a good therapist, reported, "I felt like an imposter. Someone was actually coming to me weekly for psychotherapy, and I didn't know what I was doing. My supervisors would reassure me by explaining that it takes ten years before you become comfortable doing psychotherapy. And I thought, ten years? *ten years?* I didn't expect to be an analyst after my residency, but I expected to be confident. I thought, don't give me that crap. But everyone said ten years. So I felt better, but I am still much more secure with the psychopharmacology and much less secure with psychotherapy. I feel very put off by it. It's easier to be a competent psychopharmacologist than it is to be a competent psychotherapist. The patients don't seem like they're getting better, or a patient leaves and I feel terrible. And I feel anxious, because even though I know it takes ten years and all that, still I feel sheepish and stupid with a new supervisor."

Then one must become engaged with the ideas of psychotherapy before being able to feel much ease in the practice. This leads to mild paranoia, because a resident who recognizes that there is a new way of seeing but feels he hasn't got it thinks that everyone is pointing at him. Of course, he is right. Senior psychiatrists have meetings to talk about the residents and how they are doing, and these discussions are in large part about the residents' personalities and whether they can make it as psychiatrists. "They have these meetings," Phil complained in his second year, "and they talk about us. I'm sure they think I'm too extroverted and outgoing. It's so unfair. I can't stand it."

Phil turned out to be a reasonably gifted therapist, but he was not an intellectual, and he was not comfortable in the training experience. By the beginning of his second year, he had the guarded look of the hunted. "Before I was a psychiatrist," he said, "I was innocent on the unconscious level. Now I'm guilty on the unconscious level. The year has been really hard. I'm sure psychiatric training is harder than other fields. For myself, I've had a lot of self-doubt about professional identity, about my ability to do this work, the ability to be a psychiatrist, whether I've got it inside of me. In cardiology, if someone had a specific arrhythmia, there is just one specific treatment, and if that treatment doesn't work there's a specific alternative. In psychiatry, first of all, you don't have anything to diagnose that's as concrete as an arrhythmia. But then, you can make a good clinical assessment on one level, but if you neglected something you would be called on and criticized, and you'd have to ask yourself, why did I do that? The chances are that the reason I didn't go into a certain detail was so deeply seated in myself that I'd have to do some serious self-analysis to understand why I missed it.

"There are no excuses in psychiatry. Everything you do is for a reason. Circumstance just doesn't exist in the minds of psychiatrists. Senior psychiatrists are always looking at you and judging you. I was on call the other day, and I slept from about 11 p.m. to 3:30 a.m. I went to sleep again at 6:00 a.m., and for some reason my watch alarm didn't wake me up. I was late for sign-up, and my excuse that my watch didn't wake me up was meaningless. I missed the time for some reason: some unconscious motivation meant that my watch didn't wake me up. That's understood. Any psychiatrist would say that it's understood. My unconscious is guilty of not wanting to go to morning sign-up rounds."

The final step in the learning process is developing some sense of mastery. That people feel as if they know who the good therapists are says something very interesting about this profession, where you never see the professional's work. Residents and more senior psychiatrists certainly had clear views about who was likely to be a good therapist and who was not. Often the judgments were quite consistent. The capacity to use oneself to understand another self is not, after all, a mystical quality. It is a part of human intuition that some people have naturally and that psychotherapists, who often fall into this category, learn to hone. What becomes surprising is how the process of honing can make a person feel as if he is becoming unnatural. It transforms the way he looks at people, thinks about people, reacts to people. Good psychotherapists sometimes say that they have always had the skills they have now learned to use, but that using them skillfully has changed them utterly. Or so at least they perceive.

In both of these approaches, the biomedical and the psychodynamic, what one learns to do affects the way one sees. A psychiatrist in a hospital (or a more biomedically minded psychiatrist) learns to memorize patterns and starts to use them in a rough-and-ready way. He learns to think in terms of disease and to see those diseases as quickly and as convincingly as a bird-watcher identifies different birds. For him, what is wrong with a patient is that the patient has a disease, and being a good psychiatrist involves seeing the patient in terms of the disease. For him there is a clear-cut difference between illness and health. A psychiatrist in an outpatient clinic (or a psychiatrist thinking psychodynamically) learns to construct complex accounts of his patients' lives. He thinks in terms of the way his patients are with other people and in terms of the emotions and unconscious motivations that lead his patients to hurt themselves. Here there is no clear-cut line between health and illness. What is wrong with a patient is that his interactions with other people go or have gone awry, and being a good psychiatrist involves understanding how and why. Both take the complex mess that is human misery and simplify it in order to do something about it. In the process, each approach constructs a different person out of one unhappy patient.

CHAPTER TWO

❧

THE ARROW OF HARM

Knowing what is wrong with a patient is only part of the way a psychiatrist learns to be in relationship with patients. Another piece is the way a young doctor learns to feel about patients and how he comes to judge who is a risk to whom. Unfortunately, the somewhat brutal experience of medical training tends to teach young doctors, among them young psychiatrists, that patients are a source of harm to a doctor. In psychotherapy training, the arrow of harm is pointed the other way. It is, of course, more complicated than that. But much about hospital experience invites a young psychiatrist to feel detached and distant from her patients, while outpatient psychotherapy invites a more tangled, intimate involvement.

IN THE HOSPITAL

Medical School Training

When I was an intern, I came in one morning to rounds and heard one of my classmates discussing his previous night on call. "Oh," he said, "a woman came in, and we did such and such and such and such, but luckily she died by morning." What appalled me was that I understood how he felt: if she had lived, he would have had someone else to take care of.

—Psychiatric resident

That a patient can be seen—as this one was—as a threat to a doctor's personal survival is the result of our country's approach to medical training. Psychiatrists have their initial apprenticeship in the intestines of the modern hospital. They are physicians. For five years, in medical school and internship, they confront the body immediately, directly, often horribly. They cannot, like the rest of us, hide from old age, from broken veins and sagging flesh. They see bodies fail. They see bodies mangled in car accidents and eaten by cancers. In medical school, doctors-to-be dissect the groins and brains of dead bodies, and a young student on a date sees not only a handsome face across the table but a thick neck stem of muscles, veins, and nerves whose simulacra she has sliced and pinned and studied. For five years these young adults cut dead flesh, do cardiac massage, assist at surgeries, sew up wounds, insert hypodermic needles, memorize body parts, and eventually sleep every third night in the hospital in a training so intense that few of them can imagine that any other training might be as powerful.

The experience seems to change students forever. At least, when psychiatric residents come straight from medical school and internship, they seem to be in almost a state of shock, and they talk about medical school the way anthropologists used to talk about their years in distant, savage lands. No one who hasn't been there can possibly understand, and having been there you become part of a club no one else can join. It used to irritate me, this sense that I would never understand what it felt like to be a psychiatrist unless I went to medical school and struggled through internship. One resident even explained that he deserved to earn an enormous salary because medical training was so miserable, as if thirty years of well-paid clinical work would barely compensate for his five years of pain. But I have come to believe that in medical training, there are irrevocable changes to your sense of who you are, and to some extent it is true that no one who has not had to draw blood from a dying patient in the emergency room, after having worked continuously through the previous night, can really understand. An anthropologist who did fieldwork in Turkey and then found himself enmeshed as an observer-teacher in medical school, agrees: "Not only was the language as different as Turkish and English, but the dimensions of the world that were beginning to appear—intricate details of the human body, of pathology and medical treatment—were more profoundly different from my everyday world than nearly any of those I have experienced in other field research."[1] The key difference, I think, that sets the training apart from other preprofessional experience—law school, graduate school, where the hours may also be long—is that in medicine, the student's failure to know can be the on-the-spot cause of the death of another human being. Practically speaking, of course, this is rare. Students are too well supervised and hospital emergencies too well attended for a student's ignorance to cause much harm (usually). Nevertheless, most people go to medical school in order to do what doctors do: to heal the sick, to save the dying. Especially now, when the financial windfalls of the eighties are fading under the hot glare of health care reform, they go to medical school to learn how to cure. The single most powerful lesson that students seem to learn in medical school is that they carry the responsibility for life. The second most important lesson is that they aren't responsible enough, they can never learn as much as they are supposed to know, and they cannot be as effective as they should be.

That painful tension between inadequacy and responsibility—one sociologist calls it a "training for uncertainty"[2]—is the first and most sharply obvious emotional demand in medicine. Medical students are confronted with a vast array of knowledge. Unlike in their undergraduate years, when the culture taught them to do the assigned reading in order to be rewarded with a decent grade, this culture tells them that they must master this knowledge not for their own glory—most medical schools do not give grades—but because they need it, all of it, in order to do decent work. The jejune joke is that you cannot tell a patient, "Sorry, I didn't go to class that day." Residents speak of making heroic efforts to memorize and of the stunned recognition of their own limitations. One psychiatric resident told me that he had written out the anatomy of the body on hundreds of index cards that he pinned to his walls; before exams he would pace nervously before them and memorize. He passed his exams. Most medical students pass their exams. Still, they are conscious of their inadequacy. Nobody can master the leviathan of anatomical detail, nor is there enough knowledge, in all we know of the pathways of disease, to map and chart and heal the degradation of the body.[3]

They also very quickly learn detachment. The need for detachment probably becomes apparent for the first time in anatomy lab, a class in which students spend between three months and a year carving up a formaldehyde-soaked cadaver and identifying its various parts. One sociologist who studied the learning process in anatomy lab reported that in the weeks before it and then throughout, medical students tell "cadaver stories" in which some student (elsewhere) plays a gruesome jest on, say, a bus driver by handing over the fare with a severed hand. Medical students laugh uproariously at these accounts; their laughter in the face of the bus driver's imagined horror displays their toughness. The sociologist followed medical students in their first six months of training, through anatomy lab, through visits to a local hospital for the dying, and through the unexpected death of their first psychiatric interviewee during the interview. Most of the students tried desperately not to let others know how difficult these experiences were for them, and most of them strove for an "ethic of stoicism," based on the formula that emotionalism equals weakness equals lack of scientific objectivity. A curtain of silence, the sociologist reported, falls around the cadaver experience: no one is supposed to let anyone know that it affects them, though much evidence suggests that it does. (Most of them rejected with horror the idea of donating their own body to a medical school's anatomy lab.) "The dissection of a human cadaver represents a test of one's emotional competence to become a physician, no less an entrance requirement than a high grade-point average or a double-digit Medical College Admissions Test score."[4] Yet you know, as a medical student, that the true test of your emotional competence for medicine will be in the trenches of internship. Most medical students seem to feel tremendous fear that their detachment will not hold.

That detachment is magnified by the theory of disease. Medical students are taught a profound awareness of the body as organism—not as a person. A medical student remarked to an interviewer, "I'll find myself in conversation. . . . I'll start to think about, you know, if I took the scalpel and made a cut [on you] right here, what would that look like?" An anthropologist participating in anatomy lab remarked, "I would occasionally be walking along a street and find myself a body amidst bodies, rather than a person amidst persons."[5] What doctors are taught, what they assimilate more deeply than any other professional, is that we are creatures of the body, and that bodily processes, which they know in excruciating detail, are our life. When medical students dissect cadavers, the didactic aim is that they should be able to name and know every slithering piece of it, turn what we would see as a clammy mass into a road map. As they memorize the hyperdetails of bodily process, they similarly turn the emotional horror of disease into a scientific entity. That transformation leaves the person and the pain out of illness.[6]

Thus, for young doctors, illness in those they love is peculiarly weird and upsetting. Two of my psychiatrist friends listened to family members' worries, diagnosed their metastatic cancer over the phone, and watched them die, all the while shepherding them through the tests, doctors, and chemotherapy that eventually failed to help. Most of us confront illness in the comforting obscurity of the hospital's antiseptic bustle. We believe—at least we hope—that modern doctors can cure anything if they try hard enough. Doctors rarely share the illusion that modem medicine is invincible. They do know how to ask questions about the body itself. "It's a profound shift," a resident said sadly. "I remember having a friend call from Europe, very sick. Rather than identifying with my friend, feeling how awful it must be to be sick abroad, I began asking all these clinical questions, very detailed, very careful. I knew too much, I had seen too much, and it prevented me from being as emotionally helpful as I might have been otherwise." She became the doctor; her friend was the patient. Patients are not friends. "I'll focus," she explained, "on the event as a phenomenon, not as something that happened to my mother." For a young doctor, family illness becomes a disturbing kind of double-entry bookkeeping. New doctors know enough not to be innocent of what a doctor in charge is doing. And so a young doctor may find himself the agent of his mother's death, because he knows that she needs a second opinion and whom she should call, and he knows if the doctor's reassurance is hollow or the advice sensible. Yet the more he keeps his cool, to stay on top of the specialists and the treatment options, the less he is part of her journey. He becomes the doctor, his mother is the patient. He needs to feel distant to keep his perspective. But he is her son, and she is dying.

This is a model of disease in which the body is unmindful, in which human intention and personality disappear from the body like figures from a photograph bleached by the sun. In medical school students are taught that the source of illness lies in the body and that the job of the physician is to deal with pain by locating its genesis in bodily dysfunction. In the last two years of medical school, the "clinical years," when students graduate from lecture-and-laboratory courses to trail around behind ward doctors like obedient shadows, their main task is to learn how to write down and present the salient facts of a "case," a patient's experience of illness. This is called "taking a history" and involves making a "differential diagnosis." It is an exercise in writing narrative history by agenda: to identify in the vague blur of a patient's story the specific symptoms that might be the signs of medical illness. To "take a history" means to collect the available information and present it in such a way that the potential signs of illness are clear; to "make a differential diagnosis" means to identify which illnesses the symptoms might indicate and in what order of reasonable likelihood. The narrative of a person has become a case study of a body. "When you're in a training program for medicine, you treat the problem and not the patient," a psychiatric resident said with some bitterness. "You get the person out of your face. The patient is a disease. That's the way you look at it. It's not Mr. Jones, it's the heart attack or the gastrointestinal bleed in room whatever."

The heroism in medical school lies in solving the "puzzles" of patients' complaints (what is going on with her liver?) with solutions, which are diagnoses that identify the diseases that produce the problems patients complain about. Medical students appear in a hospital unit for some short period of time (often a month or two) to learn about some specialty in medicine (psychiatry, obstetrics, surgery) as a low-level apprentice. Usually, they are given several patients to "work up": to talk to, to learn to feel doctorly with, to learn what it is to take a history. The competent medical student "presents" the patient in "rounds" to general criticism. That is, as the clinicians of the unit gather to discuss the patients, the medical student describes his patient in the approved way, listing the symptomatic history in such a way that it argues for a particular disease (the diagnosis), yet allows for the possibility of other plausible interpretations, which must be ruled out before proceeding in full confidence. A competent student, then, demonstrates that he understands how to think—in some fledgling way— like a physician. A star student solves a puzzle that has stumped the senior staff by reading the lab results more carefully or researching the journals on some topic more deeply than her seniors. And always the interpretive structure is the same: there is a biological problem that is hidden and that must be inferred.

All too often, this lesson is taught through humiliation and shame. The senior doctor in rounds will interrupt a resident's case presentation, turn to the medical student, and ask her to explain congestive heart failure. These unexpected public examinations are less common in psychiatry than they are in other fields of medicine, but students behave as if they expect them to occur, and when they do the student grows quiet and stiff. Medical students live in dread of being publicly humiliated, and vicious shaming— "God help medicine when you graduate!"—takes place often enough to keep the anxiety skyscraper-high. Medical memoirs paint the years of training as periods of cringing embarrassment and a pummeling sense of insufficiency. Very little actual humiliation is required to produce this state because of the student's intense awareness that the doctor carries the final responsibility for patients' health.

Medical responsibility asserts that it is the doctor's job to draw the correct inferences about disease. In contemporary medicine, where there is so much knowledge and yet so much is still unknown, where the interventions—surgery, chemotherapy, cell-killing and hormone-cycle-flipping medications—can do great harm, correct identification of an illness is crucial. Still, there are many conditions for which there is no blood test or scan that will reveal whether a doctor's guesswork is correct. This leads to the final powerful lesson that medical students are taught in medical school: that experience is more important than book learning, and that what counts is whether a patient gets better. A "bad outcome" is the tactful phrase used for patients who die. The good doctor has plenty of these. What makes him a good doctor, however, is that he rarely makes the same mistake twice— that he has the clinical experience with patient after patient that enables him to interpret his patients' symptoms accurately, and he has the reputation of helping them to improve. The doctor is autonomous, the doctor is responsible, and what counts in the end is his own experience as an expert. Doctors hate placing the reins of treatment into the hands of the insurance companies.

[Sample] Laws of the House of God

The patient is the one with the disease.

They can always hurt you more.

The only good admission is a dead admission.

The delivery of medical care is to do as much nothing as possible.

—From Samuel Shem, *The House of God* (p. 420), a darkly comic
   account of medical internship about which several residents independently said, "When I read it in medical school, it seemed absurd
   and extreme, but after internship I thought it was tame."

Internship

Internship is the year of intense medical apprenticeship that follows four
years of medical school. As far as an anthropologist can tell, a doctor leaves
internship shaped by two powerful lessons.

First, by the end of the year, the doctor feels like a doctor. He can do
lumbar punctures, blood transfusions, and cardiac resuscitations. He can
answer a code—a sudden flashing alert that a patient is on the verge of
death—and save the patient. He feels competent.

Second, the patient has become the enemy. In many hospitals, interns
spend more than a hundred hours a week in the hospital. They arrive at
perhaps 7 a.m. and leave at 7 p.m.; the next day they arrive at 7 a.m. and
depart at 7 p.m. of the day following (not that night but the next). Then
they repeat the sequence: one night off, one night spent fully awake and
working, the third night sleeping the sleep of the exhausted. (Some hospitals humanized this schedule after a famous lawsuit charging that sleep-
deprived interns had inadvertently killed a patient.) The work the interns
do is often repulsive. Their hands are in constant contact with diseased,
dying, often elderly bodies, with blood, feces, and spumata. They stay in
the hospital until their work is done. They are tired, overworked, and miserable. The people who are the direct cause of the work are the patients.

Even after internship, an admission is often called a "hit." House
staff—interns and residents—take turns handling admissions. In psychiatry, depending on the hospital and the level of the doctor's expertise, it
takes between one and three hours to admit a patient. This means, for
instance, that if you are "up next" but not on call, and the casual rule in
your group is that the on-call doctor is responsible for all admissions that
arrive in the hospital after 5 p.m., you have two choices if a nurse calls at
4:30 to say that a patient has unexpectedly arrived for admission. You can
pretend that the patient didn't arrive, for which the on-call doctor, one of
eight of your classmates, will hate you; or you can do the admission and be
late for your date or dinner or the movies by two hours—again. In medi-

cine, by the time tests are ordered and consulted, admissions can take longer. Like medical school, the basic struggle of internship is that there is far too much work. But whereas in the early years of medical school the work was contained in books and charts, in internship that work is the patient. And most of it is "scut" work that is disgusting, routine, and essential: doing spinal taps, drawing blood. Patients may be AIDS patients, demented screaming patients, patients with easily communicable diseases. As one of the residents said, "In internship, it's so busy that you begin to resent patients and to hate patients. It was so difficult that I loved to have a comatose patient. You wouldn't have to get a history, just check their labs."

Sometimes things become much worse. One of my psychiatric friends was assigned to an HIV unit during internship, which is not uncommon. She was new, of course, at drawing blood. Shortly after her arrival, she pulled a needle out of a patient's arm and accidentally stuck it into her finger. She tried to leave the room immediately but keeled over in a dead faint. In the end, she did not become infected. But she described that twilight period before she knew as a strange, existential desert. She had chosen medicine partly because she loved it, partly because it was safe, and now she was going to die because of that choice.

> As I'd walked into the [hospital] that morning, deflated by the transition from the bright and healthy July to the diseased neon and a-seasonal stink of the corridor, I'd passed the room of the Yellow Man [a Czech patient with a fatal liver disease]. Outside it were the bags marked "Danger—Contaminated," now full of bloodstained sheets, towels, scrubs suits, and equipment. The room was covered in blood.
> . . . The Runt [another intern] told us about the exchange transfusion, about taking the old blood out of one vein and putting the new blood into another: "Things were going pretty well, and then, I'd taken a needle out of the groin and was about to put it into the last bag of blood, and that porpoise, Celia the nurse, well she held up this other needle from the Yellow Man's belly and . . . stuck it into my hand."
> There was a dead silence. The Runt was going to die.[7]

In the novel, he wasn't, of course, and didn't. But this classic comic novel, the one I kept being told didn't convey the full gore of internship, is about overwork, gruesome elderly bodies and more gruesome illness, and the wild doctor-nurse sex that affirms life in the face of death. After years of listening to residents and walking down overscrubbed corridors, the part of the novel that seems overdone is the social bonhomie.

A cruel system breeds callous survivors. Medicine has a macho culture passed on from brutalized class to brutalized class. Those who have survived the razing process of a sleepless, difficult year often see toughness as a virtue and persuade themselves that sadism brings out the right stuff in those that follow them. Interns rank on the lowest rank of the doctorly ladder in the hospital, just above medical students, and, being in one-year positions, they are often the most dispensable and insultable members of the medical staff. "I said I loved her too but it was a lie because they had destroyed something in me and it was some lush thing that had to do with love," moans the hero of *The House of God,* "and I was asleep before she closed the door."[8] Resident after resident told me about nurses who punished interns by refusing to help them out with difficult bloodwork, or refusing to allow the intern to sign a three-hour order in such a way that he would not have to return three hours later, when he hoped to be asleep, to renew the signature. (The nurses would do these things for interns they liked, I was told.) They told me that senior doctors belittled junior doctors, junior doctors belittled residents, and everyone humiliated the interns. "You can't understand doctors without understanding internship," a first-year resident said vehemently. "I hated it. It was horrible. You know that book *The House of God?* That's what it was like, I swear."

A consequence of all this—the responsibility, the hierarchy, the autonomy, the temptation to resent the patient, and the terrible uncertainty as to what is wrong and what to do—is that a developing doctor is judged by a certain kind of cultural standard as much as or even more than by technical competence. Students make mistakes. Young doctors doing their first physical exams or lumbar punctures make mistakes. Technical errors (how much medication to give) and errors of judgment (whether to give it at all, whether the patient is really sick) are errors of inexperience. What really counts is demonstrating a willingness to learn from experience and, along with that, respect for the patient—however much you hated missing the movie that night—and respect for experience. An ethnographer of error on the surgical service titled his study *Forgive and Remember,* which, he argued, was the moral principle of that service. Errors are forgiven, so long as they are not repeated, so long as the young surgeon understands that he made the error and acknowledges his desire to learn. And unfortunate accidents do happen. A patient who was admitted and discharged with all the standard symptoms of an ulcer turns out to have had a strange form of esophageal cancer instead and dies. A rape victim admitted with stab wounds to the stomach turns out also to have been stabbed in the back, and as her stomach is stitched she bleeds to death through the back. Terrible things happen in hospitals. The unforgivable errors are actions that a reasonable person at that level of training should not make.[9]

Often, this cultural ethos becomes a profoundly conventionalizing force. In any field, of course, it helps to look like the applauded image of the discipline: to tilt your hat just so, to formulate questions in just such a manner and with just such a style. The university world of the arts and sciences is no stranger to these presumptions. Yet in the academy there is a clear and explicitly formulated understanding that the quality of a scientist/scholar is judged by her work and that age and experience may bring pomposity without authority. Doctors, on the other hand, are powerfully enculturated into the belief that there is a doctorly manner, that looking like a doctor is important, and that those with more experience are usually right. It follows, then, that the power of doctorly convention is enormous, and it influences both the dress and the bearing of first-year medical students. Every hospital I was in had an implicit dress code in which doctors looked like one another and emphatically not like the nurses. This is particularly striking in psychiatry units, where no uniforms are worn. Nurses, for the most part, dress casually and for comfort, in sneakers and sweatshirts. Doctors dress for mainstream authority. The local style varies from Indonesian casual chic to Armani and bow ties, but the markers are always clear. "I could tell that you were the doctor just by the way you dressed," a patient said one evening, looking not at me but at the woman with whom I was on call. I no longer remember what I was wearing, but I remember that I suddenly realized that to fit in with the doctors at that hospital I would have to wear linen and pumps. As with clothes, so with style: the seductive authority of age and experience leads doctors to want to look like doctors, and those who violate the normative standard are marginalized.

Young psychiatrists leave internship with a clear sense of the difference between doctor and patient: that patients are the source of physical exhaustion, danger, and humiliation and that doctors are superior and authoritative by virtue of their role. A friend of mine, a chief resident in psychiatry who helped select future residents, pointed out that her job in selecting residents was specifically to find people who had not absorbed the clear message: "When I look for good residents, the most important characteristic is their open-mindedness: being willing not to judge too quickly, to be humble. They need to be capable of listening quietly before they form an opinion. They have to be able to allow people to be heard. That's really part of what it is to be a good clinician in medicine, anyway. And there are other clinicians' traits which are also very important: the sense of responsibility, the capacity to serve the patient's needs and not your own. I look for these things. And also the capacity to be comfortable with a *wide* range of people, to be natural with people. Tolerance, responsibility, and comfort.

"What you want to encourage in the residents, once they arrive, is 'good clinical judgment,' a sort of ineffable skill best characterized by the capacity to use patients' past experience to predict their future behavior. Medicine suffers when doctors are lax in listening to the history. Sometimes people order a whole slew of tests for no reason. Sometimes they don't do the expensive tests, and they ought to. You *have* to listen, because patients don't tell the story in a straightforward kind of way.

"That's one reason why psychiatrists are experienced as good doctors, because they *do* listen. And listening saves money. We had a patient come in once who had tried to commit suicide because she was a musician and could no longer play her instrument, and she'd been told it was fatigue. Psychosomatic. Well, when she came in here, we listened. It sounded when you listened carefully that it might be myasthenia gravis [a disease of weakening muscles due to the impaired functioning of the nerves], and it was. And if the doctor had listened carefully in the first place, the patient could have avoided that expensive trip to the ICU [the intensive care unit] after the suicide attempt. That's what doctoring is all about. It's so important."

When this chief resident chooses future residents, she looks for people who survived internship with their humanism intact.

Still, the hospital training in psychiatry continues the demand for emotional detachment that is so powerful a lesson in medical school and internship. The basic activities, for instance, feel much of a piece: admitting patients, prescribing medications, daily rounds, filling in forms. The lectures on psychopharmacology recapitulate the style of knowledge presented in medical school lectures. Residents memorize lists of medications with their side effects and learn something about their mechanisms, in the same way they memorized body parts and mechanisms as students. The hospital setting in psychiatry recapitulates the medical setting of internship: hospital corridors, bustling emergency rooms, wards, rounds, team meetings. The doctor's role is understood as it was in internship: he is supposed to make a diagnosis that is more or less reasonable, for which at any rate he will not be yelled at in rounds, and prescribe a medication for that condition that is also reasonable.

What is also perpetuated by the experience of internship is the antagonism against the patient. I was particularly struck by this in a hospital system in a city with relatively poor facilities for the homeless. There was a Veterans Administration Hospital uptown, in a genteel area located on a bus line, and a large city hospital located in the middle of downtown. Each evening, residents were assigned to cover the psychiatric service from 5 p.m. until 7 or so the next morning, after which they would carry on with the day. During the period of my fieldwork, residents were on call slightly more often than once a week.

The main burden of call in this hospital system was that many of the chronically ill homeless patients—most of whom were also drug and alcohol abusers—would try to talk their way into the hospital to get a free bed for the night. Particularly at the VA hospital, they would present themselves in the emergency room at odd hours in the evening (the bus ran all night) and claim that their voices were acting up and that they felt suicidal and would kill themselves unless they were admitted to the hospital. "The most striking thing to me," a first-year resident said, "was how many patients look at the VA hospital as their home. It was very frustrating, and I ran into that over and over again. If I were in a setting where there weren't so many people who wanted to get something, I would tend to be a lot more believing of people. In this system, you wind up hearing 'suicide' a lot, and it's not always true. You get cynical." These patients were often big men, often weighing 200 pounds, often unkempt and unwashed. The security guards were supposed to search them for weapons, but they were usually too busy. The resident, as often as not a slight twenty-seven-year-old woman, would take such a patient into an interview room down the length of a corridor, away from the public openness of the emergency room waiting area. In principle, she could ask a security guard to stand outside the door, but the security guards were hard to find and often uncooperative, and anyway such a request was perceived as weak-kneed and unmacho. So the resident would be confronted with a large, possibly dangerous man, who she knew was probably desperate for a clean bed for the night. If she admitted him, based upon his claims of suicidality, and he slept off his alcoholic stupor and was cheerful in the morning, she risked being yelled at by the team director of whichever team the patient was assigned to. If she did not admit him, she risked that he might swear at her or even lunge at her in anger.

She also faced the risk that he might actually be suicidal. When I was there, one resident, jaded from a year of what she took to be the manipulative lying by VA patients, did refuse to admit such a patient, and he did make a suicide attempt. She was severely reprimanded, and the story of her error spread throughout the residency. She felt humiliated for months. The senior doctors tell the junior doctors that if they are in any doubt they must admit the patient. But those are cold words when a resident knows equally well how ridiculous she will look in the morning with an inappropriate admission. The residents, then, were the gatekeepers to the desirable good—a warm bed—but they were also servants and underlings in a house run by stern masters. Nor surprisingly, they spent a lot of time worrying about protecting themselves. "When I assess a person that I don't know," said a first-year resident, "I'm looking to see whether this person is safe, whether he can talk to me or whether he's going to try to jump over the railing and kill himself, or to choke my throat because I look like a demon or like his mother. Then I want to know whether he's just wasting my time. Does he want me just to fill out a disability form? Is he a crock or really in distress? Boy, some of those crocks are really good. They can really fool you."

One night, I was on call with one of the kinder, more compassionate residents, a petite woman in heels, in the downtown city hospital. Several hours into the evening, we got a message that there was a patient waiting to see her in the emergency room. He was a thin, middle-aged man, poorly dressed and unwashed, and after some conversation it became clear that what he really wanted was a place to sleep. He spoke about needing to "detox"—he was coming down from crack—but he wasn't eligible for the substance abuse unit at the VA and couldn't have been admitted so abruptly even if he had been. The resident, excusing herself, went to call the various shelters in town. None had room, and after half an hour or so— there may have been another task for her to deal with in the meantime— she went back into the consulting room to tell this man that there was no place that could take him.

At first he didn't understand: he kept saying, "I dream about the rock, if it was here I couldn't stop myself." Then, when it became clear that the resident, as gentle as she was, would not admit him to the hospital, he hurled himself forward and swiped at her (luckily he was lying in a bed with sidebars, which held him back). The resident stepped back, unsurprised and self-composed, and called politely for the security guards. By this point the man was screaming and thrashing, and he pulled off his belt and began to pound the buckle into his wrist. Four guards ran in and pinned him to the bed, and others went to find leather straps to belt him to the bars. Now he could be admitted: he met the criteria of being a danger to himself or others. The resident seemed cool, but later, when we had stepped into a private office and I asked her whether she was okay, she burst into tears.

Sometimes patients are admitted against their will. They are brought in by police because they began to campaign in the street for their brother Bill Clinton. They scream at the doctor, threaten to sue, and not uncommonly, after they have been admitted, they take the doctor to court. If a patient has been committed, she can demand a court hearing. If she can demonstrate that she can take care of herself—she is competent enough to take a bus; she knows who she is and where—and if she can claim that she has no plans to hurt herself or others (the laws differ from state to state), a hospital cannot keep her no matter how fiercely she is protecting herself from nonexistent CIA agents. If she is so psychotic that the courts will not release her, she may curse out the doctor in front of the staff. She may wait until there is a staff meeting, then lie down, drumming her heels into the carpet, and scream that Dr. Brown hates her. A young doctor, like all of us, likes to be appreciated for his work. These patients do not generate the warm, proud feeling doctors feel when a patient thanks them for saving his life.

The residents at this hospital had to fight to keep their compassion intact against the creeping cynicism that runs through conditions like these—not the conditions of the hospital but the unavailability of shelter care in the city, its inadequate disability services, or the fact that patients often no longer stay long enough to become better enough to be grateful for the help. In their first year, residents would spend nine months on a VA unit where the chronic patients rotated in and out. The model was biomedical, for the most part—inpatient stays weren't really long enough for psycho-dynamic work, and most of the patients, it was said, weren't capable of functioning at that level—and the new resident's primary responsibility was to write the admission and discharge notes and prescribe medications. Mostly they represcribed what had been prescribed in the last visit. Inside the hospital patients would "comply" with the prescription (that is, they would usually swallow the pills), but they often stopped taking the medication outside. Antipsychotic medication in particular often has unpleasant side effects: you feel itchy or as if you can't keep still, or your body doesn't move the way it used to.[10] Many patients, then, do not take their medications outside the hospital, but then they get too sick to care for themselves. They return to the hospital, adjust to the medications again, improve, are discharged, stop their medications, and fall apart. It is a dreary, demeaning, and irritating cycle.

"You can bring in a schizophrenic who doesn't take his meds and make him better in the hospital, and that's satisfying. But if he does it over and over again, if he never takes his meds outside, it's frustrating. And it's very unsatisfying to have someone who is suicidal and say to him, 'Well, I can't treat you because you're drinking too much.'" The chronically ill often came back in when their delusions or depression got too bad to bear. One resident told me that once when he had been on the main unit and had felt depressed about the relentless quality of these illnesses, he had had a conversation with one of the nurses. The nurse had told him that in order to cope with these patients, she transferred off the unit for a while every few years. The last time she had done that, she told the resident, she had been gone for a year. When she had returned, she said, she had recognized none of the other nurses, and all of the residents had changed. But she had known every patient by name.

That first year, these residents were also assigned to work for a month in the daytime psychiatric emergency clinic. There was always a press of patients in the clinic, many of them in for a refill of their prescriptions.

Residents were expected to be competent at reviewing patient symptoms and prescribing medications without more than nominal supervision. They managed this requirement by railroading through a patient's narrative to identify his or her symptoms and prescription needs, patient after patient. The goal was to get through the line of patients in the waiting room. For me, that clinic produced one of my favorite psychiatric anecdotes. The resident, a tough, efficient ex-bouncer, ushered in a ragged-looking young man whom I assumed slept under a bridge. He carried a diagnosis of schizophrenia, and he reported that he had run out of his antipsychotic medication. The resident began writing quickly in his chart, firing off the psychosis questions to see whether the young man had become psychotic while off his medication: "Think I can read your mind?" "No." "Think you can read my mind?" "No." "Ever get any messages from the radio? TV?" "No." "Think you have any special powers?" "No." "Had any thoughts about the cosmos recently?" "Well," said the man, "now that you mention it, I've been reading Stephen Hawking's book about the nature of time, and I say he's wrong. Even if," the patient went on, "time is like the fourth dimension of a three-dimensional balloon skin expanding in space, I say that it had to start somewhere, and Hawking says time has no beginning." The doctor looked at him as if he'd sprouted wings and wrote the prescription for the antipsychotic.

Senior doctors could probably do something to lessen the cynicism and alienation that become so marked in a young psychiatrist's first year. However, the tough, see-if-they-swim ethos of medicine tends to mitigate most attempts at nurturance. Residents' relations with senior doctors are guarded and mistrustful (or, occasionally, hopelessly and unrealistically idealizing). Most of them complain bitterly that no one is interested in mentoring them; the senior doctors shrug and say that residents aren't interested in being mentored. I saw an egregious instance of this culture of contempt around a brilliant, well-known doctor who ran a unit (in another hospital system) through which the first-year residents rotated. I arrived with two of the brightest and shyest residents of the class, one of whom was desperate to do research and eager to work with the senior doctor. He rarely saw him. The senior doctor was too busy to spend time on the unit; in fact, senior psychiatrists spent so little time on the unit that they rarely interviewed the patients these raw beginners were diagnosing and treating. The residents felt that they presented the patients in team meetings and the social worker and psychologist would advise them on appropriate medications. The residents approached the senior doctor and wondered whether they might have more supervision and fewer meetings. The senior doctor held a meeting attended by all thirty or so staff members who worked on the unit, most of whom were older than the residents. He asked the residents to present their views and then went around the room, person by person, asking everyone what he or she thought of the residents' ideas. Most people opined that the residents were inexperienced, arrogant, and confused. The senior doctor then turned to the residents and asked them whether they could think of any constructive suggestions for the unit. The residents sat in silence. The senior doctor smiled gently and asked them why they had put the unit to so much trouble if they weren't willing to say anything. Six months later, the research-oriented resident transferred to another program.

The toughness needed to survive all this becomes associated with biomedicine. As it is carried over from medicine, biomedical psychiatry is about doing something, about acting and intervening, the way doctors are supposed to do. Summarizing in his final year, one resident said, "Coming into this from medicine, a different field, the first year is pretty much organized around the medicine bottle, biological medication. Coming from internship, it really didn't feel that foreign." As the differences between psychiatry and medicine become more apparent to the young psychiatrist—the fact that the illnesses take a long time to improve, that compared to medicine there are few interventions, that patients are not always grateful for a doctor's help—the biomedical approach becomes a way to cling to one's doctorly identity. As another resident remarked at the end of his first year, "Psychiatry ranges from the very biological and medical end all the way to the dynamic analytical end. But to be a very good psychoanalytic therapist, you don't need to go to med school." One of the main anxieties residents have when they begin their training in psychiatry is that they will lose their medical skills. They speak with pride about keeping up those skills, about being able to handle cardiac arrest or emergency care. Supervisors and residents talk about psychiatrists who prescribe medication in order to make themselves feel like doctors. They tell stories about young doctors doing therapy who become nervous about not being doctors and prescribe sleeping pills to patients who don't need them.

In fact, one of the common remarks about psychopharmacology is that psychiatrists prescribe medication in order to avoid the awkward intimacy that is created with a patient in psychotherapy. This, of course, was the charge leveled by senior analysts against the first group of young, biologically oriented psychiatrists in the late seventies. Even now it remains a powerful critique. "At that hospital," a resident said to me, speaking critically of a group of psychiatrists she thought were too determined to prove their toughness to a top-ranked medical house staff, "the neurologists never ask for a psychiatric consult anymore because the psychiatrist always prescribes Tegretol for complex partial seizures and the neurologists think the patients need family meetings and aftercare." Sometimes a young psychiatrist explains that the emotional distance imposed by the biomedical perspective is in fact one of the appealing things about the biomedical orientation. One resident, for instance, who told me that he didn't like the intimacy and emotional closeness of psychotherapy, explained near the end of his residency that what attracted him in biological psychiatry was "the ability to maintain a comfortable distance from the patient. When I'm prescribing medicine, I don't have to establish this real close relationship with the patient."

This bias produces a kind of sex stereotyping of the biomedical and the psychotherapeutic. Biological psychiatry is said to be masculine, what manly doctors do. Psychodynamic psychiatry is women's work. Male senior analysts say, when you ask them how people respond to them, that other people think it odd that a man should be interested in feelings. Young psychiatrists point out that the women in the class tend to be more interested in psychotherapy and that after all the wider culture prepares women for talking about emotions. Supervisors say ruefully that as more and more women end up in psychiatry, psychotherapy is increasingly becoming a woman's game. It is not clear to me that the facts bear this out. But the perception is a striking feature of the culture. "Biological psychiatry just seems more masculine to me," a resident admitted. "It's pretty tough to go into psychotherapy if you're a guy. People think you're a wimp."

With psychopharmacology, it is the medication, not the doctor's relationship with the patient, that cures. That's one of the things that makes it "manly." (Another is that it is more connected to hard science.) And when the drugs work, they work relatively quickly, within weeks. One resident, who started medical school interested in Freud and psychoanalysis but in his last year of residency was among the more biomedical of his class, said, "When I first started here, my psychotherapy outpatient was this borderline patient that no one had been able to help in twenty-five years. My inpatients were all these manic patients who kept coming in, getting neuroleptics and lithium. Two weeks later they were totally switching around and becoming normal human beings. I had one lady who was deliriously manic in the quiet room, picking at the air and talking to the wall. She was a schoolteacher before she came in. Within a month she totally switched out of it. One day later she was coming up to me and saying, 'What was I doing in that room? How was I acting?' She seemed like a totally normal schoolteacher. She seemed like *my* old schoolteacher. She was back teaching within a week. On that unit, patients came in wanting to kill themselves, out-of-this-world depressed. We gave them Prozac, and within three weeks they seemed normal like the rest of us."

And medication works, straightforwardly (except when it doesn't). It is immensely satisfying to do something that soon diminishes a patient's pain. At graduation one resident said about his diagnostic and psychophar-macological skills, "I feel good about those skills. It's something people sort of belittle because it's kind of cookbook, but when you see a large number of patients and it is abundantly clear that they need their medica-tion, and you give them a medication and they come back two weeks later enormously grateful because their business is back to functioning, it's nice." A first-year resident said, "It's very gratifying to have people you're able to help and then in a few days they say, 'Boy, was I really out of con-trol that day. I'm feeling much better. I realize that I was out of control because I was not taking that medicine. I didn't know what was going on. I'm glad you helped me.' " (By contrast, a few minutes later that resident said about psychotherapy, "I've never had a long, ongoing, intimate rela-tionship with a patient. I don't know whether I would enjoy it or not. It scares me because I don't think I'm capable of it. Somehow I feel I'm abandoning all the scientific skill that I have if I go to do that.") A second-year resident explained, "It's fun to play with the meds and get them right and get the combination right and know what to expect." A graduating res-ident said, "When I'm giving someone relief from acute anxiety with med-ication, I find it gratifying." Psychotherapy is a slow, often difficult process, and young psychiatrists are often not very good at it. Even when they are, it doesn't always work. It is greatly satisfying to become quickly good at a skill that often does, even when your other skills are pretty raw.

The patient remains set apart, as a diagnosis ("our suicidal bipolar"), as a body ("that psychosis needs more Haldol"), and as a person. Despite all that, residents often are or become compassionate about even the most difficult patients, and many residencies encourage a kind of medical agape. But the social process of hospital psychiatry teaches a young psychiatrist to anticipate that harm runs from the patient toward the doctor, not the other way around. In the hospital, at least in the early years of residency, one of the primary emotions generated through contact with patients is fear. There is fear of getting the diagnosis wrong and being yelled at in the morning, and perhaps a general existential fear of madness. There are also the basic fear of threats to one's bodily safety and resentment about putting that safety into jeopardy. "Call" hurts the doctors who do it. It keeps them up all night, or maybe all but several hours of the night, and it makes them exhausted and cranky. On call, a young doctor confronts dangerous patients who are manipulative and deceitful. (An emergency room is one of the most dangerous places in which to work.) Inner-city hospitals and Vet-erans Administration hospitals generate this fear more than do the elite nonurban hospitals. Psychosis, however, is not obedient to the rules of class etiquette. In elite hospitals patients may also be dangerous and decidedly ungrateful. When young psychiatrists learn to diagnose and prescribe, they learn that a patient can hurt a doctor. They learn to keep their distance.

OUTPATIENT PSYCHOTHERAPY

When young psychiatrists learn to do psychotherapy, what they learn is that doctors can hurt patients. Psychotherapy teachers talk about psychotherapy's demands for establishing intimacy, for tolerating the needs of other people, and for responding to their emotional needs as they are, without the interference of a therapist's own anxieties and troubles. They talk about the personal intrusiveness of psychotherapy, the fact that learning to practice psychotherapy means that young therapists must learn to tolerate knowledge about their own selves that may be embarrassing and shameful. They point out the way the patient perceives the therapist and how the therapist perceives the patient, and they make it clear that both parties distort the relationship but that it is the therapist's responsibility not to act on the distortion. They talk about the need for trust in the psychotherapeutic relationship and about the delicacy and strength of that trust. They talk about the difficulties of really understanding someone else, and they repeatedly emphasize the way people mishear one another. In fact, the whole point of psychotherapy training, its basic stance, is for trainees not to hurt the patients. This is thought to be very hard.

In some sense, it is also the goal of therapy. It is not clear what causes psychotherapeutic change, but a young therapist knows that simply explaining what is going on with a patient to the patient is not sufficient to enable that patient to change. As it happens, truth frees relatively few of us. So understanding a patient, being able to explain a patient's behavior to him through these emotion-motivation-behavior bundles, is not in itself thought to be useful, because the patient may not be able to hear and understand what the therapist has to say. The goal of therapy is for a therapist to be able to use his knowledge of a patient to construct a relationship with the patient in which the patient feels safe enough, and trusting enough, to learn from what the therapist has to say. For a therapist to be able to do this, he must be able to respond to a patient according to the patient's needs rather than his own. He must be able to listen to a patient without being caught up in his own embarrassment, fear, desire. As one supervisor remarked to me, "When the patient says, 'You are a fascist,' the therapist must be able to say, 'How am I a fascist?' To explain to him that she is not a fascist serves her own needs. To understand how she appears to be one serves his."

So one of the first hard lessons for a student of psychotherapy is learning how your own self-involvement inevitably prevents you from listening as clearly as possible. Supervision confronts young therapists with the fact that the habitual ways in which they act in the world construct their perceptions of it, and moreover that what a resident takes to be objectively true can tell an astute observer more about the resident's own awkward conflicts than about the patient. "All supervision, virtually, if it is going to be any good," a supervisor remarked to me, "is going to address the most problematic issues of the supervisee. For instance, if I can't stand it when the patient doesn't like me, I'm going to work nonstop to be funny and charming and so forth. And if I present that session in supervision, it's going to take someone three minutes before they say, 'Why don't you let this patient tell you how angry he is at you?' " For me, that moment of shocked recognition came when my first supervisor said, "You've done that before. You're listening to the words she's speaking and not to the feelings she's trying to keep hidden." I felt caught out, as if in a dream when you are lecturing to a hundred students and you realize you're wearing pajamas. At the time, what the patient didn't want to tell me I was too anxious to interpret.

"I remember we had these hall meetings," Earle recalled once when we were talking about the way young psychiatrists learn how inadequate they are as unbiased listeners, how profoundly they shape the world they take to be objective. "All the patients and all the staff would sit in this big circle. There was this patient, Susan. She carried the diagnosis of borderline personality, and she'd been there awhile, and one time, near the end of the meeting—this was my first rotation in the hospital, mind you—she started screaming, 'I hate this place, it's terrible, you're treating me like a prisoner, I'm here because I'm sick and because my mother fucked up and she's a bitch.' Screaming bloody murder. I looked at the unit director, and he was relaxed, saying, 'Okay, could you lower your voice now?' Everyone was just acting like this was a normal kind of thing to happen, and I just could not tolerate it. After the meeting I said, 'That was the most horrible thing I ever sat through.' I hadn't yet picked up that they didn't think that way. The unit director said to me, 'What was it that bothered you?' and I thought, 'Oh, come *on*, you know,' and I said, 'How could anyone tolerate that?' and the nurse said, 'This is nothing.' The unit director took me upstairs and sat with me a little, and he said, 'Why do you think that this is so upsetting to you?' It was such a shock, to hear that I was the only one who was upset and that it could be something about me which was responsible. I talked with him for a while, and it occurred to me that this patient looked like my older sister, and at dinner at home my sister would frequently shout and scream and storm up to her room. We would all have to sit there and hope that she would feel better and not hit us. That kind of thing. It was such a shock to me to make that association, and it was one of the first associations I had that explained to me what transference was."

"Transference" is the term given to this insistent re-creation of the world according to our hidden emotional expectations. It is the central term in psychoanalytic psychotherapy, but, like other powerful terms, it refers to more than one phenomenon. Transference "with a little t," everyday transference, the transference we all act out of all the time, refers to the way we all see one another through the filtering lenses of our own pasts and temperaments, so that Smith sees Boggs as a kindly old man and Jones sees Boggs as an authoritative force, and this has less to do with Boggs than with Smith's and Jones's experiences of their own fathers and uncles and grandfathers. Transference in that sense is alarming enough, because when as a therapist you begin to see so clearly the way other people distort the world, it is hard not to worry that you yourself see nothing clearly, that no human being sees the world straightforwardly, that objectivity is a flickering chimera. Adapting to a patient's needs begins to seem like a distant fantasy as you begin to realize how deeply rooted are your own needs to see people in certain ways.

Transference "with a big T" refers to the fact that in therapy those needs become even stronger and more overwhelming. Transference "with a big T" evokes the emotional intensity generated by the therapy relationship itself: the focused involvement with the therapist, an endless wondering about what she does in her off-hours, what she's really like, what he's like with his family. It is common for an analysand to say that the analyst is the most important person in his life. When I was in therapy, I thought of this attachment as the "Wizard of Oz" phenomenon. For me, my therapist became a floating head that accompanied me everywhere, with whom I had conversations that extended way past my sessions, late at night and early in the morning. Psychoanalysts often explain these intense feelings as the reenactment of childhood experiences, but they probably owe their intensity to the weird asymmetry of the therapeutic relationship. In any case, transference "with a big T" points to the fact that psychotherapy is utterly and overwhelmingly emotional. Therapy, when it is working well, is a powerful, intimate experience.

From the very beginning, young psychiatrists know the great power a therapist has to hurt, as well as to heal, because most of them know firsthand what it is like to have intense feelings about a therapist who accidentally, inadvertently, does something that feels cruel. It is often said that to learn psychotherapy, you must not only do psychotherapy but be in psychotherapy, and most young therapists who are interested in psychotherapy present themselves for psychotherapy at some point in their residency. When they do, and when they become involved with the therapy, they rapidly see how fragile, dependent, and needy patients can be with their therapist and how a patient scrutinizes a therapist for slight clues to her love or hate. The hall-of-mirrors quality of a student therapist in therapy makes that fragility even more apparent than it is to an ordinary patient. "When I came in the first time," Earle said, "my therapist said, 'Why are you interested in therapy?' and I said, 'Well, you know I'm in training, and I've heard a lot of people say that their therapist is their best supervisor.' He threw that back in my face. He said, 'Oh, I'm glad you're here for training purposes.' Well, there went that defense."

Most nonpsychiatrists in therapy have very private experiences of therapy. Their therapist knows no one they know. They often tell relatively few people about their therapy, or, if they do, there is little more to report than an endless string of comments about what the therapist said and when. Their therapist can be their personal, sacred, perfect source of wisdom.

For a young psychiatrist, the experience of therapy isn't like that. Particularly if the psychiatric community is a small one, as it was in the town in which I did much of my work, most residents choose their therapist from the same small group deemed good enough to supervise them for their psychotherapy. The two roles are not allowed to overlap: you may not have your therapist as your supervisor. You are always, then, intimately involved with more than one senior psychiatrist. In my town, most residents knew that their therapist was the therapist for at least one other resident and who it was; most residents in therapy knew that their therapist was a supervisor and for whom. They called this "cobwebbing": that they knew one another's supervisors, therapists, and consultants, that when they joined their residency psychotherapy group they might realize that their T-group leader is their analyst's husband or that their supervisor supervised their therapist. In turn, their seniors have lived in a cobwebbed world for years, and their close knowledge of one another has not always made them friendly. Small-town psychodynamically oriented societies probably re-create the forced intimacy of early American small-town society better than any other institution does. As in Salem, their worlds have strains.

So in addition to the everyday intimacies of the psychotherapeutic experience, there was a world of backdoor gossip about the upsetting behavior of the senior psychiatrists on staff at the hospital. A great many residents reported to me things that their therapists or supervisors had said about senior colleagues. This illicit gossip becomes even more noticeable in psychoanalytic institutes, where analysts see their young student analysands four times a week, during which there is much time for discussion of students' supervisors and seminar leaders. Analytic orthodoxy suggests that analysts should listen silently, without comment but with confidentiality, to their analysands' tearful tales. No one I talked to suggested that this had happened in his own case. Several people spoke of being outraged when an indiscretion revealed in the consulting room made its way into the public domain. One person told me that he had nearly been dismissed from his analytic training because of some remark that had made it from the consulting room to the student evaluation meeting. (In earlier days, a trainee's chief evaluator was his analyst; not unnaturally, successful candidates were often reluctant to criticize their training in their analyses.) I went to a seminar on analytic supervision in which an analyst in training spoke about her difficulties with her supervisor, how she'd been convinced that she'd done a terrible job, and how her analyst had later told her that he'd talked to her supervisor and that her supervisor had thought she was good. Some members of the audience were predictably indignant at this breach of confidence, although it would have been cruel for the analyst to insist upon principle rather than kindness. At the same time, these indiscretions spoil the ideal of therapeutic neutrality and perfect privacy.

Meanwhile, each resident is rudely confronted with the fact that his therapist, the sacred being to whom he confesses his most embarrassing, upsetting thoughts, is shared by other people he knows and may even be thought to be less than perfect by them. I remember having lunch with a woman, a perfectly reasonable lunch in which we talked freely about our friends and activities, and as we returned to the clinic she asked me who my newly assigned supervisor was. When I told her, she blanched, and I realized that he was her therapist. She felt acutely embarrassed that I knew her therapist in a more relaxed way than she did, that I called him by his first name, that I could have lunch with him; on my side, I began sorting out the comments I'd made to check whether I'd be embarrassed if anything I'd said were to be passed on in the consulting room. I had dinner with another resident who talked about her annoying new patient who, to demonstrate his professional skills, had given her some articles to read. She would, she announced, have to ask her supervisor whether she really had to read them. She then told me who her supervisor was—and I wanted to punch her because he was my therapist, and I knew he would have advice because when I'd met him, I had of course presented him with my first book. In my therapy-anxious state, I heard her saying that my gift had been an annoyance to my therapist. This kind of thing happens constantly. There is even a tactful etiquette about how to manage the awkwardness: the more sensitive residents (who are almost all in psychotherapy or psychoanalysis) find out whom a friend is seeing for therapy and then never mention that name casually in the presence of that friend. (This habit is uncannily similar to the tabooing of powerful names in parts of India, Africa, and Melanesia.)

Even more tarnishing than realizing that your therapist is merely human and shared by others is the fact that you are able to see the insincerity inherent in his technique. Young therapists see that their own patients feel as powerfully about them as they feel about their own therapists. It scares them, because they do not feel competent and trustworthy the way they feel their own therapists are. Then they begin to wonder whether all patients trust their therapists blindly. They wonder whether their own therapist is incompetent, the way they feel themselves to be. It becomes hard for residents to trust their therapists because the residents do not say everything they believe to their patients. They know that they say things to make the patient feel better that are not entirely honest (for example, when a patient wonders how sick he is), and they know that therapists change their minds over time. Things they say casually to their patients in the first month, they have forgotten or ignored by the sixth month, yet their patients carry the words around like mantras. How, then, can young therapists trust their own therapists? All young doctors, of course, become mistrustful of their doctors when they see the imperfections of medicine. In my experience, most doctors firmly believe that you should never have surgery in the hospital—whichever hospital—in which they were interns. Rarely are their feelings so intense, and their idealizations so shining, as when they begin to see the flaws in psychodynamic psychiatry.

"It makes it very difficult, because I'm looking for the wires," Earle said. "I'm looking for the mechanism behind what he's doing because he presents this smooth exterior and he says little things, little interpretations, and I want to see the strategies he's using, the decisions he's making, the formulations that he's making and why he's doing something now and not then. He's closing up an hour by making a statement that brings us back to the beginning. I know exactly what he's doing because I do that daily. He wants the end not to be painful to me. It's hard for me not to know the truth, not to know what he's really thinking, not to know the interpretations he's not giving me because he doesn't think I'm ready for them." This double-entry bookkeeping epistemological commitment—I believe my therapist, and I understand that these are the techniques that I should use to persuade my patients to believe me—is like an anthropologist's experience of going native and trying to reflect upon what it is like to live that life unreflectively. Anthropologists do this for a year or two at a time. Psychotherapists develop it as an ethos.

Despite seeing more of the human, flawed, technician-at-work side of the therapist than the nonpsychiatrist sees (most people idealize their therapists as unflappable heroes), a young therapist learns to trust his own therapist deeply, possibly more than a nonpsychiatrist trusts his therapist. In the psychiatric culture of therapy, you learn that trusting your therapist in spite of his flaws is a mark of your own psychodynamic skill. "You begin by telling everyone you're in therapy," a senior resident explained. "You tell them about your therapist and what he said. Then you find you don't want to tell anyone anything. And then you find that when someone mentions his name, you feel hot and embarrassed and you blush, just because he knows so much, now, that you never thought you'd tell anyone." These feelings are supposed to be overwhelming. If they are not—if you do not convey the fact that you cry in therapy—your fellow residents will wonder whether there is something wrong with you (particularly if you are female, but even if you are male). I had recurrent conversations with female residents about how to walk out of a session in which you had cried for half an hour—and then take a session with a patient of your own. (Waterproof mascara.) In casual conversation, in interviews, in gossip, we talked about what our therapists had done for us and what our friends' therapists had or had not done for them. If a resident was not in therapy, it was because she was afraid of therapy—afraid of its intimacy, afraid to learn so much about her own unhappiness. In psychiatric residency, being aware of your anger and misery is good. Some residents took my involvement in therapy as a sign that I was okay—in psychiatric residency, a decision to go into therapy is a sign of health—and always in my conversations with them there would come a moment when their voice would drop, they would become conspiratorial, and then they would ask, "Are you still seeing Dr. Cohen?"

In the end, what a young psychiatrist's knowledge does is to make even clearer the basic lesson of the field: that we profoundly shape our world, that we throw ourselves against the hard wall of our therapist's personality only to discover that we built it ourselves.[11] That is one of the great strengths of having patients, for a patient experiences his reactions to his therapist as natural, as the way any sensible person would react to such a rude or loving remark, while a therapist discovers that most people believe they act as any sensible person would act, when in fact they act quite differently from one another. One patient thinks it peculiar and self-absorbed that you should ask her whether she is upset because you are leaving on vacation soon; another cries violently when you ask her the same question, because she is overwhelmed by your kindness in mentioning something she could never bring herself to say without what she calls your permission.

"It's odd," Earle remarked, "you begin to disengage your feelings about the person from the person himself, and you realize that this person is just an innocent bystander of these feelings of yours, that he has accidentally stepped into your life. The important part of that, for me, is that this realization does not get in the way of having those feelings. The feelings are just as intense and just as unavoidable no matter how much I know about the transferential process. What it *has* made me wonder about is that I'm supposed to be reproducing my early object relations, my feelings about my mother and father. Because the experience makes me think that my parents, too, were bystanders. That these are not feelings about my father, but feelings I had for my father that emerged because of the situation we were in and how he happened to be the person who was there. Some people will say that my father did this to me, or they hold their parents to blame for so many things or consider them to be responsible. I can't do that, because of my understanding of how these things evolved. I just have to think of my father having to be there at the right time and how what followed actually had to do with the dynamic interaction with my personality and his personality and the situation we were in. That's the conclusion that a lot of patients reach in the course of therapy. They sort of let go of blaming their parents and come to accept the situation that created the experiences. But I think it just happened earlier in me because of my understanding of transference and projection." ("Projection" occurs when you "project" something you are feeling, such as anger, "into" someone else. So, for example, you might feel angry, not know that you feel angry, but experience a friend as being angry at you.)

The vivid lesson of psychotherapy is that in the end we are responsible for the way we feel, that other people are bystanders to our private dramas, and that becoming bystanders to ourselves—*seeing* ourselves—is an enormously difficult task, yet essential to effective therapy. Therapists are always partially blind, preoccupied by their own troubles and driven by their own unconscious needs and expectations. All people are; the therapist at least has a greater opportunity to know the areas of his blindness, so that he can attempt to peer around them. But in the world of doctorly superiority, this opportunity to see one's own blindness comes hard and is humbling. The young psychiatrist fears that he is not saying the right thing and not doing the right thing, because (he fears) he is too narcissistic, too hysterical, too something. Often when I asked residents whether they thought that psychotherapy worked, they said that they knew it did from their own experiences in psychotherapy but not from doing it themselves, because they felt too awkward and clumsy with a patient.

What they know about why therapy works when it works just enhances their nervousness. In medical school, they have already absorbed the lesson that a doctor is immediately responsible for a patient's life. In medical school, that responsibility hinges on factual knowledge: a doctor must have the intelligence and memory to know the criteria for a diagnosis and to choose an intervention that will work. In earlier decades, that was more or less the model that explained therapeutic efficacy. Freud, although unfailingly complex, wrote for the most part as if it were intellectual insight that made the difference. An analyst was able to understand a patient's associations and behavior and presented the understanding to the patient in a series of interpretations. From the interpretations, the patient learned to

understand his or her implicit assumptions, and through this new understanding the patient changed. Psychoanalysis worked because the analyst
provided the patient with knowledge.

Over the last two decades, psychoanalysts have increasingly turned
their attention to how an analyst relates—not to what he knows. In the
1950s, a psychoanalyst named Heinz Kohut began to write articles and
books couched in an obscure jargon about "self-objects" that made much
psychoanalytic discourse seem simple by comparison. Nevertheless, his
work revolutionized American psychoanalysis, because he essentially
argued that the therapeutic relationship was what made the therapy work.
Many psychoanalytic patients, Kohut claimed, came from emotionally
deprived backgrounds in which they were not allowed to be genuine but
were forced to live out their parents' needs. The children became narcissistic adults, incapable of empathizing with others because no one had truly
empathized with them. A therapist's job was really to reparent them, to let
them experience trust and steadfast affection, and from this experience the
patients would remake themselves as more confident adults. To put it
crudely, in the Freudian model a therapist's job was to interpret a patient's
unconscious conflicts; in Kohut's "self psychology" a therapist's job was to
repair a patient's emotional deficits through the relationship in therapy.
What a therapist did became at least as important as what he knew, and
transference became an even more complex, weighty concept in which not
all the feelings were just about the past.[12] "We were all less stiff than the
Freudian was supposed to be," one analyst confided to me over lunch. "It
was just that you weren't meant to say anything about it."

From a young psychiatrist's perspective, however, contemporary
changes in psychoanalysis have sharpened the recognition that when a
therapist meets a patient, he must do so without a shield of elaborate theory. In the 1960s, a young, frightened therapist could bolster his confidence
by seeing himself as a scientist. He could hide behind the belief that he
could be a scientist observing some data. He could protect himself from
intimacy with a fantasy of intellectual authority. These days, that protective
fantasy is simply less available. A psychiatrist's psychotherapy is no longer
conceived of as the encounter of a scientific and theoretically trained mind
with a needy patient. It has become the naked emotional encounter of two
souls.

There is, in fact, much to fear. Therapy relationships are emotionally
intense in ways that are quite incomprehensible to an outsider. A resident
has some patients who love him, others who loathe him, and some who
threaten to kill themselves when he goes on vacation. Many of his patients
cry copiously into his Kleenex. Sometimes he buys Kleenex by the case.
When he is in psychotherapy, he too weeps copiously, apologizes for it, and

then weeps some more. Young therapists are often taken aback by the strength of their own and their patients' feelings. Some of them make decisions about where to live on the basis of where their analysts live. "My analyst is unwilling to relocate to San Francisco [to which this resident had planned to move at the end of residency]. Well, I like this city, even if it isn't San Francisco. So for now I'll stay." Or, as one resident more simply said about his analyst, "God, I like him."

To learn how not to hurt a patient, how to construct a relationship in which a patient is not limited by the therapist, creates a world of paradox. The blunt, peculiar worldview shaped by this training embodies therapists' inherent inability to meet the impossible demands of this profession, the impossibly difficult task of listening without desire or memory (to borrow a phrase), to be perfectly compassionate and objectively intimate. On the one hand, psychotherapeutically oriented psychiatrists place great value on honesty. Yet therapists are often dishonest, for they are always forming hypotheses about other people and holding back from using them, and they are psychologically coy, in that they value the ambiguity that comes from seeing too much complexity to be certain about anything. They value emotional openness, a kind of alert willingness to listen that many of them call "being available" but what they mean by that is less of an emotional presence than an emotional reserve, a capacity for responsiveness that is very different from directness. They value having a rich understanding of a human being but they often see people as types, so that one graduating resident complained that he couldn't read novels anymore, because he had immediately seen that Lawrence Durrell's Justine had a borderline personality disorder and Emily Brontë's Catherine Earnshaw was histrionic, and so the novels lost their mystery. This world admires honest emotional expression, yet many psychiatrists are hesitant to reveal themselves to their colleagues because they are afraid of being interpreted (and shamed) by them. This world admires people who are courageously honest, who understand their pain and can express the complex contradictions of human emotion—yet because a therapist is the one who must encourage that honesty and understanding, she becomes indirect, manipulative, and quiet. As Earle observed, "The thing that's most odd is to undo your socialization. My style is to be right in there, as you would at a cocktail party, to oil the social intercourse. I had to learn not to do that, not to nod so much, not to agree instinctively but to step back, to say, 'You're asking that question, and it's important. Why are you asking? What's behind it?' It's really a perverse act, because you are taught socially to cooperate, and as a psychiatrist you learn to resist, to introduce some discomfort in order to create the space for them to discover something. That is why shrinks are strange, because they've unlearned all that stuff. Shrinks will pause and think."

The counterpart of "transference" is "countertransference," a term that refers to the way a therapist feels about a patient (transference refers to the way patients feel about therapists), and the interesting thing about the diagnosis of disorders most specifically associated with therapy is that the skill is taught not through a disease model but through an interaction model. The diagnosis of personality disorders is informally taught through countertransference, through the way the interaction with a patient makes a therapist feel. Here the lesson is that identifying those feelings gives the therapist knowledge and that ignoring them can wreak chaos in the therapeutic relationship and damage the patient's ability to heal.

In psychotherapy, diagnosis is not terribly important, at least as it is taught in psychiatric residencies. When I asked a second-year resident whether diagnosis mattered when doing therapy, she looked at me as if I'd said something very stupid and snapped, "No, it's a waste of time, it's absurd. There is no diagnosis in therapy." She went on, "We all know the feel of a borderline, but the diagnosis isn't relevant. If they're schizophrenic, you're going to write them a prescription; if they're borderline, what are you going to do?" In long-term therapy, a resident's only important senior is her supervisor, who tries to teach a way of interacting with the patient, a way of thinking about people in general or one person in particular, that crosses diagnostic boundaries. I rarely—I am inclined to say never—heard a psychodynamically oriented psychiatrist discuss diagnostic categories in a supervision. (For a time, I had a clinical psychologist as a supervisor; she did think more diagnostically than the psychiatrists, but that was in part because her academic interests included personality disorders.)

Nevertheless, there are diagnoses for which the primary treatment is psychotherapy (although medication is also usually prescribed). These are the personality disorders, which are described as long-standing character difficulties. In the diagnostic handbook, they are separated from the other serious psychiatric disorders such as schizophrenia and depression, which can become acute. The acute disorders are called Axis I; the personality disorders are identified on another axis, Axis II. The personality disorders come in three groups, the "anxious," the "dramatic," and the "odd." The "anxious" include the avoidant, dependent, and obsessive-compulsive personality disorders; the "dramatic" include the histrionic, narcissistic, antisocial, and borderline personality disorders; the "odd" include the paranoid, schizoid, and schizotypal personality disorders. Like the Axis I diagnoses (schizophrenia, depression, psychotic depression, bipolar disorder, obsessive-compulsive disorder, and so forth), each personality disorder is defined by a list of specific criteria. The patient must meet a specified number of criteria in order to qualify for the diagnosis. But because personality disorders are not by themselves generally considered to be valid reasons for hospital admission (they are not thought to become "acute"), a resident never has to memorize their criteria and never prototypes them as thoroughly as the Axis I disorders. A resident rarely has to write an admissions note for a patient that demonstrates that the patient meets the official diagnostic criteria for an Axis II category. Hospital admission forms are likely to be examined by people whose job it is to determine whether the admission was necessary, and failure to display evidence that a patient meets criteria for an Axis I diagnosis can lead to disqualification for payment. An Axis II diagnosis by itself commonly does not qualify the admission. Even if a clinician believes that a patient's borderline personality disorder is responsible for her suicidal rage, he will list a diagnosis like "major depressive disorder" on Axis I, and "borderline personality disorder" on Axis II, and usually his admission note will demonstrate the criteria for the Axis I depression more systematically than for the Axis II personality disorder. Access to outpatient psychotherapy is not controlled by disorder status in the same way, and the outpatient intake form, for admission to the outpatient clinic, does not have to provide evidence for a diagnosis to the same degree that a hospital requires. As a result, residents do not pay as much attention to the diagnostic criteria, and most of them have much hazier notions about the content of a personality disorder diagnosis than they do about the other common diagnoses.

Instead, these categories are taught by the way a patient makes a doctor feel. The category "borderline personality disorder," for example, identifies an angry, difficult woman—almost always a woman—given to intense, unstable relationships and a tendency to make suicide attempts as a call for help. At one outpatient clinic, the category "borderline" was taught through the "meat-grinder" sensation: the chief resident explained to the others that if you were talking to a patient and felt as if your internal organs were turning into hamburger meat (you felt scared; you felt manipulated by someone unpredictable; still, you liked her), that patient most likely had a borderline personality disorder. That internal feeling was insisted upon as a diagnostic tool in a way that bypassed the usual emphasis on "meeting the criteria." When I presented one of these patients in a meeting at the outpatient clinic, the team leader stopped me before I got to the diagnosis and asked, "How would you describe this woman's experience?" I cautiously said, "Well, she's got a lot of anger, no coherent sense of identity, experiences a sense of inner emptiness"—I was listing diagnostic criteria for the borderline personality disorder—and the leader cut me off, smiling, and said, "No, that's cheating. What does she *feel* like?" Had I been presenting a patient with schizophrenia, the team leader would probably have taken that time to focus on the criteria. But I wasn't. I explained that in the interview I had felt intensely needed and flattered and a little scared by her anger at the world. When you feel that way, the team leader said, think "borderline."

When residents first encounter the personality disorder categories in the inpatient setting, those categories usually appear as an aside, as a means of explaining why a patient does not want to take the medication she has been prescribed. And it is the general idea of the personality disorder, with shades of awkwardness and annoyance, rather than a specific diagnostic category, that is invoked. In the first year of residency, a common phrase is "Axis II flavor." A junior resident will present a newly admitted patient and diagnose him as depressed, possibly secondary to substance abuse—in other words, he's an addict—then put down the notes and say, "But you know, there really was an Axis II flavor to this guy"—which means that the resident mistrusts the patient, may not like the patient, and probably doesn't quite believe everything the patient told him. (On the specific occasion I'm remembering, the fact that the patient had announced in the admissions interview—he was admitted for depression—that he was HIV positive but that his test came back negative was seen as strong evidence of his Axis II character. He was seen as manipulative and deceitful.) Or a resident will say about a patient she has just interviewed and diagnosed as having panic disorder, "There's something really weird about this guy. I couldn't put my finger on it. Probably Axis II."

The personality disorders become insults in the way new psychiatrists learn to gossip. Your fellow residents are people whose work you have to do if they don't do it, who may get pregnant and dramatically increase the amount of overnight call everyone else in the class must do, who may overinterpret you, show up late for your meeting, and take all the attention in seminars. A new resident learns to describe those unendearing traits as personality disorders: the other residents are narcissistic, obsessive, hysterical, and borderline. The patients whom they begin to call Axis II are the ones who've come to get all they can from the system and see a resident as a means to that end. Such patients are the tough thugs who come in (the resident thinks) because they want a prescription for their street drugs. I remember sitting in one intake interview where a patient was meeting his outpatient psychiatrist for the first time, when the patient began to go on and on about how his last doctor had prescribed Xanax (a tranquilizer not unlike Valium) and how helpful it had been, and the doctor began looking more and more stony. When the patient left, I asked what had been going on. "This guy has a problem," the resident said. "His problem is that he wants a prescription to abuse." Residents refer to such patients as having an "antisocial personality disorder." ASPD is the other major personality disorder category commonly used by residents, the first being "borderline." A shorthand recall for the diagnosis is that the ASPD patient is a male criminal; the borderline is a female who grew up in a criminally abusive household.[13] Personality disorder patients are the patients you don't like, don't trust, don't want.

One of the reasons you dislike them is an inexpungable sense that they are morally at fault because they could choose to be different. This is the inherent danger of the interaction model of psychiatric illness, the fact that believing that someone has the capacity to change his behavior can lead you to blame them for the way they behave. Let me quote a resident who said clearly what I have heard others say less directly: "I have more respect for Axis I. I feel better about it. If they're really depressed, have all the neuro-vegetative symptoms, you feel like they came by their diagnosis honestly. The same thing if they're manic, have classic psychotic symptoms— it's exciting. You think, oh, they have a real diagnosis, you can treat it with medication, and you also give them the benefit of the doubt. They've got genetic loading to have this terrible disease. On the other hand, Axis II is almost like an insult. You kind of attribute more blame, even though that's not true. In Axis II, I think there may be some genetic linkage, but there's probably a lot of early childhood experience. It's not their fault. But somehow you have a worse feeling about them."

In psychodynamic psychotherapy, treatment involves helping a patient take responsibility first for his or her behavior and then for changing it. Therapy may be based on the premise that a patient is not responsible for the circumstances that led to such maladaptive behavior—a cold or abusive parent—but it must be premised on the belief that the maladaptive behavior that developed out of those circumstances is under the patient's conscious or unconscious control. This is a major difference from the disease model. When schizophrenia is treated as a disease, it is presumed that the patient cannot control his symptoms. Working from the interaction model, a patient's symptoms are much more a part of him, much more a part of his intentions, and hard to conceptualize as disease. It is easy for a resident to skip from this complexity to the irritated sense that the personality disorder patient is intentionally creating havoc. As one explained, "On the psychosis unit, the staff agreed about what the person had and how to treat it. People didn't really judge the person, as if he'd done something wrong. On units with people with personality disorders, people do judge the patients. [Some hospitals have units for patients who are admitted because of a suicide attempt but whose most important problem appears to be their personality disorder, not their depression; the admission note is still likely to justify the admission on the basis of the suicidal depression.]

I'm not wild about that but it does feel like those patients act out with more volition. They're not having hallucinations, they're throwing chairs across the room. It's like sabotage. It may be driven by unconscious needs, and in that sense it's not chosen. But nevertheless, their illness is more problematic than for someone who has a frank psychosis. When someone has a frank psychosis, the staff doesn't argue about whether or not the person has contributed to their own difficulties." As another remarked, when patients have Axis I problems, "they have a real diagnosis; you can treat it with medication."

Yet while the personality disorders may make a psychiatrist angry, that anger also makes him feel guilty. Most residents said that it was harder to be empathic with personality disorder patients because it felt as if they had more choice, but they were embarrassed by the admission. The woman who talked about having a "worse feeling" about people with personality disorders awkwardly explained a year later that she no longer felt that way. Another resident said, "Somehow you think that they should know better, it's their fault, you say to yourself, 'Straighten up.' It's harder with them, especially people with borderline personality. You feel like they're persecuting you on purpose. That's how I feel. But I can't defend that intellectually." Gertrude had started out her outpatient year focused on learning to be a good psychotherapist. She wanted to present her patient in the psychotherapy seminar that an analyst ran for her class. She was eager to take on psychotherapy patients. Then she rotated onto a unit that was known for its borderline patients. She acquired a patient who would wait until the team meeting to which Gertrude was assigned began. The patient would then wander onto the corridor on which the meeting was being held and begin to scream how much she hated Gertrude. Had Gertrude been an experienced therapist, this would not have fazed her greatly (perhaps). As it was, she felt humiliated, the other staff on the unit saw that she felt humiliated, and the story that circulated about her was not about the patient's anger but about Gertrude's shame about her hatred of the experience.

These kinds of patients are the most difficult to work with. Borderline patients cause fighting and confusion. The patient typically tells some of the staff that they are the very best, most wonderful doctors, nurses, psychologists, and so forth that she has ever known. Others she decides she dislikes. Unless the staff is well managed, it "splits": some staff members, whom the patient has told are wonderful, think she is a lovely woman, misunderstood and badly treated by all the other staff members, who are mean. The "good" staff then confront the "bad" staff. There are scenes. These patients threaten to commit suicide when the doctor leaves town for the weekend, and he does and they do. At least, a patient may make a suicide attempt that lands her back in the hospital, but sometimes she is unfortunate and succeeds and then the doctor must struggle with guilt and a lawsuit. These are patients who because of their volatile intensity engage their doctors deeply, and the doctors sometimes believe that they can save them and are also terrified by the idea that the suicide attempts might someday work. These are patients who have usually been badly abused and oversexualized, and they are often seductive, charming, and thoroughly absorbing. In 1987, Robert Waldinger and John Gunderson published a book, *Effective Psychotherapy with Borderline Patients: Case Studies,* detailing six case studies, which examined the use of psychotherapy to change borderline behavior. (The answer was that a great deal of therapy over a great deal of time made a difference.) The case studies were anonymously written. One of the authors, who was married with children, remarked of one patient that he had never felt more involved with anyone in his life, ever.

As a result, precisely because the patient is engaging, exciting, and dangerous, the borderline patient becomes for a psychiatric resident what a schizophrenic was thirty years ago: the tough, difficult patient who makes her a psychiatrist. That is because to do good therapy with these patients— to help them feel safe, to help them talk frankly, and to talk with them in a way that they can hear and from which they can learn—requires one to have the capacity not to act on one's love or hate or anger for them, which in turn requires one to recognize those emotions in oneself and also in the patient. Young psychiatrists are scared of these patients but also proud when they can work with them. I was interviewing a chief resident once when one of the newly minted second-year residents came by, essentially to get some support but also to show off. She had a patient on the (mostly) personality disorder unit, she said, who was infuriating the staff. "Borderline, of course," the chief resident said. "Of course," she replied. This was a patient, she said, who talked about horrible sexual abuse, who showed other patients pictures that her brother had supposedly sent to her, with abusive phrases scrawled on the back. "Once she has the unit in hysterics, she goes to sleep. She's *really* lethal," the younger resident continued excitedly. "She hoarded some of her tricyclic antidepressants [these older-generation antidepressants can kill you if you overdose on them] and hid them and they were discovered, maybe by accident. The hospital can't possibly let her out," the resident said, "but the unit staff wants so much to let go of her that she packed her bags on Sunday and they didn't even call me. So she left and put a note on my door saying how wonderful I was." The chief resident chuckled. "You're in the thick of it. Most residents wouldn't take a patient like this. Do you think that Jones [a supervisor whom the chief resident didn't much like] would take a patient like this?" "No, but

Judith [another supervisor] might. I'm going to go process this with Judith for an hour." And she left.

Young psychiatrists learn in psychotherapy, as they do in medicine, a kind of twinning of responsibility and imperfection. They are taught that in psychotherapy, it is a psychiatrist's responsibility to understand how his feelings shape his interactions with a patient, that the efficacy of therapy depends on a therapist's self-awareness (and also on the self-awareness of the patient), and that a therapist will never be as aware as he should be. What makes a borderline patient so compelling is that if a therapist can get drawn in to the intensely emotional world of that patient and still use his feelings as a tool in the service of the therapy, he has mastered the nearly impossible task of being a bystander to himself, at least well enough to help. Before this point, he will be taught that he might hurt the patient instead of help.

But in a medical setting, young doctors learn (more or less by accident) to fear and resent the hospital patient. The conditions under which they work make that inevitable. Those conditions are less marked in psychotherapy. That is, borderline patients and other difficult patients may lead young therapists to fear, resent, and guard against their patients. But these patients are not such an assault on the young doctor as is internship and, later on, night call in the psychiatric setting. Moreover, the teaching in psychotherapy insists on the doctor potentially being a source of harm to the patient in a way that biomedical teaching does not. Residents learn in psychotherapy that the arrow of harm flies from doctor to patient, not the other way. To the extent that the initial training and experience in diagnosis are frightening and exhausting—and they nearly always are, and for a significant length of time—the emotional experience of doing a psychiatric admission signals the need for a psychiatrist to guard himself against a patient. To the extent that the early training experience in psychotherapy is experienced as hurtful to others—and it nearly always is—the experience of doing more psychotherapy signals the need for a psychiatrist to protect a patient. These are powerful responses. And a psychiatrist who is anticipating the need to protect herself is alert for very different cues from those anticipated by a psychiatrist who feels the need to protect a patient.

CHAPTER THREE

⁂

THE CULTURE AND ITS CONTRADICTIONS

People laugh at the contradictions their culture sets up for them. They laugh at the paradoxes, the idiocies, the inanities, their attempts to do what they must do under impossible conditions. Meanwhile, their conventions adapt to the contradictions to make them as bearable and reasonable as they can be. Treating psychiatric patients can be a near-impossible task. People who do so collapse with foxhole hilarity around the stress and the demands. Depending on their model of illness, though, they laugh and adapt in different ways. Like the interpretive patterns that lead psychiatrists who are thinking psychotherapeutically or biomedically to evaluate patients in different ways and to anticipate different kinds of emotional responsibilities and responses to them, the psychotherapeutic interaction model of illness has a different impact on the life of a hospital unit than the biomedical disease model of illness. Working with these different models changes the way the staff joke, the way doctors relate to nurses, and even the sense of the unit's ultimate goal. Ultimately, these differences help to produce different moral sensibilities about mental illness.

Hospital units are small societies. Typically, a psychiatric unit—the older name was "ward"—is a corridor or small building where the patients sleep and spend most of their days and where doctors, psychologists, social workers, mental health workers, and so forth come to treat them. These different professionals have very different training. The doctors have medical degrees. They have spent a year in internship, and on the unit they are either in training, as residents, or they have completed a three-year residency and are now on staff. Some of them may have additional training though fellowships (for example, in substance abuse) or more extended residency training (as in child psychiatry). All (or nearly all) orders in the

patient's chart—from allowing smoking privileges to prescribing medications—must be signed by a doctor, even if the primary responsibility for the
patient rests with a psychologist or a psychology intern (a psychologist in
training). In that case, the psychologist makes the decision about whether
the patient should have smoking privileges. Nevertheless, a doctor on that
unit must cosign the order for it to take effect.

Psychologists are trained in nonmedical university departments, and
they take doctorates. They read a great deal about normal and abnormal
psychology (more than the psychiatrists do) and are often (depending on
the program) well trained in psychotherapy. They do not have any medical
school training. They are also usually trained in "psychological testing."
Psychological testing refers to a complex battery of written and oral tests
such as the Rorschach, the Thematic Apperception Test, the Minnesota
Multiphasic Personality Inventory, Draw-a-Person, and others. The goal of
these tests is to reveal underlying psychological issues by using more
"objective" measures. Sometimes, especially if the Rorschach (the ink-blot
test) is used, the test report will have a psychodynamic flavor. In one case
conference, the summary for a report began, "The patient has grown up
with an intense sense of inferiority spawned by her sense of neglect by her
parents, especially her mother. In her efforts to be found pleasing to her
parents, she created a shell identity which others would find acceptable
and which shielded her inner world and its insecurities." Different psychologists and different hospitals use different tests, but almost always the
tests take several hours for the patient to complete and many hours for the
psychologist to analyze. If there are psychologists or psychology interns on
the unit, they typically do psychological testing on each patient. However,
that depends on the unit. In one hospital I visited, when the length of
admission dropped to under a week and the hospital grew panicked about
its financial stability, the administrators cut out all psychological testing.
(Psychological testing had been billed to the patient or the insurance company at around $700. When the hospital was forced to cover the costs of
patient stays for a basic daily fee rather than billing each service separately,
many services were simply dropped.) Then they cut out the psychology
interns altogether. In another hospital, the psychology interns did not
always do psychological testing on each patient, but they were given primary responsibility for about half of the patients on the unit. Each intern
and each resident would be responsible for the care of three to four
patients at a time. Even so, the residents had to countersign all instruc-
tions for the care of the psychologists' patients.

Social workers typically have a master's degree and are less likely to be
given primary responsibility for patient care. A social worker manages the
interaction between a patient and the patient's life outside the hospital.

The social worker finds an aftercare program willing to accept the patient after discharge and handles the transition into that program (this is called the "disposition" of the patient). The social worker is often also the primary interface with the family. Some social work programs train their students to do psychotherapy. Usually, the fewer the hospital's resources, the more powerful the social workers' roles.

Mental health workers often have no formal academic training for their jobs (although they are sometimes required to have a bachelor's degree). They are paid to sit with patients, to walk out with them to their appointments and to lunch if they must be escorted, and in general to keep an eye on things. Some mental health workers become very senior and keep the job for decades. Many others go back to school to pursue better-paid careers in mental health. In one of the units I visited, the director of the unit—an older, highly experienced psychiatrist—had first worked on the unit as a mental health worker some twenty years before.

In many ways, the nurses are the most formidable presence on the unit. Nurses handle most of the hour-to-hour care of the patient. Psychiatrists move into and out of the unit over the course of a day because they also work in the emergency room, in admissions, in research, in the consulting service for the main hospital; they go to lectures; they give lectures; they go to and give supervision. The same is true (in different ways) for psychologists and social workers. Like the nurses, mental health workers take shifts on the unit, but mental health workers make few decisions about the patients' care and cannot dispense medication. Nurses do both. They dispense medication and take care of patients' medical needs, and they carry out the doctor's orders. There are always nurses on the unit, and they stay on the unit for hours at a time (shifts often run for eight hours). Because they have the most contact with patients, they are often very knowledgeable about the patients and their care. When a psychiatrist (or psychologist or social worker) is in training, the nurses know far more about the patient and how to treat him than the new trainee does. A new resident is in the awkward position of giving orders to a nurse who knows what he should do better than he does. The relationship between nurse and resident, then, can be a nurturing apprenticeship or a tortured, humiliating power struggle, depending on the graciousness and maturity of each party and the general climate of the place.

The climate varies widely, and units vary widely in the way they organize these roles. Some units are formal and hierarchical. Some are not. Some allow psychiatrists and psychologists nearly the same power and authority. Most do not. Some are rife with power struggles and territory wars, some are not. One of the most important factors in determining the organization of a unit is what the staff takes to be wrong with the patient, what an anthropologist would call their "model of illness." Why is the patient sick? The answer to that question tells the doctor what she is treating and how best to treat it, and her answer to that question in turn structures her relations with other staff in surprisingly predictable ways. That is because different models create predictable problems for the unit that the culture of the unit has to solve.

A BIOMEDICAL UNIT

On a biomedical unit, the model of illness is that psychiatric patients are rational adults with medical problems. The implicit presumption is that the patients have come into the hospital with brain dysfunctions, just as the patients down the hall have come in with liver failures and cardiac dysfunctions. It follows from that implicit model that the doctor should discuss the medical problem with the patient, as if he in fact had liver disease. And indeed, many conversations on these units imitate other medical discussions. A doctor walks into a patient's room and says, "Well, Mrs. Jones, how is your depression today?" or "How are your voices?" I once heard a doctor ask his patient how her psychosis was doing. But psychiatric illness, of course, inhibits patients' rational capacities. That is the problem this model creates. A doctor needs to talk to her patient about his illness, the way any doctor consults with her patient, but the patient has been admitted because he was blocking traffic and explaining that he is the risen son of God.

San Juan County Hospital is the safety net for psychiatric patients from a forty-mile urban stretch of northern California. Anyone in this area who falls between the many cracks in the medical insurance floor ends up in the county's system. They tend to stay in the system a long time, shuttling into and out of the community hospital and its associated clinics, halfway houses, rehabilitation centers, and so forth. Because the seriously mentally ill tend to drop down through the class levels, these patients are usually the poorest and sickest. Many of them carry the diagnosis of schizophrenia. Most of them live in marginal conditions. When they are outside the hospital, many of them use crack or vodka instead of antipsychotics to control their symptoms, so that when they are released from the hospital, it sometimes takes no more than a few weeks—and sometimes only a few days—until their harassed relatives call the police to take the ex-patients back. The police handle this part of their job with understanding but distaste.

The practical demands on this unit were staggering. It worked with a biomedical model not out of choice but because the patients spent too little time in the unit for the staff to do much else besides medicate them and because the patient turnover was so great that the staff found it hard to spend much time with any of them. This was a community hospital. It accepted people without insurance, without documentation, without any-thing, and it received some special funds from the state for this purpose. That was what it was supposed to do. But it had never been intended to handle as many patients as now came flooding through its open gates. As the health care system went into crisis, nearby hospitals had begun to refuse more and more of the bottom rung of patients because they couldn't afford to care for people without insurance. In earlier days, these other hospitals had covered a certain amount of the expense of that care, and the federal reimbursement policy for the care of the poor had been more gen-erous. Now the homeless who showed up in these other emergency rooms were shipped out to the community system immediately, and as the long-term care facilities in the county had decreased, the demand for beds in this hospital had become intense. Patients who clearly needed care were pushed out of the units to make room for people even sicker than they. An ethnographer of a similar psychiatric unit entitled her terrific study *Empty-ing Beds* to make the point that, in times of such pressure, the goal of the unit could be summarized as making room for the sickest of the sick.[1]

They were indeed very sick. When I arrived at the hospital for a week in 1995, one of the new patients was a handsome twenty-year-old man who, while wearing nothing but boxer shorts, had walked onto the busiest free-way near San Francisco and attempted to herd the cars, a kind of postmod-ern sheepdog for the mechanical age. He refused any medication after the police escorted him onto the unit. When the young psychiatrist tried to persuade him to change his mind, saying that the staff really thought that medication would be useful, he shook his head decisively. If it would help, he said, he would agree to eat the food. But medication was out of the question because he was training for the Marines. Throughout the day he proceeded to "train," now wearing a hospital gown and socks in addition to his boxers, by jogging around the nurses' station in short, determined, high-kneed steps. He jogged for six hours.

Most of the patients on the unit were as flamboyant and as sick. There were two women married to God; one also claimed to be a samurai warrior. She walked around the unit with her arms stretched out before her, trem-bling but stiff, occasionally holding an open plastic bag as if it were a ritual offering. When she was distracted, her arms would drop down to her sides, but at the end of the conversation they would rise again and she would continue her tremulous sleepwalker's tread. There was a woman who had already been admitted twice that month. She was a large African-American woman, and she wore a platinum blond wig that perched on her head like a moth-eaten hat. She was pregnant with her ninth child. All of her previous children were with relatives or in foster homes. She was not always psychotic. At times her eyes gleamed with what looked like irony, and then she would pinch her arm and say, "Look, the hospital hasn't helped, I'm still black." She called herself Shirley Temple. There was an even larger woman who, when she was admitted, had not bathed in five weeks. She had lain in a depressed stupor on her bed, and body cheese and fungus fell out from the folds of her flabby skin when her husband finally brought her into the hospital.

The average length of stay on the unit, adjusted to exclude the few patients who stayed on and on, was around eight days. Roughly twenty-nine patients could be accommodated. The month before I arrived, around a third of the patients were new to the unit, but the rest had been admitted to the unit at least one time previously. The unit worked like that, as containment for the sickest periods in the lives of the sickest patients. They would come in, be stabilized, get discharged, come in again. Many of them came in refusing to acknowledge that there was any reason for the admission and sometimes unable to understand that they were on a psychiatric unit. They often refused to take psychiatric medication. They were often admitted under a three-day "hold," meaning that they had refused to come into the hospital and that the psychiatrist who had interviewed them had decided that they needed to be in inpatient psychiatric care nonetheless. In these circumstances, they could be kept in the hospital for no more than three days (this was also called a "commitment"). However, to force a patient to take medication or to keep him in the hospital for longer, a psychiatrist had to go to court (or, more commonly, court, in the form of a judge, came to the unit to hold a hearing). The standard of measurement was pretty basic. Unless the patient was actively suicidal or homicidal or could not explain who and where he was, a psychiatrist could not force him to do anything and was unable to provide care the patient didn't want. As a result, blatantly psychotic patients often left the hospital as disturbed as they had been when admitted.

Terry, for example, was the kind of derelict beatnik who makes some Berkeley citizens proud and most a little nervous. He was a child of the sixties and had worked as an artist for twenty years, supported by his wife. Eventually, she had thrown him out. He had either refused to get a job or failed to keep one. His family had supported him for a while and then stopped. By the time he came into the hospital, he had been living in a van on Telegraph Avenue for several years. He was brought in by police because he had jumped through security at Oakland Airport and begun to scream. He hated being hospitalized. He saw it as a form of state oppression. He saw me as the neutral recorder of truth, of higher status than the patients' but not on the staff's side, and so he hovered around me to discuss his sense that psychiatry perverted human justice and constrained people against their will and their rights.

When the judge came to hold commitment hearings—Terry was on a three-day hold—Terry became so anxious that the judge would hear his case without him that he hung around the door to the room, periodically pressing his nose against its tiny, wire-reinforced window. During his turn (the judge heard eight cases in just over an hour) he explained to the judge that he had run through airport security because he was being pursued by big, bad, dangerous people. When the doctor later referred to him as paranoid and psychotic, Terry jumped up, obviously agitated, and demanded to know what evidence there was that he was psychotic. The judge was a large, practical man. "Probably the big, bad, dangerous people," he said dryly. But he then went on to point out that Terry had both the resources and ability to care for himself and the hospital could no longer hold him unless he chose to stay voluntarily. Terry smiled jubilantly and left the airless room with pride. But then he refused to leave the ward. He went to stand in the door of the nursing station. When he was told that he could leave now, he announced pugnaciously that he was a free citizen and they could not make him leave. He was offered the opportunity to sign in to the hospital voluntarily and thus stay on as a patient. He declined. He was then told that he would have to leave. He began stating his rights, loudly. Meanwhile, people kept trying to get into and out of the nursing station, where all the charts and medications were kept. Eventually Terry was escorted out of the hospital by police. "He's more realistic than he seems," a resident said sadly. "He's afraid of us, but he's even more scared of living on the Berkeley streets."

The staff here were faced with an increasingly impossible task. The hospital's resources were excellent for a county hospital, but they were woeful in relation to the need and declining fast. The patients were chronically ill. There was little chance that most of them would improve. Most of them could not get adequate care at home. Many of them were homeless. As the pressure to handle more such patients continually mounted, resources declined even faster. Neither the laws nor the circumstances permitted the staff to take charge of patients who felt they could manage on their own. (I heard one psychiatrist wonder wistfully whether the current legal situation didn't infringe on the patient's right to treatment.) The problem, then, was that the staff essentially *had* to treat patients as rational adults capable of making reasonable and informed choices about their illnesses, and most of them obviously were not.

There was, then, a begrudging, wry, self-deprecating tolerance of the fact that patients could decide what they wanted, which usually had a nonobvious relationship to what the psychiatrists thought they needed and what the county would provide. "He's back *already?*" someone said of a recently re-admitted patient. "Take him for a walk and see if you can lose him." Or to me, "If you really want to know about discharge planning, go to the Round Table Pizza around the corner. There's a table in the back that has a lot of the patients who've been here already and a lot of the others who haven't been here yet." The psychiatrists resigned themselves to putting the patients back on medications and discharging them to some less expensive facility or to their families. "Let's go over the patients tomorrow," a senior psychiatrist said with a sigh. "Maybe some of them will leave by then, and all that work would have been wasted." "That's our job," someone remarked to me on the first day. "We get them into the hospital, and then we get them out." Doctors on an elite unit might invest considerable time pointing out to a patient that her belief that she was not ill was part of the illness and persuading her to stay in the hospital for a few more days. These doctors more pragmatically accepted the fact that if a patient wanted to leave, he would leave, and there were plenty of others who needed help. Here, they saw themselves as just barely keeping pace. When someone actually *did* want their help, though, they were delighted.

For example, on my first day on the unit I watched a resident admit a man whose father had died three weeks earlier and who hadn't eaten or drunk for six days. It was a slow and relatively nonlethal suicide attempt. He had been admitted thirteen times before and been given a diagnosis of schizophrenia. He had not been taking his medication recently, because he claimed it made him worse ("They're giving me a lobotomy") and he didn't want any. He said he had no hallucinations—"Except for the Devil," he added, but it wasn't clear what he meant. He was obviously deeply depressed and was unable to talk about his father. Several times he started a sentence with "My father" but couldn't complete it.

After we left the room, the resident remarked, "Poor guy. In some ways this is a social admission. He's suicidal, but he's not going to die tomorrow. He wants to come in, though, he needs the help, and maybe we can persuade him to get some food and even some medication." She dictated the admission note and wrote out some prescriptions. "He's probably going to refuse them, but you have to do it for the liability issues we love so much." She gave him an antipsychotic, an antianxiety agent, and a medication for the side effects of the antipsychotic. She also wrote orders for the nonprescription drugs that patients often want in the hospital but cannot get unless the doctor has agreed: Tylenol, Mylanta, Nicorette. "He doesn't look like a smoker, but so many of them are, and they can't smoke on the ward." But Terry wouldn't stay long enough to get help; "Shirley Temple" would leave before the medication took effect; the samurai warrior would also leave, taken home by her distrustful family, to be brought back when they'd had enough. Even this willingly admitted suicidal patient would refuse the medication. The resident decided not to force it upon him, because although he clearly needed medication, he was not about to die, as she put it, tomorrow. She also felt more comfortable leaving him without medication because it was Monday. If it had been Friday, he might not have seen a doctor again for three days (there would be a doctor on call, but that doctor would not be required to see him; on-call doctors handle emergencies and admissions). That was too long a period for a patient to go untreated, she felt. It *was* Monday, however, and on Tuesday another doctor would see him and he would be assigned to that doctor's team and be that doctor's responsibility. Such small details are the stuff of hospital life.

On the unit, patients participated in countless "groups": on substance abuse, on discharge planning, on goals, on weekend planning, on living skills, and so forth. These were not the touchy-feely gatherings that we associate with the term "group therapy"; they taught the patients how to function in the most basic way. The goals group, for example, tried to teach the patients that they should have goals. The weekend-planning group tried to teach the patients that you could make plans for your free time. I had run a similar group once, with someone else, as a volunteer. The group I had run had been for outpatients and for people who were less sick to begin with, but it had still been a demoralizing experience. People didn't talk about their feelings or their reflections or their relationships with one another. When they spoke, which was not so often, they talked about how it was more difficult to get to one prison than to another and how when their son came home on probation they really hoped he wouldn't keep a gun in his car the way he had last time. The patients in the San Juan groups lived in that world, but they had less ability to cope.

For instance, in the discharge-planning group I attended, the leader asked each person in turn what his or her plans were for after discharge. "Sam?" Sam didn't answer, but he shifted in his seat. When she asked him again, he said, "I'm going to the place I was at before." The group leader want around the group and asked each person what his or her plans were. Her own goal was to make sure that they knew that there were plans for discharge and to underscore the importance of patients taking their medications, of complying with the rules of the halfway house (if that was where they were headed), and of getting along with other people. (Halfway houses, sometimes call "board and cares," are boardinghouses with varying degrees of supervision over cooking, cleaning, personal and medical care, and so forth. They are "halfway" between the hospital and independent living.) The conversation was often prosaic in the extreme. It was also geared to childhood standards of politeness. "It's not your turn to speak now," the leader (always a staff person) might say when a patient suddenly started talking "inappropriately," as a staff person would say. "Stanley is speaking now, and it's not right to interrupt him." Asking each of the eight or so patients and getting answers took the entire hour.

There was an intensely practical ethos to the place. When a patient kept dropping his pants in front of women, the resident arranged for the nurse to buy him overalls. When another patient claimed he didn't live at the address the computer listed for him but at another one, a resident drove out to the two apartments to check. Because it had become more complicated to place patients outside the hospital (there were so few beds, and the halfway houses just said no to the difficult patients), one of the nurses had arranged for people from all the relevant facilities to meet once a week for a "disposition meeting." People from every place to which a patient could be discharged met over coffee and doughnuts to discuss where each patient would go. "This is where managed care really works," someone whispered to me unironically when I attended. There was someone from each halfway house. There was someone from the overburdened long-term placement hospital, someone from each of the community out-patient services, someone from each homeless shelter, and so forth. This meeting, the nurse explained, created a "put-up-or-shut-up attitude."

The day I attended, there must have been thirty people in the room. The meeting went person by person through the people on the list of current patients. Most of them were known to at least some members of the group. After all, on average two thirds of these patients had been inpatients on the unit before, and some came in several times a month. The discussion began with an account of a man who had described himself as "suicidal and hearing voices." The speaker had spoken in a monotone, but a nurse winked at him and the room collapsed in laughter. Apparently, the patient wanted to avoid being sent to jail (he had stolen a purse) and had gotten himself diverted to psychiatry by claiming that he was mentally ill. Discussing another patient, one nurse presented a long, compelling argument about why she needed long-term care; that whenever she left the hospital she went back home, took drugs, was unable to care for herself, and was getting worse, and she needed a lengthy spell of treatment to reverse the pattern. People nodded in agreement, but then someone else said, "Good luck—she wants to go home, and she's got a hearing this Friday that she'll probably win." People talked about a patient who had done badly at one board and care and whether it would be possible for him to return to it, and they reluctantly concluded that he should not. They talked about whether there was any way to persuade "Shirley Temple" not to have yet another child, a tenth, that she could not care for. It was a good-natured, task-oriented gathering, nonhierarchical and casual.

In the disposition meeting and in the staff room people laughed about the craziness. They told stories about these patients and other patients and what the patients had done. They chuckled about the women who were married to God—that week, God was a bigamist—and about the mad, strange, funny things the patients said. They came into the staff room (it was inside the nurse's station, which was a kind of booth in the middle of the unit) when the man in the boxer shorts jogged determinedly around the nurses' station, and they chortled. "Who's the Energizer bunny?" His doctor and I went out to talk to him. We had to stand at a corner of his route. We could do a two- or three-sentence exchange per circuit. In between these exchanges we chatted idly and joked about jogging alongside. The staff here were clearly overburdened. The whole system groaned. A little humor helped.

The adaptations and contradictions on this unit—that people laughed at the craziness, that the roles were so clear that hierarchy became irrelevant, that there was a crazy contradiction between treating patients as adults and treating them as incompetent dependents—become even sharper on a unit that works with the disease model deliberately and has the resources to deliver more conclusive care.

For two months in 1993, I spent perhaps ten hours a week on a biomedical psychiatry unit in Gertrude's hospital.[2] It was known for its explicitly "scientific" orientation. The senior psychiatrists conducted empirical research on schizophrenia and bipolar disorder. One had an international reputation as a researcher. Residents rotated onto the unit with the idea that they would get a taste of how to combine scientific research with clinical practice. The unit was acknowledged throughout the hospital to be effective and harmonious. There were no wars, no hostilities, no attempt to turn rounds into ideological skirmishes. No one pulled me aside to explain what was wrong with the unit director and how someone else would run the unit better. This was, in my experience, rare. Most psychiatric units seem to generate cross fire about the way the unit director does his job, mostly because the job can be done so many different ways.

The unit could accommodate just over twenty patients. For the most part it remained full. It catered primarily (although not exclusively) to bipolar patients, who became acutely and unmistakably ill and then more or less recovered. This may have explained some of the good cheer. Not unnaturally, psychiatrists like being told by their patients that they are doing a good job. But in a world of short (five- to ten-day) admissions, few patients recover enough to feel gratitude. Sometimes bipolar patients do. The unit was a satisfactory place to work for that reason. And the patients themselves were colorful and interesting and did not lead you to have depressed thoughts about the human condition. For the most part the patients came in manic: very energetic, wildly talkative, uninterested in sleep, grandly confident, and usually very, very psychotic. That is, they seemed to have no grasp on reality. They had written the greatest American poetry, they had solved unified field theory, they had arrived at the airport shouting to the world about this important news and taken offense at an airline's request for a ticket. Psychosis is one of the most frightening psychiatric symptoms, because psychotic patients are unpredictable and unconstrained by everyday common sense. Yet someone who is psychotic can be exhilarating for the same reason. His or her imagination is free to fly. Patients who came in psychotic with mania tended to have grandiose, dramatic thoughts. When they were not manic, they were often delightful people, more than usually intense, focused, and energetic, and as often as not successful in the wider world.

So the place was full of professors, scientists, doctors, and others who came in because they had been working harder and harder at their jobs and then had stopped sleeping, started speaking rapidly and incomprehensibly, and begun acting in strange, extravagant ways. Their exhausted families could no longer cope. Sometimes it was not their families that brought them in but the police, because they had been behaving so flamboyantly and bizarrely in some public place. Once I was sitting in the dingy anonymity of some midwestern airport when a man in a charcoal gray suit strode down the corridor swinging his briefcase, shouting about moral purpose and corruption. He was loud and scary and obviously psychotic, and everyone else suddenly became still. The police wrestled him to the ground in front of our gate. That is the kind of thing that happens during mania. Manic people make noisy, disturbing, frightening scenes, and then the police take them away and deliver them to a psychiatric emergency room. Often, patients have no sense of why the police have taken them into custody. On this unit, for instance, there was a visiting foreign scientist whom the police had brought in when they had found him wandering crazily around the streets near the university. When they had stopped him, he had volubly explained his new solution to a physics problem they could not follow. He clearly was unfit to care for himself. He had been unable to eat, clean himself, or find his way back to his apartment. Yet he was quite offended that the police had detained him. He didn't see himself as ill, didn't understand that he had been brought to the hospital, and demanded to be released immediately because he had to represent his country at an important conference where his new ideas would make him famous.

This was a locked unit. (When I arrived at the hospital, I had to sign out a fist-sized ring of keys.) The large, heavy door to the unit, hospital pink, had a metal plate around its lock. The key was cumbersome, and the door swung open slowly. Sometimes the door had a sign on it that read "Split risk." This meant that the staff thought that one of the patients might shove past someone coming in and bolt for freedom. In fact, the passage between the inside world of madness and the outside was closely monitored. On the wall next to the door there hung a large whiteboard with a hierarchically ranked list of what were called "privileges." The first privilege was to go out onto the porch with other patients, at designated times, to smoke. (Many psychiatric patients smoke; some researchers think that nicotine may help control depression and psychosis.) The next was to go out on the grounds for an errand or appointment with a staff person. Then patients could go out in a group, accompanied by a staff person, usually for a meal. Then one patient could leave the unit with another patient; then by himself, as long as he telephoned back when he reached his destination. Then patients could have total freedom, except that they were never given a key. Facing the list of privileges was another list, on a blackboard, of all the patients, their dates of admission, and their privilege levels. There was another list of daily activities and the privilege level required for each. On the unit, patients wandered from room to room or sat in the large shared areas and watched television. Often they seemed groggy and disoriented (that was the medication), and they also often seemed unsure. The patient population was quite transient. Patients would generally be admitted for a week or less, then discharged. Occasionally there were real problems with "discharge placement," finding a facility that would accept a patient. (These hard-to-place patients were often drug abusers, violent, or simply underinsured.) Then, a patient might stay for weeks, once, for three months. But those patients were unusual. More common was the patient who would be seen in two or three of the twice-weekly team rounds and then vanish.

The patients here were understood to be suffering from a dysfunction of the brain, and although there were undoubtedly things about their families, their spouses, or the way they lived their lives that made things much worse, none of that really mattered except as a practical concern. The doctor's task was to identify the disease clearly enough to treat it effectively, which he usually did with medication. He would also try other interventions, such as electroshock therapy, if the medication did not work. The goal of the hospitalization was to keep a patient safe so the acute problem could cool down enough for the patient to leave without obvious risk that he might hurt himself or others. Most of the patients on the unit came in psychotic, and antipsychotics work quickly enough to begin to de-escalate them within hours or a few days, but other medications would not take full effect until days or perhaps weeks after discharge. (Antipsychotics and antianxiety agents take effect within minutes or hours; mood stabilizers and antidepressants often do not work until the patient has taken them for weeks.) The goal of the unit, then, was explicitly minimal: to prescribe the medications, to make sure a patient did not have a toxic reaction to them, to begin to see whether they might work, and to be sure that a patient was sufficiently stabilized so that she was neither suicidal nor at risk of killing herself by accident—by "insanely" reckless driving, by wild promiscuity, by the invincible manic confidence that leads to very poor assessment of risk.

Because of the emphasis on medical science, doctors were more respected on this unit than on many. One of the difficulties of being a psychiatrist is that many of your skills, particularly the more psychodynamic ones, do not seem to be the kinds of things one needs to go to medical school to learn. Even the biomedical skills seem like things nondoctors can learn. Psychologists, social workers, and nurses know a lot about medications, even if most of them can't legally write prescriptions. They spend more time with the patients than psychiatrists do. (Psychiatrists typically spend less time on the unit than any other staff people.) When new residents arrive, fresh from internship, nearly every other staff member on the unit knows more about psychiatry than they do. Meanwhile, psychiatrists are paid far more (after residency) than anyone else on the unit. It is easy for the rest of the staff to regard psychiatrists as arrogant, overpaid extravagances.

On this unit, the doctors were accepted as experts in dealing with disease. This was because there was a medical research emphasis, because doctors were associated with science, research, and "real" medicine, and because when the psychiatrists spoke about psychopharmacology they spoke as connoisseurs, with an expertise genuinely beyond nonpsychiatrists' grasp. The young psychiatrists were not resented by the other staff. The hierarchy of power replicated the hierarchy of knowledge. There was no question—given the biomedical model of illness—that the psychiatrists knew more about the patients' problems than any other staff members did, particularly if the psychiatrists were doing research. Psychologists did not compete for equal time and authority with them. Nurses presumed that while the residents needed nurturing now, in a few years their knowledge would exceed their own. Secure in that expectation, the residents could tolerate being mentored by people of lesser status. Moreover, just as a patient's personhood was not integral to his disease, a staff member's personality was believed not to be intrinsic to the performance of her job. Staff were, of course, grateful for people who were cheerful and effective. But the complicated, messy analysis of what people really felt about one another and why never took place. The kind of people staff members were and the feelings they had were regarded as irrelevant to the business of doing the job. As a result, staff members never "processed" very much about social life on the unit, they never found out how much they disagreed with each other about specific issues, and so they had, relatively speaking, few fights.

The unit modeled itself on other, nonpsychiatric, hospital units, as if the illnesses really were like heart attacks in the brain. We met for rounds in two different teams, twice a week, for two hours each time. There were lithium graphs pinned to the wall and a sleep chart that listed how many hours each patient had slept each night. It was always consulted during these rounds. Each team was led by a senior psychiatrist called an "attending," who not infrequently wore a medical doctor's white laboratory coat. For the first hour, the attending doctor, the resident, and assembled nurses, social workers, psychiatric workers, and others (the anthropologist, for instance) sat in a separate locked room to discuss the patients. (Nurses on the other team remained outside to supervise the ward.) The conversation was full of comments about how one patient was suitable for the first break study and why benzodiazepines rather than neuroleptics might be more helpful for a certain condition. "If you want to endear yourself to Dr. Smith [the local psychopharmacology researcher]," the senior psychiatrist would say to the resident, "call him about this patient and put her on his study." Relatively little time was spent discussing anyone's personal psychodynamics. The issues were practical: whether the dosage of antipsychotic was high enough, how to deal with the fact that the staff knew that such-and-such a patient was HIV-positive and had been found trying to seduce another patient, who because of doctor-patient confidentiality couldn't be told of the first patient's diagnosis but who nevertheless had to be prevented from sleeping with him; how far the social worker had gotten in the discharge planning for a patient who was ready to leave the hospital but clearly could not return home.

In fact, the whole tenor of the place was briskly practical, as if the staff were all working mothers planning play dates. I would later sit in psychodynamically oriented units and participate in staff meetings where everyone would gather, without an agenda, to "process" the week's experience for several hours at a time. On the biomedical unit, staff meetings were brisk, matter-of-fact, and agenda-driven. People held them to plan the end-of-year barbecue and to figure out how many nurses and mental health workers would be needed in the coming weeks. The senior psychiatrist never bothered with people's finer feelings. Once one of the patients decided to explain to the other patients that she liked torturing animals. She told them that she liked to stick pins into rats' eyes and listen to them squeal, that she would chop them up and drink their squirting blood. She remarked that she drank her own menstrual blood and that she liked to rape herself with carrots and then eat them. She apparently liked to share these things when she saw people sitting around in the common room, preferably at night. When they became hysterical, she would decide to go to bed. Her attending doctor did not try to explore with her what she was trying to communicate with these stories. Nor did he warn her pet-owning neighbors. He walked in to see her during rounds the morning after this was reported, the group of us following behind him, and asked her whether she wanted to spend her entire life behind hospital walls. "If you feel like you want to harm animals and babies and you need some help controlling those thoughts, tell us," he said. "Otherwise, don't tell us, because no hospital can legally discharge you if you do." She stopped making the comments. When the social worker spoke with her mother, it turned out that they were fantasies.

A senior psychiatrist once said to me that pain can metabolize three ways: in anger, humor, or wisdom. Few of us have the spiritual depth to be wise, he said, so it is important to us to find humor. This unit was downright funny. The staff were playful, relaxed, and hilarious in rounds. They laughed about the craziness and how utterly, impossibly crazy it was, and they named the craziness with irreverent, colloquial, nonspecific names. In otherwise sober team meetings, a resident might present a newly admitted patient's symptoms and diagnosis, then lower the notes to say, "Frankly, this person is totally out to lunch." Or "He's bonkers. Bouncing off the walls." Patients were crazy as a loon, nutty as a fruitcake, major-league wacko, out there, in space, really "something else." A presentation might begin, "Mr. Hill has been traveling in outer space for two days now, and we have failed to establish contact. He is our forty-one-year-old white single male admitted on . . ."

When psychosis is not brutally awful, it *is* funny, and sometimes looking for the humor in it makes it more possible to handle the pain of seeing a human being lose his mind. One of the patients on the unit decided that another patient was trying to poison him and gave up eating. The patient he chose as the villain was so depressed that the staff had been worrying about how to get him out of bed, let alone do anything that required as much energy as diabolical crime. Another patient came onto the unit somewhat violent. He had already broken one of his legs. By the end of the first evening, he tried to smash his crutch into a patient (who ducked), broke it against the wall, and then ripped out the public phone box, more commonly known as the patients' phone. When the doctor tried to talk to him the next morning in rounds about losing control, the patient paused, opened his eyes wide, and asked, "Me?" In practice, the joke could run the other way as well. There was, for example, the very psychotic patient who had been raving about his astrophysics articles. This had been taken as further evidence of his psychosis until a curious resident looked them up in the library and found them. There was the narcissistic patient who spoke grandly about his personal friendship with the director of the hospital and other important people. His resident was touched by what he took to be the needy loneliness of the old man and mentioned it to the director at a social function. "Sam's here?" the director said. "Why didn't anyone tell me? I must go see him. He's been an important friend to the university."

The point is that the staff made jokes about the craziness—not about the patient himself, not about the staff, not about prescribing medication, not about doing therapy. Laughter circles around the contradictions in our world.[3] Here that contradiction was the commitment to the patient as a rational person with a disease. The patient was, and wasn't.

Nick, the attending doctor of the "rats and pins," was smart and quick, a little out of place in these patrician surroundings but rather pleased to be in charge of them. (Some of the staff referred to him as "the cowboy.") He had entered medicine to be a psychoanalyst, but during internship one of his friends had fallen asleep, driven off the side of the road, and woken up, as a psychiatrist would say, crazy as a bedbug. It had taken antipsychotics and weeks in the hospital to calm him down. The friend had survived (he had eventually become completely normal), but the psychiatrist-to-be's commitment to psychoanalysis had not. He said that the accident had persuaded him that the brain had more of an impact on who you were and how you got sick than the kinds of complicated unconscious motives that psychoanalysts talked about. I once saw Nick in a therapy session with a patient. They talked briefly about her classes, her flower arranging, her son. She brought in a letter that her mother had written to the last psychiatrist to explain that her daughter's low self-esteem was not her (the mother's) fault. "Anyone would be crazy with a mother like that," she said. These are things that a psychodynamic psychiatrist would talk about. But Nick wasn't particularly interested in the psychodynamics: what she really felt about her mother, why she felt that way. Nick wanted to figure out how the new medication was affecting her. He wanted to learn, by listening to her and asking her questions, whether she was concentrating better, whether she was feeling more energetic or more depressed, and when, and what kind of energy or anxiety or depression it felt like. So he chatted away amiably about the details of her life while trying to hear the underlying phenomenology. The patient was telling the doctor about her soul's history, and he was hearing through it the shape and balance of her brain.

Nick was the senior psychiatrist who led my team. We met on Tuesdays and Fridays, a collection of residents, psychology interns, social workers, and mental health workers who were responsible as a team for about half the patients on the unit. After the first hour of discussion in the team meeting, we would all get up and stroll around after Nick, stopping at every room to visit with each patient we had discussed. (This is the way nonpsychiatric medical rounds are often organized, but not psychodynamic rounds. In psychodynamic rounds, team members often do not actually speak with a patient. If they do, the patient comes to see them in a private room.) Those patients were not allowed to go out of the unit during these rounds. They were made to wait patiently (or not) until the team came to see them, much as they would be forced to wait during medical rounds in a general hospital. When we arrived at a room, Nick (or sometimes the resident, if this was her patient) would enter first, followed by the rest of us. Nick would sit down in a chair facing the patient while the rest of us stood around him as he spoke. He would ask the patient how he was, how he was feeling, and what his plans were. Sometimes this was quite painful to watch. Because manic patients often do not realize, in the grip of their mania, that they are ill, the discussions occasionally became hostile confrontations over the patient's right to leave and the doctor's insistence that he stay. When the patient got a little better, the discussion tended to center on the illness as if it were a separate, malfunctioning organ. Then Nick wanted to know how bad the black despair was, whether the patient was hearing voices, was able to sleep, was able to sit through a meeting, and so forth.

Often, this approach worked well. A patient admitted to the unit after intentionally driving her car into a tree was able to say, on the sixth day, that even though she still felt awful, she had been able to get out of bed and walk about. During the rounds just after admission, she had lain in bed without moving or speaking. By her second rounds (so perhaps the fourth day after admission; her doctor and some other staff would have seen her daily), she was able to talk about the depression as "depression." Following Nick's phrasing, she talked about "symptoms" and about her despair as an "it," about how she was handling "it." She seemed to conceptualize her troubles as an illness; she knew that the illness made her feel terrible, and she wanted to treat it so that she would no longer feel so awful.

Other patients, however, were not able to behave as if they grasped the disease model of illness (at least, they were not able to behave as if it applied to them). There was, for instance, the patient whose husband brought her in after an altercation at home. She wasn't manic; in fact, she seemed quite reasonable, except that she believed that there were laser beams in her house that were poisoning her, and her husband said that when she was at home she would become hysterical about the laser beams and hit him. She denied this, refused the antipsychotic medication, and demanded that she be allowed to leave. She had been hospitalized many times previously for suspected psychosis and violent outbursts, and after a week on the antipsychotics and in the hospital she had always calmed down. She said to Nick that she knew what was best for her and wanted to go home, that she was the person who knew herself best, wasn't she? Nick answered, "Well, that's a complicated question." Then it turned out that when her husband had brought her to the hospital, the physician on call had actually suggested that she might go home. At this she had become more paranoid and delusional; had begun to speak about the laser beams that cut through her house, and had refused to leave. During the entirety of her time in the hospital, in every rounds meeting she followed the team around, explaining how she needed to go home, almost bleating in her efforts to change Nick's mind after he had negotiated with her a willingness to stay a few more days, refusing adamantly to leave when he seemed to relent. She never spoke as if there were a dysfunction in her body.

There was the person who seemed totally lucid in rounds but was in the hospital because after two years of psychodynamic therapy she had suddenly told her therapist that she was worried about the green blobs on her therapist's legs. She also never spoke in terms of an "illness." Then there was the brilliant young graduate student in physics. He was recovering from his first manic break. His father had been manic-depressive, and the son's first break had occurred at the same age as his father's. The son had calmed down after his first few days on an antipsychotic and lithium and then in rounds explained that he no longer wanted to take the medication. He was not going to write his thesis, he said, while taking psychiatric medication. (There is some point to this. People not infrequently report feeling that lithium takes the edge off of their creativity.) Nick patiently explained manic-depressive disorder to him—"Many excellent scientists have been bipolar; it's nothing to be ashamed of"—and pointed out that if he did not take his medication, he would have another manic episode. The patient explained that he knew his mental state better than those who were treating him. And this is a great ambiguity in psychiatry: Who owns a person's mental state? Who has the right to know it? Your model of mental illness makes a difference in the way you answer this question.

For all Nick's efforts to hear the structure of the disorder through the flow of conversation, a person remains the best reporter on his or her own psychic state. I know whether I am sad, anxious, or happy better than anyone else does. Psychiatrists know this. Yet they know that people can mislead themselves and that they lie. Thus a person may not see himself as unhappy because he thinks he should be happy. It is also true that being wrong, intentionally or not, about my mental state can change that very state, at least sometimes. If I insist to myself that I am happy despite a stock market tumble, that the sky is blue, the flowers are blooming, and it was only money on paper anyway, sometimes I can make myself happier than I was. Sometimes people who come into the hospital depressed decide to leave when they have regained just enough energy to go home to commit suicide, and they know perfectly well that if they tell this to the doctor, he won't let them go. So they lie and then go home and kill themselves. So how seriously should a psychiatrist take a patient's words about himself if the patient is the best source on his own mental state and yet the patient can be wrong?

Psychiatry is straightforward when a person is starkly crazy, very psychotic. You know that you cannot trust what he says about himself. A doctor knows he has to be in charge, the way a mother is in charge of her child and makes decisions for him (no ice cream before dinner) that violate his wants and yet are better for him in the long run. It is easy to say that there is an illness affecting that person's judgment. But if it's not like that, if a patient is depressed but says she's fine now and wants to leave, or, as this young man said, he thinks that psychiatric medication slows down his thoughts and he doesn't want to write his dissertation on lithium, how does a doctor decide who really knows best? Who gives a young psychiatrist the authority to say, "You're more depressed than you think"? That "you have an illness that impairs your thinking and so I cannot believe what you say"? A more psychodynamic approach handles this major epistemological issue by emphasizing that all mental states, including the psychiatrist's, are inherently complex, layered, and to some extent unknowable. That, as we shall see, creates its own problems. When a doctor takes that perspective seriously, it becomes much harder for him to believe that he understands a patient. From a biomedical perspective, there is more of a direct contradiction. The new resident on that unit told me that it really bothered her when she had to take control over an adult as if he were a child: "I think if I could just see the person as crazy, that these patients aren't themselves and you have to deal with them as if they were crazy, it would be much easier," she said. "But I still see that there is a person there, whose personality is showing through even in his psychosis, and that makes it hard for me to treat him as a child."

On this kind of unit, with this kind of model of illness, the residents wanted to see the patients as reasonable, responsible human beings struggling with physical illness as all who are in the hospital struggle. In general, we believe what people say about their pain in the hospital, and the expectation was that this was also true for these patients. When it was not true, what the patients said became part of their illness, not part of them. When a patient said she wasn't sick and the resident didn't believe her, her statement became a symptom. She became an irresponsible, incompetent dependent, who had to have decisions made for her and be managed by someone else's authority. The person was either a rational person with a sickness or an irrational person whose irrationality *was* the sickness. But people aren't really like that, either crazy or rational. There are genuine uncertainties. Perhaps the physics student was right, that his thesis would be better if he were off lithium. Only he can know if the risk of another manic episode is worth bearing.

This is a real dilemma in psychiatry. The patients on this unit could not take care of themselves, so a psychiatrist had to take over. Yet this authority has many risks. Psychiatrists can make mistakes. They can interpret someone as incompetent who might indeed be able to manage without hospital level care. Over the last few decades there has been a shift in psychiatric and legal thinking. It used to be that all that was required to commit a patient was a doctor's signature. Now there must be the kind of proof that a judge will accept in court, and sometimes patients who need help cannot be forced to get it unless they hurt someone. Yet patients are more protected from psychiatrists' misjudgments. This kind of dilemma is particularly complex for a unit such as the one described here, both because the disease model has a harder time dealing with ambiguity and because psychosis debilitates a person more profoundly than any other symptom does.

This unit's culture dealt with the ambiguity by making the line between the patient's person and the patient's illness as clear as possible. No one spoke (for the most part) as if an illness were connected to what made a person tick, to that person's unique personhood. No one thought of the nurses and mental health workers as being there to understand the patients. They thought of them as keeping the patients safe. Staff did not talk (for the most part) about the way they identified with patients or the way patients made them feel. They treated privileges not as rewards for good behavior but as practical means of protecting patients while their disease dominated their rational faculties. So, for example, a patient was given smoking privileges not because she felt that she needed that respect or that freedom. Her hopes, fears, and anxieties weren't really relevant. She was given smoking privileges because the staff thought she could manage outside the unit without being uncontrollably crazy in the way that had gotten her admitted in the first place but wanted to test this out under reasonably well supervised conditions—"although no one explained that to me logically," the resident on the unit said to me, "and it was strange to take away these things that other people took for granted." (When patients go outdoors to smoke—and it is always outdoors, even in a New England winter—staff members go with them to chat, watch, and keep control.) In this culture, interactions with patients were discussions around organic illness only, so that the understanding of patients' intentions was never muddied by dynamic complexity. Even when meeting a patient for the first time, the senior psychiatrist rarely spoke about the subtleties of personal history and desire. Instead, he focused quite explicitly on drugs and mood and attempted as far as possible to understand the patient's response as a rational self-report. The doctor would say, "If there was anything you could change about your mood now, what would it be? Are you frightened? Anxious?" as if he were palpating the abdomen, as if he could palpate the mind, even though he knew he could not.

Meanwhile, the doctors managed the contradiction between patient-as-child and patient-as-adult by defining those states as different aspects of a patient. They then acted out those differences in their relationships with patients. Doctor-patient relationships were negotiations about how to categorize patients' intentions—which parts were part of the disease and which were part of the patient's rational, reasonable personhood. For example, I once watched a well-heeled but psychotic young man try to persuade the attending doctor to let him leave the unit. He said he was fine. He explained that he was determined to go to Chicago Law School (to which he'd been admitted) that autumn, to spend the upcoming July weekend at the Hamptons, and to buy some khakis for the weekend. He said that all this was not going to be a problem for him and that if he was going to law school in a month he'd better get out into the real world now. The doctor did not interpret what the patient said, and he did not allow the patient to develop and explain his wishes. He said that the patient needed more time to recover. When the patient said, tell me what specifically you would have me do before you let me go, the doctor behaved as if there were no point explaining. He told the patient that he would have to trust the doctor's judgment and strode off down the hall. There, the desire to leave was seen as a symptom, part of the illness. The patient's illness left him still in the dependent position of a child.

When that young man could say that he had been ill and begin to discuss the problem of being ill, his intentions and his reports on his state of mind began to be treated like responsible, reasonable assertions. That part of him moved into the adult category. He became a person with an illness, not an illness in a body. The unfortunate but accurate implication here is that if you wanted to leave the hospital, you were still sick, but if you agreed to stay, you were treated as if you were getting well. This is not an unreasonable inference, because hospital stays are now so very short that if the police have brought you into a psychiatric emergency room and two days later you think you are not sick, chances are that your denial *is* part of the illness. Still, the presumption can make an observer uneasy. "Do you realize that you have been ill?" Nick asked a patient (a biochemistry professor) on the fifth day of her admission. "Don't be an idiot!" she snapped back. "Do you take me for a fool? You've been forcing my illness down my throat so much it would be impossible for me not to notice." Three days earlier when he had asked her this, she had looked at him as though he were insane. The turning point in a patient's stay (as perceived by the unit) was when she understood herself to be and have been very sick. If a patient could realistically discuss her plans for discharge, the doctor would negotiate which part of those plans were appropriate: whether it was reasonable to consider going back to her job, her apartment, her life. Patients who wanted to leave and were not "committable" (they were not suicidal, not homicidal, they knew who and where they were) generally had to file notice three days before they were allowed to walk free. During that time, the doctor would repeat in as many ways as he knew how that the staff thought that she was too sick to leave and that the desire to leave was part of her illness. Despite my uneasiness at watching the way the desire to leave became construed as a symptom of the illness, when I was watching these exchanges, I rarely felt that a patient was unjustly confined. I was far more worried that if the patient left, he would start screaming on the plane to New York and lose his job; that she would tear up her apartment in a paranoid fit; that he would go to a conference and make an utter, irredeemable fool of himself before his professional peers and seniors.

Finally, the staff on this unit, as on any psychiatric unit, worried that psychiatric illness was misunderstood by the wider world. But they had a very different take on what had to be communicated to the public or (to be more specific) what I should communicate to what they took to be a psychiatrically naive world. The more psychodynamic psychiatrists tended to assume that other people thought that psychiatric patients were strange and different. They were likely to tell me to tell people how similar we all were. At the end of my visit to a psychoanalytically oriented hospital, a senior clinician told me that when he had been a resident, he had rotated onto a unit and discovered that one of the patients was a man whom he had known in college. One day the man had reached out, grabbed his cigar (psychiatrists used to smoke cigars more frequently), thrown it down, and ground it into the floor with his heel. "This taught me," the psychodynamic director said, "that psychiatric illness is merely a powerful magnification of the emotional currents in all our lives."

By contrast, on this biomedical unit the staff were more likely to assume that other people thought that the patients are like all of us and that the problem was that the public did not properly understand how different they were, that they were far more sick than most people imagined, and that this sickness was a terrible, terrible accident in their lives. Once a nurse on the unit asked me what I was going to do with all the data I was gathering. I replied that I was going to write a book, and what would she write if she were I? "The public," she said, "does not understand these illnesses. Even my husband has no idea of what I'm working with. No one conceives of the severity. You ought to write about that."

even psychosis?

A PSYCHODYNAMIC HOSPITAL

From a psychodynamic perspective, a patient is ill because he has learned to interpret and respond to other people in maladaptive ways. (At least, that is part of his problem. These days, most psychodynamically oriented psychiatrists acknowledge that there is also a biological vulnerability.) One helps him by helping him to be aware of those unconscious patterns. But because all people, including psychoanalytically trained staff, are limited by their own unconscious, no one person can be an authority on what is going on with any other. No one can state definitively what is a mental illness and what is not. That is the problem. You need to identify what is maladaptive in the patient's unconscious to help the patient cope, but you cannot know clearly whether you are seeing the patient's craziness or whether you are looking at the patient through your own craziness. To understand patients, the staff on a psychodynamic unit talk about how they perceive the patients, how they perceive one another, and how they perceive one another perceiving the patients far more openly and exhaustively than in any other setting I have ever seen. But because none of these comments about the people one works with intimately are objective and most are personal, the emotional temperature of such a community can run rather high. Most psychoanalytic encounters take place behind closed doors, within confidentiality, with a person the patient will never see outside the session. Once the psychoanalytic context broadens to include the office, the cafeteria, and the assembly hall, a certain kind of public culture emerges to keep the potential chaos in check.

The Norton Inn is a small psychodynamic hospital in western Virginia, widely thought to be among the best of its kind and certainly among the last, a determined tortoise in a world of eager hares. It has the feel of something that belonged to a different generation but has not outlived its usefulness, like an old and beloved desk. When I arrived for two weeks in 1995, there were somewhat more than forty patients. They stayed in a large white colonial building called the "Inn," or in smaller, porch-wrapped clapboard houses within easy walking distance. Next to the Inn there was another elegant building, which housed the staff offices and the conference rooms. This twin building used to be called the Medical Office Building, but after the new director arrived to help the hospital face the changing health care world, he added the phrase "and Administration" to the small green sign on the front lawn. He felt that this was only fair. That year, for the first time in many years, the hospital settled its accounts in the black.

142

This was an open hospital. It is harder now than it would have been twenty years ago to convey the sense of what this means. Twenty years ago, there were many open units. Now almost all psychiatric inpatient settings are locked. Patients are escorted onto psychiatric units, the doors are locked behind them, and over their stay privileges are doled out to them that hinge on the locked door: going out to smoke, going to the cafeteria to eat, and so forth.

In an open hospital, there are no privileges, no seclusion rooms, no security guards to wrestle an out-of-control patient to the ground and place him in restraints. In an open hospital, patients come and go as they please. In the grand hallway of the old colonial Inn, the door swung free. Patients went out for walks, to work out at the local gym, to see their therapist, to see friends. Occasionally, they went out into the woods to hang themselves. That is the danger of an open hospital, and one reason that more hospital units are locked these days than in earlier decades is to deflect insurance companies' argument that if the patient isn't sick enough to need a locked door, he isn't sick enough to need a psychiatric admission. This hospital, however, argued that the locked door was infantilizing, demeaning, and ultimately counterproductive to the psychiatric treatment, because the ultimate goal was to enable people to feel responsible for their lives. It is hard, one staff member remarked to me, to feel in charge of yourself in prison. Most of the patients in the hospital had been admitted first onto a locked psychiatric unit somewhere else, and most had found the experience humiliating. Nevertheless, the admitting physician at this hospital had to explain to a potential patient (and, often, the family) before admission that he or she had to take responsibility for staying alive and would be admitted only if he or she took that responsibility, despite the fact that many patients are suicidal when admitted. Suicide threats are only occasionally theatrical. Fifteen percent of depressed patients eventually kill themselves. The day I left, the hospital admitted a woman with a bright pink scar on her throat that ran from ear to chin: she had sliced into her carotid artery because she had had thoughts, she said, of shooting her children.

Some patients had been at the hospital for years. Many of the staff looked back nostalgically to the times when all patients were expected to stay at least a year. When I was there, the average length of treatment was about eight months, although usually that figure included many months when patients would stay near the hospital for partial care but would not receive "hospital-level" care, in which all needs are provided for and nursing care is always available. The hospital had developed a variety of less expensive "step-down" residential and outpatient programs, in which patients took more or less responsibility for their food, housing, and self-care but could still participate in most of the hospital activities, such as community meetings and other group meetings. Insurance would invariably pay for some of this, and the hospital was, compared to others, cheaper both for full care and for step-down care. Once, the director said, an insurance company had sent the hospital a letter of thanks for the (relatively) low cost of its treatment of a patient who had bounced from inpatient unit to inpatient unit in the years previous to her Norton admission and afterward had not needed readmission. Her year at Norton had cost significantly less than her previous year of revolving-door hospitalizations. Most patients at the Norton Inn had "failed" treatment elsewhere, by which is meant that multiple hospitalizations, medications, and psychiatrists hadn't really helped. Some of the insurance companies would pay for a longer-than-average stay for these patients out of desperation, in the hope that one long stay would "stabilize" the patient and enable him to function as an outpatient. (A five-day inpatient admission can cost $5,000. Multiple short admissions become extremely costly.) But many of the patients and their families would pay directly out of their own pocket bills that were more than $20,000 for the first month of hospitalization and evaluation, then sank as low as $9,000 per month for residential care, and $2,700 for after care, but not lower.

These costs, the open-door policy, and the reputation the place had for tertiary care meant that the patients were mostly upper middle class, very smart, and young, often under thirty. They were (for example) Yale students and Columbia medical residents who had arrived at school, done well, then fallen apart. Most of them—roughly 70 percent—were women. Why there were so many women no one seemed to know, although it is a psychiatric cliché that disturbed men tend to act out their aggression on others and end up in jail, whereas disturbed women tend to act out on themselves—slash their wrists, take overdoses—and end up hospitalized. Most of the patients were depressed or bipolar (or had some kind of mood disorder) and also had personality disorders. A few were psychologically minded patients with schizophrenia. That the patients also had personality disorders is not surprising. An uncomplicated, "easy" depression or manic state can be treated well in a short admission that "brings down" the mania or "relieves" the depressive suicidality with medication. This is not the case if the patient also has a personality disorder, which a course of antidepressants will barely impact. Those were the patients who ended up in this hospital. Mostly, their personality disorder was of the type called "borderline": as before, women with a history of intense but unstable relationships, deep identity confusion, and anger. Such patients wind up in the hospital because they can be astonishingly destructive to themselves and others.

Tracy, for example, was a beautiful, blond, twenty-eight-year-old Southern belle with high cheekbones, a body conditioned by long winters on the ski slopes, and a taut, forlorn stillness. (To protect patient confidentiality, "Tracy" is a composite of several different patients.) She had ostensibly arrived in the hospital because, she said, her relationship with her mother had become too difficult for her to live at home. Her chart told a more dramatic story of violence, alcohol, sexual abuse, and suicide attempts. In her first interview with her treatment team, she announced that her mother had given her free access to her bank account. She needed to use the money wisely, she said, to make it last as long as possible.

Within a few days Tracy had slept with one of the few male patients. Sex between patients was actively discouraged. Officially this was because it was supposed to create dyads that pulled against the cohesive quality of the group. It was also, no doubt, because psychiatric patients can be stunningly nonchalant about their sexual practices—in these times, unprotected sex can be a form of passive suicidality, and in this population it not uncommonly is. In any event, the patients held a meeting to talk about the divisiveness of sexual dyads (the sex had not been particularly secretive) and the need for commitment to the community. Tracy essentially shrugged and remarked that it hadn't been a big deal for her, that sex was sex, and that she had slept with the man only because she had been horny. Two days later she saw him sitting on a sofa next to a newly admitted female patient. To show her displeasure, Tracy picked up a large bowl on the coffee table and hurled it through the closed glass window. She was angry.

As the staff understood it, Tracy's treatment rested on a tripod of psychosocial interventions: intensive psychodynamic psychotherapy, the therapeutic community program, and the "interpretation-free" zone of the art studio. Psychopharmacology was also important, and in keeping with standard hospital practice, most patients were medicated. Tracy was placed on Paxil for her depressive symptoms. She was assigned a therapist, whom she saw four times a week. At Norton, all patients saw their therapist four times a week. This therapy was insight-oriented psychotherapy, psychoanalytic therapy, the kind of therapy in which (as the more orthodox analysts conceive of it) therapists do not reassure, console, or soothe. I sat in the corner one afternoon as Tracy's therapist was supervised on her sessions by a senior staff member. The young therapist, reading from notes written after the sessions, reported that Tracy had said, "I've got to get rid of this stuff with my mother." The supervisor interrupted, "That's great, she's in the language." The therapist continued, reading what she had said to Tracy: "I think that this is a core issue for you, that in your relationship with your mother you were never sure of what other people felt, you felt teased and criticized." The supervisor murmured in approval, "You've joined her." The therapist continued reading: soon thereafter, Tracy had said, "I begged you for something for sleep, and you never gave it to me." The young therapist looked up from her notes sheepishly and told the supervisor that she had responded by explaining to Tracy that she had tried to help but Tracy had refused her help at the time. Now the supervisor said, "Look at the process. You say, get into the transference, and she says, 'You don't give me what I need.' That's what you want. It's great; and then you panicked. Give with the one hand and take with the other, that's what my teacher said. Keep backing up, and she'll lay it all out."

There was a sense at the Norton Inn that patient and therapist were locked in mortal combat. "You couldn't engage with her," a young therapist said about one of his patients, proud that the patient had improved under his care, "unless you could accept that she thought that there would be death, and that it would be either yours or hers." Indeed many of the patients—witness Tracy—were angry, at everyone. The therapeutic focus on aggression was understood to be appropriate to these patients; there was a sense that patients who "failed" at other hospitals and were sent to Norton were likely to be the kind of patients whose anger made them hard to handle. Some of the clinicians drew from a theoretical perspective often attributed to Melanie Klein and Otto Kernberg, analysts whose work teaches that hostility—not loneliness, not love—is a driving emotion behind human experience, that idealization can be a mask for persecutory anger and affection a subterfuge for sadomasochism.

"What's missed in the field's dominant model of the therapeutic interaction is Klein's perspective," one of the senior clinicians said. "The more the patient sees you as a good parent, the more it leads to envy, malice, and a desire to kill." A patient is perceived to be using the therapist to advance her own pathological goals of selfhood: to defend against connection, to induce guilt, to punish herself and others. The only hope for therapeutic success is for a therapist to confront a patient's need to bend the world to serve her needs by helping her to see the awesome destructiveness of her own rage. This is not comfortable for young therapists. One of the young fellows had grown up in a religious background that directed her to look for the good in human nature. When she had chosen psychiatry, she had seen it as one way out of a world that covered over the unpleasantness of human life. She told me that when she had been sixteen, the truck carrying her horse had jackknifed and crashed. She had sat by the horse's body, waiting for the police and ambulance, asking God how he could allow such unfairness and pain. Norton pushed her to the edge of her ability to tolerate the contradiction she lived within. "It is very disillusioning," she said, "to think that I have to believe that all of these good people have murderers inside them. You would think that it would be reassuring to discover that we are all alike, but it's not. They teach me," she continued, "that for the patients I am a coatrack to hang coats on."

If therapy is the naked encounter of two souls, these souls are imagined as wrestling in a mud pit. A case report about a patient who was being discharged described her as having entered with a "black, despairing and fragmented psychic state." In therapy, "she has easily, repeatedly and ragefully experienced empathic breaks." Her previous therapist had said that "the metaphor of a hurricane was appropriate in describing Ms. Deever's emotional struggle. He states that, like Ms. Deever, in a hurricane there is a hole in the center which is a vacuum and the hurricane swirls around it, trying to fill that hole." She had been hospitalized at Norton for three years. Her most recent therapist—she had run through a number; a senior clinician said that this patient was more difficult to work with than any other he had seen—presented her case to the staff. He was a laconic, low-key man, once an English major, who said that he had not understood racism until he had worked with this child of racial intermarriage and seen her rage and guilt. He spoke about her for more than an hour, without notes. He talked about the way she had told him how pathetic he was, how little he, an ambitious Jewish Long Islander, knew about the world. It was clear that she had made him feel small. He said that she had gone for his defenses, the ways he hid to protect himself against a patient's rage. He frequently said, when he was reporting such an attack, that she was right. When he finished speaking, he had tears in his eyes. "The patient has made him honest," a senior clinician said with respect.

One of the patient's problems, as her therapist saw it, was that she failed to perceive herself as having a psychodynamic problem. She needed to be persuaded of her responsibility for her experience. "This work is difficult," a senior clinician said, "because analytic work is about responsibility, taking responsibility. There's a fine line that separates responsibility from guilt, and this patient has a huge amount of guilt." The case report said, "Over the course of the meetings with me over the months, Ms. Deever has demonstrated an increased capacity to experience her symptoms as a result of psychological stressors rather than biochemical imbalances." Patients at the Norton Inn learned to see problems that seemed to be uncontroversially biological in psychodynamic terms. A bipolar woman told me that privately, she thought her illness had something to do with the brain but that a person like her needed to understand it as dynamic. One of the patients told me that his psychosis was a defense against his angry feelings, which had something to do with his family's lack of boundaries (in other words, he had become psychotic because he couldn't emotionally handle his family). The patient of the case presentation could not make this shift to psychodynamic thinking, and this was seen as a problem for her. She had a dream about hummingbirds, which she interpreted as her GABA receptors crying out for Ativan [a Valium-like tranquilizer]. "Actually," her therapist murmured, "I thought it was about separation anxiety."

The second leg of the psychosocial treatment tripod is the psychotherapeutic community. In this "therapeutic community," the patients, with the help of some staff, essentially manage the social and some of the administrative life of the patient group. The large community meeting was held four times a week for fifty minutes and included everyone who was willing to come; at the largest ones, it seemed that most of the people in the patients' building (patients, nurses, and psychiatric workers) and some of the therapy staff and social workers were there. There might be thirty or more people in the room. The agenda (reports from community groups, for example, and reviews of people's difficulties and relationships to staff) was just a mechanism to generate discussion. There was a sense that the group should meet, that someone would speak about something that had been bothering him, and that as other people began to contribute to the discussion, everyone present would learn what "the issues" were. Staff assumed that this public airing would help people learn to handle those issues. The goal here was to give patients another mirror in which to see how they came across to other people and to give them a sense of being responsible members of the group. Much about these meetings reminded me of a small boarding school.

There were also smaller groups. There was an activities group, which controlled a significant annual budget (more than $10,000 per year) and a task group, which dealt with social problems in the community. If a patient kicked in a plate-glass window, he or she was "referred" to the task group, and roughly eight patients and three staff members discussed with the patient the community's perspective on his or her behavior and its impact on the group. There were groups for each house outside the main hospital, as well as a women's group, a men's group, an eating disorders group, a substance abuse group, and a relationships group. Patients were elected to major positions in these groups and through their election acquired certain responsibilities, such as chairing meetings, running discussions, and, in the case of the activities group, allocating money. One patient who left the hospital and subsequently prospered in business said that her experience of being community chairperson and its associated responsibilities had been the single most important preparation for running her business.

Emotions could run high. I attended one smaller meeting where the discussion turned to the larger meeting, where a patient who hadn't been present had been criticized. She was, however, now sitting in the smaller meeting. People began to use convoluted sentences to explain how distressed they had been that someone had been criticized in her absence without telling the victim who it had been. She sat knitting obliviously until one of the patients said, "Oh, hang it, Kate, you're the one they're talking about. They think that you're a little uptight." This was, of course, an understatement. Kate was one of the most anxious people I have met, a tense sparrow with a drawn, well-bred face. "Well," she said, "you're just annoyed at me because I'm more competent than any of you are." The sympathy for her evaporated at once, and various people explained crisply just how uptight, defensive, and pretentious she was: "I mean, the other day you told me you were writing the most amazing novel, and finally you showed it to me. All you had was a page, and that page stinks." For the next few days, Kate drooped like a withered balloon. She would come up to me and say plaintively, "But it was an accident, really. You must know that. I really didn't mean it. Really."

"Eighty to ninety percent of behavior is a function of expectation," a senior clinician told me. "If you make it clear to people that they have the capacity to engage in the community process and that their treatment is their responsibility, they will respond. The culture must give them responsibility." The counterbalance to the stress of public unveiling is supposed to be responsibility. You are supposed to learn, through such interactions, how to be responsible for your feelings and their impact on others.

In general, these meetings were remarkable for their tone. Discussions were usually straightforward, calm, and inquiring. They were often psychologically astute. People often took responsibility for something that had bothered others: unwashed coffee cups, a monopolized phone. The content of the discussion tended to circle around an individual and his or her role: as a member of a community, as a member of a meeting, as a group leader, and so forth, with a kind of insistent focus on the expectations of the group. ("Why do you feel the need to use the phone in that room, where we can all hear you? How do you conceive of your role here as a patient, and where do the rest of us fit in?") They called this "examined living": all behaviors were up for discussion.

In this spirit, once a month there was an all-hospital meeting of patients, clinicians, nurses, even the cook. It lasted about an hour. As in many meetings, technically there was no agenda, but there was often a sense of what "needed" to be discussed. When I was there, the issue was confidentiality. A patient in the hospital had thrown a glass of water at another patient, and there had been a great deal of communal distress about why and whether it might happen again, and so forth. The water throwing had been a major discussion point for the community meeting on more than one occasion. In a therapy session, the water thrower told her therapist that it had been only a joke. This was not something she men-

tioned to anyone else. Afterward, a social worker (who was not her therapist) came to the community meeting and when the water-throwing incident was raised again, the social worker pointed out that it had been meant
as a joke. She had intended to calm the patients down. Instead, when the
patients talked to the water thrower, they became very distressed. They
saw the social worker's remark as a violation of patient-therapist privilege.
They assumed that what they told their therapists was confidential. Yet
here was clear evidence that their sessions could be discussed in meetings
in which they were not present and with people they had never meant to
hear them. They wanted what they said in therapy to stay behind closed
doors.

So in the meeting, once the sixty or so people had gathered in the conference room, a patient raised the point with the director of the hospital.
Several patients spoke; some staff spoke; the discussion occupied most of
the allotted time. "We don't know the truth of what happened," the director
said. "There may be many truths. In this case there seems to have been a
boundary violation. But we must recognize that therapists must talk to
other staff members and that they try to be thoughtful about issues of confidentiality." The hospital discussion didn't set any new rules about what
was sacred to therapy and what not, but it did point out that there were
inherent awkwardnesses in the combination of therapy and communal life.
"It's hard to get hold of the ethic of examined living simply by making
rules," the director said. I was sitting in back with some of the patients.
The discussion seemed to resolve the tension.

The goal of this community structure, as staff conceived of it, was to
provide what the analyst Donald Winnicott called a "holding environment": a place where people could act out their feelings without retaliation
or withdrawal by others. Within the resilience of a good psychotherapeutic
community, staff members argued, a patient should be able to play out the
developing parts of his or her personality, see how people reacted to them,
and learn from the reaction without actually risking anything in the real
world—a job, a partner—in the process. I was impressed by how well it
seemed to work. That is, I was impressed by the effectiveness with which
patients could define their roles as members of the community to one
another and to new patients, who entered the hospital irrational and deeply
disturbed. There was a kind of insistence on maintaining the limits of
acceptable behavior that seemed as if it might be comforting if your world
were falling apart. But it is a strange society, in which the unconscious
intentions of all its members are the focus of its intellectual and social life.
"The issue is," a patient said in community meeting, "what is the meaning
of these unwashed cups? What do we want to say when we leave our coffee
cups on the table?"

Tracy told me that before she had been referred to the task group, it had never occurred to her that her actions had an impact on people. She had felt voiceless, as many psychiatric patients do, inadequate and without self. The community, however, was clear that her voice was strong. They had noticed the broken plate-glass window. However, it was not until the incident with Stoddard that she heard them tell her how powerful she was. Stoddard was a tall, round man about Tracy's age, with intellectual pretensions and a scraggly beard. He announced one evening, in one of the smaller community meetings, that he would never sleep with a slut like Tracy. Few people in the room seemed to believe this, but some hours later, when news of the comment got back to Tracy, it did not occur to her to chuckle. She called Stoddard, cursed him, and declared her intention of coming over to see him in person. Stoddard then promptly called the town police, who were there to greet her when she arrived. (He was a citizen of the town. He could call the police.) Tracy was profoundly humiliated (this probably was what Stoddard had intended). She ran out of the building into the woods, pulled out a razor, and made twenty parallel cuts up the side of her arms and in her cheeks. She returned to the building dripping blood. By then the police had gone, and the nurses patched her up.

Over the next two days, I saw Tracy in various group meetings. I have never been as viscerally aware of someone's anger. Tracy sat in the meetings quite silent, pulsing with rage. I think she was on the cliff edge of control. I know that I was seriously worried, for the first time in a psychiatric setting, about where I sat in the room lest she should suddenly decide to leave and kick her way out. Patient after patient said, "You scare me; use words instead of razors." She said only, "Stoddard is an asshole. If he says one more thing about this, I won't be responsible for what happens." I had not realized until those meetings that the members understood themselves to be involved with keeping Tracy safe in the community and keeping the community safe with her, and how much senior patients saw themselves as coaching patients who had not yet learned to manage.

The third leg of the tripod was an "interpretation-free zone"—the studio, where patients painted, worked in clay, and did other crafts. "These creative activities," a history of Norton recounts, "aimed to uncover, explore, preserve and enlarge those areas of activity which were relatively free of conflict for each patient." Intensive psychotherapy is said to be "regressive" for patients, to throw them back into a more infantile, more emotionally overwhelming experience of the world. Some psychiatrists argue against long, psycho-dynamically oriented hospital admissions precisely because, they say, such intensive therapy encourages already shaky people to fall apart, not to cope. That was the point of arguing, back in the sixties, that only people who were actually pretty healthy could tolerate the strains of psychoanalysis: the intense emotions that helped neurotics to see themselves more clearly would throw the seriously ill into psychosis. Norton argued that the regressive pull of intensive psychotherapy was counterbalanced by the progressive demands of the therapeutic community and the art. Patients in therapy were *supposed* to fall apart. Then they could put themselves together in healthier ways by using the art studio and the therapeutic community to bolster their creativity and personal authority. In 1994, artwork was sold in a crafts store for summer vacationers; the annual play auditioned both townspeople and patients. Over the course of her stay, Tracy became a weaver. She would bend over the angled loom, open like a mechanical butterfly, and concentrate on threading and then passing the shuttles through to create her pattern. Her blue-and-purple chenille scarves sold easily in the crafts store, even for extraordinary prices. She began to feel like a craftswoman.

The goals at Norton are very high: not simply to keep a patient safe until he can survive outside but to come as close as possible to curing him, to restructuring a self-destructive personality. "Psychiatric units these days do good work," one of the most respected (non-Norton) senior administrators in psychiatry told me. "They do good medicine. But if my daughter were ill, I'd send her to Norton. At Norton they adopt their patients and keep them until they get better." If the biomedical world takes responsibility for a patient's body, the psychodynamic one takes responsibility for a patient's soul and for teaching that person how to take responsibility for himself. That is a more taxing role in a person's life. It is much harder on therapists, who become, as it were, surrogate parents for these bright, promising, and profoundly destructive patients.

Therapy is hard on therapists. It is harder the more they identify with their patients, and it is harder the more they feel attacked by patients or the more patients attack themselves. At Norton it is easy to feel involved with the patients because it seems that if you could only change them a little, they could do so very much. When one treats the cynical ne'er-do-well derelicts who haunt many of the places where psychiatrists train, it is hard to convince oneself that they will change, let alone make a difference to the world. At Norton, the patients come from families that are often wealthier and more distinguished than the psychiatrists' own. It is easy to fantasize that they could be powerful and effective doctors, lawyers, professors, philanthropists. Because they are young, bright, and rich, their prognosis, if the illness can be dented, is far better than that of people who are old, dull, and poor. Patients like Tracy seem to have everything but happiness. They desperately need and want help; then, when a therapist reaches out to them, they bite the hand—hard. Most analysts do not take extremely disturbed patients into intensive psychotherapy, not only because their theory suggests that the therapy will be too powerful but because they fear that as therapists they will get too involved, that these patients need help so badly that they will want to help equally badly, and then, because the patients are so disturbed, the patients will hurt them more than the therapist can bear.

Norton took these very ill patients and gave them intensive psycho-analytic psychotherapy, and the psychiatry and psychology fellows—fresh from residency and its equivalent—felt beaten up and hollowed out by them. When I was there, the hospital had five full-time senior clinicians and seven fellows, a mixture of psychiatrists and psychologists. Fellows work there for two to four years. If they are psychiatrists, they are likely to spend their last year of residency there. Each fellow sees a maximum of four patients, and each full-time therapeutic staff member sees usually one and occasionally more patients.

The fellows dreamed about their patients. They said that the patients got under their skin and into their lives in ways that were nearly intolera-ble. "I live with them in me, and it makes me crazy," a new fellow said. "But then I really see how the theory works, because I *see* it, the way I'm project-ing, the way I get angry and then paranoid. You're forced into really grasp-ing that you construct your own world, that your language is drenched in your history." These are not the obedient conflicted patients of Upper West Side New York who worry about their unconscious aggression in paying their bill three weeks late. These patients walk into sessions furious that their therapist (they say) is sadistically torturing them with his or her sexual feelings for them. They try to make the therapist confess those feelings. (Psychiatric patients can be unnervingly insightful.) They talk about their hatred for their therapist and their therapists' hatred for them. They threaten to commit suicide. One fellow, confident and poised, with five years of psychotherapeutic experience behind her, found herself so shaken after the sessions with one patient that she vomited after the therapy hour, session after session. "I feel things first in my body," she said, "all this anger and rage. It was too much." Feelings about patients, particularly for new fellows, seemed barely under control, or what the staff would call "con-tained." Sometimes they spilled out from the therapy session to the thera-pist's dealings with the nurse, social worker, or check-in person at the local gym. And these are patients who talk about suicide and go back to a hospi-tal building without locks, who talk about their therapy to nurses who may question the therapist's wisdom. There is always a hovering question in a nurse's mind about the doctors anyway, particularly new doctors, because doctors conduct their work behind closed doors.

The heart of this culture, confronted by its terrible uncertainties and risks of emotional chaos, lies in a paradox: that feelings are its insistent focus, yet its public culture repeatedly and consistently defuses strong feelings. That is the way this culture manages the greatest threat its intellectual commitments pose to its existence. Emotions are to be spoken about, not expressed. "The whole damn place is affect-avoidant," a social worker grumbled. Tears were utterly unsanctioned. In any meeting of more than four people the correct tone of voice was deadpan. When people mentioned that a first-year fellow had cried in a team meeting, they lowered their voices and raised their eyebrows. A therapist's inability to manage his feelings in public would lead the general staff to question his ability to manage the intense emotions of the therapy relationship in private. In the staff's culture, the psychotherapeutic culture of examined living—in the clinical case conference, when all staff meet for two hours twice a week to discuss one patient; in the thrice-weekly clinical meetings, when all staff meet for an hour to discuss all the patients; even in the smaller twice-weekly team meetings, when ten staff members meet to discuss perhaps a third of the patients—there was a style that took the wind out of overwrought passion as effectively as a damp English afternoon.

These meetings set a premium on formal, crafted, eloquent speech. The senior staff spoke in sentences rounded out with caveats and considerations, with deliberate, complex rhythms. They spoke well and fluidly in psychoanalytic prose: "For this patient, connecting to her feelings and communicating them to the other is fraught with peril." My notes on one patient presented in a team meeting read, "Youngest of five, can't leave home for fear of what will happen to parents or to her—possible history of sexual abuse—that may in turn contribute to her difficulties in being sexual, may be afraid of being *father's* wife, as *re* morning seminar—fears of oedipal victory over father's wife, who doubles as her mother—rage at mother for unavailability—may have contributed to eating disorder at time of puberty—fearful, insecure attachment style." Presentations were done with an implicit bow, not a sense of brisk efficiency.

Defensiveness was bad. In this public culture, when staff or patients were confronted with criticism in public, they were expected not to deflect the criticism but to address it. At one staff meeting, a senior staff member announced that the executive committee had decided to hire a senior staff member's wife to serve as a therapist from time to time, and did anyone have any feelings about that? One of the fellows—the one who vomited after difficult sessions—stuck her hand up aggressively and said, "You've made the decision; we won't influence it, so why are you bothering to ask for our response, which will just leave us vulnerable and won't have any impact?" I was watching the senior clinician at the time. He did not, as I thought he would, stiffen up. After a moment, his shoulders relaxed.

154

"You're right," he said. "We have made the decision, and unless you feel very strongly about it we won't change it. But if you do feel strongly that it is inappropriate, we will consider changing our minds."

There were jokes here as well. "The patient," said the therapist for the interracial woman, "had a dream that she would die in a plane accident and on the weekend she was scheduled to fly to Canada, she learned that the East Coast would experience its worst winter storm of the season. She was superstitious and became quite agitated in the session. Now, as it happens, I am a little superstitious, too. I told her that she might consider the train." But the humor was not about madness. It stabbed at the high seriousness of the therapeutic endeavor, and it was self-deprecating for the therapist. Staff laughed comfortably at themselves. When they laughed at the patients, they immediately became apologetic and nervous. In this case conference, the therapist remarked that the patient, who kept saying that she was desperate to leave, had developed striking neurological symptoms before discharge. Everyone listening laughed, because to them this meant that despite her many protests, she liked her therapist and wanted to stay in the hospital. But they quickly became contrite. A senior clinician immediately said that the laughter might be a way of "breaking out of the confining frame that the patient has set." A fellow pointed out that the patient's symptoms were real for her. The director remarked that laughter was a healthy response to the countertransference. Clearly, at Norton you are not supposed to laugh at madness. But staff members laughed at doing therapy. They laughed at therapeutic blunders, at the ambitions of the therapist, at the difficulty of being what they would call "in role." That is because the contradiction in this culture, its impossible model, is about the therapist, not the patient's madness. These therapists did not think that patients are rational people with a physical illness. They did not put much stock in anyone's rationality, or at least in his ability to think clearly and independently of his unconscious desires. What was funny, then, was not the patient's madness but the very attempt to do therapy, to comment objectively on a patient's superstitious comment when you yourself are a little superstitious and think she ought to take the train. The stories they told were often about the doing of therapy: how a patient worried that her boyfriend would kill her and the therapist made a psychodynamic interpretation of that fear and the patient then brightened with visible relief and said that she was so relieved that there was a psychological explanation, because her boyfriend's brother had gone after *his* ex-girlfriend with a gun. They laugh at the way a patient turned an interpretation around and suddenly the therapist was the one receiving therapy. They traded stories about the way senior clinicians had been narcissistically preoccupied and failed to attend to something they thought was obvious about a patient, and how that had backfired. They laughed at the attempt to step outside one's own dynamic frame to understand another person, which is what a therapist is supposed to do.

And I have never seen an institution so focused on the roles, hierarchical and otherwise, of its members: discussion of how a patient had not improved until her therapist had assumed his appropriate role with respect to her; the role of the hospital in interaction with the insurance company and the patient's parents; the role of the community with respect to the behavior of two patients. The reason for this is, no doubt, that people were not, in fact, defined by their roles. In a biomedical unit, the hierarchy of power can reflect what was assumed to be the hierarchy of knowledge in an unproblematic way because the possessing of knowledge is not problematic. In a psychodynamic setting, knowledge is complex, ambiguous, and uncertain. A patient can see things about her therapist, about a nurse, about the director of the hospital that these people do not recognize, and the structure of the hospital life is set up to allow the patient to point out to these people what she perceives about them. It becomes easy to doubt that someone has accumulated knowledge, no matter what his credentials. In any event, this institution was profoundly conscious of its social structure. What the social workers did was clear, and it was not what therapists did (much to the distress of the social workers, who wanted to do individual therapy and were not allowed). Even the small lunchroom was informally segregated, so that senior clinicians ate at one table, fellows at another, administrative staff in a separate room, and patients, nurses, and mental health workers in another building. Patients would have long discussions about whether the eating disorders group would still be the eating disorders group if its members met without their leader, whom they had decided they didn't like; they concluded that without a leader, however irritating she was, it would not be a group. "You have to stay in the role," the supervisor earnestly told his supervisee, a fellow. "Educating the patient, doing reality testing for him, telling him whether his responses are appropriate—that is not staying in role. Staying in the transference is your role as a therapist, allowing yourself to be trapped, to be stuck in an enactment, and then taking a step back to ask what this has to do with the patient's inner life." The explicit emphasis on role definition—far more explicit and formal than in the biomedical setting—becomes a way of clarifying the realistic differences in training and stature despite the interest in unconscious fantasy that dominates the intellectual life.

In the end, it seemed to me that one could summarize the complex culture of this place around four paradoxes. First, emotion was the content, focus, and most important issue of most clinical discussions, yet feeling was not to be displayed; it was to be discussed formally and calmly. Second, psychotherapy took place in private and was confidential, yet the environment of examined living demanded that everything be open to discussion. Third, this hospital hierarchy was as clear and as solid as I have ever seen, yet it was consistently flattened in the service of an egalitarian democracy of open discussion. Fourth, there was a great deal of discussion about limits and boundaries—whether patients should have sex, whether throwing a glass of water was an effective means of communication—yet the hospital had no real constraints, no doors, no security guards, no watchdogs. Thus, to live in the culture successfully as a doctor (or another staff person) meant that you had to talk about your own emotions in public and in depth, but not express them; you had to keep secrets but know when to share them; you had to behave democratically but with a deep respect for hierarchy; you had to substitute talk about responsible living with your patient for taking responsibility for that patient's life by keeping her under lock and key. It was a hard transition for the new clinicians, who felt the deep strain of living rubbed raw in open view of other people. "They are used to controlling people, to managing them," a senior clinician said severely. "They have to get used to doing therapy."

Norton is a very special hospital. The psychiatrists at San Juan would probably love to do this kind of work, but they can't. Even if they could, their patients would not have the success that Norton's seem to have. They do not have the money. They do not have the time. They must handle thousands of patients each year. Norton handles perhaps several hundred, with more staff. Norton's patients are young, bright, often wealthy, and usually struggling with disorders that, when managed, can leave the patient highly functional and effective. The upper reaches of our society hold many depressed and bipolar high achievers, not to mention mild borderline personality disorders. San Juan's patients are often uneducated, unemployed and unemployable, and older. Their prognosis is poor. It would be poor no matter where they were treated. They struggle with substance abuse, and are treated and then discharged into a community where crack and heroin are rampant. They struggle with depression, and are treated and then discharged into the realistically depressing world of the underclass. They struggle with schizophrenia, and though medication will stabilize them it will not make them self-sufficient. Psychiatric illness, like all medical problems but more so, is mired in the ugly realities of the American class structure. This is one reason psychiatric illness presents our society with moral choices.

CHAPTER FOUR

❖❖

THE PSYCHIATRIC SCIENTIST AND THE PSYCHOANALYST

What does it mean to be a good psychiatrist? Who do you aim to be? The biomedical and psychodynamic domains each has its own ideals. Most young psychiatrists do not in fact choose a route into rigorous scientific research or lengthy psychoanalytic training. Nonetheless, their sense of what it means to be the best is framed by the models of those who have been held up to them as epitomes of excellence. Because psychiatry has been dominated by two competing models of illness, and because true excellence in either has historically been understood as attained through the kind of training that precludes true excellence in both, the two ideals of excellence are quite distinct. In the one domain, there is the scientist, the fearless investigator of truth. In the other, there is the psychoanalyst, the wise wizard of insight. These two ideals embody different moral sensibilities, different fundamental commitments, different bottom lines. In some ways the differences are subtle; in others they are sharp and striking. The differences become part of the way the young psychiatrist imagines himself with patients, the way he comes to empathize with patients, and, ultimately, the way he comes to regard his patients as moral beings.

THE PSYCHIATRIC SCIENTIST

"I hate it," a resident wailed at the end of her second year. "They seem to think that if we don't go into research we've failed somehow." The practice of medicine rests on scientific knowledge. That knowledge is the justification of the practice. Yet the practitioners, the pure clinicians, do not produce the knowledge. Knowledge is produced by researchers, and in the late twentieth century the promise of medical science is that knowledge will always increase and always increasingly achieve its aims. Research scientists, then, are the sine qua nons of contemporary medicine. They are also its secular ascetic priests. They are paid less than their clinical counterparts for generating the knowledge that the clinicians sell in the marketplace for a higher price. They are rewarded with prestige and, occasionally, fame. They tend to have positions in medical schools and to do at least some teaching of medical students and residents. Students and residents meet the researchers during a period when their own identities are still being formed and their sense of the "good psychiatrist" is still emerging. They meet many other kinds of psychiatrists as well: the senior psychiatrists who run their unit teams, the psychoanalysts who supervise their psychotherapy sessions, the somewhat older residents or young faculty members who are mostly deeply involved in the teaching process. But the research scientists have the greatest halo in the hospital and medical school context, particularly in the very good schools. When bright residents decide not to pursue research—and most of them do not—they must struggle with a sense of letting down the teachers they have admired and even idealized. Most residents in the prestige-conscious residencies I visited had considered going into research at one time or another. When they decided not to, they felt not regret, but shame.

This shame is curious to the outsider, because in many ways our society sees clinical work as the more noble and more moral task. Clinicians deal one-on-one with human suffering. They see the intimate pain of individual lives, and they try to heal that pain. We allow them to put their hands where no other stranger's would be allowed because we trust them to help us and at least to some extent believe they can. Most people go to medical school because they want to work with people who are suffering and to heal them. This is what medical school (more or less) teaches its students to do. Researchers do not help individual sufferers—at least, not directly nor do they, when they are doing research, do anything they were taught to do in medical school. They are distant from human pain. They do not see it, do not deal with it, do not cure it, at least not face-to-face. They are not, as we would say, in the trenches or the soup kitchens. They stand back. Yet young psychiatrists can speak of choosing to be "mere clinicians."

This moral hierarchy owes much to the knowledge hierarchy between the clinician and the scientific researcher. The American Psychiatric Association convention is the meeting for general clinicians, who hurry between large panel discussions designed to deliver sound bites from the academic front—"Attention Deficit Disorder," "Schizophrenia and Depression"—and smaller sessions—"The Pregnant Resident," "Smoke-Free Psychiatric Units: Progress and Problems." There are usually more than ten thousand attendees. The large panels are held in huge, dark ballrooms filled with rows of metal seats. The speaker's face is projected onto a hanging screen behind his back as he speaks, so that people in the thirtieth row can see him, and people wander anomically in and out as one graph after another goes up beside his image. The task force for the next edition of the diagnostic manual presents the latest thinking on various topics to rooms packed with more than a thousand people: how coherent the personality diagnoses are as a group; whether it has decided to change the criteria for, say, obsessive-compulsive disorder; whether a new antipsychotic really works as well as the earlier reports suggested. The American Psychiatric Press's *Review of Psychiatry* presents symposia on new research on (for instance) schizophrenia, bipolar disorder, posttraumatic stress disorder. "Hot" topics, such as sexual abuse or managed care, may fill a large room to standing room only. Through all this there is a sense of grand spectacle, of theater and crowds and entertainment; and in fact the conference information booklet is full of special events, trips to the Louisiana bayou or around Capitol Hill, tax-deductible vacations for the frugal. Those who put on the spectacle—those who perform, who write the chapters, do the epidemiological surveys, and run the validity studies, who collect and analyze the data—have enormous symbolic power. They are the scientific researchers. It is because clinicians must keep abreast of the new science that they fly from Minneapolis to Washington, D.C., and spend five days in an overpriced Hilton.

The Society of Biological Psychiatry meetings are utterly different. Gone is the attention to clinical matters and the air of frenzied holiday. The hundred or so scientists who attend the meeting—not the most elite of its kind, but attended by many elite scientists—are colleagues. They present their work for information and critique, not as bullets of truth condensed for an unsophisticated audience. The atmosphere is competitive, ambitious, and democratic.

The word that marks these meetings is "data." Data are good or bad, massive or thin, coherent or messy. If data are good, they are convincingly the result of an experiment, and they tell a story. Good data help support one or more hypotheses and cast doubt on others. Participants in these conferences talk about good data and bad data and who has which. They stand around after sessions and gossip about the way people interpret their data and what the correct interpretation ought to be. It is said that you can figure out whether the talk was good just by looking at the way the data were presented—if the speaker spent too much time summarizing previ-

160

ous work or concentrated too much on the demographic characteristics of the patients, the data were thin and unconvincing, there weren't enough to fill a talk. Poor papers present the data raw and undigested; good papers explain the scientific problem, what the scientist did, why the data are significant. There are poster sessions in which the people who don't give spoken talks type up their work on pieces of paper and pin them to bulletin boards, the conference organizers set out cheap Chardonnay and plates of Cheddar cubes with cellophane-decorated toothpicks, and conference participants walk around with little paper plates and read the posters to see who is doing what and how. Sometimes the posters are more eagerly anticipated than the spoken talks. At humanities conferences, participants might say that they go to sessions to find out what is trendy. These conference attendees say that they go to sessions to find out what other people's experimental results are. And they look at data in other ways as well. These are government-funded grantees, people given more than a half-million dollars to carry out their experiments, who support their staff, their salaries, and their laboratories by the money they are able to raise by writing dense, careful grant applications. As I sat in one paper session of the Society of Biological Psychiatry meetings, listening to a group of eminent scientists explore the use of a new brain-imaging technique, another scientist leaned towards me and whispered, "Now, do you think those data were worth three hundred thousand dollars?"

Data ultimately create knowledge; knowledge creates intervention; and intervention is what the clinician uses to treat the patient, as both scientists and clinicians tend to frame their respective roles. In that sense, there is something of an intellectual food chain between research and clinical practice. Clinicians use medications to treat the patients they diagnose. Some researchers (clinical psychopharmacological researchers) do drug studies. They try out not-yet-approved medications (the next generation of anti-depressants, for example) on suitable patients who agree to participate in their study. Neither patients nor researcher know which patients receive the actual drug and which receive sugar pills; thus, these studies are called "double-blind." While some researchers in this domain are very serious, many of the studies are routine and what the researcher does is close to clinical work.

Then there are researchers who try to develop new diagnostic categories to replace older ones or to explain underutilized diagnoses. They develop interview "schedules" and "recruit subjects" that meet the criteria for some diagnosis; then they try to demonstrate that a subgroup of those patients can be more accurately described with the new criteria or explain some characteristics of that group that have been ignored. Or they explore an under-studied phenomenon: they try to figure out, for example, why so many psychiatric patients smoke, and they begin by taking smoking histories of a wide range of patients. This work is further away from everyday clinical work, and a researcher, not a drug company, develops the topic to be investigated. These researchers are still called "clinical." The word "clinical" simply refers to working with people, or working in the clinic. Usually, the word "clinician" is reserved for someone who does not do research, and always refers to someone in the capacity of a treater of patients, not as a researcher. A "clinical researcher" does his research in a clinical setting, with patients, and though he may do some treatment-oriented doctoring, which he calls his "clinical work," his primary identity is as a scientist.

Scientists who are not clinical are at the beginning of the food chain. They do not work with people. They often work with rats. They work on brain mechanisms, and they work in laboratories. They study the processes that create (or accompany) an actual disorder, what might be termed the "source" of the illness, and their work, though in many ways incomprehensible to clinicians, is seen as the most important and most exciting of all psychiatric science.

In the summer of 1994, I called Randy Gollub because a senior psychiatrist had described her to me as a star. (Unless otherwise indicated, the psychiatric scientists in this chapter are identified by their real names.) She was a laboratory scientist. Because she was female, she was an unusual scientist. There were some well-known female psychiatric scientists, but few of them conducted "basic" research, research about mechanisms in the brain, the kind of research that commanded the field's deepest respect. By 1994, only one woman, Paula Clayton, had been named to the chair of a prestigious department of psychiatry (chairmanship is far more powerful in medicine than in the arts and sciences, as a chairman controls a department's financial resources, which can be considerable, and holds the chair more or less until he or she chooses to resign). Some psychiatrists thought that the lack of women in this role was due to the kind of science the women did. In any event, I was not interested in the political future that other people envisioned for Randy; I wanted to know what it was like to live life as a laboratory scientist.

We arranged to meet in her office, which meant that I traveled the length of Boston to find the dockyard skyscraper into which the Massachusetts General Hospital, a Harvard affiliate, has deposited its laboratory scientists. MGH (Massachusetts General Hospital) East is a strikingly beautiful building. Randy's lab lies above a red-marble-walled lobby with a sparkling fountain, and, in its first years as laboratory space, it is elegant: there are fresh offices, space for the secretaries, newly laid carpet. This is a world of scientists: of postdocs and lab technicians, small offices and large laboratories with long, cluttered work spaces. It is obviously not a hospital space. There is no bustle. The cafeteria is small and gracious. No one is dressed in surgical scrubs or, for that matter, in expensive doctorly suits. There is not a patient in sight.

Randy turned out to be a lean, lanky woman, rather attractive, very determined. At first, she said, her scientific zeal had indeed been fueled in part by her feminism and by her determination to advance the status of women in science. "I didn't want to earn as much as a man," she recalled. "I wanted to earn more." So she credentialed herself well. She took a medical degree not because she wanted to do clinical work but because she had been advised that as a neuroscientist she would do better in the grant world with an M.D. The lore says that doctors are better funded, because they have more resources to tap for funds and more prestige. The lore also points out that a medical degree is superfluous to their work, at least in comparison to their academic training, that it is graduate and postdoctoral work that teaches a doctor to think like a scientist. Many future scientists get their medical degrees nonetheless.

Then she fell in love with the science and, more remarkable to her, the clinical side of medicine. "Much to my surprise, I really enjoyed the clinical work, and I couldn't give it up now." Randy did an M.D./Ph.D. at Duke and a postdoc and residency at Yale. Eighteen years after she started her undergraduate degree (four for the B.A.; four for the M.D.; four for internship and residency; six for the Ph.D. and postdoc), she took her first nonstudent job. She was over thirty-five. In 1994, the American Psychiatric Association Press published a book coauthored by one of Randy's mentors—the director of the lab in which she was given space—that set out the intellectual basis for this kind of serious psychiatric science. *The Molecular Foundations of Psychiatry* by Steven Hyman (then at Harvard, now the director of the NIMH) and Eric Nestler (at Yale) describes the neural structure of the brain. It is a brilliant book, written with a sophisticated understanding of the interaction between genetic abnormality and environmental influence. It is also strikingly technical, with paragraphs for the "general" reader distinguished from paragraphs for the reader who wishes to pursue material in depth. It displays the brute fact that psychiatric laboratory science exceeds the everyday medical student as graduate-level work exceeds the freshman and is beyond the grasp of the average psychiatric resident. The determination and early dedication needed to choose this professional road winnow out all but the very few. This makes a person like Randy very rare. The existence of people like her can make a young psychiatrist who discovers this kind of psychiatric science in residency feel awed and humbled.

Like many psychiatric scientists, Randy had at first wanted to solve the problem of schizophrenia. (Schizophrenia is perhaps the least understood and most important, because most debilitating, of the major mental illnesses.) Her tack was to focus on a discrete issue in the hopes that twenty years further on she might have part of the general answer. In her fellowship in electrophysiology, Randy had learned to read the electrical signals produced by certain kinds of cells. In these days of elaborate techniques, a postdoctoral fellowship is often focused on learning to carry out a specific technical process. Her MGH workstation consisted of a microscope, a petri dish, and what looked like expensive stereo components, piled up in a rack of six or so beside her. She would slice a piece of living rat brain into a petri dish—the slice continued to live in a complex, soupy bath—and poke at the sliced brain with a sensitive electrode attached to the layered components. Once she found a "good" neuron ("good" meant that it was easy to take readings from it) she added various fluids to the bath to see how the cell reacted.

What she had discovered was that there are certain kinds of rat brain cells that no longer respond to the neurotransmitter serotonin when the new antipsychotics clozapine and risperidone are added to the bath. Those new medications target what are sometimes seen as the true, core symptoms of schizophrenia: the listless apathy and emotional withdrawal, the "negative" symptoms. All antipsychotics target the flamboyant delusions and hallucinations (the so-called positive symptoms). But psychosis is a symptom of many conditions—mania, psychotic depression, and so forth. Only schizophrenia, the most intractable mental illness, generates the flat disconnection from the world. Cells that respond so powerfully to these new antipsychotics as to ignore a basic neurotransmitter such as serotonin might be important indicators of the schizophrenic process—particularly if they could be localized in one region of the brain. Randy had already localized them in the long, thin interneurons of the rat cortex and had used the data to suggest a potential site of action for these drugs. As is typical of psychiatric medication, psychiatrists know far more about a drug's efficacy— whether or not it works—than how or by what mechanisms.[1] It was not unreasonable to hope that she might eventually find a similar site in human brains. She thought she probably could.

To a young psychiatrist looking in from the outside during residency, this is a glamorous, powerful world. From the inside, it often seems less romantic, and the noble pursuit of truth seems chained to pragmatic expediency. Randy had an enviable position: an academic title, start-up money for the lab, the support of a powerful university's name. But her salary support was not guaranteed beyond a few years. In a time in which perhaps 10 percent of all scientific grants were funded, the medical school expected her to generate her own salary from grants. Any grant submission requires an intense period of work; many people suggest that a reasonable scientist should devote an entire month to the preparation and submission of one of these twenty-five-page, single-spaced packets, which have accompanying pages and pages of appendices, human subjects clearances, cost estimates, budgets, summaries of previous work, and so forth. After a year or two, Randy would be expected to pay for all her expenses: petri dishes, lab technicians, postdoctoral fellows, secretarial support. Her mentor then had fifteen people on his payroll, and their livelihood depended entirely upon his capacity to generate funds. "As a scientist," he said, "you must live with a combination of great confidence and great fear."

These days, science is about generating money. Very few psychiatric scientists are paid by their universities to teach and do research, the way historians and anthropologists and classicists are, even though they too have academic titles and teach in academic settings. Almost all of them must, like Randy, raise their own salary from grants as well as pay the costs of running their labs. (Actually, some portions of their salary may be generated by clinical work. The actual structure of an academic physician's salary can be fearsomely complex, with "X," "Y," and "Z" components subdivided and assigned to different grants, different clinics, and so forth.) To be a working scientist—to pay your mortgage, buy your groceries, clothe your children—you must be funded. Not only must you be funded once, but you must work on projects that can be reliably funded year after year until you retire. Most scientists, then, cannot indulge themselves in good but speculative ideas. The peer review system that awards the grants tends to be conservative, and speculative projects often fail. Those projects do not, by their nature, have much preliminary data. The system is intensely competitive, and your chief rivals may be the ones to review your grant submission. The whole setup makes many researchers bitter and tense. "What I hate about science," said one of Randy's senior colleagues with a grimace, "is the financial structure. If you don't get the grant, you can't do the work. So you go from gig to gig. You go where the money's good because you can't afford not to. I've been one of the lucky ones. But you worry about when you'll be forced to leave Broadway and take a cheap soap opera job to make ends meet."

To handle such a job well, you need to be able to handle stress well, or at least develop a modus vivendi. While I was writing this chapter, I had lunch with a biologist at my own university. He told me—he is a very accomplished scientist—that he would become so tense about grants and laboratory results and whether the laboratory would produce enough data for him to give talks and get funded that he had developed long-standing problems with his jaws. (It is quite possible for a very bright postdoctoral or doctoral student to work on a project for an entire year and get nowhere, with no data to present. If a senior scientist has a small laboratory, with perhaps one to three people working there, it is quite possible for the lab to produce no data for a year or more and thus to fail to be funded again and be forced to close.) He then recounted the back problems of a score of other scientists. He explained that one of the most important issues for a scientist was whether and how he was able to relax. He himself, he said, read pulp fiction. It is not pleasant to live on grants or even to have to rely on grants to be able to do your research. Historians, anthropologists, and literary critics can continue to work and think regardless of whether they get funded. Scientists can't.

The hours are also long. Experiments often don't work, data are often jumbled and messy, techniques fail more often than they succeed, and getting data means interpreting an array of results that may be largely due to error. Young, ambitious scientists are expected to spend all their time in the lab. One postdoctoral fellow in a large lab, where corridors of tables were lined with beakers and little plastic cartons and young people in sneakers were perched on high swivel seats, told me a story about such-and-such famous lab, where the lab director—the gray-bearded senior who directed the lab's research—would come around the lab on Saturday nights and Sunday mornings to make sure that the students and postdocs were there. It may be an apocryphal story, but the postdoctoral fellow swore that it was true.

Young psychiatrists do not see all of this when they look up to a clinical researcher or a laboratory scientist. They don't really see the pragmatism in the way scientists tailor their science to ensure their funding. They don't really see the stress. That is, they know that it is hard and competitive to get grants, and many of them chose not to enter scientific careers because they seem too hard—and because they like treating patients, which is why they chose medical school in the first place. But they do not know on a visceral level what it is to wake up in the night in a cold sweat when your wife is pregnant and you don't know if a grant will come through. Nor do they really know what research is like and how tentative and controversial the results can be.

On the other hand, they sometimes don't see how much fun it can be. Randy loved what she did, and she loved the doing of it. She seemed to have a wonderful time collecting data, chatting about how to analyze it with colleagues, flying around to conferences delivering talks. For her, science seemed like an intellectual sandbox. And it was the playing that fascinated and satisfied her. She wasn't that tied to the specific topic she worked on. She couldn't afford to be.

Despite her long training in electrophysiology, Randy herself switched out of her first field into the world of neuroimaging. Neuroimaging is the new chic darling of psychiatric science. It is a technology-heavy field that uses various methods—magnetic resonance imaging (MRI), positron-emission tomography (PET)—to take what looks like a picture of the brain. The functional MRI, for example, takes advantage of the coupling of neural activity and blood flow. A scientist exposes a subject's head to a high magnetic field and in effect measures the amount of blood flow to any region. The appeal of these methods is that the subjects appear to experience no side effects. So for the first time, scientists can study the brains of living humans without damaging them. With these new methods, psychiatric scientists are able to study the way blood flows to different areas of the brain when the subject performs different tasks. Scientists put people into these brain scanners and ask them to read words, remember phrases, so forth. One of Randy's colleagues, Scott Rauch, had done an experiment in which he put patients with obsessive-compulsive disorder into a brain scanner and then asked them to touch some object—a soiled paper towel, for instance—that was at the center of their obsessive rituals. Touching the object triggered unbearable feelings of dread and contamination. And the blood flow to certain regions of the brain increased.[2]

"In psychiatry," he explained, "disorders are syndrome-based. You see how people behave and label the illness based on some set of behaviors. In internal medicine, we usually know *something* about the physiological process, and that helps the internal medicine people to develop better treatments and better diagnoses. In psychiatry, we're still trying to figure out whether eating disorders, for example, are really just a sign of an underlying depression, or whether they're a different disease. We don't know. And sometimes diagnoses that look pretty much alike are grouped in very different ways across the diagnostic manual. Take OCD [obsessive-compulsive disorder], for instance. There's Tourette's syndrome in a section on movement disorder, body dysmorphic disorder in the somatoform disorders, trichotillomania in the impulse disorders, OCD itself in the anxiety disorders. They all involve problematic, compulsive repetition. But then, so does sneezing with hay fever. How do you figure out what goes with what? My hope is that neuroimaging will help psychiatry do better at pathophysiological classification. We've got a while to go yet, because we've had no way to distinguish the physiology of these illnesses at all. And if we can do that, our diagnoses and, ultimately, our treatments will get a whole lot better."

Because the granting agency shared these hopes, there was money in abundance to carry out neuroimaging studies and few people to compete for it, because neuroimaging was a new technique (relatively speaking) and not many scientists had learned to use it. Randy's mentor wanted her to apply for at least one grant because the grant-giving body had put aside money for the area and that meant that the odds of being funded had improved from something like one in twenty to one in four or less. For the same reason, it also became clear that with a little background work, Randy stood an excellent chance of getting a highly prestigious five-year award if she went into the area full-time. "We were virtually guaranteed to get the money for the first grant if we applied for it," she told me. "My mentor was really excited about the possibilities of this technology. He worked hard to recruit me for the project. He didn't back down for months, and finally I began to listen. . . . And I liked the people I would be working with. In physiology, I worked by myself. Me and the petri dishes. I thought it would be interesting to work with a group of people. We laughed a lot when we were writing the grant. It felt like good energy. And we got a fantastic score on the grant.

"Initially I'd been pretty skeptical about neuroimaging because I didn't think it could give me the answers I was interested in. I thought that the tool would smush together too much of the brain, that it was too crude. So I went to the neurosciences meetings—you know, there are these enormous meetings, thousands and thousands of people—and I specifically went to all the talks on neuroimaging, and I was really impressed by the quality of information that people were getting from this tool. I learned that if you were clever about how you used the tool, you could learn a lot. Then I found out that the same Washington source that had funded the first grant was looking to recruit new people to the field, and by luck I was at one of the best places in the world to do the work. It was like a sale on money. If you had a good idea, with good people to help you and the support of your institution, you had a really good chance of getting the money. They would pay my salary and my lab costs for five years to train me to do this.

"So I wrote a grant, and it got funded. And you know, that was really lucky. It turned out that the project I abandoned was a sinking ship. There were other, more experienced people using electrodes to look for that localized area in the human brain that responded so well to the new antipsychotics, and they couldn't find it. They just couldn't find it. In humans, it doesn't exist."

She found a way to make the new project fun. She enjoyed the way the data would crystallize on the computer screen. It was a little like taking photographs of different slices of the brain. Randy got excited as she showed me the different slices and what you could see in them. She also decided that she liked doing the experiments. Once she took me to one. Her subject lay in a darkened room with his feet sticking out of what appeared to be a large metallic doughnut. In the antechamber, Randy and her colleagues sat in front of computer screens and monitoring devices. Her subject, a cocaine user who was being paid well for participating, was being fed intravenously with a sequence of cocaine and sugar water. He reported to the team when he felt high and described how high he felt. They were scanning his brain to be able to learn, eventually, what areas of his brain seemed to be active at different moments and how the activity correlated with his physical and subjective state. Randy frowned at the controls and entered data into the computer. At one point she turned to me and grinned. "I like working with people," she said. "I mean, there's a lot of technology here, but at least I'm working directly with people. I don't have to get to people by going through rats."[3]

The play here is important. There is an entrepreneurial quality to the skills that make one a successful scientist. They are not entirely unlike the skills a scientist needs to figure out how to stay funded, although they are not the identical skill set. Scientists can be very good at grant writing and rather poor at interpreting data and formulating, and also the reverse. But still there is a kind of overlap, an ability to see in a boring experimental outcome the edge of something interesting, something that other people think to be important, something people will "buy."

At their best, these scientists do what is in essence a complex sorting task, making unusual distinctions and then trying to figure out whether they are significant in some way. The point of that sorting is to look, always, for useful but unrecognized distinctions or clusterings, often in a particular group of patients. Is there a consistent pattern of behavior in this set of people who have often been called schizophrenic or depressed that would lead us to think that they have a different problem altogether? That question led to the development of the "borderline personality disorder" category. Some depressed patients seem to have an elevated cortisol level. Is that true for a large enough percentage of depressed patients that it could be something like a blood test for depression? The answer to that turned out to be no, but in the meantime there were great hopes for the "dexamethasone suppression test."

What you hear when you listen to many researchers is a continuous, creative, sometimes slightly zany pairing and splitting apart and repairing. Jonathan Cole, for example, is a well-known clinical researcher who ran the first NIMH psychopharmacology center when it was established in the 1960s by Nathan Kline and Mary Lasker. He is a warm, jocular man known throughout his hospital not only for his quick mind but also for the bottle of M&Ms marked "Happy Pills" that he keeps on his desk. Like many of the other smart scientists I knew, he is what a psychiatrist would call "hypomanic," not manic but talkative, boundlessly energetic, with a capacity to generate multiple ideas. Only some of those ideas would eventually make it into research protocols and be analyzed with comparison groups, controls, and the various slow constraints of scientific study.

"Play with the data," I once heard Cole say to a much younger colleague. "Play with it until something interesting emerges." He seems to chop standard categories apart and lump the segregated pieces together in unexpected ways: What (for example) are the differences between schizophrenia and dissociation when it comes to hearing voices? Will the ways in which the two disorders respond to medication tell you anything? "Many people believe, you know, that research purity is next to godliness, that if you can't ask the question right you shouldn't ask it at all. I tend to believe that if you've got some data on a messy area you may be better off than if you have no data. Good psychiatric problems," he continued, "ask interesting questions which can be clearly answered. One of the problems of research in psychoanalysis is that it is very hard to make a prediction that could be proven right or wrong, and one of the nice things about drug studies is that the placebo at least gives you a chance of showing that something is different from something else. They're interesting. We did a study of drug abuse liability for a drug somewhat like trazodone [an older-generation antidepressant]. Most college-age kids didn't like it. But some did. Why? [It turns out that most psychiatric drugs are abused on the street. This is a genuinely puzzling fact, given that many have unpleasant side effects and are often described as unpleasant to take.] But drug studies don't solve all the problems of the world. As I get older, I am increasingly interested in things that give big differences. I've been trying to get a resident to do a project on epilepsy. Psychiatric patients with epileptic features will, if you give them one word in one ear and another in the other, eighty percent of the time be able to tell you only one of the words. Other psychiatric patients can usually tell you both words. It's as if patients with epileptic features can't grab both words at the same time, and because most psychiatric patients can tell you both words, this struck me as interesting. But I haven't found a resident yet to do it."

Another example of psychiatric scientific play, linking unconventional ideas together and then seeing which are foolish and which are powerful, comes from a man who is trying to restructure the field's ideas about personality disorders. I first saw Hagop Akiskal in one of these giant American Psychiatric Association sessions, where he stood in front of a thousand attendees and presented a remarkable theory of mood disorders. Akiskal argues that many of the problems that are now diagnosed as personality disorders—borderline personality disorder, for example—are really mood disorders, disturbances in the regulation of mood the same way depression or mania are disturbances in the regulation of mood. He retreats (astonishingly) to classical antiquity to find his categories, citing Aristotle, Soranus, Aretaeus, and Avicenna. He points out that in Graeco-Roman medicine there were four temperaments: the sanguine, which made people active, amiable, and funny; the melancholic, which made them lethargic, brooding, and contemplative; the choleric, which made them irritable, hostile, and given to rage; and the phlegmatic, which made them indolent, irres-olute, and timid. In excess, he argues, the same four temperaments become manic, depressed, borderline, and "avoidant." In the official diag-nostic manual, these last two are personality disorders.[4] Leaving out the phlegmatic as possibly more associated with thought disorders such as schizophrenia, he argues for four basic "affective" (or mood) tempera-ments: the depressive or dysthymic, the manic or hyperthymic, the irrita-ble or labile (depressed and hypomanic at once), and the cyclothymic or cycloid (a rapid cycle between depressed and hypomanic). "Dysthymic individuals were gloomy, given to worry, self-reproachful and self-disciplining, and possessed such character traits as nonassertiveness, pes-simism, and incapacity for fun. Hyperthymic individuals, by contrast, were habitually cheerful, sociable, self-assured, eloquent, boastful, improvident, and uninhibited. Cyclothymic individuals *alternated* from the hyperthymic extreme to the dysthymic, while irritable characters were hypothesized to possess hyperthymic and dysthymic traits *simultaneously.*"[5] Cyclothymic and irritable people often, he suggests, get diagnosed not only as borderline but also as a range of other personality disorders: narcissistic, histrionic, and so forth.

These personality disorders are thought by most psychiatrists to be cop-ing responses to unfortunate circumstances—bad parenting, bad home environments, or bad luck in life—that have become chronically dysfunc-tional in dealing with other people. If Akiskal is right, people diagnosed with personality disorders struggle because they were born that way, and their life history sounds messy because life has always been difficult for them to handle. Psychotherapy might teach them how to manage their vile humors more effectively by being more self-aware, he argues, but the only thing that will really check their mood is medication.

Akiskal is a flamboyant, provocative man, and he enjoys perturbing what he sees as a placid psychiatric pond. "This is something that would offend the humanistic mind, to think that these more abstract issues of the human being, which have defied explanation and understanding, could have some material base." He has, as many scientists do, a "discovery story," an account of how he came to recognize that there are (as he sees it) underlying mood problems in patients diagnosed with personality disor-ders: "There was a group of people in the seventies who were called char-acterological depressives. It was believed that these people really did not have depression, but that their character structure was depressive—unfor-tunate experiences made them perceive the world and people in a depres-sive way. It was thought that they developed that way and they were serious, they were pessimistic, they were somber, low in self-esteem, and they *suffered*. If you ask them how long they have felt this way, they say, 'I brought depression to this world.' Or 'I've never felt joy in my life.' This is a very fascinating group of patients who until then were being put on the couch because, to put it in psychoanalytic language, they had sucked the 'bad breast.'

"I seem to be making fun of this way of thinking—and perhaps I am, because this was a crazy way to think about these patients. Okay, it's a metaphor, the bad breast, but to think that something like a pervasive alteration in one's personality arose from early misfortune has never made sense to me. If that were true there should not be one sane person on the planet. At any rate, we didn't know how to treat these patients, and one day such a patient was sent by an analyst to our laboratory because the patient was sleeping on the couch. The roles were reversed"—here he chuckled—"the *patient* was sleeping. Anyway, the patient was sent to our sleep laboratory and he didn't have narcolepsy, didn't have sleep apnea, but his latency to REM sleep was very short, forty-five minutes. That you see only in psychotic depression and rarely in outpatients. So this rang a bell, that this so-called depressive character might have a real underlying depression and the depressive character was really secondary. This gave me an idea, that we should study a large number of these patients, and we did that, and the next step was to give them medication. But in those days the medications had a lot of side effects. It has taken a decade until the medications came along with an acceptable profile of side effects [the Prozac family] and patients can now take them for a long period of time. This observation, which was made in the late seventies, has made a difference in the lives of three to five percent of the population. What is the psychotherapeutic part? That comes in your approach to these patients, because they can't just take the medication and get well. They have no social skills, they are loners. And one of the things that may happen if you treat a patient like this is that you may get a wedding invitation. For the first time in their life they feel good enough to date, to fall in love, and to marry. That is a lot of change fast, and psychotherapy can help them."

Akiskal's story also points out that psychiatric science is now configured, at least for many of the more senior scientists, as a rejection of the psychodynamic approach to mental illness. This rebellious aspect of psychiatric science might well vanish in two decades. But now it is very real. Many of the more senior scientists (particularly those who went to medical school when the psychoanalytic model still dominated psychiatry) tell their career story around that turning point. One brilliant, maverick scientist was still angry at his analytic supervisors from a residency of decades earlier. He told me that one of his patients had complained of sudden attacks of intense anxiety in public places, the symptoms of which would now be called "panic attacks." When he wondered out loud to his residency super-visor whether the problem could be organic, his supervisor chided him for his fear of therapeutic intimacy. Now the standard psychopharmacological line on panic disorder is that 95 percent of the cases are manageable with antidepressants. The maverick scientist still has not lost his fury at an explanatory system that told him that he was emotionally inadequate when he questioned the standard psychoanalytic explanation of his patient's pain. Neither have many others who became the first large generation of psychiatric scientists and tell stories about psychoanalytic supervisors who questioned their motives when they questioned the psychological cause of illness.

Many of these older scientists adopt a style that seems deliberately to signal that they are not the tweedy, reserved psychoanalysts of their super-visors' generation. This is not true of all scientists. Neither Cole nor Akiskal has chosen this style, nor, in my experience, have any female scientists. The male scientists who do display little stern abstinence. They pump iron, play squash, and are the aging athletes of psychiatry. They go drinking and dancing with their lab technicians and junior colleagues. They talk quickly and loudly. Their ideal is the scientist—usually the laboratory scientist, even if they themselves do clinical research. They are fiercely scornful of Freud, some of them the more intensely because they came to Freud after being philosophy majors and initially saw Freud as a means of putting philosophical skills to practical use. Many of them came of age in the era not only of Thorazine but of LSD, and many came to the recognition of brain rather than mind through youthful experimentation during college. "One of the things that was pretty important was getting into the drug scene," one of these men explained to me. "That was what you did then, but it was pretty striking for someone interested in psychodynamics who had been taught that our experience of reality is shaped by our history with our parents. I mean, one day I went along to my professor's office—and he was a pretty well known analyst, as well as being a professor, and I was trip-ping my brains out and the swirls in the carpet stood up and walked around the room and I thought, if a drug can do this to my sense of reality, what am I doing taking all this psychoanalytic stuff at face value?" Above all, these men present themselves as people to be judged by their accomplishments, not by their personalities.[6]

George Banks (a pseudonym) is a good example of this kind of psychi-atric scientist, although no one, of course, is "typical." I met him on a balmy spring day in California. He had an elite, rugged, sailing-on-the-bay look. He was Protestant. He was in his forties. He lifted weights. He iden-tified himself primarily as a scientist. He was a clinical researcher and was looking for interesting connections between behaviors and drug response, and he also had an extensive clinical practice in psychopharmacology. He had, however, started out planning to be a psychoanalyst.

"I went off to college to study philosophy, and it was great," he told me. "I was definitely on the humanities track, not natural science, not even social sciences. I wanted to know how people had conceived of the great problems throughout human history. They were heady, passionate times. We would stay up all night, talking about Suzanne Langer, thinking exciting thoughts. I did some pretty good work, actually. But you couldn't really go to grad school then [in the middle 1970s]. I had sent off for applications to a number of graduate programs. One of them—I think it was the University of California—sent me an application with a frank letter, thanking me for my interest and not wishing to discourage me but wanting me to know, before I committed myself, that there were no jobs currently available in the field. I went to Europe for a time, to be a little closer to the sources of Western ideas, and I visited Freud's house in Vienna. That was pretty powerful, and I thought that medicine was kind of practical, and that was good. I had what seemed like an inspired insight at the time, that to be a psychoanalyst would allow me not only to reflect on life but also to provide a service that would guide others through the philosophical way of life. So I went to medical school to be a psychoanalyst."

Many of the older scientists first chose psychiatry in order to learn about psychoanalysis. A psychiatrist who initially conceived of himself as a future psychoanalyst and then rejected that view is likely to be quite clear—and angry—about the conceptual orientation that sets the two approaches apart. George continued, "I'm sure I read more of Freud's work than any of my colleagues. I read at least three quarters of it by the end of college. It was fascinating, that he recognized that the attraction the patient felt towards him seemed to be transferred from other relationships, that he could sit back and say, this isn't just me. I had never been in psychotherapy myself, had never seen it done, and I didn't really have any clinical experience. It was all very interesting, but it was all pretty theoretical. That probably is one of the reasons I became disenchanted by the model. It's much harder to become disenchanted once you've paid for your own psychoanalysis." (This is probably an accurate remark. To go into analytic training and claim at the end of the more than one hundred thousand dollars it costs you that the enterprise is misguided demands a great deal of our limited human capacity for disinterested objectivity.)

"So anyway, I entered medical school having done all this work in philosophy and psychoanalysis, but right at the beginning, I think I had a really strong interest in neuroscience. Neuroanatomy, neuropharmacology, the brain. And the psychiatry teaching was dumb. Like, you should be kind to your patients because they are people just like you. I was insulted. Then

I signed up for a course that turned out to be about the leading ideas in biological psychiatry by the leading researcher into the genetics of schizophrenia. I had the sense that things were moving, that these people were in the forefront of something, and meanwhile there was this dull course taught by a psychoanalyst who was presenting Freud in a really diluted way. I had the impression that I'd read more than he had. He spoke as if he had no understanding that there were several Freudian models of mind and many post-Freudian ones, as if he had no awareness of his intellectual roots. I tried to ask questions, and I would be given various responses, like 'You're going to have to delve further,' but it didn't seem like anyone could tell me exactly what they were seeing that I wasn't. It was like the analysts had this knowledge but they couldn't impart it. And if they did really understand, why weren't the patients getting better?

"Still, I entered my psychiatry rotation with contempt for psychopharmacology. But within three days, I remember this guy came in from the street absolutely psychotic. His mind was splattered on the wall. He came swinging onto the ward, everyone's tugging on their neckties [to get them off in case he tried to choke them], and he gets an injection of Haldol [an antipsychotic], and within a hour and a half he was a normal human being again—idiosyncratic, mind you, but making sense in his own way—and I was stunned, absolutely stunned that a very simple and intrinsically uninteresting intervention could so dramatically transform the subjective universe. I had been completely in the psychodynamic camp, and this just woke me up to the fact that there is this other dimension, and it is real. It is concrete.

"I was still pretty dynamic. I was trying to do psychoanalytic research, which was completely obsessional and now, I think, pretty meaningless, trying to define undefined terms and at the same time getting pretty angry at some of these psychodynamic diagnoses which let you claim victimhood. But then in residency I started out on a largely biomedical unit, and it was a completely unanticipated delight. Patients were getting better. If the first medication didn't work, you tried another, and there was always a solution to a problem. And you felt so powerful and effective because you were actually doing this action. It was really exciting. One of the key questions was whether all people with psychotic symptoms were schizophrenic or whether some of them were manic depressive. This was terribly important, because if they were manic you could give them lithium, which you wouldn't do if they were schizophrenic. And it was very exciting to see the way the doctors approached the problem and the impact: these guys were changing the way psychiatry was done in this country. It was totally different from the psychodynamic unit, where the patients were treated for much, much longer periods of time, with minimal medication interventions and maximal interpretations. There the patients never got to go home and the staff were always second-guessing you and talking about you behind your back and the emotional tone of the place was incredible. The nurses were always irritated or offended by something you did or didn't mean to do, and you would be called to account for these tiny slights you weren't even aware of. You were always apologizing for something, you never did anything right. Part of the staff's task seemed to be to expose you as completely as possible. On top of it, the patients really didn't get better.

"And it didn't make any sense. Even then I thought that the psychoanalytically oriented physicians weren't listening to the right part of the patient's story. They might be listening, but they'd already made up their minds that the illness was due to something else. And from my perspective, to see a college student doing fine and suddenly end up manic and then come down with lithium and be back in control, it really is much more consistent with acute episodes of the brain than it is with childhood conflicts that are so quickly erupting and resolving. And [in the late 1970s] I could admit a patient and write a great dynamic summary and present her to a case conference and someone might suggest a psychopharm consult and then another person would say, 'Why do that?' And yet I sort of felt that another dynamic formulation might be as plausible and it wouldn't really matter if I'd chosen that and in retrospect of course it doesn't, what matters is that the patient has classic major depression, she's not thinking well or eating well and she needs an antidepressant, fast.

"I had this analytic preceptor, who wasn't pleased that I didn't have complaints about the biological unit and was pretty explicit about not spending time with those types because, he said, people take up sides around here and you'll find yourself on the wrong side. Watch who you chat with at lunch, that kind of thing.

"And gradually, my confidence just eroded. I realized what had happened when I read this book about language and the brain which had a really coherent view of brain function and the way it affects speech. I couldn't believe that anyone could still believe, as they did, that stuttering was rooted in childhood conflict. I mean, you'd see psychoanalytic interpretations of ulcers, that the introjected mother was eating the stomach lining, before they realized that ulcers were caused by bacteria. And I realized that whenever an effective biological treatment or explanation emerged, there went the psychoanalytic explanation, and I thought, what next?

"I saw an intellectual pattern emerging, that psychoanalytic theory was so plastic that it could explain anything. That that is the nature of psychoanalytic principles. You just can't test them. You can make any conclusion consistent with the story, and I started to learn that I had patients that I treated with one psychoanalytic supervisor one year and another the next, and with each different supervisor I'd be given a different causal story about the patient. And the analysts, after all those years in therapy, maybe they improved in some ways, but judging by what I saw they seemed to be every bit as human and every bit as unenlightened. I got involved in my own research and found an incredible wealth of new information and ways of looking at things. Every once in a while I'd contrast it with other views, but I just found them wanting. The biomedical model just seemed to be more exciting and to offer more chances of new insights and better treatment, better understanding."

Banks is describing a time when there seemed to be an either-or choice between the biomedical and the psychodynamic. Leaving that aside, his account captures a central feature of the psychiatric scientist: that the personhood of neither the psychiatrist nor the patient is relevant to the efficacy of psychiatric treatment. By "personhood," I mean the idiosyncratic features that make someone who he is: how and when he gets angry, what he fears, how he raises his eyebrow, whether he is abrupt or rude or gentle. Those features (unless they are diagnostic) simply aren't salient to whether the psychiatrist has chosen the right medication or whether the medication will work. The independence of personhood and the things that count repeats itself through most aspects of psychiatric science.

For a start, scientists can be indifferent human beings and still have good reputations as scientists, whereas a psychiatric therapist, whose authority rests on being perceived as a good, kind, reliable listener, a non-surgical Marcus Welby, damages his professional reputation and his income by becoming known as a jerk. The same is, if possible, more true for psychoanalysts, whose authority rests in addition upon their own experience of and response to their personal psychoanalysis. We know psychiatrists who might be regarded as narcissistic fools, and some of them are remarkably successful, in part because of a social context that persuades their patients that it is they who are the inadequate parties. But calling a psychodynamic psychiatrist a jerk has a different implication for his work than insulting a scientist in the same way. A therapist's work depends directly on his human capacity. A scientist's does not; and many esteemed scientists have been known for their human incapacities as well. We think more warmly of scientists who are generous and kind, but those qualities do not make their science great. This was the unsettling revelation for those who read *The Double Helix,* that the most capable of scientists could at times come across as an accomplished lout.

The scientist's personal qualities do matter if they affect the reliability of his empirical reports. "Data" emerge out of the morass of real-world particularities—the skewed measurement, the contaminated sample, the imprecise assay—that embed the general mechanism that the scientist wants to identify. Scientists strain to see the data through the specificity of the experimenter who conducted the experiment and the lab where it was done, through the crankiness of the equipment or the humid weather. They reach for what they take to be the regularities beneath the surface noise of individual events. They need to be able to believe that the experimenter's report is an accurate reflection of what happened; that he does not publish without double-checking his results; that his laboratory is orderly enough that his published work is likely to be replicable. "Scientists know so much about the natural world," the sociologist of science Steven Shapin remarks, "by knowing so much about whom they can trust."[7] It is so hard to get evidence for one's scientific theory that one's reputation for coming by it honestly is terribly important.

When a scientist is trusted, what is trusted is the data. The individuality of both patient and doctor fade to unimportance. From the point of view of his work, the person of the scientist is less important than the data he collects and the papers he writes. George Banks was morally offended by the discovery that different psychoanalysts describe the same patient in different ways; that psychoanalytic theories might not be disprovable; that psychoanalysts lack interpretive caution and controls. He was shocked by analysts' relationship to their description of psychiatric patients and by the way they treat what he calls "data." He assumes that good descriptions of psychiatric patients must be extended beyond the individual: that a door blew open not because the wind was strong that day but because when the wind blows with such-and-such a force, it moves objects whose resistance is below a certain threshold. Banks wants psychiatry to make claims that are independent of the particularities of the psychiatrist and his patient.

This ethos is very different from that of a clinician, a person who treats patients to help them, not to study them. A clinician—psychodynamic or psychopharmacological—is interested in what can be done for a person right here, for this unique person with his own story and his idiosyncratic responses to different medications. What matters is whether a patient gets better. A scientist—even though she may be a good clinician when she works in a clinic as a doctor—is interested as a scientist in patients as data points. When she goes to conferences and wanders from poster to poster, she is interested in the experimental results that have been generated. Often she is more interested in experimental results as additional data points than she is in a researcher's more general theory. When she refers to conferences as having "lots of good science," she means that she saw good data on interesting problems rather than (usually) that she acquired an approved and agreed-upon conclusion that she can take back to help her with her patients. Scientists go to conferences to look at data and to get ideas about data that will eventually produce interventions that clinicians can use to help their patients; clinicians go to conferences to learn from the scientists what to do to help their patients.

The joy of doing science seems to come from this sense you have as a scientist that you have discovered something "true." Randy Gollub felt in doing each project that she was doing something fundamentally important. The psychiatric scientists I knew saw themselves as finding things out about the world that no one else yet knew. They did behave as if their own discoveries were contingent: true given what we know now, true given the questionable accuracy of the categories we now use, true subject to revision. Still, for all the subtlety of this decade of strained awareness of the flimsy hold we have on the real, these scientists really seemed to feel that they were on a search for a bodily mechanism that could explain some aspect of mental illness, that they would find one, and that "true" for them meant true for all people of a certain type, true beyond the surface, the appearances, and the individual idiosyncracies of human beings. They felt so strongly that they were doing this that they were sometimes shocked when everyday human politics got into the interstices of their science. That, for instance, was what happened to my friend Susan.

Susan (a pseudonym) had trained at an elite residency program. Then she spent some years at a research institute where the brightest young psychiatric scientists are invited to spend a postresidency fellowship. She had decided to become a scientist in part because of a premenstrually psychotic woman she'd encountered during residency: "I saw a patient who was quite psychotic, and we didn't know the etiology, couldn't figure out what was going on. My unit director said, 'Don't medicate her until we have a better sense of the problem.' The next thing you know, she walks into my office and she is crystal clear and she has her period. It turned out she had gotten psychotic in response to her menstrual period. That was pretty fascinating. We followed her, did serial taps on her spinal fluid, and we found that during her period her dopamine/serotonin ratio went off kilter. We could track that for her and medicate her appropriately, and she no longer became psychotic with her menstrual cycle."

Susan wrote a paper on that in residency. To turn the anecdote into a scientific study, she advertised for more subjects, collected more spinal fluid, and analyzed the data. When she arrived at her research institute, she continued the work and found that women often had higher prolactin levels and lower thyroid levels than usual during their premenstrual phase. She reasoned that sleep deprivation might reverse those trends, and it did. She found a research group working with people suffering from seasonal affective disorder, who respond with particular intensity to the lower level of light in winter and become depressed. As she became involved with the project, she began to talk to the patients. The women said that their premenstrual syndrome improved when they were treated with light for the seasonal affective disorder. Susan speculated that the light suppressed their melatonin. Indeed, she then discovered that the good effects of the light therapy could be reversed just by giving the women doses of melatonin. She moved into the field of "chronobiology"—"Hormones and neurotransmitters are connected all over the place," she said. "It gets messy"—and started flying around the world to attend meetings on circadian rhythms. She became widely known for her work on women, hormones, light, and psychiatric illness.

When the official psychiatric diagnostic manual was being revised in the middle eighties, Susan was part of the battalion of psychiatrists who helped evaluate the existing diagnostic structure. She and others argued that there should be a category for "late luteal phase dysphoric disorder," which by this point was more commonly thought of as PMS, or premenstrual syndrome. To receive the diagnosis, a woman had to experience five of the following ten symptoms before her period, of which the first four were the most important: (1) marked affective lability (suddenly feeling sad, tearful, angry, or irritable); (2) persistent and marked anger or irritability; (3) marked anxiety, tension, feelings of being "keyed up" or "on edge"; (4) markedly depressed mood, feelings of hopelessness, or self-deprecating thoughts; (5) decreased interest in usual activities, such as work, friends, hobbies; (6) easy fatigability or marked lack of energy; (7) subjective sense of difficulty in concentrating; (8) marked change in appetite; (9) hypersomnia or insomnia; (10) physical symptoms such as breast tenderness or swelling, headaches, joint or muscle pain, a sensation of bloating, or weight gain. Everyone on the committee voted to include the diagnosis in the diagnostic manual.

At this point the Women's Committee of the American Psychiatric Association, aided by the Women's Committee of the American Psychological Association, held meetings, contacted the media, and in general made their distress about the diagnosis so public that the officials of the American Psychiatric Association backed down from their pledge to support the scientists. The diagnosis was printed in the appendix, as a topic for further research. Susan was horrified that a belief in what *should* be the case should override what science had demonstrated to *be* the case: that some women had premenstrual periods that caused them to experience symptoms of mental illness. It was unfortunate, but it happened to be true. "Those women just didn't want to see any difference between men and women at all," she complained. "I thought, this is *science*. This is supposed to be a scientific document based on clinical work. Some women have these problems. It's ridiculous to think that men and women aren't different. They have different endocrine systems. Hormones protect against some diseases, but they make you more vulnerable to others. That's the science. It was so upsetting to find out that you could be scuppered by the media, as if the politics could matter more than the truth."

The psychoanalytic theory of mind will never anymore be understood to provide the explanatory foundation of mental illness, because that foundation, as it is culturally constructed in this age of electron microscopes and genetic analysis, lies beyond personhood, in biological microstructures that escape uniqueness. There is a quality here of the deepest and most real. It has a moral quality: that this knowledge is what really counts, what really makes a difference, what in the end creates the greatest good for the greatest number. Even if one scientist accomplishes little, every scientist participates in the aspirations of the whole. And that is why when young psychiatrists choose to become clinicians, they can see themselves as choosing self-indulgence or lifestyle over the search for truth. For many young psychiatrists, at least in residency, the moral authority of science outranks the moral authority of helping people one person at a time. That is why they may feel shamed by their decision to leave scientific research behind and go out into the private or public sector to become clinicians.

THE PSYCHOANALYST

When I began this work, I found a mentor in a gifted senior analyst, who told me, when I spoke to him about the pathways of young psychiatrists, that I should read *Magister Ludi*. What I'd told him, he said, reminded him of the selection process for the elite players of the fictional glass bead game at the novel's center. He thought the novel would help me to understand the process of becoming a psychoanalyst.

Magister Ludi (The Glass Bead Game) is Hermann Hesse's most elaborate novel, possibly his best. It presents the putative history of Joseph Knecht (in German, "servant"), the legendary master of the glass bead game, and his rise to prominence. The game itself is never fully described, yet it becomes clear that it demands not only sophisticated intellectual skill but a kind of personal grace and purity that direct ambition will thwart. The hero "had no desire to dominate, took no pleasure in commanding; he desired the contemplative life far more than the active life, and would have been content to spend many years more, if not his whole life, as an obscure student, an inquiring and reverent pilgrim."[8] He becomes a powerful ruler of men. Most of Hesse's novels have a sometimes irritatingly noble character who struggles against a plot of human pettiness, and Knecht is his fullest characterization.

This is an unusual way to describe what is, after all, a well-institutionalized profession, but it captures a quality that is often missed by those who look at psychoanalysis from the outside. This quality is its ethos, its moral tone. Psychoanalysis has a profound moral vision, but that vision is not focused on the rights and wrongs of behavior. That is why Philip Rieff, in a famous book, *Freud: The Mind of a Moralist,* could argue that though Freud had a sternly moralistic mind, psychoanalysis by its nature was amoral because it ignored conventional standards. A world that took psychoanalysis seriously, Rieff said, would have no ethical core because its culture would have no basis for guidance. Analysts do tend—as Earle pointed out—to listen in order to understand, not to judge. They want to know why someone committed adultery and lied about it more than they want to condemn the action. They are interested in intentions, both conscious and unconscious, and in how those intentions lead to action. They see, as one senior analyst put it, action as in service to the self, and what fascinates them is not what people do but why—what self those actions serve. Analysts also believe that the "why" is inherently unknowable, because aspects of one's own psyche are always hidden and an observer can never see clearly because his own unconscious intentions distort his vision. But analysts also believe that you can come to know more than you did, even if you can never know everything. The psychoanalytic ethos, then, focuses on the honesty with which you try to know and the caring in the way you try to help another person know. If what really counts for the psychiatric scientist is knowledge, what really counts for the psychoanalyst is the process of coming to know. Joseph Knecht was a model for my mentor because he was not self-interested: he was able to act for others, to serve them, without the intrusion of his own wants, fears, and needs. My mentor did not really believe that it was possible to be like that. But he took it as a kind of analytic ideal.

A psychoanalyst is evaluated by peers first and foremost as a certain kind of person. That is, analysts judge themselves and other analysts on the basis of criteria that are primarily about who they are, not what they do. In part this is the simple consequence of a practice in which no one ever sees a practitioner perform except his patients, who (as analysts see it) are not able to have an objective judgment about an analyst's performance. In fact, satisfied customers do generate more customers. At least some of an analyst's patients come to him because they have heard about him from other patients. An analyst's reputation owes something to what other analysts have heard about the way he treats his patients. I was once standing in the cocktail lounge during the annual meeting of the American Psychoanalytic Association and, striking up a conversation with the man waiting behind me in line for wine, asked him what he thought of an analyst whose work I had been reading. The man winced, and said with contempt that the writer sounded good on the page but he was mean to his patients. An analyst's reputation also owes something to the way he appears in public. When he speaks, his listeners draw conclusions not only about whether he is smart or stupid but about whether they would send a patient to him for analysis. This fact about psychoanalysis not unnaturally shapes the way analysts present their public papers.

The main gathering of the American Psychoanalytic Association occurs in New York the week before Christmas. Despite the freezing, wintry weather, the conference is called the "fall meeting." It is always held at the Waldorf-Astoria, a hotel, like the profession itself, that is elegant and nostalgic for its past. The first time I attended, the hotel seemed full of elderly Europeans in fur coats embracing in the lobby. (One young analytic candidate told me that going to the American Psychoanalytic Association meetings was like watching dinosaurs deliberate over their own extinction.) Lately among the two thousand attendees I can see more of the young people who are, rather surprisingly, entering the profession. The demand for full psychoanalysis is declining rapidly, so that in few places apart from New York can analysts with full analytic practices be found, and few enough even there. But most people do not enter analytic training in order to establish an analytic practice. Far more, in my experience, choose analytic training because they believe, probably correctly, that the training will improve their psychotherapeutic skills. Some of them simply want to become part of what even now is thought to be a psychiatric elite. "A friend of mine said that she was interested in psychotherapy," one of the residents remarked to me, "and that she'd probably go to one of the uptown analysts, and I thought to myself, right, that's what I should be if I want to make it, an uptown analyst." But my mentor thought that people entered analytic training only if their own personal pain drove them to it.

The fall meetings of the American Psychoanalytic Association have a hushed, respectful quality. The men wear professorial jackets, sometimes a little scruffy. The women wear soft, textured knee-length suits in muted colors. These are not sharp-edged businessmen. They are people who work alone, often in little offices in their attics or basements; cramped, sparsely furnished rooms at the margins of their more capacious houses, with a narrow entrance at the back or side so that a patient need never see the wife unpacking groceries on the kitchen table. This conference is their social fraternity as well as their public examination. Their clothes are intended to display their graciousness and their carefully calibrated tolerance for the unconventional. "Anthropologists," a psychoanalyst said to me with some disapproval, "can be flamboyant. Psychoanalysts are not allowed to be flamboyant."

183

The papers given at the meetings are also intended to display their presenters' psychoanalytic suitability. It is common for an analyst to criticize another analyst not only for his intellectual argument but for his quality as an analyst, which is imagined on the basis of what he has written in his paper and the way in which he has presented it. One senior analyst, for instance, dismissed a paper he didn't like at the American Psychoanalytic Association meeting with "He struck me as somebody who really had this very limited view of what it was that he was doing and how he was doing it. I was struck by his exhibitionism. He really took off, and he was, I think, the least qualified person there. And I could imagine how he might be with a patient." In other words, the senior analyst disliked the intellectual content of the paper, formulated his dislike around the personal characteristics of the paper presenter, and summarized his criticism by suggesting that these were not characteristics that would be helpful for an analyst doing analysis. This is not an uncommon sort of comment, nor indeed is it easy not to wonder, when watching analysts deliver a paper, what they are like with a patient, what it would be like to be in analysis with them. Just being on a panel, however, can increase referrals, a term used to describe one doctor's decision to refer a patient to another doctor. The better known the analyst is, the more his name crops up when potential analysands ask for advice. "It really helps when someone has a patient coming here from elsewhere, and they get my name because that analyst heard me give a paper," an analyst remarked to me. "If they've heard someone speak, it really helps. I get a lot of referrals from the outside."

The result of this scrutiny is that the papers delivered at these meetings are often somewhat odd attempts to convey the restrained sobriety of the field's ideal representation of the good analyst: unexcitable (excitability would imply that the analyst would respond to his own needs rather than those of his patient), unimpressionable (impressionability would imply that the analyst could not retain sufficient emotional distance from his patients; the result of this hesitation to show gullibility is that the only really acceptable reference is Freud), and reserved (there are lengthy, laboriously argued papers on the question of under what circumstances it might be appropriate to touch a patient on the shoulder: none, for the most part). The technical term for this restraint is "abstinence." The analyst abstains from responding to the analysand in kind but analyzes the analysand's behavior and discourse. In demonstration of these ideal traits, paper presentations at the American Psychoanalytic Association are sometimes dull. Most papers are read in a flat monotone devoid of emotional inflection.

At the same time, some papers attempt to indicate the analyst's gift for human warmth. Warmth is not an obvious characteristic of this severe, restrained world. Yet in recent years, as psychoanalysis has become a buyer's market and particularly after self psychology began to provide a theoretical justification for paying attention to a therapist's relationship skills, appearing to be approachable and easy to talk to has become important. Analytic "stars" have acquired sufficient authority to perform their papers as theatrical events: to modulate their tone of voice; to show evidence of having practiced the talk before presenting it to an audience. They are eager to indicate their personableness, their interest in other people, and their capacity to understand. They speak of their concern for their patients and speak lovingly of patients who have been "failed" by their analysts. They talk of discovering their patients' capacity to forgive themselves. They will, if they accidentally make a Freudian slip (and analysts not infrequently make such slips when presenting papers), smile at the audience as if to say, I am human, I forgive myself, I share with you the tolerance of human weakness.

The route into this contradictory psychoanalytic world is closely guarded, and despite the fact that no analyst-to-be is ever directly observed in the analytic hour, there are certain performance criteria for success. Candidates must meet three conditions in order to graduate. They must have completed a training analysis at an institute with a senior member who has been designated a "training analyst." In analysis, a patient comes each day (more or less) of the five-day workweek, for roughly hour-long sessions (actually forty-five or fifty minutes) each day. Analysis often lasts for six to eight years. Candidates must also participate in seminars on psychoanalytic theory and practice that run perhaps six hours a week for four years. In addition, they must carry out three analyses, of which one must have reached termination and the two others been ongoing for at least two years, and each of which has been supervised weekly by a training analyst. The process is fantastically expensive. The training analysis can cost $20,000 for each of five or more years, and weekly supervision can add $5,000 per annum per case; by three years into the training, when the candidate is still in analysis, still attending classes, but also carrying "control" cases for a very low fee, the time spent in training can run more than twenty hours per week. The standard calculation made by psychiatric residents is that analytic training could generate a $40,000 drop in income for five years or more and that the total time in training would be at least eight years. (Time spent in training could otherwise generate income.) Nor is this loss necessarily recouped: nonanalytically trained psychiatrists often set their fees as high as those who are analytically trained.

In 1990, the American Psychoanalytic Association surveyed its approximately three thousand members (2,083 returned the questionnaires).[9] Analysts, the report noted, are not young. The typical analyst graduated

from training in 1972 and was in his late fifties; "his" because only 17 percent were female, although there has recently been a marked increase of
women in the profession. He earned an average of $128,000 and was a psy-
chiatrist. He worked an average of forty-five hours a week, with 76 percent
of that time spent in private practice. He had two analytic patients—training analysts had an average of four analytic patients, but the modal number
was two—with a total of eighteen patients, most of whom he saw once or
twice a week in psychotherapy. (When an analyst sees patients in analysis
four times a week, as well as patients who come in less frequently, he refers
to the second group as "psychotherapy patients." He treats his psychotherapy patients with psychoanalytically oriented psychodynamic psychotherapy.) He spent most of his time, then, doing something other than
psychoanalysis in the strict sense.

The training analyst is the most powerful member of this field. A training analyst is one of a subset of analysts associated with a particular institute who have been handpicked to do all the supervision and analysis of
candidates at that institute. The American Psychoanalytic Association sets
certain restrictions on those who can be named training analysts: they
must have carried five analytic cases since graduation and written case
reports about three of them. In the golden years of psychoanalysis, most
institutions had many analysts who were qualified to be training analysts
but who were not (or not yet) selected. This could be a powerful conventionalizing force, because training analysts were often not chosen until
years after their own graduation. The fear of being passed over could keep
an analyst's criticism of his seniors in check for a decade.

Training analysts earn more than other analysts ($139,000 compared to
$112,000 for the just-graduated in the 1990 study). They have a steady
stream of patients, because all candidates must have analysis and supervision, and the candidates pay the training analysts for their time. Training
analysts run the local institutes, and the mystery of their selection process
has a kind of Skull & Bones mystique that reduces grown men and women
to childish panic. "To be selected as a training analyst," said one aspirant,
visibly more agitated on this topic than he had been during our talk about
theory, "they have to scrutinize your character, which is a whole mysterious
process. Talk about being subject to their moral attitudes! God knows who
says what about you and in what context—I mean, they integrate what they
hear from the couch, and it is this *totally* bizarre process."

The history of psychoanalysis is a history of schism. Analytic institutes
are famous for their tribalism and the smallness and ferocity of their quar-
rels. "They *all* act like they haven't been analyzed," an analyst said bleakly
in an interview about psychoanalytic social life. More than 20 percent of
the respondents in the 1990 study complained about institute politics.

(The authors of the study pointed out that the complainers were not training analysts.) One respondent fumed, "On the national level, virtually every decision of the American [he refers to the Association and, for example, the decision to allow non-M.D.s to receive training] seems to have been wrong or ill timed; opportunities to unify psychoanalysis have been squandered or allowed to slip out of its grasp; on the local level, pettiness abounds."[10] Many local institutes have splintered after terrible fights.

Some of this death-grip infighting over trifles must have to do with the odd quality of these relationships. Most analysands, after the emotional drama of psychoanalytic treatment, walk out of their analyst's office and never see him again. When analytic candidates finish their treatment, by contrast, they join their analysts as supposed equals in the intimate setting of the committee room. All of a sudden, the lopsided power relationship of the consulting room becomes a relationship between peers. The transition is hard and, some would say, never complete. Small squabbles become family dramas with contingents of angry, loyal, competitive siblings. This stems from the terrible contradiction of consulting room relationships: that they generate feelings of intense emotional attachment that violate most of the standard cultural expectations of human closeness.

Even the architecture surrounding these relationships is unusual. The analyst has an office, which often has been architecturally rebuilt so that arriving and departing patients never lay eyes on each other. The door to the clinical consulting room is extra thick, like the "piano doors" of music practice rooms, or doubled with two doors to insulate the room from the outside world. The consulting room itself is quietly spare. I met only one analyst whose office resembled the sprawling collectorly chaos of Freud's own, with a kelim-covered couch and antiques strewn around the room. Usually there is an unadorned analytic couch—a flat bed with a slightly raised headrest—in leather or tweed and some abstract art. The couch's headrest is covered by a paper napkin, freshly changed for each patient. The analyst sits behind the couch's head, often on a comfortable black leather swivel chair. Directly across from him is another, often identical, chair for the psychotherapy patients whom he sees sitting up. The chairs are identical so that the patient will not feel belittled by his own chair's inadequacy.

In analysis, an analytic patient lies on the couch, from which he cannot see the analyst. Analysts often say that it is easier to do therapy when you don't have to look at the patient. It is easier because you do not need to observe the social niceties; you can, as one analyst observed, scratch your behind. It is easier, also, because violating the social niceties is what analysis is about. An analyst is silent about the common subjects of everyday conversation. He does not tell analysands about the people he knows. He does not talk about his family, his work, or himself. He does not respond to his patients with the usual conversational latency. Often, he says very little. He waits and lets them say more. If he tells his patients that he will be away on vacation and they ask him where he is going, he is more likely to ask them what their fantasies are about his vacation than to reveal where he is headed. This habit, which is useful in the consulting room, is sometimes maddening in ordinary social conversation, into which it sometimes creeps. When an analyst does speak, he rarely says all that he knows, infers, or speculates about the other person when in conversation with that person. "You're taught never really to say anything during the analysis," a senior analyst explained.

This is a profession that you enter to help other people. Yet its method demands that an analysand, the person in analysis, lie on a couch so that he or she is unable to see the analyst, and the demand of abstinence further dictates that the analyst not reveal herself, not talk about her home life or her feelings. In analysis, a patient is asked to reveal his most private thoughts and emotions, an act that usually entails reciprocity. Not only is an analyst not expected to reveal herself, she is expected not even to respond with normal emotions. "When the young man in one of his first hours with me on the couch took out a cigarette and lit it," a well-known analyst reminisced in a famous text on psychoanalytic technique, "I asked him how he felt when he decided to light the cigarette. He answered that he knew he was not supposed to smoke in his previous analysis and now he supposed that I, too, would forbid it. I told him immediately that all I wanted at that moment was to know what feelings, ideas and sensations were going on in him at the moment that he decided to light the cigarette."[11] Analysis is a deliberate frustration in the name of caring. "You're on the couch," one analyst explained, "on my lovely couch staring off onto the blank wall and window. I'm sitting here, and you say something. You don't know whether I'm yawning or frowning or smiling or whether that funny look of interest is on my face."

The structure of the psychoanalytic relationship is one of great emotional deprivation. In a conversation in which one person is pouring forth a tale of pain, the psychoanalytic relationship does not allow the other listener to respond with his face, with a touch, nor even much with his words. It does not allow him to reciprocate or respond in kind.[12] At the same time, the analytic relationship permits the analysand an extraordinary degree of freedom. Here, for the first time, he is encouraged to say anything—everything—that enters his mind, without worrying whom he might offend or what social mores he might violate. It permits him to say everything and places him in a passive, dependent, exposed position from which to do so. The combination of the analysand's confessional experience and the analyst's inhibition makes for a very asymmetrical relationship. The asymmetry makes the confessor—the patient—feel extremely vulnerable. And the consequence of the vulnerability is a rush of emotion.

It is a remarkable rush, over the top and out of control. Within months, weeks, or even minutes of the first analytic encounter, patients develop powerful feelings about their analysts or their analyses. The content of those feelings can be wildly varied: hate, love, fear, anger, anything. But the intensity is undeniable and obvious. Residents become deeply uncomfortable when they catch sight of their analyst in the hospital. A young woman I met on the plane to the American Psychiatric Association meeting said, smiling nervously, that she actually felt quite shaken and insecure these days, that she often cried without reason, but that this was to be expected in the first year of analysis and she was sure the analysis would eventually help. Young psychiatrists hear their peers report, as I heard a resident do, that a resident had been saying thus-and-such in his session with his therapist and then "He"—using the pronoun in a hushed, reverential tone—had said such-and-such. They become suddenly, deeply, awkwardly, pinkly embarrassed when they talk about their analysts and unexpectedly and excruciatingly shy when they attend one of his lectures at the local institute. They arrive at their analyst's office and burst into tears, because it is her office. Wherever they come from, these feelings grip an analysand with such iron teeth that it is not unusual to hear people declare that their life was profoundly disrupted for the first two years they were in analysis and that their analyst has become the most important person in their life. The violence of these feelings cannot simply be attributed to the cultural expectations about psychoanalysis. The feelings are too sudden, too unexpected, too strong.

As I have said before, the analytic explanation of this intensity is that the feelings re-create the experience of earlier relationships from which they are transferred. As one analyst wrote, "The important and enduring aspect of the concept of transference neurosis [is]: it defines the analytic process as [a] repetition of early pathogenic experiences and their intrapsychic pathological vicissitudes."[13] Hans Loewald, who is known for the brilliance and subtlety of his work on transference, goes on to pry gently loose the idea that transference only evokes feelings from the past, and he and later analysts do articulate the complexity of transference as incorporating an analysand's present relationship with the analyst and the great range of experiences incorporated in an analysand's response to the analyst. But the analytic discussion of transference tends to ignore the far more basic (and anthropological) question of why these feelings are so very, very strong.

I suspect that the structure of the analytic relationship itself, and particularly its emotional deprivation, generates the intensity of the analysand's response. Not the content: undoubtedly the content of each analysand's emotional response to the analyst is the result of the personal history of that analysand's experience. But it may be the case that the intensity of the feelings, this great amplification, is the consequence of the unusual communicative structure of the analytic relationship: that the analysand tells the secrets of his soul to a person who does not reciprocate, does not respond in kind, and whose face he cannot even see. In a "normal" relationship—one that conforms to standard expectations of human relatedness—when one person makes himself vulnerable to another person, that person reciprocates by being equally vulnerable, telling the story of her personal afflictions and struggles. In a "normal" relationship, one person's expression of love or hatred is met by a symmetrically powerful feeling, not a cool voice inquiring in what way the analyst is lovable or despicable. In a "normal" relationship, you see the face of the person to whom you are talking, and you read immediately the emotional response of your companion. That none of these normal features is present in an analytic relationship makes that relationship most unusual. Yet the emotional strength of the analysand's experience probably stems from a very general feature of human relationships, the fact that emotions intensify the way we communicate. Emotions help us to reach one another. If I tell you that my foot hurts, you may listen; if I scream in pain, you will help me or flee.[14] When one person opens his heart to another and the response is not "normal" but not a straightforward rejection (the beloved has not said no, but perhaps the beloved is a little deaf), the emotional volume may go up in a desperate attempt to get through. Psychoanalytic relationships have a distorted reciprocity in which one person is powerful, distant, and withholding and the other is vulnerable, yearning, and revealed. They are relationships in which the patient feels forced to scream. This is useful to the psychoanalysis, because when a patient screams—or rather, amplifies her emotions because she feels that she has not been heard—the analyst can see the emotions all the more clearly.

If the emotional deprivation of the analytic relationship turns the analysand's feelings into forced hothouse blooms, it also removes the analyst's ordinary emotional resources. "Empathy, when you're not looking at someone, it's clunkier, it's less . . ." The analyst I was talking to broke off and looked at me in perplexity. "First of all, I don't understand empathy, and I don't think anyone does. There's a lot of mysticism and hokum about it. But empathy is basically the sum total of what you pick up and ways you have of sort of identifying with other people and comparing their experience to your experience and then imagining that we're in similar situations. But when they're on the couch, you don't see their face. Somebody could be silently tearing up, and you don't know it. It puts pressure on the patient to verbalize, to put everything into words. The advantage of the couch is that there are experiences you're not going to talk about sitting in a chair. When you're the patient, you can see the analyst sitting there, looking at you. You're going to tell him that you masturbate to the image of a meat loaf? It's not so easy to say that. On the analyst's side, there is more room to, in a sense, miss what someone's up to and leave them alone." Analysis may make it easier for a patient to talk about his most embarrassing problems than face-to-face psychotherapy does. In Catholic confession, as well, he who confesses does not have to look into the eyes of someone he respects as he reveals his shame. But though it is easier to confess when you do not have to look someone in the eyes, it is harder for the person to whom you confess to understand. As the philosopher John Searle remarks, we know that our dogs are conscious when we look them in the eyes. Our faces are remarkable tools in emotional interpretation, and in analysis they cannot be used. Even when the analyst sits facing the patient, the asymmetry of the relationship remains.

What are these peculiar relationships like for those who engage in them as a professional occupation? Whereas each analysand has only one analyst, who is in some ways and for some time the most important person in the analysand's life, someone about whom the analysand dreams and fantasizes and to whom he attributes nightmarish power, each analyst has an average of eighteen patients. Some of them are analytic patients, whom he sees four to five times each week; some are psychotherapy patients. The general rule is that the more frequent the visits and the more orthodox (more abstinent) the technique, the more powerful the patient's feelings. Still, even in once-a-week psychotherapy a patient's feelings may be vivid. Not only does each patient have powerful feelings about his therapist, but people come in for psychotherapy and psychoanalysis because they are in pain. They pour their anguish of loss and misery into the therapist's lap and leave.

The short answer to the question of what analysis is like for an analyst is that analysts often say that they never quite manage to adjust to its demands. "I would defend myself with curiosity," one analyst explained. "I tried to think rather than to feel, to protect myself from being overwhelmed by feeling. I could deal with the obvious feelings I had for this person by trying to find out more about them. That was productive, because it helped me to figure out what was going on. But it also protected me against the suffering that you have to feel because patients suffer in your presence. They suffer. But I don't really think that analysts do handle their patients' pain. I think that's one of the big sources of stress. Obvious and deep sources of stress. It will not go away, and psychoanalysts never resolve it." Yet there is often great pressure, professionally, to deny the emotional stress, to deny even the emotional connection to the patients. Analysts are supposed to treat their patients with clinical indifference. Any sign of attachment can indicate a patient's manipulation or a doctor's error. At least that was standard theory in the field until recently, when analysts began to suggest that the feelings analysts had for analysands were not simply "false" feelings, figments of a relationship with somebody else, or a countertransference mistake. (In recent years, psychoanalysis has become more relaxed, more open.) One paper at a recent American Psychoanalytic Association meeting argued that analysts should not distance themselves from their feelings of love for their patients by calling them "countertransference," as if they were delusions rather than the real thing.

The longer answer is that an analyst has intense feelings about his or her analysands that are as entangled as the analysands'. I interviewed a number of analysts in depth. I remember being taken aback at first by how excited they were about their patients' achievements, as if they were parents or teachers or lovers. One analyst had a patient so brilliant and so exciting that he had to force himself not to discuss literature; another analyst had a patient who would be one of the greatest writers of her generation; yet another analyst had a patient with such courage that he nearly cried explaining it. Yet the content of their interactions seemed so banal. One analyst explained that a female patient had walked out of his office and dropped her sweater on the carpet. He had picked it up for her—and that was what they had talked about for three weeks, the sweater and the fact that he had picked it up. There is some sense to this. Just as you hear emotional style more clearly when someone screams than when he whispers (there is more emotion to listen to), you can see much in the microcosm of that moment. When the analyst picked up the sweater, did the patient feel he was being chivalrous? Aggressive? Flirtatious? Intrusive? But it is not just patients who have strong feelings.

After the 1989 San Francisco earthquake, *American Psychoanalyst*—a news sheet sent to members of the American Psychoanalytic Association—carried an apparently inane article. It explained, anecdotally and at length, that after a rush-hour jolt that had destroyed freeways, buildings, and bridges, many San Francisco analysts were worried about their patients. "If you know psychoanalysis, it wasn't a silly article," an analyst explained to me. "What was striking about that article was that here are a bunch of psychoanalysts who are surprised to learn that they cared deeply about their patients. You know, 'I was in my office and I heard about the earthquake and I thought, "Oh, my God, my patient lives on that street where that house collapsed." "Oh, my God, I hope my patient is all right." ' They're *surprised* to learn that. That was what I found so amazing about that article. That's a different generation of analysts than me and my friends. If there's an accident on the freeway when my patient is driving in to see me, I'm concerned, because I know I have a tie, a real relationship with those people, which is very intense. When you meet with somebody four or five times a week and talk about very intense issues for two, three, four, six, seven years . . . you don't talk to your *wife* that much. In psychoanalysis you have very intense relationships, and they are really quite private. It's a very strange business, doing analysis."

This man, Ethan Bass, is a young analyst (in analytic time; he is fifty) who is also a training analyst, a warm, feisty man who initially treated me with the gingerly respect one might accord an ink-spitting squid but who then decided to trust me. He was one of the most desirable supervisors at the hospital at which he held an appointment; he was also among the most feared, for he was blunt and smart. He ran the main psychotherapy seminar for residents and taught at the psychoanalytic institute. He had six analytic patients, one person who came for psychotherapy four times a week (that patient did not lie on the couch but instead sat facing the analyst), and another who came three times. He was an experienced, respected, articulate analyst. One of the things about which he was most articulate was what he described as the emotional nakedness of doing this work and its weirdly exhausting quality.

"It's different from psychotherapy," he told me. "It's more intense, it's more intimate. . . . I always tell my patients or a potential patient' that doing psychotherapy is like renting the movie and analysis is like going to the theater. It really has much more impact, and it's really more— you know, the theater's dark and you can't get up and go to the bathroom, you're really surrounded by it, and it grips you. In psychotherapy, you come in on Tuesday and the next week you come in again. You've had seven days to get away from whatever was going on. So analysis is really marvelous, but then again it is much more stressful than psychotherapy for the analyst. The treatment itself is also very gratifying for the analyst. But it's intense."

The analyst's experience of nakedness is, of course, paradoxical in this context, because it is the analysand who feels exposed and defenseless against the cool imperturbability of the analyst. But such is the strange power of the relationship that the analyst too feels exposed and visible, even though he cannot be seen. The formidable barriers to reciprocal emotional communication with the analyst press the analysand into hawkeyed attention to responsive detail. This is another reason analysts sometimes find it hard to do psychotherapy, because their face is so carefully scrutinized for emotional indicators. "You can't hide in analysis," continued Bass. "I mean, the patient really begins to know who you are, and if you have a little trouble with this or that, or, you know, you'd really rather not be sad today, thank you very much, the patient sort of—since you are the place where they are doing their emotional work, they get to know pretty well where it's solid and where it is not, and they poke at you in your most vulnerable places.

"My first control was very, very difficult. I had a very brilliant, very disturbed man in analysis, and he was not going to be a classical patient. He was not going to be the kind of patient that I had read about and that my teachers knew about and that they wanted to teach me about, and I wanted him to be that. We had a big-time struggle, which was not good for either of us, and my supervisor was, of all potential supervisors, probably the worst I could have chosen for this case and I didn't know any better. This was a guy who really needed me, at times, to hold his hand. Now, I was not going to hold his hand any more than I was going to sleep with him. I just couldn't do it. I still don't think I would hold his hand, but I would be able to deal with that now, and that kind of need and that kind of hunger, and that kind of anxiety, but I couldn't deal with it then. I really didn't know how, I wasn't competent enough or confident enough to know that I could find a way to help him with that. So it made me anxious, I made him anxious, it was very difficult. The path to analytic nirvana is not a simple one."

Certainly the analytic path forces the analysts who follow it to unlearn many of their basic expectations of human interaction. As psychoanalysis confronts analysands with emotional deprivation, it confronts analysts with a strange combination of omnipotence and a kind of perpetual absence. An analyst is often for a time the most present person in an analysand's life, the person around whom his fantasies revolve, a homunculus he carries in his head to comment on his actions. Yet the same analyst remains, with respect to the outside world, his analysand's silent shadow. If an analysand breaks through his creative writing block while in analysis and writes a brilliant novel, the analyst cannot crow his victory. If an analysand turns out brilliant or wealthy or a national figure, the analyst cannot boast that he helped. If an analysand is a famous writer and commits suicide and years later a biographer approaches the analyst for tapes of the sessions and he chooses to give them over, having decided that this is what the analysand would have wanted, he will be vilified by his peers.[15] Most of us rely on some public affirmation for our achievements. An analyst has little. His clinical work is private to all but his patients, and in their emotional upheavals they cannot be trusted in their judgments. An analyst is hired help, employed by a client who tells him about her life and loves him and hates him, in the interest of a development in which he plays no future role. In the same way that kids develop their coordination and people skills through playing tag and capture-the-flag, psychoanalysis is like a large emotional sandbox in which analyst and analysand play at relationship to prepare the analysand for real life.

"My role is to be the sidekick," remarked Bass. "In the child consulting room the kid's got the toys. He says, you stand there. Then he throws darts at you. You're the one who loses at checkers, the one who is always frustrated. But what you are in charge of is the only certainty, the ground rules. I'm in charge in some ways. In other ways I'm the employee, the guy who's given a script or told to stand over there.

"I mean, you try to create the space in which someone can use the space, the freedom to get into whatever they need to get into. I think of it as a kind of light play. I think that the transference is a playing out of something. It's as if the patient comes in and you say, 'Tell me about it, what was it that went on when you were a kid that is still so problematic for you that you can't get married or it's ruining your love life?' And it's as if they say, 'I can't talk about it, but let me show you.'"

It is remarkable and often moving to hear analysts talk about their patients, because it is so clear that they are caught up in their lives and idealize their patients as much as their patients idealize them. But what gives the analyst's role its piquancy is that analysts never see their patients outside the consulting room—analysts know everything about their patients except what they are like in normal human relationships—and that for them, it is a job. It is something they do for money, and it is a hard job, for change comes slowly and reluctantly to most human lives.

Certainly the fact that an analyst is doing a job helps him to handle his everyday frustrations. "God knows, most of us do work in which we are not free to express ourselves, whether we are shoveling peat or doing psychoanalysis," Bass said once. "That's why they call it work—like anything you start out knowing how to do and then you do some and you get pretty good at it and you do some more and you get better. And you know, you can be sitting there having had a disappointment or an upsetting hour with the previous patient and still what is happening in this hour has its own logic and its own meaning and is compelling enough so that you can sort of forget the other stuff." Analysis is, nonetheless, a job that asks that someone have feelings for the sake of money and in which an analyst feels a close and honest connection to someone whom he also believes not to be telling the truth, because that person can't.

"You're immersed in feelings every day," Bass continued. "And it isn't possible in the moment to separate it out. I mean, when you're dealing with something sad, when you might find yourself crying, you can't distinguish the sadness the patient has experienced and is inducing in you from your own sadness, which is the source of the way the patient induces sadness in you. The way you get sad is for some sadness of your own to be mobilized, touched. But at the same time you're working, you're doing your job. You're thinking about this, you're making interventions about that, you're noticing the way you are responding to the patient. So there's something comforting about that. It's like when you go into work, into the office, and people say hi to you and they recognize who you are and whatever was happening before, you know there's something normal. Well, when you're functioning in the analytic situation and you're functioning well, that has its beneficial effect. But it is complicated because you are functioning by emoting and being touched and being intimate with someone. And one of the tenets about psychoanalysis is that people don't tell you the truth. They tell you things for a reason, and they tell you things in a particular way."

This relationship blows apart most American notions about good relationships: the separation of friendship from commerce, the association of intimacy with reciprocity, the affiliation of trust and honesty. These are among the reasons that people have pointed to psychoanalysts' amoralism: hiring a friend is like renting a prostitute, they murmur. Analysts are usually acutely aware of the oddity of these relationships. Their patients, of course, insistently confront them about their irritating refusal to reveal where they are headed on vacation or whether they are married. But the analyst too struggles against the constraints of abstinence: the desire to name their patients' names in public, touch their shoulders when they cry, or join them in an intellectual jousting match. "He's so smart and creative," an analyst commented regretfully about a patient, "that I really have to work not to engage on that level, it's so much fun." The struggle itself becomes important to analysts as a "place" in which the psychoanalytic work is done.

Milton Spyer is an elegant man with a soft voice who worries, despite his evident reserve, that he may be perceived as too flashy a dresser, too outspoken a thinker, too prolific a writer to be made a training analyst at his local institute. He has an attentive, uneasy, Jamesian alertness. He is much sought after as a supervisor and has eleven patients in psychoanalysis, a figure that is remarkably high for his geographic area, where most analysts do not have full practices. He speaks, in the same way that young therapists do, of using his own experience to interpret someone else's, but his description of that process is, like most analysts', more nuanced: "I do find that the experience of being an analyst with each patient is different, because I think that what I do is wittingly or unwittingly—all at once to coalesce around someone else's nature or the nature of their personality and, at the same time, to use the French term, do violence to it. Not in the sense of trying to cause someone pain, but a useful collision. Enough to provide a complementarity that lets someone look at what they're doing at the same time, but enough of my adaptation to someone's nature to get into it, to know what they're experiencing."

Spyer thus understands himself to act in two ways. He tries to understand the analysand's experience from the inside, as it were: "The first thing I'm doing, trying to listen to what someone is feeling as they describe an event, as I sense them with me. And I'm always trying to understand what I'm feeling." He also comments on what he calls "the unconscious," ways in which he says the patient's experience is determined or defended against or not quite experienced because of prohibition or conflict. In this he is standing on the outside, looking in. He is "doing violence": "As I listen to the content, then I start to think more about the unconscious part, what they might not be aware of, what in their conscious experience may be defending against something else. For instance, when someone says, 'I'm sorry for being late,' and I think to myself, you're not sorry for being late, you've been late frequently. You may regret it at some level, because you feel that you might be hurting me or insulting me, but we both know that you want to hurt me, and yet you're very critical of yourself about that wish. That would be the kind of thing I might say to someone at a particular point. If I really knew it was true."

We are usually unconscious of our motivations when we would be embarrassed to know them; the analyst's job is to point these out. That is why Spyer describes interpretation as "doing violence." An unproven interpretation can create a high cost in pain—and if Freud says that "no damage is done if, for once in a while, we make a mistake and offer the patient a wrong construction as the probable truth," he also says that "a mistake, once made, cannot be rectified." [16] Yet it is impossible to know whether an interpretation is correct or whether this is the time, of all possible times, to make it. In recent years, analysts have begun to argue that it is the moments of misunderstanding, not of understanding, that provide the greatest opportunity for the patient to know himself. This is also what Spyer argues.

"These little points of interaction between the patient and the analyst, these little shifts, become so crucial," he reflected. "More and more I see those moments as related to a countertransference-transference impasse, where you get into listening in a particular way and you're not really getting it in some way. You're listening but not getting it. Then something happens in a way which allows you to see who you are to this person in the transference, what you feel like, what you are doing not to put forward some mutual understanding, what they're doing with you not to let you. Not that the seas part when you make these awarenesses known to the patient. But sometimes they do, and sometimes they give you a new working model.

"I think I know less and less about technique, and I believe less and less about technique. I really believe that technique is something that each analyst and patient discover together—guided, certainly, by principles that I could articulate, and they're important principles. This is not a completely wild process at all.[17] But when you read what people write about as abstract principles of technique, they're really stupid. I mean, I guess I'm more skilled now at figuring out how to work with each person individually."

For the expert therapist, the dilemma of therapy is that on the one hand, there is the demand to identify, to imagine patients' deepest idiosyncracies, to try to understand what makes them individual, what gives them specificity, to feel with them what they feel; on the other, there is the demand to step back from the identification and to understand through comparison with others—to wonder whether a patient's sense of inferiority does, as Charles Brenner suggests it might in *An Elementary Textbook of Psychoanalysis*, emerge from some form of self-attack.[18] Psychoanalysts fret about the ways in which the pattern-identifying interferes with connecting to the patient. Often, like Spyer, they talk about suppressing the temptation to think with detachment—the temptation, literally, to analyze.

"The way I listen now," Spyer continued, "is very different from the way I used to listen. I find I don't rely so much on formulations now. I almost try to undo formulations. I don't like thinking in that way anymore. I mean, I make formulations, but I'm more struck by how they get in the way as I'm listening. A formulation would be that a man fears castration by his mother in some way and out of fear identifies with her and becomes her in some way, and that there is an underlying wish for a father who will protect him from his mother and blah blah blah. Now, I wouldn't say that I don't form impressions like that, dynamic understandings of each person, but I don't feel that they are on my mind as much as they used to be."

This, of course, is a conceit on the same order as that of a professional photographer who talks about the wisdom of the untrained eye. Spyer feels free to dispense with formulations only because the art of constructing them has become so automatic for him. But the conceit is revealing. Analysts pay a great deal of attention to their inevitable failure to understand perfectly. They struggle to understand everything, to realize the meaning of all acts and wishes, while deeply believing that the project of complete understanding is doomed. One might call this the paradox of human knowing: that the more we understand someone, the more we realize how little we can know them. Sophisticated analysts entangle themselves in the contradictions of this paradox. To quote Spyer, "Listening without memory or desire, nobody can do that. I mean, what a horrible idea. How can the field believe in the unconscious and say that anyone can do that?" Analysts often focus upon the difficulty of doing therapy. Unlike specialists in other fields, they publish accounts of cases that *didn't* work, as Freud did most famously with *Dora*.[19] They talk and write about the impossibility of ever fully understanding, of listening without filtering the other through the self. They teach that you must accept uncertainty and that you must give up the need to be right.

From that sense of failure emerges a powerful sensibility: that what is admirable is not *behaving* in a certain way—analysts are often quite tolerant of patients' less conventional behavior—but *understanding* one's own behavior as honestly as possible, despite the impossibility of the task. There is a firm moral commitment to trying to see yourself clearly, with your inadequacies, your awkwardnesses, your discomfort, your own dishonesty about the very process of coming clean. Psychoanalysts, of course, have personal moralities in which they abhor murder, lying, embezzlement, and so forth. But those moral stances are not particularly psychoanalytic. The specifically psychoanalytic ethos involves a commitment to the process of self-understanding.

"Are they trying to be true to themselves?" Spyer continued. "With a big emphasis on *trying*, because many people lie, and it's a very wonderful thing when someone can talk about lying and how they lie to themselves and to the people they love and look into it and understand it more and change it. And I think there's something about someone who wants to overcome pain. Some people would call that taking responsibility. I think there's something else that's valued, too, which is the suppleness with which someone can look into themselves, delving into affect. Someone who can look at their interior map in a very rich way and work with it. To know what they feel, so if they decide to take a new job with different risks, they've checked in with the part of them that's ambitious or grandiose or the part of them that's not feeling creative enough and the part of them that's self-destructive. So what are these things? They're some sort of courage. One more thing: I think there's also value placed on someone's capacity to bear affect. To bear intense emotion. Love, passion, pain. Aloneness, intimacy, cruelty, excitement. You know. The whole range. To experience them, to enjoy them. To bear them."

Philip Rieff understood that the entire field of psychoanalysis rests on an innocent, noble hope. Strictly speaking, there is no reason that learning to know and experience our feelings, which is more or less what Spyer means by "bearing them," should make us good. "Freud gives no reason why unblinking honesty with oneself should inhibit unblinking evil."[20] There is no guarantee, Rieff points out, that once people unrepress their murky depths, those who have greater awareness of those depths will act more justly or caringly. Perhaps the neurosis actually inhibits the patient from acting on scurrilous impulses. After all, much of what Freud said about our unconscious was alarming. If he was right, there are desires in our dark cauldrons of hatreds and sweaty yearnings that no one would let loose upon humanity. But psychoanalytic practice proceeds as if knowledge (and the care of the analyst) will lead to goodness, at least for those who come into therapy because they are unhappy. Rieff underestimated the degree to which analysts see the attempt to achieve authenticity as an ethical stance. Analysts do seem to want genuinely to believe that if you know and accept yourself, you will be loving to others. In the footsteps of Hannah Arendt, they want to presume that evil is not done by those who learn to think and feel.

"Psychoanalysis helps people," a senior analyst reflected to me once (I had heard him defend a notorious analyst once at a public meeting on the grounds that she had meant well, even though she had acted naively and to disastrous effect), "but its truths are not appetizing. You get a sense of man's fallibility and the constant way in which he tries to protect himself through illusion. In the acceptance of oneself, there is a giving up of the grandiose fantasies that one could be anything or that there will be this idealized parental figure who will take care of everything. You give up the sort of everyday dishonesty that gets people by. The positive side is that you can bear it alone, you can stand on your own feet, you can accept the failures of your spouse, your work, and your own capacity, and find a way of making a place for yourself that is fulfilling. The psychoanalytic experience can confront you with your dishonesty, the sort of everyday dishonesty that gets people by."

Psychoanalysis is a powerful expression of the modern age's belief in authenticity. If we are able to understand who we "really" are, somehow we will become ourselves. We will be able to acknowledge the ways in which we are other people, the ways in which other people have made us, the ways in which we are unique because of the particularities of those of whom we are both a reflection and a transformation. Our uniqueness lies in part in our limitations. To live without lying to ourselves about those limitations is to be ourselves—and to be free. This conviction of salvation through self-discovery is a real feature of psychoanalysis, and Rieff is right when he points to the weakness of this claim. At the end of this self-involved and destructive century, the claim that knowledge, particularly self-knowledge, will inevitably lead to goodness seems naive.

But psychoanalysis also embodies an older, more religious impulse that Rieff did not really grasp but that runs through the practice of psychoanalysis in the way analysts respond to their patients, the way they judge one another as analysts, and the way they see themselves acting in the world. Freud remarked, in a letter to Carl Jung, that psychoanalysis is a cure through love. The philosopher and analyst Jonathan Lear develops this theme in a book entitled *Love and Its Place in Nature*. Love in Lear's sense really means wise nurturing. He sees that nurturing embodied in a fundamental analytic commitment: that for therapy to be therapeutic, an analyst must engage emotionally with a patient and must empathize and sympathize (to some extent) with the patient, and that through this process the patient may grow into a better-formed individual with a more developed sense of inner responsibility and freedom. Analysts believe that respect and love for others grow along with respect and love for oneself and that respect and love for oneself can be nurtured by a caring analyst. Analysts talk about their patients as if they thought of themselves as wise mentors or parents. They obviously care for their patients, and they care deeply. No other word but "love" quite captures this emotional tone of an analyst's involvement with his patients (although the presence of love need not imply the absence of other feelings). No other word captures the tone in the way that analysts imagine themselves to help patients "become" themselves. As Lear puts it, in psychoanalysis "the creation of the individual and the caring for the individual are of a piece."[21]

This, too, has its naiveness, but it is naiveness with a genealogy as old as human faith. There is, in fact, a somewhat Christian feel to contemporary psychoanalysis, though most psychoanalysts might be taken aback by that characterization. Their love for their patients is rarely stated in such bald terms as to make the comparison striking. Nonetheless, the love represented in the Christian tradition is not so dissimilar to the way that analysts conceive of their care for the patient. The psychoanalytic credo that self-knowledge and authenticity are good and help to make us good really must be understood as framed within a belief that love will make us loving and that when we love we trust others and protect them. We become good friends, good citizens, good, whole people. More and more psychoanalysts emphasize in their writings and discourse the necessity and power of analysts' love for and acceptance of their patients. They quickly qualify the kind of love they mean: not carnal, not possessive. They seem to mean the kind of belief in another's capacity for goodness sometimes captured by the word *agape*, brotherly love, the unselfish love of one person for another, the love of God for humankind. This is the kind of love that the great teacher Elvin Semrad invoked when he spoke about loving the patient: "The most important thing, the thing that makes the difference, the thing that we as psychiatrists are dealing in, is love and humanity."[22] One analyst explained to me that she could not accept a war criminal in therapy, nor indeed anyone whom she was unable to love in some way. This is a common sentiment, though it is more often expressed through practice than articulated as a principle. Most analysts really do behave as if they love their patients. In this sensibility there is a rock-bottom commitment to the belief that an unhappy person will flourish and become a decent person when he is nurtured, mentored, and accepted as a wise parent loves, nurtures, mentors, and accepts a child. At least, there is a commitment to the belief that such love is necessary for that unhappy person to become good and trusting, even if, as in the case of war criminals and sociopaths, it may not be sufficient. This is the kind of sentiment that motivated my own mentor, I believe, when he told me to read *Magister Ludi*. A psychoanalytic patient carries out his process of self-discovery in the presence of his analyst's love, just as Joseph Knecht carried out his work in the presence of his love for those he governed. In the psychoanalytic framework, to serve is to love, and to love is to accept people and to nurture them so that they grow healthily and wisely. "This book is an interpretation," Lear writes. "As such it is an act of love."

The senior analyst I quoted above continued his remarks with these words: "I love this great tenth-century picture of this big fat Zen monk. He's holding a bunch of shrimp in his hand and he's got this exquisite kind of laughing face and he clearly has tremendous pleasure about holding those shrimp in his hands. I love that picture. It represents an image that I have about what one needs to do with oneself where you can hold yourself in your hand in a loving way and an accepting way and kind of embrace it." If the moral authority of the scientist derives from the knowledge he acquires, the moral authority of the analyst derives from the love he gives.

CHAPTER FIVE

❧

WHERE THE SPLIT
CAME FROM

Whence did this divided consciousness arise? The story of twentieth-century psychiatry is that psychoanalysis was imported from Europe at a time when the approach to mental illness was essentially custodial. Psychoanalysis rapidly became entrenched as *the* theory that explained mental illness and *the* treatment that would cure it. Like most single-answer cures, it overpromised. When new psychopharmacological treatments and theories emerged and successfully treated what psychoanalysis could not, the new psychiatric science claimed to win the ideological battle and to supplant its former rival. To the new adherents, psychoanalysis was charlatanry and psychiatric disorder was brain dysfunction. The psychoanalysts responded in kind. In practice, the more biomedical and the more psychodynamic approaches settled down in the 1980s into what one·senior clinician called a "happy pluralism." Then the economic currents changed. As managed care companies began to take control over insurance reimbursements, the ideological tension between the psychopharmacological and the psychoanalytic looked as if it presented a choice, and the psychopharmacological approaches seemed cheaper and more like the rest of medicine. Compared to the power of these economic forces, the ideological tensions seem like domestic squabbles. But together they are pushing the psychodynamic approach out of psychiatry with a nearly irresistible force.

From the patient's perspective, this is a mistake. Whatever the cause of psychiatric illness, practically speaking the evidence is fairly clear that for most psychiatric problems, a combination of psychopharmacology and psychotherapy provides the most effective treatment. The American Psychiatric Association has recently started issuing what are called "practice guidelines." These aim to describe appropriate standards for treatment that represent "the consensus of experts in the field regarding current scientific knowledge and rational clinical practice" for selected disorders. For the most part, the guidelines concerning psychotherapy for each disorder are supported by careful studies of psychotherapy outcomes for patients with that disorder, and for the most part the guidelines suggest that a combination of psychotherapy and psychopharmacology provides the optimal treatment.[1] The most widely used guide in the field says bluntly that "psychotherapy in conjunction with antidepressants is more effective than either treatment alone in the treatment of major depressive disorder"; "psychotherapy [of bipolar patients] in conjunction with antimanic drugs, e.g., lithium, is more effective than either alone"; "antipsychotic medication is not as effective in treating schizophrenic patients as when the drugs are coupled with psychosocial interventions."[2]

This makes good intuitive sense. One could fairly comfortably separate the psychiatric illnesses into three groups: those in which the brain-driven, organic quality of the illness is flagrant, as in (for example) schizophrenia, major depression, manic depression, and obsessive-compulsive disorder; those in which learning and physiological vulnerability seem to be equally important, as in the panic disorders and possibly the personality disorders; and those in which learning probably predominates, as in eating disorders and possibly trauma disorders. (I hasten to point out that this classification is controversial and merely illustrative.) The most organic are probably much like other medical problems: you carry a predisposition to the illness, and if it is a strong predisposition, you will likely get sick even in good circumstances, but if it is a weak predisposition, you will get sick only under stressful circumstances. Bad parenting can certainly play a role here, but so can poverty, a parent's illness, or, for that matter, being a temperamentally hyperactive child of a temperamentally high-strung mother. The point is that learning plays a role in acquiring most psychiatric illness. It certainly plays a role in being able to live with that illness. Psychotherapy is fundamentally a learning process. In it, a patient learns how to verbalize and to understand his difficulties. It makes good sense that teaching a patient how to understand his emotional world—how he interprets and reacts to people and how they interpret and react to him—might help him cope more effectively, particularly as he begins to regulate his emotions pharmacologically.

Certainly a fair amount of research supports this view. There have been many studies of psychotherapy. Some focus on patients suffering from depression, others on those with bulimia, bipolar disorder, schizophrenia, social phobia, borderline personality disorder—all kinds of problems.[3] Such studies have repeatedly concluded that psychotherapy of all forms helps patients to suffer fewer symptoms, to feel more effective, to stay out of the hospital for longer, and to perform more productively at work. Like those made for medication studies, this is a statistical claim. Bad therapy can make things worse. Nevertheless, studies have repeatedly demonstrated that on average psychotherapy is helpful both for the very ill and for the somewhat disconsolate. For example, a much-cited three-year follow-up of 128 depressed patients treated with psychotherapy and with medication revealed that psychotherapy alone significantly lengthened the time between recurrences, whether medication was used or not (the best outcome appeared to be the combination).[4] A 1994 study suggested that at the end of psychotherapy, the average treated patient is better off than 80 percent of untreated patients.[5]

Yet by their nature, psychotherapy studies are less rigorous than most medication studies. By the time the research parameters are tight enough to produce testable results, the conditions of psychotherapy have often left the real world far behind.[6] In research settings, therapists often carry out therapy from highly specific manuals with patients who have one and only one diagnosable complaint. But most patients do not go to a therapist because they are having trouble sleeping; they see a therapist because they are in despair. If they feel better after six months of once-a-week psychotherapy, it is hard to say exactly what the therapist did because no one knows exactly why therapy works (this is true for medication as well, but the uncertainty is considerably more diffuse when it comes to psychotherapy). As a result, a report from the Outcome Measures Project of the National Institute of Mental Health could state in 1995 that "despite hundreds of studies in this area, we can make few definitive statements about the changes brought about by various forms of therapy."[7] The most convincing controlled outcome studies are actually those done with patients sick enough to be hospitalized, because there are crude measures that can distinguish a study group from a control group—namely, how many days the patients spent as in-patients in the hospital. The impact of psychotherapy on those not sick enough to be hospitalized is harder to judge. Does staying in a marriage or a job prove the worth of the therapy or its worthlessness? To those focused on a "rationalized" medicine that ties specific outcome to specific intervention, studies of psychotherapy seem inherently fuzzy.

One way to avoid worrying about objective parameters of change is simply to ask a very large number of people who have had psychotherapy what they thought of the experience. In 1995, *Consumer Reports* reported on a survey of its subscribers, the largest ever survey on mental health care. About 2,900 respondents had received psychotherapy from mental health professionals, mostly psychiatrists or psychologists. "Most had made strides towards resolving the problems that led to treatment," stated the report, "and almost all said that life had become more manageable. This was true for all the conditions we asked about, even among the people who had felt the worst at the beginning."[8] In fact, the people who had started out feeling the worst made the most progress.[9]

Moreover, the *Consumer Reports* survey was very clear about the length of treatment: the longer people stayed in therapy, the more they improved. Obviously there were no controls in the *Consumer Reports* survey, but it did rely on real-world conditions, and it does tell us something important: that most people who chose to consult psychotherapists felt that they had benefited from therapy, and the longer they had it, the better they felt they did. The data suggest that a year of therapy "may be very worthwhile" and that "people who stayed in treatment for more than two years reported the best outcomes of all."[10] A number of recent studies support the claim that long-term therapy tends to produce better results, particularly if a psychiatric condition is chronic (as for some patients with depression) or if a patient has been traumatized or has difficulty maintaining a stable relationship with a therapist (as in borderline personality disorder, the most dramatic of the personality disorders).[11] One unusually large 1992 study reported on more than 650 German patients in psychodynamic psychotherapy (including psychoanalytic therapy). Over the course of their treatment, the patients significantly decreased their use of medications. They had a one-third decline in medical visits, a two-fifths decline in lost workdays, and a two-thirds decline in days hospitalized. The declines persisted more than two years after the end of therapy, and the longer the therapy, the more successful it was.[12]

The *Consumer Reports* survey also concluded that a mental health professional's level of training in psychotherapy made a difference. Some of those who responded had sought help from their family doctor. They tended to have done well, but those who had sought out a mental health specialist had done much better. Respondents were equally satisfied whether they had seen a psychiatrist, a psychologist, or a social worker. They were less likely to feel that they had been helped after seeing a marriage and family counselor. Marriage and family counselors typically have a shorter master's degree than a social worker and one year, not two, of supervised clinical experience. This evidence does not suggest that psychiatrists do better therapy than psychologists and social workers. It does suggest that psychotherapy is very helpful, that it should be available in conjunction with psychopharmacology, and that if someone is treating serious psychiatric illness it should be a tool she understands and can use. It may, however, reduce overall costs to have a psychiatrist deliver the therapy if a patient is receiving medication, for then the insurer need not be responsible for separate charges for medication visits and psychotherapy visits.

Yet the *Consumer Reports* study has been much criticized, not least for its selection bias. Who, the critics ask, would respond to such a survey? Surely, they answer, those who have benefited from psychotherapy and want to defend it, and surely those who have stayed in psychotherapy the longest will be the most committed to the psychotherapeutic cause.[13] These doubts also cast a shadow on the claim that training made a difference.

In fact, one of the most important problems in assessing psychotherapy is that there are now many kinds of psychotherapy that a psychotherapist can be trained to do. Psychodynamic therapy, of course, focuses on unconscious conflicts and defense mechanisms that hinder adult behavior. This is the therapy closely associated with psychoanalysis and the one in which psychiatric residents are most thoroughly trained (when they are trained in psychotherapy), although they are exposed to all kinds. "Interpersonal" therapy derives from psychodynamic therapy and focuses specifically on present relationships and communication with others. "Cognitive behavioral" therapy helps patients recognize and interrupt distorted (and negative) patterns of thinking. "Behavioral" therapy addresses specific behaviors and tries to supplant harmful ones with more helpful ones. "Family" therapy treats a family as a unit, rather than focusing on one member as the client.

In the real world, people enter therapy with a host of complaints, not one specific symptom, and therapists typically use a combination of these different approaches to treat them. Indeed, as I observed psychiatrists learn about different therapies and practice their techniques, it seemed to me, as an anthropologist, that most psychotherapies were more similar than different and that a clinician who could not switch from one emphasis to another was probably a bad clinician. The *Consumer Reports* study also explicitly supported what is known as the "Dodo hypothesis," which is that there is no evidence that one mode of psychotherapy is superior to any other, assuming the same amount of contact between patient and therapist.[14] (In *Alice's Adventures in Wonderland,* the Dodo judged a footrace and declared that *"everyone* has won and *all* must have prizes!")

Yet in the new world of rationalized and rationed medicine, such claims seem unbearably ambiguous. They provide no guidelines to anyone about the length of an adequate trial of therapy, about its type, or about who should deliver it. As one researcher in the new field of "quality of care" pointed out to me, "True or not, the long-standing assertions about psychotherapy—that therapy of all forms helps patients and that longer is always better—won't work in the resources allocation processes afoot in contemporary health care. You can't counter managed care by pushing back with broad claims like that. You have to identify focal areas where therapy has an identified role and frame this role in terms of a defined population, a clear

therapeutic process, and specified outcomes with a credible time course."
But, he continued, many psychiatrists resist this kind of piecemeal
approach, and across-the-board resistance perpetuates across-the-board
cost-cutting activity by managed care.

Some research does indicate that specific therapies are better or worse
for specific symptoms—family therapy for schizophrenia, cognitive behavioral therapy for panic disorder, interpersonal therapy for depression, and
so forth—although these claims are often controversial in the research literature.[15] But there are not only many psychotherapies but many psychosocial treatments: clubhouses for clients, residential and day treatment
programs, family education, vocational training, substance abuse counseling, community treatment programs for clients with chronic and severe
problems. To persuade a skeptical company that these interventions are
helpful demands the kind of rigorous analysis that compares one program
to another for similar kinds of patients and with numbers large enough to
make differences statistically significant.

Yet medication alone is often not effective. "You want to use a medication," a psychiatrist once observed to me, "in the first few years, when it
still works." He meant that the newness and the chicness of the medication give it a placebo aura that helps it take effect in a way it might not later
on. The mantra one hears throughout psychiatry is that *both* psychotherapy
and psychopharmacology have the same crude success rate: a third of the
time, they work well; a third of the time, they have some impact; a third of
the time, they don't work at all.[16] Needless to say, the mantra needs qualifi-
cation, but it captures some truth. It would now be considered malpractice
for a psychiatrist not to prescribe (or offer to prescribe) medication for
patients suffering from most serious psychiatric disorders. For patients
with serious symptoms, psychopharmacological treatment is imperative.
However, the medications often do not work, and they often do not work
well. About two thirds of depressed patients respond positively (50 percent
or greater improvement) to at least one of the antidepressants, but about a
third also respond that well to placebo. Meanwhile, one third of depressed
patients—a huge number, given that one in ten Americans will suffer from
major depression in their lifetime—respond to no medications at all.[17]
Eighty percent of bipolar patients respond to lithium, which is a high figure—but a fifth do not, and one to two in a hundred people are bipolar.[18]
For schizophrenic patients, relapse rates are 40 percent within two years
while taking medication.[19]

Psychotherapy helps some people who do not respond to medication or
who relapse. (At least 10 to 25 percent of patients—pregnant women, for
example—cannot or will not take medication.[20]) Family therapy reduces
the relapse rate in schizophrenic patients to the same extent as antipsy-

chotic medications do, according to one study.[21] Many studies comparing psychotherapy and psychopharmacology even suggest that they are often equally effective. For example, in one study, 150 depressed female outpatients, all of whom had responded to a common antidepressant medication (amitriptyline) in preliminary treatment, were randomly assigned to treatment with medication, with a placebo, with psychotherapy, with psychotherapy and medication, with psychotherapy and placebo, and with nothing. Treatment with medication alone or with psychotherapy alone was nearly as effective in preventing relapses.[22]

There is even evidence that sometimes psychopharmacology and psychotherapy may have the same ultimate impact on the patient, each method altering the neurotransmitter chemistry, although psychiatrists more often conceive of medication and psychotherapy as working in different ways: that drugs reduce symptoms and psychotherapy helps people cope with other people. In a now-famous study of obsessive-compulsive disorder, patients were given either medication (Anafranil) or psychotherapy. If a patient improved, his brain scan changed, and the scan changed in the same way regardless of whether drugs or talk was used.[23] Psychotherapy, after all, is a learning process that involves the brain. (There is a delightful study of the neurological reality of learning in sea slugs entitled "Psychotherapy and the Single Synapse."[24]) In 1996, *Scientific American* reported that "claims about the 'wonder drug' Prozac notwithstanding, numerous independent studies have found that drugs are not significantly more effective than 'talking cures' aimed at treating the most common ailments for which people seek treatment, including depression, obsessive-compulsive disorder, and panic attacks."[25] At least some research suggests that there are only two illnesses for which drugs are clearly better than talk therapy: lithium for bipolar disorder and antipsychotics, particularly the new atypical antipsychotics, for schizophrenia.[26]

Meanwhile, providing psychotherapy to these patients may make for cheaper health care costs. Why? At the minimum, psychotherapy helps a patient to stay on medication, no small matter because when patients stop taking their "meds," they usually get so sick they return to the hospital until they are stable enough to survive outside it—often a matter of five to ten days.[27] Refusal to take medication (it is technically called "noncompliance") is one of the chief reasons for hospital readmissions. At $60 per psychotherapy session and $600 per hospital day (both are estimates; both are frequently more expensive), a year of weekly outpatient psychotherapy saves money if it prevents even one six-day admission. In fact, there is good evidence that providing psychotherapy is cost-effective for that reason.[28] A recent analysis of English-language scientific papers on the subject published between 1984 and 1994 found that in 88 percent of studies, psychotherapy reduced the cost of treatment for patients with severe psychiatric disorders (schizophrenia, bipolar disorder, borderline personality disorder, substance abuse, and others).[29] And the savings hold across the illness spectrum. When Aetna shifted from unlimited outpatient psychotherapy in 1975 to twenty visits per year in 1976 and 1977, there were no savings because the rate of psychiatric hospitalization rose abruptly. When Champus expanded its outpatient psychiatric coverage (its costs grew from $81 million to $103 million) between 1989 and 1992, it gained a net saving of $200 million because its customers' hospitalization rate dropped sharply. For every dollar spent on psychotherapy, four dollars were saved.[30] A 1990 study discovered that schizophrenic patients who received psychotherapy in addition to medication reduced the average number of days spent in the hospital from 112 days (for controls) to 43 over a period of twenty months.[31] A 1992 study on borderline personality disorder patients found that twice-a-week psychotherapy decreased the number of days in inpatient care, emergency room care, and appointments with nonpsychiatric medical doctors; the saving was calculated at an astonishing $10,000 per patient, a reflection of the high cost of hospital care and the high risk of hospitalization for these patients.[32]

Some studies indicate that people receiving psychotherapy reduce their use not only of psychiatric inpatient services but of medical inpatient and outpatient nonpsychiatric services. A 1990 study showed that group therapy sessions had led to a 50 percent reduction in medical outpatient visits at one HMO.[33] A 1991 study reported that psychiatric consultation for elderly patients with hip fractures led to reduced hospitalization, with savings of five times the cost of the psychotherapy.[34] Metastatic breast cancer patients given a year of weekly group therapy experienced less anxiety, nausea, and pain and had double the survival rate of the control group.[35] There is a similar result for patients with malignant melanomas.[36] There have been many such studies.[37]

Yet what we do not know is how many people would avail themselves of psychotherapy if it were freely available through the average health insurance policy. Some researchers refer to this as the problem of the "hidden iceberg."[38] Seeing a psychotherapist carries a certain amount of stigma even now. What might happen to the demand if the stigma disappeared altogether? On the other side sits the worry that perhaps as many as 70 percent of all nonpsychiatric medical visits are for essentially psychosomatic or psychosocial problems. That, goes the argument, is why freely available psychotherapy would cut overall medical costs. Yet how do we know when a psychotherapy session is "medically necessary"? Most people in therapy for help with a bad relationship or a stressful job would happily accept that a suicidal patient needs psychotherapy more desperately than they do, just as most people in the emergency room with a sprained ankle accept that a patient with a heart attack needs a physician's care more urgently than they do. But then, most people make appointments with their internist for stuffed noses and aching knees, not major medical crises. Identifying equity in psychiatric and nonpsychiatric medical care is a nightmarish policy problem.

There are, of course, problems with some of the ways in which psychotherapy has been used. Most recently, there has been a public outcry about false memories "retrieved" by psychotherapy and about some of the more bizarre claims that patients have been abducted by aliens and abused by Satanists. There have been cases when therapists have been accused of inducing patients to remember events that may not have occurred. It is sometimes forgotten in the tumult that the process of diagnosis, both psychiatric and nonpsychiatric, is always subject to enthusiasm. People come into a clinician's office complaining of distress. Those with confusing symptoms are more likely to be given a diagnosis that is then receiving a good deal of professional and public attention, and the condition is thus overdiagnosed. Attention deficit disorder is an example of a now-trendy diagnosis; eating disorders and schizophrenia were trendy in their day. In the early eighties, the trauma diagnoses seemed to explain problems that had previously been ignored. It may well be the case that those who complain of bizarre trauma in fact experienced more commonplace trauma (sexual abuse, bullying) that did make them ill. In fact, the existence of Satanic and alien abduction fantasies probably tells us a good deal about the suggestibility of certain kinds of traumatized patients.

But the bottom line is that mistakes happen in medicine. In the 1960s, the "appropriate" dose of antipsychotic was hugely greater than it is today. Surgeons once recommended the removal of the uterus for menopausal women who found hot flashes troubling. Just as psychopharmacological overenthusiasm and surgical overenthusiasm should not lead one to dismiss psychopharmacology or surgery, so too psychotherapeutic zealotry should not lead one to dismiss psychotherapy as a technique. There will always be controversies. The evidence, however, suggests that the general technique of psychotherapy helps patients feel better and cope more effectively.

The dilemma for psychotherapists in the age of managed care is how to maintain medical funding for a "procedure" that they know to be useful but that lends itself poorly to the type of rigorous study that is increasingly necessary in the current health care environment.

Psychiatric medications—especially Prozac—have profoundly changed the way many Americans think about psychotherapy. When I teach psychological anthropology to undergraduates, some of them shift irritably during the lectures on psychoanalysis. Then they go to the small discussion groups and complain that they shouldn't have to read Freud because he has been "disproved." They often see an either-or choice between these two ways of looking at mental illness, the one rooted in medication with a discourse about brains and neurotransmitters, the other rooted in language with a discourse about self-awareness. This is a mistaken perception. It is also not an unreasonable inference from the history of twentieth-century psychiatry, for psychoanalysis was once the dominant key of psychiatric practice, and in the last few decades the history of psychiatry had been the story of psychoanalytic decline and psychopharmacological ascendence. But the real story of twentieth-century psychiatry is how complex mental illness is, how difficult it is to treat, and how, in the face of this complexity, people cling to coherent explanations like poor swimmers to a raft.

By the end of World War II, psychoanalysis completely dominated American psychiatry and was nearly synonymous with it. The American Psychoanalytic Association had voted to permit only medical doctors—de facto, only psychiatrists—to train as psychoanalysts, overturning Freud's explicit wishes.[39] (When psychologists won a suit against the American Psychoanalytic Association in 1986, that changed, and psychologists and other professionals are now admitted for training. Even in earlier decades, there were some exceptions.) In the decades after the war, most psychiatric residents were immersed in psychoanalysis. Most ambitious psychiatrists became psychoanalysts, most psychiatric textbooks were written by psychoanalysts, and most teachers of psychiatry taught psychoanalytic theory. Almost all psychiatric leaders (there were exceptions) were psychoanalysts. "In some quarters," mused an éminence grise in 1990, looking back on the postwar decades, "it was believed that psychoanalysis had taken over United States psychiatry lock, stock and barrel."[40]

Why? Psychoanalysis introduced a theory of mind that in its complexity and explanatory power was clearly superior to its predecessors and clearly better equipped to handle mental distress. In mid- to late-nineteenth-century America, marital difficulties, financial misfortunes, and anxiety were not the domain of professionals whose job it was to remove them. By the end of the nineteenth century, Americans apparently began to believe that rapid social change was creating an epidemic of "nerves" that was causing just those difficulties. And by the 1920s, there were numerous competitors for the personal problems clientele: neurologists, social workers, clergymen, advocates of "positive thinking," and the like. Inevitably, a professional tussle arose over which discipline would take charge of the many people who wanted help with the discords and distresses of everyday life.[41] In this setting, Freud's theories were like a flashlight in a candle factory. He offered models of the mind, elaborate theories, specific explanations (for psychosis, hysteria, even jokes), and a specific technique. The competitors had an optimistic theology and some homespun remedies. Freud's ideas decisively won for the psychiatrists the battle for jurisdiction over ordinary human unhappiness. That victory considerably broadened the patient pool for psychiatrists.

Psychoanalysis was also associated with a distinct improvement in patient care. The postwar period was not a medical era given to systematic outcome studies, so although many case studies testify to the power of the psychoanalytic method, there are little systematic data. However, those prewar decades ushered in a more compassionate and optimistic era of psychiatric care. A study of the Boston Psychopathic Hospital elegantly describes an early-twentieth-century shift from a warden's sensibility of locking up the mad to a doctorly sensibility of helping the nearly normal to adjust socially and find their bearings in a frenetic world.[42] The new psychiatrists did not have asylums; they had hospitals. Soon they had outpatient clinics and private practices. Patients were no longer imagined as weird, different, and bodily impaired, as they had been (more or less) in the nineteenth century. They were like the rest of us, victims of an ordinary struggle that wounded a patient somewhat more than those who were not patients. Psychoanalysis was not responsible for this shift in attention from the "alien" to the everyday (it was under way before psychoanalysis had much impact in American psychiatry), but as that shift occurred, psychoanalysis became a powerful theory that justified psychiatrists' treatment of ordinary people, and psychoanalysis was hailed as a powerful method that outshone any other in complexity and technical depth. Not all psychiatric hospitals held to the new standards of humanitarian care (in 1946, for example, one unnerving autobiographical novel, *The Snake Pit,* depicted a psychiatric hospital as a prison). But the tenor of patient care does seem to have grown distinctly more kindly and hopeful.[43]

World War II itself established the value of psychoanalysis both within psychiatry and within the public awareness of psychiatric problems.[44] At the front, shell-shocked soldiers were treated with various techniques, but the symptoms—incapacitating anxiety, recurrent nightmares, intrusive thoughts about one's victims—seemed to cry out for an account of something like an "unconscious." One contemporary recalled, "You didn't have to go into profound theory to demonstrate such things as symptom substitution or repression [in combat trauma]. No one had explanations for these things except the analysts, and they could mobilize them for treatment."[45] The public had been horrified by the news that at least 1,100,000 and perhaps as many as 1,875,000 men had been rejected for military duty because of psychiatric or neurological disorders, and then that more than a million patients with neuropsychiatric casualties had been admitted to military hospitals between January 1942 and December 1945.[46] Psychoanalytically oriented psychiatry seemed to promise a cure. Later, novels such as *Captain Newman, M.D.* gave (apparently) thinly fictionalized accounts of the war and the way military psychiatrists, equipped with psychoanalytic concepts of repression, transference, displacement, and above all the unconscious, could figure out the roots of a soldier's fear and restore him to effective functioning. In 1946, the National Mental Health Act vastly increased the money available for training and research, created the National Institute of Mental Health, and created a network of sixty-nine new hospitals for the Veterans Administration, mostly to deal with psychiatric casualties. Most, by then, had a psychoanalytic focus.[47]

By the early sixties, the American public had adopted psychoanalysis with gushing enthusiasm. Looking back on that era from the distance of four decades, psychoanalysis seems so alien, so peculiarly European against the postwar cheeriness of Tupperware suburbia that one concludes that the American public can have adopted it so eagerly only by not quite understanding Freud's essential pessimism. Some scholars link the popular eagerness to a peculiarly American and deeply un-Freudian optimism about the perfectability of self.[48] In any event, in 1961, *The Atlantic* devoted a special issue to "Psychiatry in American Life." The editor's introduction remarked, "The impact of [the psychoanalytic] revolution has been incalculable. To an extent not paralleled elsewhere, psychoanalysis and psychiatry in general have influenced medicine, the arts and criticism, popular entertainment, advertising, the rearing of children, sociology, anthropology, legal thought and practice, humor, manners and mores, even organized religion."[49] In the Fall 1963 issue of *Daedalus,* an issue devoted to the professions, a psychiatrist remarked, "It is hardly necessary to document the extent to which psychoanalytic thought has pervaded every aspect of modern American life."[50] The author described the widespread appeal of psychoanalysis as a "professional dilemma": psychiatrists wanted to help but could not solve all social problems and could not be everywhere at once. The assumption seemed to be that if a psychiatrist *could* be everywhere, he *would* be able to solve all social ills. This was not the psychoanalysis of devastated Europe but a bright, shiny intellectual appliance, an automated floor buffer for messy psyches. One American commentator (a nonpsychiatrist) happily described psychoanalysis as making possible "a community favorable to the emergence of a humanity more humane than any we have ever known."[51]

Power magnifies weakness. Even at the time, it should have been clear that psychoanalytic dominance could not sustain itself. There was, for a start, the problem of verification created by the theory itself. Psychoanalysis emphasizes the role of unconscious motivation in human suffering. The central hypothesis in psychoanalysis is that our deepest motivations are usually unconscious and often horrid (self-destructive, other-destructive, full of rage, greed, lust, and envy), that we create a panoply of defenses to protect ourselves from acting on those impulses (repression, avoidance, displacement, humor, sublimation, to name just the more obvious), and that the emotional conflicts we thus create drive us nonetheless. From this perspective, people fall ill because they are unable to tolerate the conflicts they find themselves saddled with. If they cannot bear the fact that in some ways they hate their mothers, they may make themselves sick and miserable so as to make her life a burden, while themselves remaining unconscious of their malice. Caught between their love and their hatred, they may feel so guilty that they refuse to allow themselves comfort and peace. The role of the analyst was (then, at least) conceived as helping someone understand aspects of his inner life he could not see for himself and then take responsibility in relation to them. The psychoanalytic process (as it was conceptualized) helped patients understand how they damaged themselves unconsciously, learn to interrupt those patterns, and live a more rewarding and realistic life.

In fact, not even Freud was certain whether an analyst's interpretations and a patient's insight together enabled human change or whether some other feature of treatment—an analyst's unwavering attention, his consistent concern, his reliable presence—was as or more important. But insight—a patient's cognitive understanding of his own psychological dynamics—has always been understood to be important to the psychoanalytic process, and in the postwar period insight was often understood to play the crucial role in therapeutic change.

By their nature, interpretation and insight are unreliable. A trained psychoanalyst, having read much and seen many people in therapy, might be able to understand a person's psychic "grammar" and so help that person understand what he is trying to hide from himself because he fears it. To make this possible, an analyst offers an interpretation, or a description, of a patient's unconscious patterns to the patient. If the patient accepts that interpretation as accurate, he experiences what the analyst calls insight (he may also experience insight independently of the analyst's interpretation). There can be no proof that an analyst is right, nor is an analyst immune to his own unconscious fears, doubts, and blunderings. A patient's rejection of the interpretation does not prove that the interpretation was wrong, nor does her enthusiastic endorsement prove its accuracy.[52]

Yet when psychoanalytic power was at its crest, psychoanalysts casually assumed that criticisms of psychoanalysis—by the patient, by the press, eventually by the new psychiatric scientists—were driven by fear and anxiety in the face of psychoanalytic interpretation. In a field dominated by the notion of an unknowable unconscious, criticisms can always be interpreted as "resistance" to the hard truths of Freud's theory. Thus, younger analysts who protested aspects of psychoanalytic theory or even the behavior of their seniors were often thought to be acting out their unconscious conflicts, like patients, rather than expressing legitimate criticism, like colleagues. In the period of its greatest success, psychoanalysis became an orthodox profession, stern and unforgiving to those who strayed outside conventional limits. "Newcomers to contemporary analysis," an eminent psychoanalyst writes gently, "are not in a good position to fully appreciate the rigidity that characterized the Freudian psychoanalytic writing and discussion of the 1950s and 1960s."[53] All patients were understood to be crippled by emotional conflict, which made them desperately unhappy. Yet the patients themselves were thought to provide the greatest impediment to the resolution of that conflict. This was their "resistance": a refusal to see the conflict for what it was, a psychically manufactured distortion of their real experience. The recognition that each of us builds the cage of our own imprisonment and then howls against the injustice of our confinement is brilliant and deep. But it can also be used to argue that the analyst is always right. The failure of therapy could always be attributed to the patient.

This arrogance, the implicit assumption that accepting an analyst's authority was the route to cure, could also have the effect of focusing attention on the interpretation of an illness rather than on the illness itself. For example, here is a text, published in 1961, that explains that the mania of manic-depressive disorder is a defense against the recognition of a painful personal reality. The author quotes Helene Deutsch, a senior psychoanalytic maven, for support:

> The patient was denying that she lacked a penis, and from this central latent denial irradiated a host of manifest secondary ones. "During the time that she was in analysis," Deutsch wrote (1933), "her husband and lover both deserted her, she lost most of her money, and she experienced the melancholy destiny of mothers whose growing son deserts them for another woman. Finally, she had to accept the narcissistic blow of my telling her that she could not become a psychoanalyst. None of this was capable of disturbing her euphoria."[54]

The modern reader is startled not only by the interpretation but by the fact that the analyst could mention as an aside the disintegration of a life she was supposedly overseeing. In the late 1990s, a psychiatrist would see the "euphoria" of mania as the mood swing that might be causing the loss of husband, lover, money, and son. In 1961, the patient's refusal to acknowledge the analyst's interpretation (of penis envy) was the "central" denial. The collapse of the rest of her life was "secondary." This emphasis on the analyst's explanation would come back to haunt psychoanalysts later, when the new psychiatric scientists accused them of ignoring patients' sicknesses altogether.

Another problem was that it was possible to attribute a patient's failure to improve not to the patient but to the therapist, and specifically to the therapist's anxiety and fear about that patient. Here the real resistance lay in the doctor, not the patient. Psychoanalysts who emphasized a doctor's struggles were likely to teach compassion and kindness to young psychiatrists. They would argue that a doctor must be taught explicitly to learn to care because otherwise his unconscious fear of intimacy and connection would inhibit him from helping patients as much as he could. Nothing in the last few decades has dimmed the salience of this concern. But again, it has a danger, which is that the approach can lead one to confuse the limitations of the practitioners with the limits of the practice. The arrogance that grew out of this approach to psychoanalysis was that the only limits to what psychoanalysis could treat were the limits of the doctor's compassion.

From 1954 to 1976, Elvin Semrad was the legendary residency director of the Massachusetts Mental Health Center, a Harvard teaching hospital where many of today's psychiatric leaders trained. Semrad was a portly Nebraskan, not particularly handsome but warm, with a deeply attentive presence. He seems to have been one of those people who makes you feel clear-headed and capable, as if you can face the reality you fear directly and decide competently what to do about it. He made people feel, as one of his residents told me, as if he listened to them more carefully than anyone had ever done before, and he taught his students that this was what their patients should feel about them. He told them that their job was to "sit" with patients, a term analysts often use to describe the process of trying to understand, to tolerate, and to accept a patient's anger and pain in the patient's presence and to help patients to look at their lives in a way that can help them find their own solutions to their problems. Semrad hated medication; he thought it was a cheap crutch that people used to avoid addressing the real issues. "If they have to get addicted," he said of the patients, "I would rather have them addicted to psychotherapy than to drugs. . . . When you take poison, sooner or later you get poisoned. And all drugs are poison."[55]

Semrad taught that doctors cure through love—of a particular, reserved kind, of course, but love nonetheless. A doctor's ability to heal was his ability to care. One of Semrad's ex-residents who was, when I knew him, a popular supervisor in his own right, still spoke of Semrad with reverence and in Semrad's tradition taught his students through stories. "When I first arrived at Mass Mental," he said, "before I'd gotten the feel of the place, I was given a patient who was a wrist cutter. She would cut her wrists with anything she could get her hands on, and it was driving me mad. I couldn't stop her, and everyone was angry at me. Well, Semrad kept his door open. He formed intense bonds with his residents. It was a very intense apprenticeship in being there for your patient, curing through care, but I really didn't understand that well then. I only knew that I was desperate, and I went to talk to him. To my great embarrassment, I began to cry. Semrad said nothing. So I pulled myself together, and I sat there thinking that my psychiatric career was in ruins. In many hospitals, those tears would have been a sign of overinvolvement. But Semrad said, in a very gentle but confident tone—it is impossible to convey the quality of that tone—'I'm sure that if you show her how much you care, she will stop.' And so I went back to her. I told her that I was confused, that I didn't know what to do, I was so upset—and she stopped." Semrad seems to have been fairly direct, but he used aphorisms, often paradoxical: that love, for example, was "the only socially acceptable psychosis"[56] or, in advice to a resident, "Go after what the patient feels and cannot do himself. Help him to acknowledge what he cannot bear himself, and stay with him until he can stand it."[57] After his death, two students collected the sayings that they could remember in a book. It is clear that they reciprocated the love.

This made sense if psychiatric illness were understood solely as a response to emotional conflict. From this perspective, the difference between psychosis, neurosis, and health was a matter of degree. True mental health was an illusion. To some measure we were all damned. We had all lusted in our hearts and loins for unallowed parents in unallowed ways, and emotionally we were all groping toward the light. Psychiatric patients were people more overwhelmed than others by anxiety or rage, and psychosis and depression were various ways of handling their otherwise unmanageable feelings. Young psychiatrists learned that their basic job was to listen empathically to the patient, to try to understand the patient's experience from the patient's point of view, and to understand and to describe (or interpret) the patient's conflicts. A psychiatrist's presence would help a patient understand that he could live a different sort of life, one less haunted by misery, and with that understanding, the patient could decide to relinquish the symptoms that, until then, had been a refuge. But the psychiatrist could work this miracle only if he genuinely accepted and understood the things the patient feared, so that those things would seem less terrifying. That was why the psychiatrist's loving acceptance of the patient was so important.

It was also, at Mass Mental, very difficult. The clients at Mass Mental were among the sickest, poorest, and most chronic patients in Boston. Most of them were thought to have schizophrenia, the darkest of all psychiatric illnesses, an illness of psychosis, emotional withdrawal, and profound dysfunction. In those days the label included the same chronic, difficult, apparently untreatable and incurable patients who had filled the state mental hospitals since they had opened. Many people, working with these patients, have a palpable sense that something has gone physically wrong with their brains. But in the period of psychoanalytic imperialism, the schizophrenic's psychosis, emotional apathy, and inability to function were said to arise from his intense emotional ambivalence. The schizophrenic's mother (she was called "schizophrenigenic") had given him conflicting signals that he was unable to resolve except through psychotic emotional withdrawal. The famous example of this kind of double bind was this: a mother visits her schizophrenic son; he is glad to see her, and hugs her; she stiffens; he draws back; she asks, "Don't you love me anymore?"[58]

To Semrad, a schizophrenic was the most exciting patient, the tough, difficult patient that made a young resident a "real" psychiatrist, particularly the schizophrenic in his first "break," or psychotic episode, because that was when consciousness broke open like a cracked skull to display the hidden workings of the unconscious inside. By seeing in the psychosis the meaning of meaningless words and gestures, a doctor could help a patient. Semrad recognized that it was hard to do daily therapy with these patients. Nonetheless, the ethos was clear. As the chronicler of the classic study of Mass Mental pointed out, "to treat schizophrenics psychoanalytically became the ultimate professional challenge at which most psychiatrists tried their hand."[59] It proved that the doctor did not fear the patient, that his own unconscious defenses were not so steep as to prevent him from making emotional contact with that patient, that he had the courage, as Semrad would have put it, to bear what the patient could not, so that the patient could see that the burden was bearable. As Semrad wrote, "In order to engage a schizophrenic patient in therapy, the therapist's basic attitude must be an acceptance of the patient as he is—of his aims in life, his values, and his modes of operating, even when they are different and very often at odds with his own. Loving the patient as he is, in his state of decompensation [his psychosis], is the therapist's primary concern in approaching the patient."[60]

These were terribly important lessons. But loving the patient did not, by itself, do much for the symptoms of severe mental illness, although it probably helped lessen the intense loneliness most schizophrenic patients fear and probably prevented relapses into more severe psychosis. Not even all of Semrad's residents believed the message of hope about the hard but rewarding work of doing therapy with schizophrenics. "It was nonsense," one said to me thirty years after the fact. "You couldn't do anything with them." That the ethos sustained itself at all was probably due to the fact that the word "schizophrenic" was more capacious then than it is now and in fact included many people who would not now be called schizophrenic and did in fact improve. (Some of them would now be called borderline personality disorder, manic-depressive, and so forth. Also, even with the current narrow definition, some significant percentage of schizophrenics—perhaps as high as 30 percent—do eventually improve. It is not clear whether their improvement has to do with their treatment.) As a result, while popular accounts described the miraculous transformations wrought by psychoanalytic psychotherapy on the very sick—*Dibs; Jordi; Lisa and David; The Fifty Minute Hour; I Never Promised You a Rose Garden; Autobiography of a Schizophrenic Girl*—many of the sickest patients remained as ill as ever.

Psychoanalysis, on its own, without appropriate medication, did not have much impact on severe psychiatric illness. Yet it was terribly difficult to make that criticism stick, because the theory itself invited the observer to blame the patient or the therapist rather than the technique. When a psychiatrist complained openly that psychoanalysis didn't work for his patients, he was at risk of looking like a fool. In the end, economic and social problems created the conditions under which the old psychoanalytic paradigm gave way. And because it gave way reluctantly, it did so without grace.

There was, for a start, the problem of whom the analysts would treat. In 1970, Arnold Rogow published a remarkable book called *The Psychiatrists* that probably represents the peak of public confidence in the psychoanalytic method. Rogow was a political scientist who justified his interest in psychiatry on the basis of the enormous power psychiatrists seemed to have over American lives: "Perhaps it is not too much to say that where the public once turned to the minister, or the captain of industry, or the scientist, it is now turning more and more to the psychiatrist."[61] He was tempted, he said, to recall Winston Churchill's words about British fighter pilots in connection with the psychiatrists: "Never have so many owed so much to so few." The paean call of the study was that far more people ought to become psychotherapists because so many Americans needed the help so badly. By 1970, the demand for psychotherapy far exceeded the number of psychiatrists qualified to provide it. Rogow wrote urgently about the need for more psychotherapists. He called on professors to lay down their books and take up training in any form they could, and he supported his call by citing a 1969 study of New York City schoolchildren that claimed that only 12 percent of them enjoyed good mental health.

In fact, by now there were many reports of high levels of mental illness in the American community. In 1962, the Midtown Manhattan Study reported that in a sample of 1,020 men and women in the "lowest" level of socio-economic status, 47 percent were "impaired" and 23 percent had "moderate symptom formation." Only 5 percent were "well."[62] The literature of the period uses data like these to document a desperate need for psychiatrists. A 1968 report prepared under the auspices of the National Commission on Mental Health Manpower presents itself as an eager recruitment plea, "an invitation to explore a career in mental health." "No state," it implored, "can meet even minimal staffing standards; *no* profession can produce enough graduates to meet the demand. The situation is now critical, and the future looms even worse, for the population is expanding while the pool of mental health manpower remains almost static." The psychoanalyst, the report promised, will "find himself in tremendous demand."[63] In the flush of their own authority, psychiatrists took up a social responsibility that from this distance seems poignantly ambitious. In the 1970 presidential address to the American Psychiatric Association, the speaker announced that "for too long we as psychiatrists have focused on the mental health of the individual."[64] It was time, he went on, for psychiatry to turn its attention to pollution, overpopulation, racism, and nuclear war.

But Rogow's own data reveal a major economic difficulty with the psychoanalytic enterprise. Analysts did not like to treat the very sickest patients, even though the promise of psychoanalysis was to treat all mental illness and even though most psychiatrists had been trained by treating very sick patients. One hundred eighty-four psychiatrists answered the questionnaire Rogow sent to every thirtieth name on the lists of members of the American Psychiatric Association and the American Psychoanalytic Association. Thirty-five were psychoanalysts as well as psychiatrists. A quarter were Jewish and most were middle class in origin. Most of them described themselves as psychoanalytically oriented and used this approach with most kinds of patients. Most of them preferred to treat "neuroses"—in other words, patients who were not very sick. Most patients were white and in business or the professions. For a fifth of the analysts, 75 to 100 percent of their patients were Jewish; for an additional quarter, 50 to 75 percent of their patients were Jewish. No analyst had any Puerto Rican, Mexican, or Native American patients. Only three analysts had any black patients, and very few of those. Only one analyst had any blue-collar patients, whereas slightly more than half of the psychiatrists had at least one blue-collar patient. Half of the patients were women, most of them housewives. The cost of an average psychotherapy visit in many cities in 1970 was $35, so that a year of once-a-week therapy cost $1,500 to $2,000 and a year of analysis cost well over $5,000. In 1969, the median earnings of a civilian American man was $6,899.[65]

The unavoidable picture that emerges from this document is of a medical profession whose most important practitioners saw the wealthiest and healthiest members of the patient population. Another study, published in 1969, unironically remarks, "Although it is true that only two percent of the adult American population will admit that they have ever consulted a psychiatrist or a psychologist for a personal problem, the importance of the people who have actually received therapy transcends the sheer numbers involved."[66] This is in damning contrast to the rest of medicine, where the patients of the best doctors may be wealthy, but they are usually also among the sickest. The important people who consulted psychiatrists were hardly in that category. In 1970, one out of every two hospital beds was occupied by a psychiatric patient, and most psychiatric training took place in hospitals filled with chronic patients. But those patients were not the patients of the most esteemed psychiatrists (although it was always true that despite the class bias, some of the best psychiatrists chose to continue to work with the sickest and the poorest of the patient population). The most esteemed psychiatrists were psychoanalysts, and their patients were too healthy to be admitted to a hospital. There was even common psychoanalytic wisdom that supported this position. Freud had written on the question of analytic "suitability" and had been clear that only patients with healthy ego strength (not psychotic) were suitable for psychoanalytic therapy. There was a contradiction, then, between the ambitious promises of the field and its actual practice. Until there were real treatment alternatives, however, there wasn't much motivation to confront that contradiction.

However, in the early 1970s, the visible failure of the community mental health movement, which was an attempt to apply psychiatric thinking to the poor and sick in society at large, began to discredit psychoanalysis, at least as a treatment for the very ill. In 1963, John F. Kennedy's presidential address on mental health had argued that "the time has come for a bold new approach."[67] The initiative had established community mental health centers, which were to treat psychiatric problems locally and preemptively, so that the hospitalized could return to their families and those at risk would not get so sick. Local psychiatrists would take responsibility for local areas and, by dint of their professional skills, maintain the community's mental health. The idealism of this time still lingers in the memory of those who became psychiatrists, social workers, and psychologists in order to participate. "It was wonderful," a psychiatric nurse said sadly of the days when she had worked in a hospital that had been founded to serve the community mental health purpose. "Spirits were so high. We were all so committed. It was so exciting. It's different now." The money never really materialized, but many of the hospitalized were released from hospitals despite the lack of local community care.[68] This was called "deinstitutionalization." Because the infrastructure of community mental health care was never established, homelessness became the only option for many of the former patients. The profound chronicity of much mental illness became evident to the public, particularly in the next decade, when the real estate market skyrocketed and much formerly affordable housing was converted into more profitable investment.[69]

Meanwhile, an "antipsychiatry" movement emerged and gathered force. Since the early sixties, Erving Goffman, R. D. Laing, Thomas Szasz, Thomas Scheff, and others (some psychiatrists, some not) had been writing vivid, brilliant books arguing that the mentally ill were not ill, just unconventional. The movement was a child of its rebellious, antiestablishment times, and it gained a wide audience. There were different ways of running the critique: Goffman pointed out that human behavior was profoundly shaped by institutional life, so that asylum patients rapidly learned to be psychiatrically ill; Scheff argued that the apparent symptoms of mental illness were better understood as nonconformity, which was labeled "deviant" by the social group. The general claim was that psychiatric illness was a problem of "labeling" and mental illness was a myth.[70] In 1974, the psychiatrist E. Fuller Torrey published a book entitled *The Death of Psychiatry*, which began, "Psychiatry is an emperor standing naked in his new clothes." Most people treated by psychiatrists, he argued, had problems in living and certainly did not need to be treated by people with medical training; all the others had brain disease and ought to be given back to the neurologists. What psychoanalytic psychiatrists saw as the emotional conflicts at the root of mental illness, these antipsychiatrists saw as a rebellious, artistic, unconventional rejection of the establishment. The fact that homosexuality had been removed from the list of psychiatric illnesses in 1973 by, of all things, a vote of the membership of the American Psychiatric Association, as if an illness label were a matter of opinion, did not help to allay these widely publicized doubts.

Indeed, with the fluid psychoanalytic boundary between health and illness, it was difficult to say who was really sick. In 1973, *Science* published an article that deeply embarrassed the psychiatric world. The author, an academic psychologist named David Rosenhan, had persuaded eight people to present themselves at twelve different hospitals, complaining that they each had heard a voice saying "Thud." Beyond this "auditory hallucination" they changed nothing in their life histories save their names and, if they were in the mental health field, their professions. Each pseudopatient was admitted; all but one were diagnosed as schizophrenic; their average length of stay was nineteen days. It was common for other patients on the wards to suspect the pseudopatients of being journalists or inspectors or in any event sane, but the staff members never did. On the contrary, they prepared notes and case reports as if the pseudopatients really were schizophrenic. One pseudo patient was described in his discharge summary as follows:

> This white 39 year old male . . . manifests a long history of considerable ambivalence in close relationships, which begins in early childhood. A warm relationship with his mother cools during adolescence. A distant relationship to his father is described as being very intense. His attempts to control emotionality with his wife and children are punctuated by angry outbursts and, in the case of children, spankings. And while he says he has several good friends, one senses considerable ambivalence embedded in these relationships also.[71]

Ambivalence was the trademark of the schizophrenic's psychodynamics. Rosenhan neatly summarized the attitude of the psychiatric staff toward the pseudopatients: the patient is in a psychiatric hospital, so he must be psychiatrically disturbed.[72]

Again, this fluidity had economic repercussions. In the psychoanalytic era, diagnosis per se was not terribly important. Many psychiatrists believed that diagnostic labels were irrelevant and used them cavalierly. Study after study bore out the unreliability of the diagnostic process; one found that young psychiatrists were no more likely to agree with an examiner's diagnosis of a patient than would be expected by chance.[73] With this level of vagueness, deciding how many people were actually ill became a significant public health puzzle and certainly cast into doubt the earlier dire estimates of the Midtown Manhattan Study. In 1978, the President's Commission on Mental Health reported that 15 percent of the population needed some form of mental health services at any one time— and then, astonishingly, mentioned in a footnote that this estimate had no data to support it: "Ideally, we would like to know the true prevalence of psychiatric disorders. . . . How do we come to terms with the fact that such data do not as yet exist?"[74] The estimate, in other words, was a guess.

This was a significant problem for insurance companies, which by the 1970s had began to cover medical care widely. In the 1960s, Aetna and Blue Cross, through the Federal Employees Benefit Program, reimbursed for treatment for psychiatric illness dollar for dollar with other medical illnesses. By the mid-1970s, Aetna had cut back coverage to twenty out-patient visits and forty inpatient hospital days per year. An official explained why:

> Compared to other types of [medical] service there is less clarity and uniformity of terminology concerning mental diagnosis, treatment modalities and types of facilities providing care. . . . One dimension of this problem arises from the latent or private nature of many services; only the patient and the therapist have direct knowledge of what services were provided and why.[75]

This, of course, was true. No information other than the diagnosis was released to insurance companies on the grounds of confidentiality, and the diagnosis provided almost no information.

In addition, the psychoanalytic citadel suddenly faced competition from the interlopers allowed in to help shoulder the increased demand for psychotherapy. In the middle 1960s, only psychiatrists were recognized as legitimate providers of psychotherapy, and, as we have seen, only psychiatrists could train as psychoanalysts. Psychologists did offer therapy, but only psychiatrists could be reimbursed by insurance companies. But because the demand for therapy far exceeded the supply, by 1972 Medicaid allowed psychologists to bill for services, first for psychological testing and then for psychotherapy, and by 1974 the government allowed clinical psychologists to be named as qualified independent providers of psychotherapy.[76] Social workers soon followed suit, and the gates swung open. Psychiatrists no longer looked as if they were doing something special, something that no one else could do.

It was around this period, in the 1970s, that a new kind of psychiatrist began to emerge. These psychiatrists saw themselves as scientists, and to them that word set them apart from psychoanalysis, to which many of them were openly hostile and which few of them regarded as scientific. (Psychoanalysts still tended to think of themselves as scientists, as had Freud. I will use the term "psychiatric science" to refer to this new movement in psychiatry.) The psychiatric scientists were committed to what they called strict standards of evidence, and they tended to view psychoanalytic theories of causation as neither provable nor disprovable by those standards. They were determined to create a psychiatry that looked more like the rest of medicine, in which patients were understood to have diseases and in which doctors identified the diseases and then targeted them by treating the body, just as medicine identified and treated cardiac illness, thyroiditis, and diabetes.

They already had the medication. Psychiatric medication had existed since 1954, when Smith Kline and French had introduced Thorazine, a medication that reduced the hallucinatory symptoms of psychosis.[77] (Actually, even earlier a drug called reserpine had been used, but as it induced depression it is no longer prescribed much.) Many psychiatrists— among them many of those who taught residents, published in journals, and set policy—were scornful of the medications in the early years, seeing them as crude instruments that addressed the symptoms but not the underlying psycho-dynamics of illnesses. It is true that Thorazine is a blunt instrument: it reduces psychosis but often leaves the patient in a daze. It can also produce muscular twitches and a shuffling gait. Residents from the sixties, when chronic patients were put on huge doses of Thorazine and the psychoanalytic model still dominated as the explanation for their symptoms, learned to talk about the "Thorazine shuffle" in the hospital. By the seventies, however, a whole crop of new psychiatric medications had appeared, many of them more precise in their action and less devastating in their side effects.[78] Lithium began to be widely used to manage the mood swings of manic depression, and it was strikingly helpful (lithium had been discovered in 1949, by John Cade, but because it can be toxic it was not used freely until the early seventies, when tests were developed to measure and control blood levels). Miltown, Librium, Valium, and other antianxiety agents—"mother's little helpers"—were often prescribed. Reliable antidepressants (the tricyclics) were available, although their side effects were unpleasant. There were medications in abundance. What psychiatrists did not yet have was a clear connection between what was medically wrong with a patient and how to tie that specific judgment to a specific medical plan.

The emerging school of "scientific" or "remedicalized" psychiatry owed its allegiance not to Freud but to Emil Kraepelin, a German psychiatrist born the same year as Freud (1856). Kraepelin had created an important taxonomy of psychiatric illness by studying symptom clusters and final outcomes, and by collecting family histories to trace hereditary traits.[79] He is famous for, among other things, applying the term "dementia praecox" to a group of illnesses that began in adolescence and ended in dementia. (The term now used is "schizophrenia.") The new psychiatric scientists argued, in effect, that psychiatry had made a wrong turn by following Freud instead of Kraepelin. (Their approach is called neo-Kraepelinian.) They tended to believe that if a disorder could be distinctly identified with specific criteria, a common clinical course, and perhaps a family history, it probably had an underlying organic cause and was a disease like any other.

Much of the initial work came out of Washington University, where a collection of researchers—most famously, Eli Robins, Lee Nelken Robins, Samuel Guze, and George Winokur—had been doing research since the

1950s. What they did was to describe a disorder and then draft criteria for its diagnosis (for example, suicidal thoughts, depressed mood, inability to concentrate) that were clear enough for different observers to give the same diagnosis to the same patient. They did this through clinical wisdom, but also by using laboratory studies, family studies, and follow-up studies. This was a novel and threatening idea, odd as that seems on this side of the 1980s. The criteria they produced are sometimes known as the "Feighner criteria," after the lucky resident who was the first author of what became a famous paper, "Diagnostic Criteria for Use in Psychiatric Research," published in *The Archives of General Psychiatry* in 1972. The paper sits oddly in the table of contents among papers with titles such as "On the Incapacity to Love" and "The Chinese Attitude Toward Parental Authority as Expressed in Chinese Children's Stories." It is modestly written, but the dry prose has a revolutionary tone: "Diagnosis has functions as important in psychiatry as elsewhere in medicine."[80]

In 1980, the American Psychiatric Association published the *Diagnostic and Statistical Manual of Mental Disorders,* third edition, called more commonly *DSM III.* The two previous *DSMs* had been slight, spiral-bound pamphlets not taken terribly seriously by the field. When the American Psychiatric Association published its first diagnostic manual in 1952, most psychiatric disorders were listed under the explicit title "Disorders of Psychogenic Origin or Without Clearly Defined Physical Cause or Structural Change in the Brain."[81] The diagnostic ancestors of the current psychiatric labels were clearly marked; but they were adjectives, not nouns. The manual spoke not of "schizophrenia" but of a "schizophrenic reaction." Its language was distinctly psychoanalytic. The "psychoneurotic disorders," for instance, were "anxiety reaction," "obsessive-compulsive reaction," and "depressive reaction," rather than (as now) "generalized anxiety disorder," "obsessive-compulsive disorder," "major depression." The early manual described all those problems this way: "The chief characteristic of these disorders is 'anxiety,' which may be directly felt and expressed or which may be unconsciously and automatically controlled by the utilization of various psychological defense mechanisms."[82]

DSM III was a fat book. There were many more diagnoses, they were more precisely detailed, and they were decked out with the accoutrements of scientific research. The psychodynamics were gone. In the place of Freud's ghost stood Kraepelin. ("It's extraordinary," a psychoanalyst said to me when I described the training of young psychiatrists. "*Kraepelin.* They're going back to Kraepelin.") *DSM III,* like the Feighner criteria out of which it had grown, was "scientific," medically speaking (at least, that was the intended point). The psychiatrists responsible for *DSM III* had assembled under the guidance of Robert Spitzer, a tall, quick, shy man trained as a psychoanalyst. Spitzer argued that the "innovation" of *DSM III* would be a "defense of the medical model as applied to psychiatric problems."[83] The minutes from the first meeting of the Task Force on Nomenclature and Statistics read:

> A diagnosis should be made if the criteria for that diagnosis are met. . . . It is hoped that this will stimulate appreciation, among psychiatrists, of the distinction between the known and the assumed. . . . The diagnostic manual will be essentially behavioral, with exceptions for conditions of known etiology. . . . It was agreed that "functional" is no longer a suitable designation for a group of conditions—schizophrenias and affective disorders—which are no longer seen as purely psychogenic.[84]

In other words, psychiatric diagnosis should matter. A diagnosis should mean that the diagnosed person was sick, and sick in a way that different physicians could reliably recognize. The manual listed more than two hundred categories (only a few are commonly used). Under each category there were criteria, often with inclusion rules: six of the following nine, eight of the following sixteen. If the patient met the criteria, the patient had a mental illness. If the patient did not, he or she did not. The patient's personal history—his or her ambivalence, potty training, basic trust, resolution of the Oedipus complex, dependency, whatever—was irrelevant. From the vantage point of *DSM III*, it didn't matter how a patient had become depressed or why. What mattered was that he met the necessary number of criteria, which could be determined (more or less) by a short interview. All of a sudden, there was a sharp, clean dividing line between mental health and illness.

And that line was thought to be determined by science. Gone was the wise clinician's sensitivity to the subtleties of psychodynamic communication. These diagnoses were based on what anyone could observe (in theory; actually, using the manual involves considerable skill), and the committee went to great effort to show that different people would give the same diagnosis to the same patient. Research on the validity and reliability of these categories was reported with numbers and with statistical terms that most psychiatrists had never encountered. A 1979 article on the diagnostic reliability of affective disorder categories, for instance, has tables that include "F" scores, "kappa" scores, "two-tailed" significance scores, cross-tabulations, differentiating and nondifferentiating criteria, reliability coefficients, and the like. "Whereas most studies of diagnostic reliability," the authors report, "yield kappas (an index of reliability that corrects for chance agreement) that range from .4 to .6, the kappas for the RDC [Research

Diagnostic Criteria] were usually above .7 and usually above .8."[85] In a bracing book called *The Selling of DSM,* two social scientists accuse Spitzer of snowing the field with the illusory precision of statistical accuracy. They say that he used a statistical term—"kappa"—of doubtful applicability and produced kappas in abundance to prove that psychiatry was a science.[86] They undoubtedly have a piece of the truth; yet it is also quite clear that these new categories were far more specific than the old ones. Consider the *DSM II* definition of schizophrenia, which could include most people when they hit their low spots:

> This psychosis is characterized chiefly by a slow and insidious reduction of external attachments and interests and by apathy and indifference leading to impoverishment of interpersonal relations, mental deterioration, and adjustment on a lower level of functioning. In general, the condition is less dramatically psychotic than are the hebephrenic, catatonic and paranoid types of schizophrenia. Also, it contrasts with schizoid personality, in which there is little or no progression of the disorder.

Now consider this one from *DSM III:*

A. At least one of the following during a phase of the illness:

    1. bizarre delusions (content is patently absurd and has *no* possible basis in fact), such as delusions of being controlled, thought broadcasting, thought insertion, or thought withdrawal

    2. somatic, grandiose, religious, nihilistic, or other delusions without persecutory or jealous content

    3. delusions with persecutory or jealous content if accompanied by hallucinations of any type

    4. auditory hallucinations in which either a voice keeps up a running commentary on the individual's behavior or thoughts, or two or more voices converse with each other

    5. auditory hallucinations on several occasions with content of more than one or two words, having no apparent relation to depression or elation

    6. incoherence, marked loosening of associations, markedly illogical thinking, or marked poverty of speech if associated with at least one of the following:
        a. blunted, flat, or inappropriate affect
        b. delusions or hallucinations
        c. catatonic or other grossly disorganized behavior

B. Deterioration from a previous level of functioning in such areas as work, social relations, and self-care.

C. Duration: Continuous signs of the illness for at least six months at some time during the person's life with some signs of the illness at present. The six-month period must include an active phase during which there were symptoms from A, with or without a prodromal phase, as defined below.

Prodromal phase: A clear deterioration in functioning before the active phase of the illness not due to a disturbance in mood or to a Substance Use Disorder and involving at least *two* of the symptoms noted below.

Residual phase: Persistence, following the active phase of the illness, of at least *two* of the symptoms noted below not due to a disturbance in mood or to a Substance Use Disorder.

Prodromal or Residual Symptoms:
1. social isolation or withdrawal
2. marked impairment in role functioning as wage-earner, student, or homemaker
3. markedly peculiar behavior (e g., collecting garbage, talking to self in public, or hoarding food)
4. marked impairment in personal hygiene and grooming
5. blunted, flat, or inappropriate affect
6. digressive, vague, overelaborate, circumstantial, or metaphorical speech
7. odd or bizarre ideation, or magical thinking, e.g., superstitiousness, clairvoyance, telepathy, "sixth sense," "others can feel my feelings," overvalued ideas, ideas of reference
8. unusual perceptual experiences, e.g., recurrent illusions, sensing the presence of a force or person not actually present

Examples: Six months of prodromal symptoms with one week of symptoms from A; no prodromal symptoms with six months of symptoms from A; no prodromal symptoms with two weeks of symptoms from A and six months of residual symptoms; six months of symptoms from A, apparently followed by several years of complete remission, with one week of symptoms in A in current episode.

D. The full depressive or manic syndrome (criteria A and B of major depressive or manic episode), if present, developed after any psy-

chotic symptoms, or was brief in duration relative to the duration of
the psychotic symptoms of A.

E. Onset of prodromal or active phase of the illness before age 45.

F. Not due to any Organic Mental Disorder or Mental Retardation.[87]

However manipulative one can accuse the task force of being, there is
no question that two psychiatrists were more likely to use the same labels
to describe the same patient when they were using *DSM III* than when
using *DSM II*. It is also clear that Rosenhan's pseudopatients would never
have been diagnosed as schizophrenic if the interviewing psychiatrists had
been using *DSM III*.

There was a great debate in the field over *DSM III* (which was nonetheless immediately adopted), and to an onlooker the debate is fascinating
because its advocates could clearly spell out the benefits and its opponents
struggled with an inarticulate dread: that in the lust for scientific
respectability, something had gone terribly wrong. In 1984, the *American
Journal of Psychiatry* published a debate about *DSM III* among four great
shaggy lions of the psychiatric field: Gerald Klerman, George Vaillant,
Robert Spitzer, and Robert Michels. Spitzer, as mentioned, had led the
DSM III task force. Vaillant was a beloved psychodynamic teacher, famous
for a book on adult development called *Adaptation to Life*. Michels was a
psychoanalyst and chair of psychiatry at Cornell and would soon become
dean of Cornell Medical School. Klerman held a named chair at Harvard.
The pro-*DSM* argument (Klerman and Spitzer) pointed out that the *DSM
III* categories enabled physicians to tease apart different psychiatric conditions and gave psychiatrists a descriptive language to talk to one another
across cities, across states, even across countries. ("In Japan," Klerman
wrote, "it was a delight to see Japanese psychiatrists, particularly the professors, carrying around the mini–*DSM III* and studying it with characteristic Japanese vigor.") In addition, the categories did not rely on anything
that had to be inferred by a complex, unprovable process.[88] The argument
against (Vaillant and Michels) pointed out that data that are reliable (who
is tall) may not be very valid or useful if you are interested in schizophrenia.
They argued that the diagnoses were parochial and reductionistic. But
mostly, the argument against claimed that there was something intrinsic to
emotional suffering with which *DSM III* could not engage. As Vaillant
pointed out, "[Psychiatry] has more in common with the inevitable ambiguity of great drama than with *DSM III*'s quest for algorithms compatible
with the cold binary logic of computer science."[89]

By this point in the early eighties, psychiatry in many hospitals had become a sprawling confrontation between what were then thought of as the "two camps": either psychiatric illness was like a disease, reliable diagnosis was important, and psychopharmacology was the major and crucial intervention, or diagnosis was not important and psychopharmacology was a crutch. In some hospitals there was a quiet war that, at least in the largest psychiatric hospital I studied, left behind a wreckage of bitterness and folklore about the days when the biological psychiatrists (as this group came to be called) and the psychoanalysts had sat at different tables during lunch and when case conferences could be cruel, covert duels. Some of the younger psychiatrists felt palpably relieved by the new approach. Scientific psychiatry removed the burden of responsibility from residents who were determinedly trying to cure their sickest patients through caring, only to find that despite their good intentions and hard work they made no impact. Psychoanalytic supervisors often took a patient's lack of progress as an indication of a young doctor's fear of intimacy and engagement: the psychiatrist wasn't "really" trying hard. (One of the problems here is that the residents were seeing patients in the hospital who were far sicker than those the analysts saw as private patients.) With the new biomedical approach, these young psychiatrists could shake off that criticism. They weren't inadequate; rather, they were doctors dealing with chronic patients whose diseases had no adequate medical treatments. "I was pretty distressed with psychoanalysis by the end of residency," one senior psychiatrist reminisced. "The psychoanalytic model really dominated, and when I had a different take on the patient, I would be told that I was resisting. I felt inadequate. When the biomedical revolution came along, it felt very familiar. And I felt vindicated."

The most famous instance of the ideological struggle emerged just before the balance of power shifted in 1980 with the publication of *DSM III*. On January 2, 1979, a forty-two-year-old internist named Rafael Osheroff was admitted to Chestnut Lodge, an elite psychiatric hospital outside Washington, D.C., with symptoms of anxiety and depression. At Chestnut Lodge, he was treated by intensive, psychoanalytically oriented psychotherapy. Despite this treatment, his depression worsened noticeably. He lost forty pounds, was unable to sleep, and began to pace so incessantly that his feet became swollen and blistered. After several months, the staff held a case conference on the treatment plan, prompted by the family's distress at the length of hospitalization and the patient's lack of improvement. The case conference concluded that Dr. Osheroff was being treated appropriately by psychodynamic psychotherapy. More specifically, it concluded that psychiatric medication might interfere with the psychotherapeutic process. Osheroff's condition continued to worsen. At the end of seven months of inpatient treatment, his frustrated family had him discharged from Chestnut Lodge and admitted to another psychiatric hospital, the Silver Hill Foundation in Connecticut. There he was immediately medicated and in three weeks showed marked improvement. He was discharged within three months and soon resumed his normal life.[90]

In 1982, Osheroff sued Chestnut Lodge for negligence. The psychiatrists he sued were psychoanalysts. They had believed that his depression was one of many symptoms of the disturbed personality style that he had developed. He was, they had decided, narcissistic, a term that carries a great weight of psychoanalytic theorizing. The narcissistic person is an adult infant, someone so wounded by parental failures in early childhood that he has great difficulty recognizing anyone else's needs. From a psychoanalytic vantage point, depression indicated that Osheroff's adaptation around this inadequacy had finally broken down. His doctors had resisted prescribing medication on the grounds that medication would not address what they saw as the basic problem and might, in fact, dampen any motivation to change. For the psychiatrists who testified for Osheroff against Chestnut Lodge, depression was a collection of symptoms—weight loss, insomnia, agitated pacing, depressed mood—and the psychiatrist's job was to treat the symptoms in their own right, no matter what else was going on. This line of reasoning broke the causal chain between the analyst's understanding of the origin of the illness and the illness itself and let the depression float free as a medical problem. Behind this reasoning lay the conviction that what psychiatrists can see is what psychiatrists should treat.

By the time the case was settled out of court (much later, in 1988) it was clear that Osheroff had scored a moral victory. In April 1990, Gerald Klerman published an article in the *American Journal of Psychiatry* entitled "The Psychiatric Patient's Right to Effective Treatment: Implications of *Osheroff vs. Chestnut Lodge.*"[91] Klerman laid out, in clear, sensible prose, what he took to have happened in the patient's hospitalization. A private psychiatrist had prescribed antidepressants to Osheroff before hospitalization, and although Osheroff had soon stopped taking the pills, it was apparent from the medical record available to the Chestnut Lodge physicians that the medication had improved his mood; the Chestnut Lodge physicians had refused to prescribe medication despite good evidence that he was depressed and the psychotherapeutic treatment was not working; and once Osheroff was under the care of new physicians who prescribed the medication, his illness quickly improved. The chilling part of the essay, however, was its judgment upon psychoanalytically oriented psychotherapy: that "there was no scientific evidence for the value of psychodynamically oriented intensive individual psychotherapy."[92] *No scientific evidence.*[93] Most psychodynamic psychiatrists perceived psychotherapy as a delicate relationship whose impact depended on the intimacy of the patient's trust and the doctor's intuition, and as manifestly not the sort of thing that could be measured in quantifiable units. They knew it worked; many of them called psychoanalysis a science; the charge was confusing and hard to grasp.

Alan Stone—a professor at Harvard Law School and once president of the American Psychiatric Association, known for his incisive wit—tried to defend the Chestnut Lodge physicians against Klerman's charges in the same journal. He explained at length that because the case had been settled out of court, it had created no legal precedent—in fact, he announced that he would not speak of "the Osheroff case"—and then conceded that the action, along with Klerman's paper, had "potentially serious legal consequences."[94] He defended the Chestnut Lodge doctors against Klerman's judgment by pointing out that standards of care had been different in 1979 and then argued that those standards were still valid. He suggested that Osheroff had improved because he had been so furious at Chestnut Lodge that a transfer to another hospital had filled him with a triumphant joy indistinguishable from good health. At one point Stone even remarked, in defense of the Chestnut Lodge approach, that "much of what all physicians do has no demonstrated effectiveness—even the prescription of supposedly efficacious medications."[95] "The rebuttal by Alan Stone, M.D.," a letter to the editor remarked sadly some months later, "may well be the best case that a clever man can make."[96]

The tortuousness of Stone's argument was partly the result of fighting on the losing side. Nobody had disputed that Rafael Osheroff had been seriously depressed. By 1990, it seemed absurd that a depressed patient, so seriously ill that he was admitted to a psychiatric inpatient unit, would not have been medicated. But the back-and-forth complexity of Stone's argument had as much to do with the sense of confronting a radical shift in argument, that those things psychoanalysts had taken for granted were suddenly not even part of the conversation. That is the feeling one has when reading these exchanges between the psychoanalysts and the psychiatric scientists from this era: perplexed groping after the argument, genuine incomprehension of what the other side has said, charging to attack a point the other side never thought it made. Throughout the 1980s, those who were groping were the analysts. They seemed to paw helplessly at the arguments, dimly recognizing that there were virtues to the other side, rarely seeming to really grasp the way the others thought because the very structure and goal of the way they thought were different. Now it is sometimes the other way around. This incomprehension is the result of the transformation of a psychiatric illness into an altogether different animal, so that the analysts, looking across at the psychiatric scientists, did not see what they worked with and the scientists, looking back, could not see why they were puzzled.

In these battles the supporters of scientific psychiatry came across as sensible and straightforward, while the psychoanalysts, losing ground, seemed circuitous, ambiguous, and complex. Sometimes they could sound shrill. Months after the Klerman-Stone exchange on the Osheroff case, the *American Journal of Psychiatry* published a flurry of letters. Most of them urged psychiatrists not to bifurcate the field into biological psychiatry and psychoanalysis and promptly went on to take sides. The psychoanalytic supporters suggested that drug companies prove that drugs work only because they want to sell them—"There is considerable pressure, unconscious if not conscious, on researchers to produce findings favoring the efficacy of a drug"—and that double-blind studies of medication response (in which neither doctor nor patient know who is taking what) are rarely genuinely double-blind (that is, doctors and patients often guess which drug is being taken). Thus, the supporters argued, reports of psychopharmacological efficacy can largely be chalked up to the placebo response to the doctor's quiet interest in the patients on the "real" medication.[97] There is, in fact, some empirical support for this position. Pharmacological medications have side effects, and it is often possible to identify which patients are taking the "real" medication from the bodily sensations they report. In a review of antidepressant medication trials using active and inactive placebos ("active" placebos produce a variety of bodily sensations), 59 percent of the studies using inactive placebos reported that medication outperformed placebo but only 14 percent of those using active placebos did.[98] However, the tone of the letters invokes a more wholesale rejection of the idea of medication and its efficacy.

Before the balance of power shifted, psychoanalytic self-defense often came across with this regrettable tone. The year Osheroff was admitted to Chestnut Lodge, before the power of the new psychiatric science was fully evident, before outcome studies became quantifiable and reproducible, the *American Journal of Psychiatry* published an article that aimed to describe how effective psychoanalysis was. The author, John Gedo, explained that "reports based on the work of groups of practitioners have created a misleadingly pessimistic impression of the potential of psychoanalysis as a therapy because such surveys have included a disproportionate number of inexperienced analysts." By "inexperienced analysts," he appeared to mean all those who do not engage exclusively in psychoanalysis; this, as it happens, invalidates all but a handful of trained psychoanalysts, as most psychoanalysts also see nonanalytic patients on a once- or twice-a-week basis. Gedo continued by remarking that he devoted himself exclusively to psychoanalysis, so that he was in a position to have perfected himself as a technician, and he would like to point out that most of the time, the technique works. This is a defense of the field by a man who wrote without embarrassment that he has helped thirty-six people in a twenty-year career, all of them of "the professional and academic elite." He claimed that all of his patients had been suffering from "complex and severe character disturbance" but that "whatever the symptoms, I adhered to an unvarying policy of accepting [into treatment] anyone with a serious commitment to seeking self-understanding." He explained that his analyses reached successful conclusions with a minimum of six hundred to a thousand sessions and that even in cases of failure, he did not "reach that reluctant conclusion" until the analytic process had "been given a chance to unfold in the usual manner over a number of years." He then explained—and this is the point of the article—that most of his patients had improved. Unfortunately, he admitted, he had carried out no systematic follow-up, but he had heard about his patients casually; "by contrast, I have seldom had news about patients who did not reach a successful analytic termination."[99] The reader gapes.

The sharp improvement of psychiatric medication in the last fifteen years has given powerful reinforcement to the biomedical approach. There are far more drugs than there were before, and they are sometimes more effective and usually more comfortable and less dangerous to take. (One of the major problems with older psychiatric medications was that the side effects were so unbearable that patients often did not take their medication after being released from the hospital.) The most important of the new developments is clearly Prozac (fluoxetine hydrochloride) and its cousins Paxil, Zoloft, and others. Prozac, which was first marketed in 1987 and is now taken by 20 million people worldwide, is not, in fact, more effective for depression than the older generation of antidepressants (the tricyclic antidepressants).[100] But when people take tricyclics, they put on weight, have difficulty urinating, become constipated, and develop dry eyes and mouth, clammy palms, drowsiness, and an increased risk of cardiac problems. With Prozac, people actually lose weight (at least for a while), and the major side effect for most people seems to be jitteriness and, for a significant percentage of men, impotence. Prozac has meant that taking psychiatric medication for common anxiety and depression has become, practically speaking, risk free. (Of course, there are no good data on the consequences of taking Prozac for decades.) Moreover, Prozac works in a relatively well understood manner: it inhibits the neuron's reuptake of the neurotransmitter serotonin (although what *that* means is still unclear). In fact, almost all effective drugs for depression have something to do with serotonin. Prozac became the first good example of a medication whose impact clearly linked it to a brain function, a problem with the regulation of serotonin. It has led many researchers to explore further the role of neuro-transmitters in psychiatric disorders.

These days, research psychiatry is a branch of neuroscience. Many of the leading researchers attend and present at the annual Society for Neuro-science conference (once a tiny academic meeting, this annual event now has more than twenty thousand attendees). Many work in laboratories. They use chemicals and petri dishes. They do experiments with rats. They scan the brain to determine relative blood flow under various conditions. The sci-entific respect for this work is reflected in the congressional funding for the National Institute of Mental Health (NIMH). In the early 1970s, Congress deeply distrusted the NIMH—in 1976 the dollar amount of funding for the institute was actually lower than it had been in 1969—precisely because there was no way of distinguishing mental health from mental illness. One of the powerful psychiatrists of the era explained to me that the political message from Congress was "Show us that you are doing real research, and we will fund you." In 1983, the budget for the NIMH increased by $20 mil-lion and then kept rising. By 1994, the NIMH budget stood at $600 million, up from $90 million in 1976. And under the leadership of Lewis Judd, the NIMH persuaded Congress to declare the 1990s "the Decade of the Brain," a decade in which neuroscience research, including research in psychiatry, would be given the highest national priority. "Neuroscience," Judd argued, "has become the fastest-growing, and arguably the fastest-moving, branch of the life sciences. . . . The prospect for a *worldwide* Decade of the Brain 'grassroots' effort emerging from the neuroscience and neuropsychophar-macology communities in each of the world's sovereign nations is beginning to become a reality." [101]

Yet the new psychiatric science did not in itself pose a life-threatening dan-ger to psychodynamic psychiatry, because for all the foolishness of psycho-analysis in the era of its great arrogance, psychodynamic psychotherapy made a significant difference to the lives of patients and most psychiatrists knew it. Despite the ideological conflicts, by the middle 1980s many hospitals had set-tled down to what many perceived as a two-tone psychiatry. Residency pro-grams spoke (as they continue to speak) of a need for an "integrated" psychiatry. In residency programs in the middle and late 1980s there were (roughly speaking) two kinds of psychiatric orientations: biomedical and psy-chodynamic. (This opposition oversimplifies the complexity of psychiatric practice, but oppositions often do simplify; one of the consequences of ideo-logical tension was to create a more dichotomous sensibility than might have been the case otherwise.) A young resident would have extensive contact with both kinds of seniors. Admittedly, many seem to have experienced a need to choose between the two, even though there was an emphasis on integration. Even in the early 1990s, many young psychiatrists felt a sharp tension between the two approaches. They said things like "By the end of your second year, you have to decide which camp you're in." Many told me that they had deliberately chosen an "eclectic" residency because of what they saw as the deep divisions in the field. I myself felt that in many cases "integration" meant no more than parallel problem solving. "I attempt to integrate the two," said a psychiatrist just out of residency, "but it's more like I shift gears but it's a little bit jerky. I'm always shifting back and forth." In the early 1990s, most young psychiatrists said that there are few models of true integration. "Do you have a sense of what the good psychiatrist does?" I asked a new resident. "I do and I don't," she said. "One thing I know is that there's a real split in the staff between the people who do therapy and the people who do psychopharm. I see people who are really good at one or the other, and I would like to be good at both. But it's kind of hard to find one person on the staff who's everything."

The real crisis for psychodynamic psychiatry has been not the new psychiatric science but managed care and the health care revolution of the 1990s. More specifically, it is not just managed care but managed care in the context of ideological tension that is turning psychodynamic psychiatry into a ghost. It is harder to think about psychotherapy, about a patient's psychodynamics, about a patient as a kind of person to whom those thoughts are relevant because what must be done in the hospital belongs squarely in the domain of the new psychiatric science, and that way of thinking has been imagined as the denial and disproof of the psychotherapeutic endeavor. It isn't that psychiatrists think that psychotherapy isn't important. Most of them do. Most of them even think that psychiatrists should learn to do it, that psychotherapy should be the province not just of psychologists and social workers. But the more time they spend on the phone with insurance agents negotiating for a six-day admission to be extended to nine days because a patient is still suicidal, the more admissions interviews they need to do, the more discharge summaries they need to type, the less the ways of thought and experience of psychodynamic psychiatry fit in, the less they seem relevant or even real, and the more psychiatrists are willing to fall back on the ideological position that the cause and treatment of mental illness is biological and psychopharmacological. I saw these two approaches diverging just as the training programs were changing. That is what, for the most part, I have described. Then, at the end of my fieldwork, I saw the balance tilt irrevocably.

CHAPTER SIX

❖❖

THE CRISIS OF
MANAGED CARE

I met Jonathan at the same hospital where Gertrude had done her residency but in 1996. Gertrude had graduated along with her class, and the hospital had changed dramatically. "They've decided to ax the psychoanalytic journals from the library. The *psychoanalytic* journals." Jonathan was a resident then, a tall, sandy-haired young man, eloquent and obviously in distress. "At times," he continued, "it feels like those in power are willing to throw anything out the window to survive. They'll do *anything*. And yet it's not like they're saying, well, we know we should retain a balanced view of humans and psychopathology, but we're going to lie through our teeth and say that we believe only in biology. It snowballs. People who believe in that method start to become the people who are more in charge of things. They get promoted, other people don't, and eventually you're surrounded by a whole institution that speaks in this language. And I think there are antagonisms from the days when psychoanalysts ruled the roosts. Some people are clearly getting back at them.

"But you know," he continued, "I view this now less as a rift between the biologically oriented people and the dynamically oriented ones. I see it now as more between those whose central idea of their identity is clinical work and those whose central idea of their identity is being part of a treatment system. There's a growing sense in psychiatry as a whole that it's not that you're a doctor and you see a patient and the patient's best interest is what you primarily care about and what you're involved with. Now it's clear that the relationship is contaminated by the needs of the institution and particularly the needs of the insurers. It was always true that the doctor's needs were involved in the relationship, but it's much more complicated now. Before, you might have wanted to see a patient five times a week because

239

you'd make more money that way. But you could wrestle with that in your own conscience. *This* is a titanic system. It goes way up past the hospital, to the insurance companies and the rest. As a doctor, you're the leading edge of this . . . *machine*. You're not a doctor in an individual relationship with a patient. And the rift seems to be between those two groups of people, people who think you're part of the engine of health care and the people who see themselves as doctors who take care of patients. The biological people tend to fit better into the machine, but not always, and the process by which this transforms the institution is so *insidious*. I used to think that I should write it down while it was happening, keep notes, but I didn't and sometimes now I sit here and think, how exactly did it happen? And I sit here with a sense of something missing, with the sense of a great loss, as if I were a refugee child. I sit here and say, the system is crazy, it doesn't *work*, and the older people say, it used to be different."

Some years earlier, in the months between the two long summers I had spent with Gertrude and her class, several of the most important insurers that worked with the hospital had hired firms to manage their ballooning medical costs. I remember sitting, one balmy afternoon during that second summer, in an administrator's office in a psychiatric hospital with a large training program, listening in increasing discomfort as a practical woman laid out what the impact of the new policies on her hospital would be. In 1988, they had had roughly 110,000 inpatient "days" for which they could bill for treatment. That year, 1993, they would have 69,000, a drop of 40,000 and a $40 million decline in a year's revenue. The average length of a patient's stay had dropped from a month or so down to thirteen days and was still going down. Meanwhile, the average number of admissions had more than doubled. This is a tremendous human cost, because the bulk of the difficult work is done at admission and at discharge—long notes are written, summaries are dictated, arrangements are made. To keep the beds full but cut the length of stay by more than half is to double the workload without adding staff. Staff would, in fact, have to be fired. The administrator figured that the minimum it cost the hospital to care for a patient for a day was more than $700, but it had just made a deal with a major insurer to cover the cost for $535. It had had to make that deal, she said, because if it didn't, those patients would go elsewhere and the hospital would go bankrupt. But, she said, there's a hospital down the road with no grounds, no students, and no senior psychiatric stars. It had offered $400. And it, she said, is the competition. At the time we spoke, her hospital faced a $9 million shortfall that year.

"People used to want to be psychiatrists because they wanted to talk to their patients," the administrator continued sadly. She didn't think that would be possible anymore. There simply would not be enough time. Psychiatrists would be more like internists, spending fifteen minutes or so apiece with their patients. They would be the team leaders of a group of social workers and nurses, too busy to sit down and get to know the patients. And patients would come into the hospital for very brief stays, for five days or two or three. The administrator compared psychodynamic psychotherapy in this new era to cosmetic surgery. "But you know," she added, "you can still sit down for six sessions with a patient and talk about the kids reaching adolescence." In the room down the hall, other administrators were busy trying to design a computer program that gave precise treatment guidelines (length of stay, medications, and dosages) for patients with specific diagnoses. The presumption was that individual doctors would no longer be allowed to make those judgments.

By 1990, health care costs in the United States exceeded $600 billion, more than 12 percent of the gross national product and a 10.5 percent increase from 1989 to 1990 alone.[1] By 1994, the total cost of health care in the United States was approaching $900 billion annually.[2] In response to these escalating costs, health insurance companies increasingly adopted strategies that have come to be called "managed care," in which medical costs are not simply reimbursed after the fact, but rather the cost of the patient's care is "managed" by prior agreement with the insurer. Before admitting a patient, a hospital (or doctor) would have to call the patient's insurer and get authorization for the admission and for its length. Companies that insured large numbers of patients, such as Blue Cross/Blue Shield, would negotiate with a series of hospitals for daily hospital rates that would include all relevant charges and were sharply lower than previous reimbursements for the same services. Hospitals would compete for these contracts. As a result of this, managed care was sometimes called "managed competition." The policy makers' hope was that free-market competition between providers would lower the overall cost of care without greatly reducing quality. In fact, they believe that market competition can improve quality. What the policy makers did not fully understand was how difficult it would be to get meaningful and feasible measures of quality that would allow competition on the basis of quality to take place.

Managed care is by no means an evil. The older psychoanalytic approach kept patients in hospitals for months, even years, even after the advent of psychopharmacology. For some of these patients, the extended time was a kind of salvation. In the safe environment of the hospital, they were able to try out and eventually master more effective ways of dealing with their difficulties. For many others, the prolonged stays were a kind of return to the nursery, where other people fed them, washed their clothes, and set the rules they lived by. Instead of getting better, those patients fell into a regressive state of childlike dependency. The theory was that a patient's defenses needed to crumble so that he could emerge out of the chrysalis of his insanity as a more mature, resilient person, but even in that era many psychiatrists were not convinced. One afternoon I sat in a psycho-dynamically oriented psychiatrist's office and listened as she grumbled about the field's idiocy in not developing reasonable measures of patient improvement. After a while she stopped and looked up at me. "Actually," she said slowly, "many of the cuts are really better for the patients. Now hospi-talization will focus on moving people to healthier levels of functioning immediately rather than doing deep, intrapsychic work. Treaters will move from working from the inside to working from without. It'll make people feel more competent, feel more mastery, develop more self-esteem. Regression is rarely good for us." Many psychiatrists look back on the era of long-term psychoanalytically oriented hospitalization with some horror. These very long stays seem wasteful and ineffective from a more contemporary perspective, and though clinicians complain bitterly about the current chaos, few seem to want a return to the almost prisonlike confinements of the past.

Moreover, in the era before managed care some psychiatrists egregiously abused the hospital, the patients, and the insurers for their own financial gain. Rent-free offices and salaried time were used to run extensive private practices. Wealthy patients were cherry-picked off units for daily psy-chotherapy, even though some of them lacked the capacity to participate in or gain from it. Some of the work, such as Mass Mental's psycho-analytic therapy with schizophrenic patients, was motivated by clinical phi-losophy; some was pursued principally for financial gain. And across the country, problems that were poorly defined were treated with methods that varied widely from clinician to clinician and were poorly understood by the patients who came in for help. Many psychiatrists now seem to feel relief that the profession is being required to focus more rigorously on treatment protocols and their outcomes.[3]

However, in the short run, the problems with managed care have been significant, and many treatment programs are in painful turmoil. Hospitals with training programs suffered in the competition with less elite facilities. For a start, it is more expensive to deliver care in a hospital connected to a medical school. The students are slow, they need supervision, and they need to be provided with lectures, seminars, and case conferences. Despite the fact that students provide cheap labor, the system as a whole is more inefficient and more expensive. Medicare and Medicaid payments to "training" hospitals have always been somewhat higher to compensate for the higher costs. Then, too, the patients sent to university centers are more likely to be sicker than those sent elsewhere, because university hospitals have a concentration of researchers and elite doctors. They provide what is called "tertiary care," a level beyond what the average hospital can provide. With patients sicker than average and costs higher than average, the new reimbursement policies have driven many university hospitals into near bankruptcy. Fields such as psychiatry faced particularly deep shortfalls, because the time needed for psychiatric treatment is ambiguous. When managed care management took over psychiatric services, there was little "outcome" research in psychiatry. "Outcome" research evaluates the relationship of treatment to patients' recovery. Drug trials necessarily involve outcome components (the research must demonstrate that the drug works significantly more effectively than a placebo) over a specific period of time. But there was comparatively little outcome research in psychotherapy (significantly more has been done since the early 1990s), little research on the difference between a ten-day psychiatric admission for any particular diagnosis and a two-week admission, and less commonsense limitation on shrinking the length of admission than there was for many nonpsychiatric medical problems. In psychiatry, there are no expensive hospital machines or intravenous drugs that require a patient to remain in the hospital (electroshock therapy might be an exception). Psychiatric care was thus more severely walloped by managed care policies than any other branch of medicine was.

The experience of revisiting Gertrude's hospital by the time Jonathan was a resident was a little like coming back to a tree-lined London neighborhood after the Blitz. Administrators were frantically trying to cut costs. Nearly all the nonmedical services—food preparation, laundry, lawn care—had been farmed out to independent contractors, and gardeners, cafeteria workers, and others who had worked at the hospital, sometimes for decades, had been summarily dismissed. Hospital units were opened and closed and moved and reorganized like circus tents. The "psychosis unit," for example, would be moved twice during that summer to make room for one new program or another that the hospital had put together in a desperate bid to come up with unique services that no other hospital could offer. Over the weekend, the patients, their belongings, their files, their medications, the bulletin boards, the kitchen—all the paraphernalia of a space that can sleep twenty people and accommodate their staff—had to be boxed, moved, and unpacked. Sometimes a new program would be developed almost to the point where patients could be admitted, and then the new business plan would chop it and the person who had poured his life into designing it would be fired or reassigned. Shortly after that second summer, a third of the staff had been fired, the base salary of the rest would soon be cut in half, and many had left voluntarily in the hope that things would be better elsewhere. The administrators were behaving in ways that seemed sadistic to those under them, as if they were hoarding food in a severe famine. (However, they also probably saved the hospital from bankruptcy.) One clinician told me that at a rare meeting of clinicians, the hospital director showed a slide entitled "Your Options in Dealing with Managed Care" with a bulleted recommendation: "Move to Wyoming." No one laughed. Stories circulated about how one doctor, who had spent his life at the hospital, had been fired over the phone, how another had been fired in an answering machine message, how the groundspeople hadn't been told anything was wrong until they had gone to an all-hospital meeting and heard in the lecture that their jobs had been contracted to an outside service. The remaining staff became hostile and embittered. "Horrible things were happening," one psychiatrist remembered. "It was like they'd take you all into a room and tell you that in a month, eighty percent of you would be shot. One month later, they'd tell you no, only twenty percent have died. You'd be so worried about your own skin that you just felt relieved at having survived."

"I left myself," the psychiatrist continued, "when a patient came onto my unit and tried to hang herself twice by the end of the first day, and then Utilization Review [a hospital office that negotiates with the insurer] said she'd only been authorized for a two-day admission and would have to be discharged. I kept thinking about what the jury would say if she killed herself and I was the one held liable." This was a realistic fear. The legal responsibility for discharge lies with the physician. If a psychiatrist thinks that a patient is not ready for discharge but the insurer refuses to cover further treatment, the psychiatrist faces having to choose between discharging a possibly suicidal patient and risking the consequences to them both, or continuing care knowing that each extra day will be an enormous financial burden on the patient's family that they may never be able to pay.

The role of psychotherapy was profoundly altered by these new policies. There is little point to inpatient psychotherapy if a patient stays just for five days, and the hospital simply stopped providing it. Patients were admitted to inpatient units to be in safe, locked settings while they were medicated to dull the crisis that had led to the admission. The goal was to stabilize them, no more. Meanwhile, the outpatient therapy program was in chaos. Policies that once had covered half the cost of weekly psychotherapy for a year changed the rules so that a potential patient would have to call the insurance company, explain the problem for which he wanted psychotherapy, and be authorized for one visit; the therapist would then have to call the company after the visit, confirm the problem, and get authorization for more visits. The process was so laborious, embarrassing, and irritating that both doctor and patient often gave up. I remember a psychiatrist grimacing as she talked about a patient who had wanted therapy for anxiety and impotence who had not been able to bear what he felt was the humiliation of explaining himself repeatedly over the phone to a dry voice in the insurer's office. Most of the analysts left or were fired. In front of the building where many of the psychoanalysts had had their offices, the parking lot was often nearly empty. Once it had been difficult to find a parking space.

The inpatient units were not in great shape, either. Most of the patients were in the worst phase of their crisis because patients who weren't in that stage were no longer hospitalized. They were heavily medicated and often angry at their doctors. This was particularly true of psychotic patients, who were often discharged before they fully realized how sick they'd been. Older psychiatrists said that in earlier days, the psychotic patients would come on the unit furious at being incarcerated; then, over the three or four weeks they were there, they'd calm down, feel depressed at what they'd done when they were crazy, and by the time they left they'd be so grateful to the psychiatrist for getting them back to normal that sometimes there would be tears in their eyes. "It made us feel good," one psychiatrist said, "and now the patients never get to that point anymore. Now they leave as furious as when they come in and only a little less crazy." So the units were tense, the staff were demoralized, and the patients were sicker than they ever had been. They'd be discharged sick and the psychiatrist would be frantic, feeling responsible for someone who often was suicidal and barely functional. There was a pervasive undercurrent of doom and panic.

By the end of her residency, Gertrude (who had become an excellent psychiatrist) was horrified at what had happened to psychiatry: "It was *very* depressing. It was so apparent, on the inpatient unit, that a lot of our behavior was dictated by managed care. There was a lot of pressure to move patients out before they were ready and a lot of anxiety because some of the patients were still suicidal. The managed care company would still say that we needed to move them out and the liability of course was on the doctor. If you discharged a patient who then committed suicide, it was *your* fault. And the managed care company would say, 'Please don't do anything you think is clinically unsound.' But then they would make the family responsible for this huge bill. It was very unfair to the family and unfair to us. And it got worse. My first year there, it was only beginning. That next year, we were doing outpatient, and outpatient was still pretty good. But then if you sent an outpatient into the hospital for treatment they wouldn't really get treatment, they'd get a Band-Aid. They'd only be there for three days because the managed care company wouldn't pay for any more, and so you had this really, really sick person to manage as an outpatient. That was bad.

"You got a real feeling that psychotherapy was shunted to the side. You learned that your goal on the inpatient unit was to stabilize them as fast as you could. In the days gone by, they would have had psychotherapy in the unit. Initially, when I was a medical student, you had to do psychotherapy three times a week. That was the expectation. Then, toward the end, that was not the expectation at all. You just did psychopharm management on the unit, and even that you couldn't do—you can't try new drugs when the patient's in the hospital for three days. The psychotic patients were easiest. You had a clear justification that they had to be in the hospital. So the managed care companies would stay away, and you could at least start them on clozapine or get them on the road. With other patients, who were really sick but not flagrantly psychotic, it was more difficult. You definitely felt that at times there was inappropriate care."

Psychopharmacology fits more easily into these time-limited constraints than psychotherapy does. As Gertrude pointed out, however, in a very short admission (three to five days) there is not even enough time to start a new medication and judge a patient's response to it. Psychopharmacology "management" often consists, in these circumstances, of represcribing whatever a patient was taking before the crisis that brought him into the hospital. And psychotherapy still exists outside the hospital. Psychologists, social workers, marriage counselors, and others will continue to practice psychotherapy, although as reimbursements have shrunk their practices have also suffered. But the issue here is not that clinical psychologists can take over the "relationship" aspects of treatment. The issue is that in the context of an ideological split, psychotherapy begins to appear less effective, less necessary, more wasteful. The psychotherapeutic way of thinking begins to seem less relevant to the task of taking care of patients.

The issue Gertrude raises is not just the risk to this effective method of treatment in psychiatry and psychiatric hospitals but the risk that its loss will damage the everyday ability of psychiatrists to deal effectively with patients, whether they are treating them with drugs or with talk. From Gertrude's perspective, the problem with managed care was not only that patients were given too little care—discharged when still suicidal, for instance, so that someone with severe depression was suddenly back home among razors, pills, and ropes—but also that training was being compromised. She felt that young psychiatrists had more difficulty diagnosing what was wrong. (She supervised them in her new job.) This she pinned on the sudden devaluation of psychotherapy. She believed this to be true even though she had clearly defined herself as a psychopharmacologist.

"There's *no* question," she said, "you *cannot* be a good psychopharmacologist without being exposed deeply to psychotherapy. It gives you your background, your intuition. That the patient's mom was depressed after childbirth and so this is going to affect attachment and so maybe she'll be less likely to take the drugs you prescribe. With psychotherapy training, you know why certain patients are so difficult. Some poor internist has no idea why this patient is so difficult, and you just listen to the case and get a sense and you think, this person sounds like a borderline to me. The bottom line is that it's all about how you were connected with your parents, which has a lot to do with how you interact with the world as an adult. People put on a facade. You have to listen for the subtle, insignificant things that they don't think are important but make you raise an eyebrow. Someone says, my mother was never around when I was growing up, and they'll say it nonchalantly. Well, that's significant. What it means you don't know yet, but you make a huge mental note of it.

"I've declared myself as a psychopharmacologist, but without that psychotherapy background you're not trained well. I see a lot of this on the unit I work on now, people who aren't well trained in psychotherapy, and they try to use medication for inappropriate reasons. In fact, they seem to have *no* training in psychotherapy at all. I mean, obviously the program has to be accredited, so there must be some psychotherapy component, but it's not the way it used to be. They think that everything's depression. Even the senior doctors. Of course, you can't ignore the pressures of managed care. If you say that this is something with the personality, they won't pay for it. But I don't think that it's all an attempt to get the patient care funded. I think there's a problem with the way they see the diagnosis, because they haven't had the psychotherapy background. If psychotherapy goes, we're in big trouble."

Gertrude is right: a psychiatrist does become a better diagnostician as a result of psychotherapeutic training. The practical training in Axis I diagnostics teaches a resident to assimilate a patient's experience into a prototype—or, as one angry psychiatrist fumed, "Biologic psychiatrists as a whole really only listen to that portion of the patient's discourse that corresponds to their biological paradigms."[4] The anger may be misplaced, but the insistence that expectations affect the way we listen is not. It is easy to listen only for the major, diagnosable, reimbursable Axis I disorder: the schizophrenia, the depression, the bipolar disorder. But people who have Axis I conditions such as depression or schizophrenia also often have personality disorders: in treatment-resistant hospitalized patients, that combination (technically called "comorbidity") may exist in as many as 71 percent of the patients.[5] "Symptoms are embedded in character structure," one textbook begins, "and the dynamic psychiatrist recognizes that in many cases one cannot treat the symptoms without first addressing the character structure."[6] In fact, one cannot always recognize symptoms accurately without having some idea of the character of the person who is ill. That was Gertrude's observation, and it has certainly been mine. What really changed as the residents went through their training was not so much their ability to recognize depression, which they could do easily in the first year, but their ability to recognize what was not depression—the fact that what might look like depression was really borderline personality disorder, alcoholism, a schizophrenic coming to terms with his illness, or an anxious, guilty student stewing in the shame of coming to see a psychiatrist in the first place. That is a recognition skill that psychodynamic training teaches and inpatient biomedical care often does not. It is for this reason that many psychiatrists argue that regardless of one's specialization, one needs the skills of both biomedical and psychodynamic psychiatry to do the task of either well.[7] The more psychiatrists focus exclusively on the biomedical model, the more difficulty they have in recognizing the personality disorders and other personality problems that may look like primarily biomedical issues but aren't.

For example, in 1993 I attended a case conference for a young woman I shall call Bonnie. She was seventeen. She seemed on balance to be schizophrenic. For the six months prior to admission, she had felt that people were looking at her and laughing. She thought they knew embarrassing details about some physical illness she had. She knew that some of her classmates were talking about her. She saw one of them across the street. That person read her lips and reported her thoughts to other people. Those other people followed her and made fun of her. They commented on her. Later, they talked to her even when they weren't there. Their voices called Bonnie "a little shit." She saw one of their cars outside one afternoon and tore the antenna off. A neighbor called the police when this happened, and Bonnie was brought into the hospital. She did not seem manic and reported no history of rapid speaking, racing thoughts, or high energy. Her performance at school had deteriorated markedly over the previous year. She was slightly obsessive. It took her sometimes three hours to eat her meals, and she would wash her hands repeatedly.

What made the diagnosis more complex than simple schizophrenia was that Bonnie's mother colluded with the illness in many ways. She had searched vigorously for physical explanations of Bonnie's difficulties. She had had Bonnie diagnosed with a vast array of allergies to ordinary foods, taken her out of a school because the air at the school was polluted, and attributed her distress—including her visual and auditory hallucinations—to a series of bowel disorders. She had kept Bonnie home from school to tend to the bowel problems. Bonnie reported in the hospital that she would not move her bowels unless her mother told her to, and in many respects the relationship between mother and adolescent was more like a relationship between a mother and a much younger child, seemingly at the mother's choice. The mother found it impossible to do anything other than care for Bonnie and was unable to clean the house, so that the house was disorderly and chaotic.

What do you do if you are a psychiatrist who sees this patient? At the least you must be able to be interested in the family setting of the illness, and you must realize that there is a kind of folie à deux in the life of this young woman. Then you must be able to know that medication alone will truly not solve the problem. Schizophrenia does not in general clear up and go away; family therapy is often very helpful in managing the disruption that such patients generate in the lives of those who live with them. But here in particular, understanding the disorder meant understanding that the mother's behavior may have exacerbated the problem; that there may have been an underlying problem with obsessive-compulsive disorder that Bonnie's mother may also have shared; that treating the designated patient meant also treating the mother; and that engaging the mother in therapy was central to the possibility of change. Bonnie's problem was not only her psychosis but her enmeshment with her mother. A psychiatrist would have to see all that to help the patient, and a psychiatrist encouraged by the educational and economic environment to look only for the organic brain dysfunction might not.

Moreover, for psychiatrists to be effective, they must be able to discharge patients into a setting that they will accept, and they must be able to discharge patients on medications that they will be willing to take. Making these quick assessments of a patient's abilities—being able to judge her integration into this or that group home, being able to predict her reliability in taking medications—is undoubtedly enhanced by the person-focused specificity of psychodynamic training; building a relationship that enables a patient to trust a doctor involves investing the time that psychotherapy allows. Under the new conditions of managed care, when doctors have very little time to evaluate patients and make decisions about their treatment, the skills of being able to anticipate rapidly the particular needs and vulnerabilities of each person become even more important.[8] Expertise in psychopharmacology involves skill in the knowledge of how drugs interact and an intuition of what drug will work well for what patient. Expertise in psychodynamics involves skill in the ability to judge what kind of person the patient is and how he or she will react to a given set of circumstances.

I saw unmistakably, in my time at the hospitals and in my discussions with staff and patients, that psychotherapy had been muted under the impact of managed care policies. This was happening to meet the concerns of the insurers. It was not because the new developments in psychopharmacology and biological psychiatry had led psychiatrists to think that the more talk-oriented approach is not important but because psychotherapy just didn't accommodate as well to the short-term approach insurance companies understandably favor. There are, of course, psychiatrists who would like to dispense with psychotherapy altogether. "Psychotherapy," a psychiatric scientist said to me once in irritation, "is what ministers can do. We are doctors." Most, however, believe that psychotherapy training makes psychiatrists more effective with their patients. But the overwhelming reality was that insurers would not pay for the length of hospitalization that would make psychotherapy possible inside the hospital, and they were very hesitant to pay for outpatient psychotherapy, particularly by psychiatrists, whether or not a psychiatrist was already seeing a patient for psychopharmacological treatment. By the middle 1990s, I knew very few psychiatrists, regardless of their disciplinary commitments, who thought that reimbursement policies enabled most psychiatric patients to get adequate care. Very few thought that the current training practices would teach psychiatrists to deliver that care.

The real problem is not just that money has become very short. The problem is a financial crisis in the context of lingering ideological tension. Faced with the fear that psychiatric care would not be reimbursed, many psychiatrists, psychiatric lobbies, and patient lobbies (the most effective probably being the National Alliance for the Mentally Ill) have argued that psychiatric illness is a medical disease like any other and deserves equal coverage, or "parity." Most health insurance plans have annual and lifetime limitations for mental health coverage that are far lower than the caps for nonpsychiatric medical coverage. The argument for the medical nature of psychiatric illness is a good argument, but as the debate continues, it encourages psychiatrists and nonpsychiatrists to simplify the murky complexity of psychiatric illness into a disease caused by simple biological dysfunction and best treated by simple pharmacological interventions.

Meanwhile, the institutional structure of psychiatry, again as a consequence of this ideological tension, continues to separate the psychodynamic from the biomedical. These approaches are presented in different lectures, taught by different teachers, associated with different patients, learned in different settings. The new policies have sharply enhanced that separation and severely truncated the psychotherapeutic side. Psychotherapy is no longer even nominally part of inpatient treatment, except in particular patient populations (psychotherapy remains effectively the only intervention for trauma patients, and therapeutic relations established in that inpatient setting are often continued on an outpatient basis). Even the close contact with the patient, the "intense, intimate relationship," has become nearly impossible on an inpatient basis, given the volume of work and the short admissions. In one of the hospitals I visited, a resident used to have on her unit one or two patients who were primarily her responsibility. At that time she might spend half an hour a day or more just talking to the patient. Now that same doctor may have four or more patients to see in the same time, and the patients come and go very quickly. She can't see each patient every day. She can't do much more than talk to each patient when he is admitted to the unit and see him for a few minutes before or after the team meeting. Outpatient psychotherapy has been radically curtailed, and outpatient psychopharmacology patients are not uncommonly expected to be seen in visits scheduled by the clinic in fifteen-minute intervals. Psychotherapy is no longer what most psychiatrists expect they will do upon graduation from residency.

As a result, young psychiatrists have an increasingly harder time seeing the point of the very different approach that psychotherapy presents, and their teachers have a hard time knowing how to teach in a way that speaks to the realities of these different circumstances. Psychodynamic teachers find this depressing. "I asked the first-year class," one teacher gloomily remarked, "what would go through their minds if a patient in psychotherapy with them called them by their first name, rather than calling them Dr. So-and-so; I asked them to think about how they would handle it. One of the residents said that she'd think that the patient was hypomanic." In other words, it didn't occur to the resident to imagine that therapy is often experienced by people as intimate and personal; she didn't understand that the point of the question was to explore how to maintain that intimacy while still maintaining the boundaries appropriate to a doctor-patient relationship. Instead, the resident thought of this encounter as diagnosing a sick patient rather than as talking to a troubled person, and her dynamically oriented teacher was floored. "What do you *say*?" the teacher continued. "What could you possibly say to get that resident to understand what the patient felt like?" I often heard such demoralized remarks from psychodynamic teachers who had taught in a different time. "I mourn," sighed a senior psychiatrist. "So few of the residents have any interest in learning how to get close to a patient. And so I mourn. I mourn at the passing of the torch to the biologists, however desirable it may be in some ways. I feel that something very special is going to be lost."

The mourning is widespread. In 1995, in the beautiful hills of northern California, I attended a small, elite meeting of psychiatric department chairpersons. In their seminars they presented service utilization charts and financial flow sheets. They knew who used the services, how often, and for how long. They explained for what, in their respective states, they were reimbursed and how those reimbursement patterns were changing the future of psychiatry and, ultimately, the structure of psychiatric residency. All of their residencies were going to survive, and none of them had any real doubt about whether psychiatry would survive as a profession. Most of them had made their names as scientists and biomedical researchers. Yet nearly all of them spoke of their despair. They seemed to look at the new psychiatry of managed care with horrified resignation.

These were men and women who were in many ways the architects of these changes. They had helped psychiatry to survive despite the corporate perception that psychiatric illnesses were not really medical and thus not really the domain of health insurance. They had succeeded in persuading governmental agencies and insurance companies that psychiatric illnesses were medical diseases and thus needed medical insurance coverage, but at the cost of almost destroying the sensibility that had defined the field and drawn them to it. "You have the opportunity," an eminent psychiatrist quietly remarked to me once, "of seeing our profession in the beauty of its great sunset."[9]

Jonathan was right. This is not the story of the triumph of brain over mind. The loss that is felt so keenly in psychiatry is the loss of a close clinical relationship with patients in which a doctor knows and understands his patients well and takes full responsibility for their care. This has been the model for clinical care across medicine, and as managed care bureaucratizes and rationalizes our health care, the loss of these long-term, personally resonant relationships is mourned across the disciplines. But nowhere else was that relationship as rich as in psychiatry, particularly psychodynamic psychiatry, nowhere else was the relationship understood so deeply, and nowhere else is its loss so striking. Under managed care, psychiatrists have begun to move from one-on-one relationships with patients to being merely the heads of treatment teams made up of psychologists, social workers, and nurses. Of course, in hospitals psychiatrists have worked as members of treatment teams for years already. They are, however, the most expensive members of those teams and, as a result, the ones the insurers want least to pay. Increasingly, psychiatrists are being pushed into management positions in the teams, or out of management positions and intoconsultant roles, and out of intense, unmediated relationships with patients.

As a result, there has been a loss of an entire dimension of a way of thinking about people and their interaction in groups. The same year Gertrude's hospital began to change in 1993, I visited another hospital in that state. By the early 1990s, Lacey Hospital had long been a place for intellectual mavericks. It was a public hospital that served the local urban poor. The offices were small, dingy, and insufficient in number: residents were sometimes assigned three to a room, so that therapy hours had to be carefully negotiated in advance. In the entire psychiatry department there was only one accessible fax machine and only one photocopy machine. The corridors were in need of paint. One of the treatment programs was housed in a trailer in a parking lot. Yet the residency program in psychiatry was one of the most competitive in the country and among the most elite. Most of the doctors had been well and expensively educated. They followed contemporary fiction. They were often aggressively liberal. During my stay a young analyst at the hospital decided to give the psychiatry department seminar. He spoke on the concept of time in Joyce and Heidegger. Not only was this topic considered suitable for the formal didactic purpose of the occasion—in other hospitals, such seminars commonly featured titles such as "Dopamine and the D2 Receptor"—but the hall was full.

At the center of this ethos sat an odd but charismatic man. Like Semrad in Mass Mental's heyday, Harper Frank was celebrated for his work with severely disturbed patients. He was particularly good with paranoid patients. In an interview he would set his chair side by side with the patient's and ally himself with his crazy, skewed vision of the world—the patient would whisper, "Doc, I feel like they're all after me" and Frank would whisper back, "Yep, you can't trust anyone around here, turn your back and someone will plant a knife in it"—until the patient was chuckling and chiding the doctor for his outlandish beliefs. The residents usually felt that they couldn't make that technique work. They came to Harper Frank less to learn the explicit knowledge he had to teach and more to participate in his sense of the world. He was given to aphorism and metaphor, to an intransigent scorn of institutions, and to a crabwise, quizzical peering at the world that the young residents found deeply appealing. "What he taught me," a resident explained, "was that one could have all the facts and still not be in possession of the truth."

The unit I joined for more than ten weeks was sometimes described as a time capsule, a psychiatry unit run the way units had been run before the psychopharmacological revolution. The two directors identified strongly as psychotherapists. They would say that understanding the patient was more important than diagnosing the patient. When they referred to what they did day to day, they spoke of "the task" and "the work." Several times a week they held "community meetings" attended by all the patients (there were twenty-one beds on the unit) and most of the staff (almost as many as patients: seven psychiatrists, five of them residents; five psychologists, four of them interns; five social workers, four of them interns; a fluctuating population of full- and part-time nurses and mental health workers). Community meetings of staff and patients lasted for half an hour. There was no set agenda. People were supposed to talk about whatever was important to them. They usually talked about the director and the associate director, who usually remained silent as the conversation went on around them. Afterward, the staff met for half an hour—this was called "wrap-up"—to discuss the meaning of what had been said. Staff meetings were run in the same way, though without the official wrap-up. To understand the patients, they thought, they needed time to talk.

On this unit, it was assumed that everything was open to scrutiny; that no behavior was unmotivated, but that knowledge of its motivation was always incomplete; that the leader existed not to take command but to take responsibility and to demand that all others take equal responsibility for whatever happens. The key to helping patients was assumed to be understanding their feelings, but because psychic process was said to be often unconscious for both staff and patients, in order to help the patients, the staff were assumed to need to talk to one another about what the patients made them feel and why they made them feel that way. It was assumed that the young psychiatrists would experience feelings that were intense and overwhelming, both because the patient's anguish would catch, like a contagion, and because the group process that "the work" demanded was so stressful that they would find themselves retreating to the defensive styles they had used as children. Behind these expectations lay the weighty theories of Wilfred Bion.

Wilfred Bion is the giant behind the influential group relations model in the psychoanalytic world. A difficult, dense writer, he was a psychoanalyst's psychoanalyst, and his observations about the analytic process—for instance, that an analyst should listen without memory or desire—have seeped deeply into analytic theorizing. His work on group relations generated the Tavistock Institute of Human Relations and the A. K. Rice Institute, both of which, over several decades, have seen thousands of people pass through their experiential training conferences on group dynamics. In *Experiences in Groups,* Bion set out the premise of his approach: that people become emotionally childlike in groups: "The adult must establish contact with the emotional life of the group in which he lives; this task would appear to be as formidable to the adult as the relationship with the breast appears to be to the infant, and the failure to meet the demands of this task is revealed in his regression."[10]

Essentially, this approach takes Melanie Klein's dark model of infant life and applies it to groups. Klein had argued that young infants were unable to integrate their conflicting powerful feelings about their mothers' breasts, that they felt both loving dependence and rageful frustration, and that in consequence they swung between perceiving a good breast and perceiving a bad one. Klein's theory is no longer taken as a plausible description of the infant mind, but what makes it powerful as psychoanalytic theory—like all powerful psychoanalytic theory—is its evocative, metaphorical power in describing adult emotions. When Bion applied the theory to groups, he did so analogically and loosely, and he suggested that while groups could occasionally, after many years and much determination, behave maturely, rationally, and scientifically (these were called "work groups"; the phrase is presumably the source of the oracular term "the work"), the rest of the time they swing in their collective perceptions from depending on their leader's goodness or the hopefulness of an emergent pair within the group to fighting with or fleeing from the leader, who is perceived as bad.

As one reads Bion, it becomes clear that many of his subjects regarded the theory he derived from them with some astonishment. He describes one group thus:

> Three women and two men were present. . . . One woman had brought some chocolate, which she diffidently invited her right-hand neighbor, another woman, to share. One man was eating a sandwich. A graduate in philosophy, who had in earlier sessions told the group that he had no belief in God, and no religion, sat silent, as indeed he often did, until one of the women, with a touch of acerbity in her tone, remarked that he had asked no questions. He replied, "I do not need to talk because I know that I only have to come here long enough and all my questions will be answered without my having to do anything."
>
> I then said that I had become a kind of group deity; that the questions were directed at me as one who knew the answers without need to resort to work, that the eating was part of a manipulation of the group to give substance to a belief they wished to preserve about me, and that the philosopher's reply indicated a disbelief in the efficacy of prayer but seemed otherwise to belie earlier statements he had made about his disbelief in God. When I began my interpretation I was not only convinced of its truth but felt no doubt that I could convince the others by confrontation with the mass of material. . . . By the time I had finished speaking I felt I had committed some kind of gaffe; I was surrounded by blank looks; the evidence had disappeared. . . . The woman who was eating, hurriedly swallowed the last of her chocolate.[11]

It is very hard, when confronted with this deliberate prose, not to wonder whether the theory creates the evidence. Bion himself admitted that there was no independent means of validating his theory but for the reader "to recall to himself the memory of some committee or some gathering."[12]

Yet it is undoubtedly the case that after several hours in such a group, with such an interpretation-making leader, group members have powerful and childlike feelings about one another and particularly about the leader. Bion has captured a real phenomenon of human experience in groups. On the unit I joined, the chief resident might tell the director of the unit, in public (although not in front of the patients), that at the previous meeting she had been furious at him. Other times she might cry; other people would cry; by my third medical staff meeting, after a general staff meeting at which my presence on the unit had been a central topic of discussion ("We can't talk openly in front of an anthropologist," someone had stage-whispered. "It's dangerous") and during which the primary discussion was the residents' rage at the director for being passive when he was attacked, I felt gripped by an emotion that somehow was not quite mine, that was bigger than I was, and that made me feel indissolubly a member of the group. The psychiatric premise was that the staff would act out the tensions felt among the patients, and vice versa, so that to keep the unit safe it was necessary to know who was mad at whom and deal with it. In 1954, a detailed anthropological study of Chestnut Lodge indeed extensively documented a relationship between the tension among the staff and the severity of the patients' symptoms.[13]

This unit was now in crisis. The pace of hospital life had shifted abruptly since Medicaid and Medicare, federal insurers that cover most patients in community hospitals such as this one, had adopted managed care strategies. The average length of inpatient stay had dropped from thirty days to twenty days since the autumn; it would drop to eight days by the following spring, one year later. In consequence, the number of admissions had risen abruptly, and the work on the unit had increased greatly. In February, the directors had announced that they could no longer carry out their work without more staff and that with the current staffing, trainees were learning how to bill insurance companies, not to understand patients. The hospital administrators rather drily replied that no one was very happy with the changes but they were here to stay and (to be blunt) the staff should damn well get used to it. The directors threatened to resign. The hospital administrators nodded politely, wished them good luck, and began to make plans to restructure care on the unit. The directors decided to go through with their resignations, and the unit sank into shock.

It did seem as if the crises among the patients grew more acute in the aftermath of the shock. "We will kill someone," the unit director announced dramatically the second day I was on the unit. I had arrived for Morning Report, the meeting in which the events of the previous day and night are summarized for the staff. Psychologists, social workers, nurses, mental health workers, and psychiatrists were clustered into a small room around a long table. After the patients were presented, the unit director said softly and deliberately that he had "closed" the unit on the previous evening, that although not all the beds had been taken, he had refused to accept any more admissions. He had done this, he said, because the unit was not safe. "Some team members have kept things from other team members because they did not want to hurt them. This is chaos and confusion," he said. "In these circumstances," he said, *we will kill someone!*" suddenly belting out the last sentence like a minister. A shocked, silent staff listened to the rest of the report. Later that day, when I walked out with him for coffee, he said that what you had to do on a psychiatric unit was to manage the unconscious life of the unit.

But talk about "the unconscious life of the unit" fares poorly in a world that is increasingly short term. One of the residents openly scoffed. Mary saw patients as savvy manipulators of the system. "You know," she said, "the director was a little hysterical. I mean, I think he was referring to my patient, who earns about twenty-eight thousand dollars a year. The patient ran out of benefits and had the choice of staying on in the hospital at his own cost, to the tune of seven hundred dollars a day, or being discharged to therapy at a hundred fifteen dollars a session. So they discharged him—he said he wasn't suicidal—and he went home and overdosed. It got him back into the hospital for free. That's what the director was referring to, but it didn't have anything to do with the way we treated him. It was finances, and it was a reasonable thing for the patient to do."

The director had inferred that the patient's overdose had been an act of pain and misery and that the patient might have been pushed over the edge of what he could handle by the stress and frustration on the unit. The resident thought that this interpretation was too dramatic and a little irrational. She, thinking as her environment encouraged her, assumed instead that it was perfectly "reasonable" for a patient to swallow enough medication to kill himself, call 911, be rushed to the hospital by ambulance, and have his stomach pumped on arrival, because he wanted to persuade his managed care officer to authorize a few more days in the hospital.

What was being lost on the unit and would be lost irretrievably as the directors left for other jobs and were replaced by different people was the subtlety of human interaction, the sense that it mattered to the patients that the unit was in tension. Noticing group dynamics had become a luxury. Thinking that tension among the staff could generate or reflect tension among the patients became an extravagance. Talk of unconscious this or that perplexed the residents who had not encountered it before, even though they had come to the hospital to learn it, and they often treated it dismissively. The resident whose patient had, she thought, made a suicide attempt to get readmitted for a few days went on to say, "When I first arrived, we had a six-hour meeting about shaking the patient's hand: Was it violating boundaries, or did it communicate something you hadn't intended? *Six hours.* And I thought, it's a social *convention.* You're a doctor, you can shake the patient's hand. And they'll talk about switching an appointment on the patient, is it a loss for a patient, and I'd think come on, you're a doctor, you end up switching appointments.

"Then there are the chairs," she continued. "The chief resident always sits in the same chair for the community meetings. No one else can sit there. At first I thought it was pretty weird. Now it seems natural to tell a patient not to sit there. But in my first medical staff meeting [which was held in the director's office], there was a desk chair and I didn't sit there, but then when I sat down I was told that this was the associate director's chair, please move, and then when the director went on vacation the associate director sat in the director's chair but the chief resident didn't sit in the associate director's chair and that's what we talked about for the entire hour of medical staff meeting, the meaning of who sat where. There's a whole lingo: we talk about work, safety, and containment, you know. It's good, in ways. I've begun to think about the unit as having 'frame' and 'content.' And although it's irritating, it teaches you stuff. It's kind of like a New York theater experience."

Medications increasingly took the place of relationships with patients. Another resident, a mild-mannered, generally dutiful man I shall call Stefan, had as a patient a sixty-two-year-old woman whose brother had cheated her out of tens of thousands of dollars. She had been admitted to the psychiatric unit (on the day her mother died) after threatening to kill her brother's girlfriend. She was slightly retarded and extremely chatty, and she said that when she was at home, she thought that her mother and father and brother were all in the room. She knew it was a fantasy, but it was nice, she said, because they talked to her and warned her off certain people. Stefan thought that she might be psychotic and prescribed Trilafon, one of the more potent antipsychotics, although he laughed wryly and said he'd really rather be an old friend of the patient's, talking about the Red Sox, than diagnosing any symptoms. But soon he decided that she wasn't psychotic and wanted to lower the dose of Trilafon. The associate director told him to raise the dose level because the nurses said that she was becoming more agitated. They worried that she was psychotic.

Then Harper Frank interviewed the patient at the weekly case conference, when all the staff gather to hear an outsider interview and discuss one of their patients. In front of the staff, Frank announced that the patient was overmedicated. (She may have been agitated as a side effect of the medication.) Stefan felt immensely relieved and vindicated, and he and the other residents took me down the corridor into a meeting in which they talked about how the nurses wanted the patients overmedicated because they were afraid of them. Afterward I walked into the staff room to find the chief resident in distress. She had been supporting the associate director's insistence upon more Trilafon for this patient, because she trusted the nurses' intuition. She had also seen the patient herself. And she knew, she said in tears, that Harper could be rude about the unit, that he thought that the patients were all overmedicated and that the real role of the psychiatrist was above all to connect to the patients. It was great to believe in this, she said, it was important and fundamentally right, but these days it didn't work. It was medically naive. It *wasn't* the role of the doctor when the patient was on the unit barely long enough to unpack. "She's *not* a sweet old lady," the chief resident said despairingly. "She came in with a plan to murder a woman and then kill herself." Then she looked disconsolate. "Harper understands the humanity of the patient better than any of us. But she still needs the Trilafon."

Stefan had wanted to understand the patient's intentions. He was very attracted to the idea of the psychodynamic model. He wanted to persuade her that she didn't need to feel murderous or suicidal, and he felt that his relationship with her might help her to feel less isolated. He could feel this intensely because it genuinely was not clear whether she was psychotic. There was a real ambiguity about whether this patient had described fantasies she had never intended to act on or whether in fact she had crazy delusions. After all, when she had been admitted, she had talked about killing her brother's girlfriend, but she had also recognized that some of her crazy thoughts were fantasies. But because she was in the hospital for only a week, the most reasonable, pragmatic, safe approach was to treat her as if she were psychotic and medicate her. There is a kind of Pascal's wager here. A patient who is medicated even if she does not need the medication is not as dangerous or unpredictable as an unmedicated one who does need medication. The less time a patient spends in the hospital, the more the doctors feel forced to medicate ambiguous symptoms. There may be good reasons for shortening the length of hospital admissions, but the inevitable response is to medicate the patients more aggressively.

When medications take the place of relationships, not only do patients suffer the side effects of aggressive medication, but they lose the healing power of the relationship. Training in psychotherapy teaches a doctor something that becomes relevant to all encounters with patients, which is the importance of the relationship between doctor and patient and the importance of understanding that relationship in some depth. That relationship can be integral to a patient's ability to respond to treatment, to feel comforted, to trust a doctor and so to take the medication he prescribes, to feel that if the voices become violent and disturbing there is a safe place to go for care. Stefan may have romanticized the relationship he had with his patient, but at least his attachment to her gave him a willingness to listen for the ways in which she was not psychotic and gave her a conviction that someone cared for her and about her.

Managed care has disrupted relationships even in the emergency room, where patients come and go very quickly. The psychiatric emergency services in this hospital worked as well as any I had seen, and did so because the staff behaved as if they had long-term relationships with the patients. I spent hours down there, in a small, windowless room like the cabin of an intrepid submarine. One staff person, a man with a ponytail and a sharp sense of humor, would periodically go out to rescue patients who holed up and refused to leave home, but mostly the staff dealt with people who were brought in by family, friends, or police. They knew many of them, perhaps a third. Some just walked in off the street. (One of the startling consequences of the cost of psychiatric illness is the way state administrators sometimes offload patients onto other states. In southern California, patients would show up in the psychiatric emergency room and explain that they had been in Minnesota or Illinois and had gone to the bus station and a nice man from the county mental health had bought them a bus ticket to San Diego, which they thought they'd like to visit. When I was at Lacey, one patient showed up after having had a bad conversation with the Devil, who had been traveling with him on the train. Apparently, the patient had found himself in New York's Pennsylvania Station and an officer had asked him whether he wanted to go away and paid his fare so he could.)

Many of the patients, though, were local people known to the staff. The emergency staff already knew what medications worked and on which wards they did better, and they were able to keep an eye on them in the community (more or less). When a familiar face showed up, which with these patients happened often, the staff knew how to handle them effectively. The staff seemed comfortable with the patients, and compared to other emergency rooms there was less violence and less apparent manipulation, with fewer patients feigning illness in order to get a bed for the night. (The homeless shelters in the city were better serviced than most.)

Those relationships were being broken by the system, however. Managed care policies had been put into place alongside a decision to privatize the mental health hospitals. Many hospitals had closed, and the competition for beds had become intense. Patients were shipped around like sacks of onions to people they did not know, who made judgments based on less information than was needed. This is more technically known as "fragmentation of care," and it represents the most basic breakdown of the doctor-patient relationship.

Because insurance companies now contract with particular hospitals, because many hospitals compete for these contracts, and because many hospitals have been closed, the old community hospital ideal has largely vanished. Lacey had been founded as one of these hospitals. The idea had been that it would handle the needs of all (or most) of the people in its "catchment area," the geographical area it served. Patients would have long-standing relationships with the hospital and its staff, and when they came in crazy, people knew who they were and what was likely to help.

This was particularly helpful for psychiatric patients. All of us benefit from long, knowledgeable relationships with particular caregivers. We don't need to explain our medical history in detail every time we fall sick, and we know that our doctor more or less keeps track of us. For psychiatric patients, who are often fearful and angry, that trust is even more important. When people have illnesses that bring them back to the hospital frequently—schizophrenia, bipolar disorder—they do better, and stay in the hospital for less time, if they know where they are going and who will take care of them, and can be persuaded to follow their advice when they leave.

Until managed care, perhaps half of Lacey's patients were "frequent fliers." "There'd be patients in the community," explained someone in the psychiatric emergency service, "who'd just stop by the unit once in a while. They'd walk in, say hi to the folks up there, and leave. It kept them pulled together, and then, when they did get admitted, they knew exactly what to expect." When I was there, however, chances were that when such a patient showed up in the emergency room he'd be shipped off to another hospital, either because his insurance company didn't have a contract with Lacey or because there were no beds since the unit was full of patients who had come from elsewhere. In a short admission, there was rarely time to get the old medical record chart from Lacey to the hospital where the patient ended up. So not only was the patient disconcerted by his new surroundings, but his doctors, who had never met him before, would have to make decisions about how to medicate him without any knowledge of his history apart from what he was able to report. Patients who once might have been admitted to Lacey three times in the course of a year might now be admitted to three different hospitals, acquire three different and unconnected charts, and be placed on three different medication regimens. The commonsense wisdom down in the emergency room was that this was costly and dangerous, that the patients got sicker, and that a great deal of psychiatric work became redundant. By the time I arrived, the staff in the psychiatric emergency room seemed to spend half their time on the phone, calling insurance companies and getting approval for care, while the patients sat listlessly in the next room. Usually there were few beds available in the hospital, which was full of patients from other catchment areas; local patients would then have to go off to other hospitals. Sometimes they were sent off even if there were beds available because their insurer had negotiated a contract with another hospital. None of this seemed to be much help to patients.

The sharply limited relationship with patients imposed by managed care makes most sense with the biomedical model and offends the practitioners using that model least. If psychiatric illness is a brain dysfunction and medication is its primary treatment, relationships with patients can seem to be irrelevant. Because of the ideological tension, it makes it seem that the biomedical approach is right and the psychodynamic approach is wrong. As the argument evolved in the seventies and eighties, if psychiatric illness is biological, it should be treated with drugs; if it is psychological, it should be treated with therapy. Now many people draw the inverse conclusion: if a disease is treated with drugs, it must be a biological illness. Never mind that short-term hospitalizations and medication trials often do not work. The history of ideological warfare invites us to infer from the use of biomedical treatment the failure of the psychodynamic approach.

But that is a mistake that blinds us to the cost of this great loss. Patients are less well off without psychotherapy. They do less well, are readmitted more quickly, diagnosed more inaccurately, and medicated more randomly. As a result, doctors who came of professional age before the health care revolution see managed care, and the loss of psychotherapy that has accompanied it, as a moral problem. They feel that they are doing something ethically wrong when they abandon their close clinical relationships with patients. They feel that they are giving bad care, that they are uncaring, and that the patients suffer.

"What's true is what is worth fighting for, and that is also what is good," a senior psychiatrist told me. "What is good and what is true are united. You cannot adhere to untruths without being immoral in some way." Michael Griffiths (a pseudonym) had in some ways rejected his psychoanalytic training, but he found himself in moral despair at the inroads made by managed care. He was a chiseled, handsome man, like many psychiatrists blunt and acute. "Michael is free," one of his colleagues said enviously. "It doesn't matter to him whether his patients like him or not. It makes him very good at handling these very sick patients." Michael Griffiths had trained in Semrad's Mass Mental program but had become famous in part by demonstrating that insight-oriented therapy—intensive psychodynamic psychotherapy—was not particularly helpful for schizophrenics. He had disrupted a main tenet of the midcentury psychoanalytic worldview, and he had been integrally involved with the development of the *DSM* diagnostic categories. But his ultimate commitment was to the complexity of an individual life, and while he thought that many of the analysts he worked with were mistaken in some of their beliefs, he was shocked by the unfettered biomedical vision and profoundly saddened by the loss of psychiatry as he knew it.

"Perhaps I had a little more distance than most when I was doing my psychoanalytic training," he explained to me one afternoon. "I didn't come from an urban Jewish background, so culturally it wasn't part of me. I didn't have the overwhelming personal problems—a history of failed relationships or difficulties at work—that would have made me hope ardently that the training analysis would be deeply therapeutic. And when I began my training, psychopharmacology was making its first inroads into psychiatric practice, and while it was still, at that time, viewed with suspicion by the mainstream psychoanalytic community, it was also clear that here was something that was empirically based and could not be discounted. So the eventual rift in psychiatry was already part of my experience in training.

"But why did I drift away from mainstream psychoanalysis? Over the course of my training, first in psychiatry and then in psychoanalysis, I felt very confident as a psychotherapist. All along the line I had very positive feedback for my abilities. The problem was that the patients weren't responding so well. Not just the schizophrenics, all patients. Despite the beauty of the insights and the depth of the theory. Well, I was still in training. Then I was placed in charge of a long-term treatment unit. The patients would come and come and come, and all the wise people in the community were their therapists—there was no question of adequate training for them—and hell, sometimes it was clear that the patients were worse. Here were these therapists, doggedly pursuing this method with belief and commitment, and the patients weren't getting better. I came to see many analysts as blinded by theory and self-interest. They were guided by ideas that were wrong and which could not be tested. It was like a religion, and slowly but surely this pushed me toward a multifactorial model of illness and treatment. It did not disillusion me about the place of psychoanalysis in the lives of healthier people or as a system for understanding much of what we were seeing. It wasn't as if the explanations given by psychoanalysis were wrong. But they were insufficient. You had to look at the family and the organic side; you had to see how social rehabilitation—teaching the patient to sit at a table with other people without being grossly inappropriate—was so important and so undervalued by psychoanalysts."

So he challenged the assumed usefulness of insight-oriented psychotherapy for the sicker patients and began to offer alternative kinds of psychotherapeutic interventions. He began to look at the social context of patients' experience and to provide therapy that taught patients how to function within that context. He used medications. He was seen by some in the older generation as a renegade. However, he balks at the shifts of the biologic revolution. He thinks that medication alone is less clinically effective than medication in the context of psychosocial treatment. He still thinks that psychodynamic understanding and psychosocial therapies are essential for the adequate treatment of patients. The purely psychopharmacological approach, he fears, is even more narrow than the narrowness of the psychoanalytic perspective he first protested against.

"These days," he continued, "the psychoanalytic or even psychosocial explanations are sometimes given the same kind of blindsided dismissal that the earlier generations of exclusively psychoanalytic thinkers gave to social or biological factors. I remember a former colleague who zealously spearheaded the shift toward a biological paradigm in my hospital here. He said that the patient who is reacting in an unusual and unhealthy way which is diagnosable has an illness, meaning a brain disorder. It was a very powerful message, and the inferences drawn from that message are *wrong*. If you put a person in a closed room for ten years, their brain chemistry is going to change. Take them out, and it may or may not revert. That brain chemistry is not fixed by the genes. It is alterable and greatly influenced by psychosocial factors. Childhood events register themselves in the brain, and they influence its neurochemistry, and the fact that you can see something in an adult brain which may be altered by medication doesn't say a whole lot about etiology. And to suggest, by using a term like 'brain disorder,' that the mind is not involved and that psychosocial factors are not involved is not right. You can get the same effect from psychosocial treatment as from medication. It just takes a little longer. It may also be longer-lasting and, depending on the patient, more effective.

"What really bothered me was that my zealous colleague was blind. He was not seeing what was there in front of him. The people. Complicated people with life histories, with very individualized prognostic options, with a great deal of uncertainty about how they got that way and a great deal of ambiguity about what the effects of his interventions were going to be. He treated every aspect of that in black and white. As if he knew. And he didn't know. Like a blind man touching an elephant, he *couldn't* know."

Once when I went to see Griffiths, it seemed that he had been waiting to tell me about something that had greatly upset him that week. He had just done a consultation with a young man who had been diagnosed as schizophrenic. There was some justification for this diagnosis: the young man was withdrawn and intermittently psychotic, and his life had become disorganized. But what the psychiatrist in charge of the case hadn't considered, Griffiths explained, was that his parents had divorced shortly before he had fallen ill. And in this health care system, the belief that he was schizophrenic, with its expectations of schizophrenia, would condemn him. His caretakers would assume that he would have a chronic, debilitating course. They would disconnect.

"Of course, the economic pressures are changing how psychiatrists must work," Griffiths said. "There is so much pressure to move patients out of the hospital, and any psychosocial treatment gets shortchanged because at present you cannot document its effectiveness the same way you can document the effectiveness of medication trials. Even now, I wake up in the middle of the night angry at the wrongheadedness of clinical decisions. What they've done is understandable. Managed care companies have a primary interest in cutting costs, and they need to have rules to guide what they pay for and what they won't, and it leads to inappropriate clinical decisions. I become reconciled to this over time. I see it as part of an historical process. I can't personalize it—the forces pushing this are very large, and I would end up aging very quickly and unhappily if I were going to the mat every day for things I care about but couldn't win." Then he paused, and an expression of great pain came over his face. He seemed to want to believe in what he had just said, and he clearly didn't.

"I've got to stop," he said, shaking his head and looking out the window. "You come in here and ask me about these things I feel passionate about, and I've tried so hard to retain my equilibrium in the face of these terrible affronts. It is so difficult for me."

CHAPTER SEVEN

⁘

MADNESS AND MORAL RESPONSIBILITY

This book might have ended with the previous chapter. But there is a profound moral dimension here that transcends managed care and ideological tensions. The way we as a society conceive of mental illness matters. It affects the way mental illness is experienced by those who deal with it. It affects the way we vote on health care policy, the way we react to the homeless on the street corner, the way we care for those we love who struggle with mental illness, the way we deal with our own anxiety, depression, and despair. Above all, the way we conceive of mental illness affects the way we conceive of ourselves as people, and particularly the way we conceive of ourselves as good people when we are confronted by another person's pain. It affects our moral instincts about what it is to be human.

The disease model of mental illness has been a tremendous asset in the fight against stigma and the fight for parity in health care coverage. And it is clear that the disease model captures a good measure of the truth. Mental illness often has an organic quality. People can't just pull themselves back together when they are hearing voices or contemplating suicide, and their illness is rarely caused by bad parenting alone. Yet to stop at that model, to say that mental illness is nothing but disease, is like saying that an opera is nothing but musical notes. It impoverishes us. It impoverishes our sense of human possibility. And it cruelly punishes those who struggle, like Laocoön wrestling with writhing snakes, with mental illness at its most savage.

"I'm on the California Mental Health Planning Council, as a consumer appointed by the state director of mental health." Now in his fifties, John has dealt with schizophrenia for thirty years. He is lucky, because in the last ten years his symptoms have abated somewhat. He still meets the criteria for the disorder, but he is what is called "high-functioning," and he has become a powerful voice for clients in the California mental health policy arena. His views about diagnosis are shared by many clients whose lives have been devastated by mental illness. "When we come around for introductions, what I say is, 'My name is John M. Hood III, and I have a diseased brain,' and they all laugh. It's part of my routine, my camp humor. Can you imagine how insulting it would be if you turned to me and said, 'I'm *sorry* you have a diseased brain'? When it gets right down to it, the medical model is an insult to me. To say I have a diseased brain does not validate me. I have a complicated thought system, with different behaviors."

John is a highly intelligent person, once a teenage math whiz. He said that even in kindergarten he had been withdrawn, not "socially appropriate," a phrase he has learned from the mental health treatment world. "Then, at the end of sixth grade, I said to myself, I will be a heavyweight, I will go out and make friends with the most popular people in school. And I did. It worked. I still wasn't able to deal with reality, in the psychological sense. But I was elected to be the Boys Federation representative from my homeroom and the Red Cross representative from my homeroom, even the homeroom representative from my homeroom. I did some wild stuff. I skinned a cat in physiology and pinned it to the door of a young, beautiful English teacher. I think she had some identity issues around her sexuality and the emerging sexuality of these high school boys. I became notorious for that. Then once I spent an entire class reporting on a meeting that never took place. I just looked up 'Red Cross' in the encyclopedia. I'm good at that sort of stuff, looking things up."

When his father moved to London the year John graduated from high school (his father went to pursue a doctorate at University College), John ended up pumping gas in Colorado and living in a trapdoor attic above the station. He never showered. There was no shower in the station, it didn't occur to him to find one elsewhere, and he had no friends. He lasted three months. "All this stuff is pathological in some sense, but the real symptoms, when I became aware of them as symptoms, came later." He went to college—an excellent one—for a year and did moderately well. There he became involved in the counterculture. "If I could have made an adjustment within the counterculture, I would have been okay. The counterculture kept me stabilized that first year."

That summer, he went off to visit his parents in England. The Vietnam War was under way, the Beatles were hot, teenage men grew their hair past their ears and took drugs and made trouble at home. John was hardly unusual in that respect. But on his way from California to see his buttoned-up parents, he stopped for a night in New York. There, in a cheap hotel room he shared with a stranger, he felt his mind take off. "It whirled, and it would not stop." Nonetheless, he arrived in England without incident. It was a bad summer, lonely and isolated. He knew no one and argued constantly with his parents, who were frightened by the drugs he was taking and horrified by his hair, his clothes, his lifestyle. He came back to California, but because his parents refused to support him when he was using drugs, he had no money for a room at school. He camped out on friends' floors instead. He felt he had many friends. Still, someone made an appointment for him to talk to a psychiatrist about "the workings of the mind." The night before the appointment, John stayed up all night and wrote page after page about his own philosophy of mind. "I expected that *I* would teach *him*." During the appointment, the psychiatrist asked him whether he'd like to stay in the hospital for a while, and John agreed that it might be a good idea. After all, he pointed out to the psychiatrist, he was homeless. John was diagnosed as paranoid schizophrenic in the hospital and discharged after ten days because his parents wanted to care for him at home in England. He found it difficult to concentrate there. He knew no one but his parents, and he got on very poorly with them. He returned to California eight months later, after his father finished his doctorate.

Since then John has been hospitalized about a dozen times, although he hasn't been hospitalized for more than fifteen years. He has been on psychiatric medication for more than thirty years and takes some powerful anti-psychotics. He doesn't entirely like his medication and would like to be off it, but he finds it helpful. John has never heard voices, but he hears the walls creak loudly and repeatedly. He feels that the creaks are punitive: "I am obsessed, as I am to this day, by the idea that there is a supernatural force that makes creaks in the walls, and that they are God telling me what I am doing wrong. There is a real creak. You might not notice it, but it would be there. I know, I've spent thirty years trying to deal with these creaks." As a young adult he became aware of what he calls the "social game," which is the way people signal to him that they are attacking him and defending themselves against him by scratching their chin or their ears or shifting position or leaning on their elbows. He says now that this was a delusional system—but it is also part of his training in shamanism, and he now thinks of himself as a shaman. He doesn't really believe in any one religion's god, he says, but from a very young age he began to think of himself as the risen Christ and to prepare for his much-anticipated return: "I thought there was this job, a good clean job, which was the Second Coming, and I thought I fulfilled the conditions for it, even though I don't believe in biblical prophecy or anything like that. So I saw myself as able to have more authority and power than was appropriate. That was delusional." In his home he has a collection of different-sized medication bottles. His walls are hung with another collection, the awards he has received for his work in the mental health field. He has been on many state policy planning boards and has been recognized for his work by these awards, and by ceremonies and further appointments. In 1998, he was awarded the most prestigious local prize in the mental health field, the Mental Health Person of the Year, a prize given annually to a client or provider. On receiving it, he addressed an audience of seven hundred. He has been an enthusiastic producer of newletters for the mental health community. He also writes plays and poetry. He is employed as a peer counselor at a county psychiatric hospital, where he works on a locked unit where many of the most dysfunctional patients in the county can be found.

John is active in what is called mental health patient advocacy, a lobbying effort on behalf of those diagnosed with severe mental illness. There is a variety of such groups. Some refer to themselves as "psychiatric survivors" and take a strong stand against mandated psychiatric medication. There is, for example, a magazine called *Dendron* that is specifically focused on alternatives to what its writers call forced psychiatric drugging. *Dendron* has a circulation of 6,000 and an estimated readership of 15,000. Its Winter 1997–98 issue features Burch House, a treatment center in New Hampshire modeled after R. D. Laing's communities in England, where patients with acute psychosis are stabilized without psychiatric medication. Many of the patient advocacy groups recognize that the Burch House treatment approach is not feasible in a managed care world. Nevertheless, they strongly tend to prefer a community-centered and therapy-centered model over a medical model.

This is not true of all organizations that lobby for psychiatric patients. The National Alliance for the Mentally Ill, for example, has been a powerful voice in defense of the medical model and a powerful voice in Congress. It is one of the largest advocacy groups, with more than a hundred thousand members nationwide. It has used the medical model to argue effectively that more research in psychiatry is desperately needed because mental illness is not the result of poor socialization and inadequate parenting but rather a medical condition in need of medical attention. Its publications are full of MRI scans, psychopharmacological studies, and epidemiological surveys. Its policy statement describes it as a grassroots organization for "individuals with brain disorders and their families" and states that the organization promotes "the prevailing scientific judgment that 'severe mental illnesses' are brain disorders, which at the present time are neither preventable nor curable, but are treatable and manageable with combinations of medication, supportive counseling, and community support services." It uses this approach in an effort to destigmatize mental illness and, as a corollary, to persuade the public and Congress that mental illness is an illness like any other. NAMI is widely respected within the psychiatric community as an excellent organization with powerful political clout and striking efficacy. But many within the patient-run advocacy movement are skeptical of it, seeing it as a "parents' organization" committed to erasing parents' guilt (NAMI is, in fact, deeply committed to the view that mental illness is no one's fault; its policy statement states that the strongest weapon against the stigma of mental illness is science). The patients' skepticism focuses on NAMI's support for the medical model.

Like many clients, John is adamantly opposed to the medical model because to him it makes his thoughts, his goals, and his desires seem as if they are not really his own but due to something separate from himself. He disapproves of NAMI's stand: "The whole NAMI emphasis is trying to avoid looking at the upbringing. You could say, 'John Hood thinks he's a wizard, and has a very animated emotional style, he has too much dopamine, he's not responsible for what he thinks.' But as a peer counselor what I focus on is: take responsibility for your actions, treat other people as they should treat you, and have a sense of humor. If I have a client that comes up to me and says, 'I jumped over the moon last night,' I will validate that belief. As far as I have to go. You cannot live without validation. And you cannot live without doubt. That's where the medical model comes in. Everyone's looking for an answer. For something. But there's no simple answer. There can't be."

Madness is a terrible thing. It is hard to treat, hard to live with, hard to comprehend. Most people do not grasp how strange and horrible and recalcitrant the problems are, how frightening it is to look into the eyes of a crazy person and see no answering recognition. Many would rather brush past a psychotic panhandler than deal with him, would rather pretend that the mentally ill do not exist. We are right to be terrified by psychosis and depression, because mental illness distorts the defining features of person-hood, and, seeing that, we are reminded that the foundations of our being are built on sand. The mad are people who deliberately hide razors and then, in private, when their mothers have gone to bed, slice into their flesh until blood seeps into the bedsheets. They hoard sleeping pills for months, collecting new prescriptions even though the old ones are untouched, then wash them all down with vodka and leave a voice-mail message on their doctor's line. They refuse to take out the trash for months, until the stench offends their neighbors and the janitor comes in to find a crawling pile. They skip lunch and eat only one tomato and one can of tuna fish each night, chopping the food carefully into a thousand pieces and eating forkful after tiny forkful for an hour. They act on the basis of voices we cannot hear and beliefs we cannot share. They intend; they decide; they choose.

Their illnesses are a part of who they are in a way that seems very different from the alien invasion of a cancer.

In our society, we usually see people with cancer, heart disease, or a broken leg as innocent sufferers, and we usually feel that they have some claim to our help and that it is good and right to support them through a misery they did not ask for and do not deserve. In psychiatric illness there is no such clarity. We often find it difficult to respond to psychiatric patients as innocent sufferers, because taking an overdose seems deliberate and chosen in a way that having cancer does not. We sometimes even find it difficult to respond to them as people, because when a man is psychotic he loses the ability to behave like a person among people. That makes it difficult to empathize with madness and hard to know how to respond appropriately. That awkwardness is embedded deep within our religious heritage.

We are not supposed to destroy ourselves. Fate, to borrow a Homeric phrase, has woven the thread of life with pain, and that can reflect poorly on a supposedly benevolent creator. But if (as people in earlier centuries did) you accept that there is a God who allows this sharp misery, if you grant that God sends pain for a reason, then what is the right stance to take toward it? Do you embrace bronchitis as God's gift until he removes it? Or do you attempt to cure it yourself, in effect arrogantly challenging God's wisdom?[1] Martin Luther resolved the puzzle (as others also did) by arguing that God asks of humans that they take responsibility for their own well-being.[2] "A farmer does not commit the care of his field to God in such a way that he himself does none of the things that pertain to agriculture, does not plow and does not cultivate the land," he explained.[3] "Many argue rashly about the necessity ordained by fate and say, 'If God wants to preserve me, I will survive in a time of plague and famine even without food and medicine; but if I am to perish, all those things will not help me at all.' These thoughts are impious and have been forbidden by God, for He has not rendered to us His secret counsels as to how or when He wants to help you."[4] In other words, to refuse to seek health is to demand of God that he do for us what we can do for ourselves.

By the same reasoning, to hurt oneself intentionally is to spurn God. It is hubris. "The body has been given to us by God," wrote Luther, "not that we should kill it with fasting or vigils, but that we should care for it with food, drink, clothing, sleep and medicine."[5] From this perspective, self-hurt is sacrilegious and possibly evil, even if done in the name of worship: "Do not choose your own affliction. . . . God gave you two eyes, and these you are not to injure or gouge out; also two legs, and these you are not to cut off. On the contrary, if your members are ailing, God wants you to employ medication for healing them. But if it should occur that tyrants

271

murder you or otherwise persecute you, then you must suffer it and let God rule."[6]

Luther here used an old religious distinction, which I shall call the distinction between inessential and essential suffering, between the suffering one can act on and suffering that, as a Catholic priest might say, one must offer up to God. Essential suffering is what we are not able to prevent but must survive if we can. Essential suffering is the inherent difficulty of human life, our troubles, the way we struggle in the world, being the specific people we are, of a certain character, in this specific place and time. The particular history of our pain molds our characters further into the people we become. Human pain is inevitable, and all the knowledge and fervor in the world will not wash it safe and pure. Nadine Gordimer tells a tale of a young South African radical, burning to save the world from apartheid, who one day takes her lunch to the park and finds a park bench across from a man who is quiet and untroublesome. When a pigeon perches on his shoulder, she realizes, her sandwich gone, that he is dead. When the revolution comes, she thinks, and there will be justice, equality, the brotherhood of man, and human dignity, there will still be this, and she throws away the cellophane wrapper from her sandwich and vanishes into the crowd like a thief.[7] Human life is hard. Our personal histories are trails through small circumstances filled with hurt.

Inessential suffering is the pain we can treat. We can remove it because it is the result of some fact that can be altered. When it is gone, it is inessential to us. It has not made us who we are. Luther argues that illness that can be cured, hunger that can be fed, and chill that can be warmed are inessential sufferings, and it is our duty to remove them. He also argues that those fervent worshipers who scourge and starve and otherwise torment themselves to honor God are terribly misguided. Only suffering that is unavoidable must be accepted. We must ask for God's beneficence to our crops only if we have tended the fields with love and care. "Fool!" remarks the Talmud. "From your own work, do you not understand that . . . even as the plant, if not weeded, fertilized and ploughed, does not grow . . . so is the body of man. The fertilizer is the medicine, and the farmer is the physician."[8]

As this distinction has been inherited by our Judeo-Christian culture, medicine handles the inessential suffering, religion the essential suffering, and intentional hurt falls into a limbo, neither treated by medicine nor tolerated by religion. The physician's role is to treat what is treatable and to manage what is manageable. Doctors are not trained to handle the patient's existential crisis or, in extremis, his confrontation with death. That is why there are priests, ministers, and rabbis attached to hospitals, and while doctors can hardly avoid the personal tragedy created by a diseased liver, it is not their task to attend to it, and an emergency down the hall preempts a patient who has been treated but is in despair. Doctors are taught how to understand disease processes and interrupt them. A priest or rabbi is taught how to help us through moments of the irrevocable.[9] We go to doctors to solve the problem of our aching joints and stuffed noses, as if the doctors were glorified technicians of the body, and we go to church to solve the problem of our loneliness in the infinitude of time and space. That, among other reasons, is why people in their thirties and forties often begin to feel a need for religion, because by then they have realized that life is an accumulation of forced choices, with consequences that could not be foreseen; that bad things happen to good people, sometimes in terrible ways; and that to see life as good despite this can require the kind of wisdom one finds in spirituality. Or in great novels. Mary Gordon wrote that she had read *Middlemarch* three times. In her teens, she yearned for Dorothea to marry the romantic, dashing Ladislaw. In her twenties, she fumed that Dorothea had lived her life in the shadow of men who were clearly not her equal. In her middle forties, she realized that the intense and passionate Dorothea had lived as best she could, in the circumstances in which she had found herself, and Gordon saw for the first time that *Middlemarch* was a sad book, about grace and dignity and faith.[10]

The power of religious comfort lies in its ability to reframe and reinterpret the inevitable pain of life. In church we come to terms with the life that circumstances have carved out for us, and we learn to make the best we can of it and accept our struggles as essential to ourselves. We learn to understand pain as part of life and, in some senses, as a spiritual lesson. Modern medicine, by contrast, separates a person who is ill from the illness that he or she has. Intentions are cordoned off from the physical problem. No doctor refuses to set a broken arm if the patient broke it because he acted like an idiot on the soccer field. She treats lung cancer whether or not the patient smoked. In medicine, the complex circumstances that led to and result from pain are bracketed away from the injury in order to treat the injury. Even doctors who see themselves as healing the whole person or as engaged in social justice are trained to treat, act upon, and remove. We have institutionalized the distinction in the phrase "medically necessary," the central policy concept in managed care. Medically necessary care is, in the words of a Medicaid statute, care that is "reasonable and necessary for the diagnosis or treatment of illness or injury or to improve the functioning of a malformed body member."[11] Doctors fix abnormal conditions, ameliorate inessential suffering, and ignore the troughs of ordinary life. "If one were asked to select the single most important idea upon which medicine is based," writes a medical historian of medicine, "it would be . . . that abnormal conditions in the body can be recognized."[12]

273

Psychiatry fits badly into the dichotomy between abnormal, treatable problems and the flow of life because when someone carves her initials into her arm you cannot cleanly separate the treatable problem from its personal setting. There is no tumor to excise. There is nothing specific you can set aside and say, here, if we cure this, the pain will go away. There isn't even much of a clear-cut sense of normality—healthy people are like this and unhealthy ones like that—at least compared to medicine, where it is complicated enough.[13] Psychiatric problems are bound up with the unique life each person leads because they are bound up with the way someone willfully chooses, the way she wants, intends, decides. In psychiatric illness, the injury *is* the complex intentional circumstances that surround the pain. What is broken, metaphorically, is that the patient *wanted* to get hurt or to fail, and the want is not like a benign and operable tumor but is connected to many other wants, fears, aspirations that are knitted into the person that patient has become.[14] The problem of intention is inherent in psychiatric illness. Yet we live in a culture with religious traditions that condemn intentional suffering and medical practices that bracket intention away.

And so our models of psychiatric illness are solutions to the problems that psychiatric illness presents to us. The facts, as I have pointed out, are that major psychiatric illness has a complex cause and that a combination of psychopharmacological and psychotherapeutic treatments provides the best outcome. Practicing psychiatrists often come to have a rich, complicated, multicausal understanding of an individual's struggles. But each of the two approaches they are taught has emerged as a solution to the problem of intention and, in particular, to the problem of feeling compassion for self-destructive intention. In our Protestant, individualistic culture, we help those who help themselves. We want to help people who lose their houses because of hurricanes, floods, or other natural disasters; we have little sympathy for those who burn down their houses and then claim they have no place to live. Psychiatric science and psychodynamics are among our culture's choices about how to make sense of self-inflicted suffering so that we can feel compassion for those who suffer, so that we can want to help.[15]

Psychodynamics manages this by focusing on the unconscious. That makes some intentions effectively unintentional, but it leaves the cause of suffering embedded in a complex intentional web. Psychiatric science manages by aggressively minimizing intention, so that what might seem to be intentional (suicidally pulling the trigger of a gun, swallowing barbiturates and rum) becomes a bodily dysfunction to treat. Both psychodynamics and psychiatric science are attempts to come to grips with crazy, incomprehensible, self-destructive intention in ways that help us to feel compassion. Both explain self-destructive intention by effectively making it nonintentional. But they do so in different ways, and the difference has profound consequences for the way we feel compassion for the person we need to help.

Compassion depends upon empathy, and empathy is always imperfect. We can never really feel another person's pain. Instead, we feel the echo of the emotional pain that we perceive, in the person we think we see, as the person we would like to be, with the expectations we carry of a person, in the way we feel able to express ourselves around that person. We *learn* to perceive. This is perhaps the most basic anthropological insight. People are never "in themselves" to other people. Who they are is mediated by the person *to whom* they are, by the way they are understood, responded to, engaged with. We are not transparent to one another. So empathy is never pure. We empathize with other people from within our own expectations. Those expectations have what I have come to think of as an "architecture." They are built from the way we conceive of and imagine the persons we see before us, the persons we hope to be ourselves, the way we expect suffering persons to treat us, the way we learn to treat them. And that architecture is often not visible to us: we simply empathize, and feel compassion, for certain people in certain ways.

When a psychiatrist, or for that matter a nonpsychiatrist, empathizes with someone like John, he empathizes differently depending on the way he understands the patient's pain. Who is this person, and why does he feel his pain? From the medical perspective, his pain is inessential suffering. It has not made him who he is. It does not come out of the complexities of his past, and it does not lie at the center of his future. This is the great gift of that approach to psychiatric illness. The pain is not your mother's coolness or your father's preoccupation; it is not your disastrous choices, your embarrassments, your inadequacies. The pain is no more you than a winter's cold is. Thus the medical model can rescue someone from stigma, which is a real and horrifying feature of our social life. There should be no more embarrassment about depression or schizophrenia than there is about diabetes, but in fact there is, because of the awkward problem psychiatric illness poses for our religious heritage. The medical model solves this problem by treating the illness as something external, imposed from outside the intentional self the way a broken leg or dysfunctional kidney is outside of and separate from our personhood. When we learn to empathize through the medical model, we learn to empathize with someone who is a victim of external circumstances, and we are invited to empathize with that person as a member of a category of other people: those suffering from depression, from schizophrenia, from floods or other natural disasters. When psychiatrists see patients in a biomedical setting, when they must diagnose and prescribe, what they are taught to see is the category of illness: a patient is depressed, anxious, psychotic, schizophrenic, bipolar. For the purposes of treatment, a patient is the category indicated by his symptoms.

From the psychodynamic perspective, the pain of psychiatric illness is an essential suffering. It is intrinsic to a person, to his experience of life, to his growth and future. The pain may have some bodily cause, but the psychodynamic enterprise tries to see the way the experience of the pain is at the center of that person's struggles. The therapist tries to help the person to understand how he has chosen to handle his depression, how his depression has figured in the way he loves and works and plays. The gift of the psychodynamic model is that the illness is not external, arbitrary, and other. At least part of what is dysfunctional is the way the patient has chosen (unconsciously) to handle his distress: his repetitive self-accusatory thoughts, his angry explosions at his loved ones, his chaotic attempts to shake off his anxiety. The illness, then, is not out of his control but something over which he is potentially a master. When we empathize with someone through the psychodynamic model, we empathize with the unique life course of that person: his hopes, his losses, his mistakes, his frailties, his courage, and his strength. When psychiatrists see patients in a psychodynamic setting, what they see is the complexity of a particular life: how a specific person dreamed, feared, yearned, avoided, chose.

A psychiatrist becomes different people, too, depending on his model and on who he aspires to be in that relationship. To be a certain sort of self, appropriate to a certain setting, has an aim: to be like, to be thought of as like, to be respected as being like the best that are respected here. "The very way we walk, move, gesture, speak," remarked the philosopher Charles Taylor, "is shaped from the earliest moments by our awareness that we appear before others, that we stand in public space, and that this space is potentially one of respect or contempt or pride or shame."[16] In a psychotherapeutic setting that public space is shaped by the model of the psychoanalyst, a complex, contradictory, elusive character conscious of the multiple roles one person plays for another, constantly questioning, eternally uncertain, curious about what is hidden, opaque, elided in our interactions with one another. The psychoanalyst sees the tragedy of human lives, which is one reason we have thought of psychoanalysts as the priests and rabbis of a secular age. Here the bottom-line commitment is to a kind of nurturing, loving relationship with the patient and a belief that self-knowledge is inherently good. In a biomedical setting, that public space is shaped by the figure of the scientist, who is a person of knowledge. A scientist is a person of data, of testing, of experimental outcomes and future outcomes. A scientist is not, in his capacity as scientist, a clinician, but he or she creates the conditions under which future medical treatment can be generated. This is a powerful moral good, but it is good in relationship to all patients in general. A relationship with a particular patient is not a powerful part of what it means to be a scientist. The expertise of psychiatric scientists lies in their knowledge of neurotransmitters and brain mechanisms; the expertise of psychoanalysts lies in their knowledge of and care for individual people.

Reality is, of course, more complex than this; and psychiatrists have much more that shapes their involvement with these models of mental illness than the rest of us (their sense of who is at risk from whom, of where the contradictions of their culture lie). Still, there is a different ethos to an approach in which the problem is a disease and the ideal is the scientist than there is to one in which the problem is in choices and interactions and the ideal is the psychoanalyst. For those of us who are not psychiatrists, there is a difference between the way we empathize when we think in terms of a person with a disease that medication will cure and whose ultimate cure rests upon a scientific advance, and when we think in terms of a person with a messy past who can be helped by being understood and mentored.

One might call the empathy structured by the biomedical model "simple empathy." Your job in caring for a person with psychiatric illness (if that is your job) is to treat the inessential suffering to the best extent that you can and to hope earnestly that better research will produce better ways of handling this class of problems. You feel empathically for a victim of psychiatric illness; identifying with the scientist, you feel moral urgency in removing this blight from the earth. The empathy is simple because the problem is simple. There are no complicating intentions.

By contrast, one might call the empathy structured by the psychodynamic model "complex empathy." The suffering is not really inessential, because while the self-destructive intentions (to kill oneself, to fail, to be imperfect) are unconscious, they are still intentional, and they are interwoven in the complex web of the person's past. They are part of him. They are who he is. You cannot feel for this person simply that he is a victim of a depression the way he might be a victim of the latest hurricane. The hurricane of depression is part of who he is, and to empathize with him is to empathize with his self-destructiveness as well as with his despair.

And simple empathy and its compassion help sufferers only when the suffering can go away. When my broken leg is in its heavy cast, I want someone who will laugh and cry with me about the indignity and pain of my broken leg, someone who will understand how much it hurts, someone who can tell me, as I struggle upstairs on crutches, that it doesn't really matter. I want someone to help me see that everything will be okay despite this terrible, painful, frustrating predicament, that nothing has really changed. But if I were to break my back, if I were to be in a wheelchair for good, I would not want a friend to tell me that the wheelchair didn't matter. The wheelchair would become part of who I was in a way that my broken leg did not. If I saw myself as the same as before, just with a wheelchair, I would always be inadequate compared to that former self. If I saw myself as a different person, a different self but still a fully human self with meaning, I might be able to live with pride and optimism. John knows he is different. He knows he can never hold a high-paying job. But he thinks he has a valid way of looking at the world, that he has the right to be here, and that he contributes to the lives of others. Thinking of his thoughts and feelings as "diseased" makes him want to cringe in shame.

Understanding a person as separate from his psychiatric illness works well when the illness climaxes and dissipates, when the depression lifts and the person emerges from her suicidal fog, when the mania abates and the person no longer believes that he has wings with which to fly. When psychiatric illness clears, it makes eminent sense to see that person as having suffered primarily from a disease. Doing so removes the threat of stigma. The misery wasn't really that person's fault, nor was it the fault of his or her parents. No one is to blame. Nothing but the body (and maybe a little stress) was the cause. The gift of this perspective is profound, because in the years of psychoanalytic dominance, the vulgarized psychoanalytic model was used to humiliate and insult the parents whose children suffered.

But when the psychiatric illness is unremitting, the medical solution is not so good. If people's personhood is independent of their psychiatric illness but the illness never goes away and the illness lies in the way they think, feel, and act, they can see themselves and be seen as never fully human. Their brains are diseased, their intentions are sick, and if (as happens too often) medication does not make the disease clear up and go away, they feel that there is nothing they or anyone else can do about it. What it is to be human in them—thinking, choosing, feeling—is sick, and it is out of their control.

When a psychiatric patient conceives of himself primarily as a victim of a disease and the disease is unremitting, he loses a reason to struggle. Vernon has been involved in patient advocacy work for close to thirty years. He speaks slowly but with passion, and he has thought deeply about these dilemmas. As a child, he was diagnosed with childhood schizophrenia—"I had to live with that all my life"—but now he is more often called bipolar or "schizoaffective," an amalgam of a mood (or affective) disorder (in his case, depression) and more schizophrenia-like symptoms, such as hearing voices. He is better now than he has been since he was first admitted to a hospital thirty-five years ago after stabbing five other boys. He has been off medication for more than a year. He credits that success in part to his joy at the birth of his first grandchild. Mostly, though, he attributes it to the way he learned to live with his illness not as an alien disease but as part of the way he is: "I still hear voices. But what I discovered was that it's complicated. When my wife died back in 1985, when I was at that air force base, I thought I was having a complete nervous breakdown. The psychiatrist told me no. He opened the door for me to understand psychology from another point of view. He asked me, did I ever read [Elisabeth] Kübler-Ross? He said, that's what you have, grief. Grief is like the beginning of acute mental illness. Knowing that, I knew how to take care of myself rather than have a psychiatrist tell me what to do. I help patients now the way organizations like NAMI don't even want to try, because it takes too long. It's taken me thirty years to not take medication. It's been difficult, but I have a life. A lot of this came about by searching for the right alternatives. After reading Kübler-Ross, I saw myself as grieved, not mentally ill. I think of mental illness now as a life situation, kind of an extension of Kübler-Ross."

Why does it help, I asked him, to shift the label from "disease" to "life situation"? "I had a psychiatrist" he said, "who put all of my problems in one category, 'schizoaffective,' and he didn't see how it could be anything else. I think if you think about it differently, you realize it takes one step at a time, and you realize you can do something. I have a system I call 'SENAP.' S is Self-awareness and freedom of expression. E is Energy activation, in a way that's free from stress. You have a right to be treated in a way that's comfortable to you, in a controlled environment. N is New awareness of self. If I'm going to get better, I need to take a look at my eating habits, my clothes, and wean myself away from bad habits. A is an Awareness of reality. Really, I mean that there is a meaning to psychosis, delusions, hallucinations. There is a social and artistic meaning. You have to see that. P is Problem solving. You take things one step at a time. You have to see that there's a creativity there."

So, I wondered aloud to him, when someone says you've got a disease, why do you feel uncomfortable with that? "When I got involved with the California Network of Mental Health Clients, we never could come up with an answer. Even now, we still haven't come up with an answer. The only thing we do know is that we're not accepting biochemistry. Clients will accept physiology, some neurology. They all agree that you can never get rid of the phrase 'mental illness,' though they would like to. But it's like this: Say I have diabetes. It's going to go on for years and years until maybe I lose my eyes. If you create the disease of mental illness, you've got to be prepared for the final outcome. I've lost over twelve friends to suicide since 1983. With an illness, you can do something. The common flu is an illness, and you know how to take care of it. With mental illness, knowing that there are different avenues to getting there and two avenues to cure—the drugs, but also talk, the community, places like the meeting place [a place downtown where clients can drop in and talk to each other], the psychosocial dimension—it gives you hope. It makes you real. A psychiatrist or a NAMI person does what they can, but it's still up to that person, that client, to say, I am ready to go up to the next level. Like me, if I hadn't gotten involved with the political work, I'd be a lot sicker. I'd be in a state hospital or in jail. I'd have just given up."

Vernon cannot maintain his sense of himself independently from his psychiatrist's and his society's sense of who he is. He lives, as do we all, within the implicit expectations of others. And just as the way he conceives of himself is entangled with the way we conceive of and empathize with him, our expectations become entangled with our moral judgments in insidious ways that rebound upon our judgments about how to deal with mental illness. Empathy often implicates morality. To echo James Wilson's remarkable discussion of sympathy, to empathize—at least beyond the toddler stage—*is* to judge.[17] To empathize is to assess someone else's circumstances and character, to interpret that person according to one's profession, one's society, and one's own personal history; to infer, on that basis, what that person feels; and, inevitably, to make a judgment about the rightness or wrongness of what has happened. To be able to empathize, you must understand why a person has acted and whether he intended the outcome of the act.[18] In that sense, empathy is one of our primary moral resources.

Morality, of course, has several faces. The anthropologist and psychologist Richard Shweder points out that across cultures, there are three primary discourses about what is right and good. There is an ethics of autonomy, with talk about justice, harm, rights, and human freedom; an ethics of divinity, with talk about purity, sanctity, and the will of God; and an ethics of community, with talk of duty, obligation, and the collective good.[19] Different societies organize the importance of these various ethics in various ways. But no matter whether yours is a society that sets duty to family above all or one that emphasizes individual rights, the basic tool for judging human action is to understand why a person has acted as he has done and whether he has intended the consequences of his act. You must judge what you think of the other person, who you wish to be in relation to him, and how you think he should be with you.[20]

This is not, perhaps, the way it should be. Certainly the Enlightenment argument between David Hume and Immanuel Kant centered on the role of emotion, and of sympathy and empathy, in moral judgment. Hume argued for the all-important role that sympathy/empathy played in our motivations; he claimed that moral behavior and good conduct are based, like everything else, upon our passions. Kant countered that our moral requirements, as we understand them, are absolutely not conditional on our feelings and inclinations. Moral considerations are what provide us with reasons for actions that are, and indeed must be, independent of our mere desires. In Kantian philosophy, morality does not tell us how to treat people based on whether we happen to feel empathically for them; it defines and limits how we may permit ourselves to treat people even when we do not like them and neither experience empathy nor feel compassion for them.

But what is a person? That is the kind of question that anthropologists and philosophers answer very differently. A philosopher argues about the world as it should be: how we should conceive of persons and their rights, how we should conceive of our moral responsibilities, why we should think, as Kant insisted, that every person must be treated as an end and not as a means. An anthropologist, less ambitious, tries simply to describe the world as she has found it. And she has learned that the cultures she studies are quite different from one another, not merely because some societies build skyscrapers and others, mud huts, but because the basic building blocks of human understanding are quite distinct. In this Melanesian society, for example, what counts as being a person is not, as we would see it, being alive, being human, but having a role, having a status, being the one with rights to a certain pig. In that African tribe, you are not really a person unless you are the legitimate child of a lawfully wedded woman. Prejudice or genocide in any society hinges on the refusal to recognize members of a group—women, Jews, African Americans—as being fully human.[21]

Anthropologists see not what moral judgment should be but how people in a particular time and place strive to be good people. We live (as one ethnographer has remarked) in a world of urgency and necessity, in what T. S. Eliot called "the endless struggle to think well of oneself."[22] Anthropologists describe, in a rich and complex way, how one should be with others in that society, what it really means to be a person *here*. In fact, that was the primary achievement of one of the best-known attempts to understand morality in anthropology. The "Comparative Study of Values in Five Cultures" project was run out of Harvard from 1949 to 1955 and eventually published as *The People of Rimrock* in 1966. Evon Vogt and John Roberts organized a team of students from various social sciences and took them off to New Mexico, where they found within a single day's drive a Navaho reservation, a Zuni pueblo, a Spanish-American village, a homesteader community of Texan and Oklahoman farmers, and a Mexican village. As a formal, scientific attempt to pin down the definition of "values" in any society, the project was an abysmal failure because no one could agree on the abstract terms. But the fieldworkers were easily able to describe what counted as moral behavior in each community.[23] They wrote about ideas to which people were emotionally attentive, that motivated them, and that rose from the way they had learned to be in relationship with one another in their community. That—the way we imagine people to be, how we imagine ourselves to be with them, how we come to feel deeply that something is right and good and true—is the cornerstone of human relationship, of the strenuous demand to be a certain kind of person in a certain setting.

And that involves empathy, because empathy is the name for the local process through which people carry their implicit expectations of one another as people with hopes and needs that are meaningful and worthy of respect in their community. I find "empathy" a useful way of thinking about these implicit expectations because few of us recognize how much our everyday emotional responses owe to the submerged icebergs of our cultural models, how much a particular local setting shapes what it is to be a self relating to other selves effectively and well.[24] Our moral instincts rest on a complex foundation in which we have expectations about who we are with, the kind of person we would like to be when we are with them, and the right way to behave throughout. When someone does something we believe to be morally wrong, we are shocked; if we are not upset, we are likely to think of that person as being "merely" eccentric or unconventional—not immoral. When we act in a way that we feel is immoral, we feel terrible; if we do not feel bad, we are likely to say that what we are doing cannot really be wrong, because it "feels so right." People in a community learn to relate to one another emotionally and to use their emotions to interpret, judge, and shape those relationships as good or bad.

And the way we conceive ourselves as and are conceived of as moral agents affects our agency—even when we struggle with schizophrenia. John Hood hates the medical model because it makes him feel like a nonperson. It is not that he thinks that its facts are inaccurate. At least, he does say that the model is wrong, but he stumbles over why it is wrong and he admits that there is something dysfunctional and organically different about his brain. He knows he needs his medication. But the way he thinks and talks cannot be separated from what it is to be schizophrenic. If schizophrenia is a brain disease, what we see as his humanity and his personhood—that he thinks, that he feels and wills and wants—is irrevocably corrupted. He must then see himself as someone whose disease should be cut away, discarded, removed; but it is also his essential "who-ness."

A psychiatric diagnosis of schizophrenia presents a major problem for someone like John Hood. He needs it because the diagnosis entitles him to benefits—health care, housing, a stipend—he would not otherwise receive. Yet to acknowledge the diagnosis as a medical condition is, he thinks, to say that his mind and self are biologically substandard. Dealing with this, the way he explains himself—as shaman, schizophrenic, wizard, master therapist, dependent, client—can become fearsomely complex. "I have a very complicated truth, which no one can figure out," he says. "I work with it in a dynamic kind of way. The bottom line is that my system is so complicated that it has got me through a lot of binds." He consistently resists thinking in diagnostic categories. I asked him once what diagnosis had been given to the founder of a client-run drop-in center. He frowned when I asked him. We were standing upstairs in a run-down stately house, its has-been elegance replaced by the mess of a communal lounge and kitchen. The founder's photo hung upstairs in the art studio, next to bold, colorful paintings with odd perspective. "We don't really talk about diagnosis here," he said. "It's not the way clients like to do things."

John wants to be seen as a responsible person. He is not, he thinks, responsible for being ill. Thirty or forty years ago, the psychoanalytic model would have held him (and his mother) as being in some measure to blame. One of the great advances of psychiatric science has been to free people from the guilt of that horrendous burden. And John does admit to having an organic problem. But he resists thinking about his schizophrenia as a disease because his schizophrenia affects his mind and he wants to think of himself as responsible for his choices, his ideas, his writing, his political work. He wants to be a trustworthy member of society. He wants to be seen as someone who admittedly has limitations but who within these limitations is reliable, reputable, and upstanding. That is why he makes such a good counselor. He teaches clients that no matter what their limitations, they can be and must be citizens.

Like many clients, John casts his struggle in a heroic light.[25] "It's the most stigmatized group in the country," he told me. "I can see guilt on my mother's face even to this day when I pull a pill out of my pocket and eat it. That I have a sick mind and have to take pills—it's enough to make you hate yourself." Instead he creates a kind of nobility in the way he survives by affirming the value of the craziness. He calls this "validation." "How do you feel about me being a wizard?" he once asked an overly self-confident mental health worker. The mental health worker said that of course he wasn't. "So I said, 'Listen buddy, I spent thirty-five years leaning how to be a wizard and I had fifteen hundred books and I knew what was in them and you have the gall to tell me I'm not a wizard?' And then I said to him, 'Okay, now I want you to tell me how you felt about my reaction.' He said, 'Well, you were out of proportion.' So I said, 'You have just failed to validate my system of emotional stability *twice*. Don't go into psychiatric nursing.'"

John wants to see himself as a special kind of person because he has managed this terrible affront. He is, he wrote in a speech, like a person in a wheelchair: "[I] have lived in sheer hell much of the past thirty years. Now, due to the skills I've learned and my personal growth, I am stable enough to be a mental health provider of services. I can honestly say that mental illness is no joke, requires realistic funding resources, and during the process of recovery, a compassionate community who accepts you."[26] A belief that you are a responsible person and that you have (some) control over life and a compassionate community that accepts you: those are the key ingredients in John Hood's recipe for recovery and the key elements of most client advocacy policy positions.

John Hood recognizes that his ability to teach psychiatric clients that they can become responsible members of society, to whatever extent they can, depends upon whether they are able to understand themselves as morally responsible human beings, and that in turn depends to some measure upon whether they are perceived as moral actors by our society. And that cannot be divorced from the way we choose to empathize with them, to understand their experiences, to imagine ourselves in their shoes, to feel compassion for their suffering.

There is no question that psychiatric science, and the new paradigm of biomedical psychiatry, has been an enormous advance in the battle against psychiatric illness. The treatments have improved dramatically. The loathsome stigma that attached itself to sufferers and their parents has abated greatly, though some remains. No more must "schizophrenigenic" mothers struggle not only with the horror of losing a child to madness but with blame, guilt, and self-accusation. No more must depression be treated with secrecy and hidden in an upstairs bedroom with yellow wallpaper, nor suicide disguised as a household accident. The ability to understand more of the brain's processes has spawned tremendous growth in the exploration of new psychopharmacological treatments, such as the new antipsychotics, that have transformed the lives of many with schizophrenia.

The danger is that the biomedical approach will become the only approach to mental illness within psychiatry and the dominant popular understanding of psychiatric illness within our culture. This is a direct danger for patients, because (to repeat the mantra) research indicates that a combination of pharmacological and psychosocial (or psychotherapeutic) treatments is the best for the patient, and the research also suggests that the combination is cheaper in the long run.

But there also is a moral danger that lies in the way we see patients and the way they see themselves. The popularized, vulgarized medical model invites us to see the mentally ill as not quite human, particularly if their problem is chronic and unremitting. It invites us into a moral instinct in which our very efforts to remove the stigma lead us to say that these ill people are not as human, not quite as alive, as we are. This is because psychiatric illness is not like liver dysfunction. It disrupts a person's reasoning and feeling. And to say that someone's reasoning and feeling are diseased, when the disease never goes away, is to say that she is not fully human. In the vulgarized biomedical model, the mentally ill have been struck by something that came in from the outside. It was not under control in the first place, and it remains no more under control than a doctor can control it.

The medical model offers tremendous hope to those for whom a cure is found but condemns those whom a cure does not redeem. On the facts, the medical model alone is wrong. An illness such as schizophrenia is, after all, a mysterious one. It is influenced by genes but not entirely genetic (if one identical twin ends up with schizophrenia, the chance that his twin will be or become schizophrenic is only 40 to 50 percent). It is also influenced by the environment. The prognosis for schizophrenia is much better in rural areas than in industrialized urban settings.[27] And its prognosis in any environment is variable. About a third of schizophrenias seem to remit spontaneously after thirty years. If we as a society understand schizophrenia—and depression and bipolar disorder and other life-threatening and incapacitating psychiatric problems—as *only* medical, we deprive people of hope when their medication does not fully work. We deprive them of their sense of mastery over themselves, of full personhood in our world, of their ability to see themselves as thinking and feeling, just differently from other people. They become lesser persons, lesser agents, lesser moral beings. We deprive them of the commitment we feel toward full-fledged human beings.

This is not particularly a dilemma for psychiatrists. Psychiatrists who are exposed to both biomedical and psychodynamic approaches seem able to maintain a rich, complex understanding of these disorders. Most psychiatrists shift between their different tasks easily, as all of us shift among the morally appropriate ways to relate to students, clients, friends, children, parents, and partners. It is true that if a psychiatrist rejects one approach, she often does feel moral outrage toward it. George Banks, for instance, felt this kind of moral outrage at psychodynamic psychotherapy. There are biomedical psychiatrists, such as Banks, who simply cannot understand how in good conscience analysts can continue to accept an approach to human suffering that refuses to separate the disease from the person. These psychiatrists see psychodynamic psychiatry as a cruelty that blames the patients for their pain. Then there are psychodynamic psychiatrists who simply cannot understand what they perceive to be the biomedical psychiatrist's cruelty to those in pain, who are shocked that a doctor might treat a depressed patient the way a surgeon might treat a cardiac patient. When you as a psychiatrist commit yourself to one side against another, you feel that someone using the other approach is doing something wrong, and because a suffering human being is at stake, you feel this deeply, passionately, morally. But most psychiatrists are not in this position. They feel the moral edge to the profession only when they are prevented from caring for people in the way they feel is right. This is why managed care is a moral crisis for doctors, particularly for those psychiatrists whose primary identity is psychotherapeutic.

The despair of psychiatrists who see the medical world changing around them is not—even though some think it is—just or even primarily a despair about money. Psychopharmacology pays better than psychotherapy, and hospital jobs, though rather more stressed than before, are still lucrative (and a psychiatrist who has been doing psychotherapy can always get a job as a psychopharmacologist). The despair comes from a sense of moral violation, from the horror that they cannot care for people in the way that good doctors—as they understand good doctors—do, that they have been forced to break their trust with their patients, that they can no longer respond empathically. They feel like bad people. They feel that they have been trained to see and understand a grotesque misery, yet all they are allowed to do is hand out a biomedical lollipop to its prisoners and then turn their backs. They feel as if they have been eating lunch on a park bench while the man across from them died, and they watched and did nothing.

The real dilemma is faced by our society. It is whether we will allow the seductions of the vulgarized biomedical model to overcome our own responsible commitment to a complex view of human life. As one reads the popularizations of the successes of psychiatric science, the wider culture seems to seek in biomedical psychiatry the possibility of temperamental perfection, a kind of technovision of the robotic soul. "Shy? Forgetful? Anxious? Fearful? Obsessed?" asked *Newsweek* in February 1994. "How Science Will Let You Change Your Personality with a Pill." The cover article goes on to describe what is known, or thought to be known, about the neurochemistry of shyness, impulsivity, obsession, anxiety, and concentration and the medications used by various psychiatrists to regulate them. "For the first time ever," the neuropsychiatrist Richard Restak is quoted as saying, "we will be in a position to design our own brain."[28] Some psychiatrists now speak of "cosmetic psychopharmacology" and argue that we should take seriously the possibility that in coming years we may be able to use medication to "cure" shyness, rejection sensitivity, and other temperamental states that cause people distress. The vision is way out of step with current capabilities, but the idea of the "designer" personality, the personality trimmed and shaped with a kind of psychopharmacological plastic surgery, has, I believe, powerful directive force. The psychiatrist Peter Kramer, who came up with the term "cosmetic psychopharmacology," wrote in *Listening to Prozac* about patients who became "better than well," more focused, less anxious, more confident, serene. Though many psychiatrists objected that those people were few in number, at least compared to the genuinely depressed, there is no doubt that Prozac appeals to the middle-class consumer in search of that ideal (this was not the point that Kramer was trying to make in his thoughtful inquiry). Also, it is hard to get psychiatric care without a diagnosis; diagnoses are treated with medication; it seems as if a new diagnosis becomes chic each year and thousands more people are placed on medication. An American pharmaceutical company executive recently speculated that in twenty years, a third of the world's population will be on psychiatric medication.[29]

Meanwhile, there has been fury at Freud. Prozac—or, at least, the existence of reasonably effective and easy-to-take medication that deals with problems once treated by psychoanalytic psychotherapy—allowed people to become furious at Freud because, for the first time, there was another plausible account of human unhappiness rich enough to be a genuine alternative. By the time Prozac emerged in 1987, it had become evident that not only the big-ticket items of psychosis and suicidal despair but even everyday blues could be handled by the medicine shelf, at least in part, and increasingly one could talk sensibly about unhappiness as a matter of neurotransmitters, not as denial or conflict or anger turned against the self. And there was a whole world of people and practices based upon the premise of unhappiness as a brain dysfunction treatable by drugs, a whole culture with its own sense of what a good, responsible doctor does with patients. There were famous researchers, funded generously by the government. There were clinics, hospital units, and clinicians who specialized in psychopharmacology and sometimes claimed that psychopharmacology was the only useful intervention in psychiatric illness. There was a model of the person that was strikingly different from Freud's and a set of conventions based on that model that were as well developed as those in the psychodynamic arena. There were popular books that translated the research and the practice into the mainstream—*Mind, Mood and Medication* in 1981, the wildly popular *Listening to Prozac* in 1993—and, by the early 1990s, a health care debate desperate for anything that looked cheaper than its predecessors. And so, for the first time, it became possible for someone to reject Freud's vision of human nature without leaving himself vulnerable to the charge that a person who rejects psychoanalysis is simply too embarrassed and too weak to look at himself with honesty. It became possible to have believable moral outrage.

In 1995, a curious debate appeared in the leading journals of the intellectual world. The Library of Congress, which owns many of the unpublished Freud documents, had been planning to put up an exhibit in honor of Freud. The hundredth anniversary of the publication of *The Interpretation of Dreams* was approaching, and it seemed an appropriate time for a commemorative testimony to a man whose impact on the twentieth century had been far from negligible. The Library of Congress assembled an advisory board of psychoanalytic scholars and went to work. Six months later, the exhibit was postponed. Fifty critics had signed a petition denouncing the proposed exhibit—Gloria Steinem, one of the signatories, complained that the library had actually planned to honor the man rather than to present him as a troubled individual—and ad hominem attacks on the advisory board (the exhibit plans were "an obvious attempt to whitewash" and "a complete cave-in to the Freudian faithful") were appearing regularly in the media. Peter Swales, one of the more vociferous critics, explained, "I'm acting in the name of consumer protection."[30] (The exhibit has now been opened to a bemused public.)

In the last few years, declarations of psychoanalytic inadequacies—"Freud bashing"—have been announced like major scientific findings. Freud, these writers proclaim, was a scientific charlatan, his methods corrupted, his personal integrity a sham, his entire enterprise a vehicle for a narcissistic imperialism that, since it could not depend on the truth, resorted to brazen fictionalizing. He is said to have been sexually unfaithful—with his sister-in-law, Minna Bernays—and to have doctored not his patients but his cases by suppressing the realization that his female patients had been abused by their fathers in order to retain their fathers' patronage. "Is Freud Dead?" asked *Time*'s cover in Thanksgiving week of 1993. The *New York Review of Books* ran a series of hostile essays, whose authors continued to write to the letters-to-the-editor section for months, long, careful, joyless exchanges between psychoanalysts and antianalysts, each side launching missiles that sailed past its opponents, each side surprised and confused that the other would fail to grasp evident truth.

"That psychoanalysis, as a mode of treatment, has been experiencing a long institutional decline is no longer in serious dispute," began Frederick Crews in a *New York Review* article about recent Freud criticism entitled "The Unknown Freud." "Nor is the reason," he went on. "Though some patients claim to have acquired profound self-insight and even alterations of personality, in the aggregate psychoanalysis has proved to be an indifferently successful and vastly inefficient method of removing neurotic symptoms. . . . The experience of undergoing an intensive analysis may have genuine value as a form of extended meditation, but it seems to produce a good deal many more converts than cures."[31] In the course of the essay, Crews referred to psychoanalysis as an "epistemic sieve," as "fatally contaminated," as derived from "misleading precedents, vacuous pseudophysical metaphors, and a long concatenation of mistaken inferences."[32] "He questioned "whether anything is salvageable from a once respected body of theory whose evidential grounds have proved so flimsy."[33] He denounced not only the validity of Freud's claims but the quality of the man himself: "It is not recorded whether Freud ever expressed regret for having destroyed these four lives, but we know it would have been out of character for him to do so."[34] "He was also quite lacking in the empirical and ethical scruples that we would hope to find in any responsible scientist, to say nothing of a major one."[35]

Jeffrey Moussaieff Masson, to take another example, is (or was) a dashing, colorful analyst whose rise and fall from power Janet Malcolm chronicled in *The New Yorker.* He became disenchanted with psychoanalysis and in 1990 published *Final Analysis,* an account of his seduction by and eventual rejection of the discipline. It is at times a petulant book but at one point the reader feels a sudden sympathy for the crestfallen young man looking out from the pages. "All of the analysts had their blind spots. . . . And yet all of them thought it legitimate to offer themselves up as models upon which their individual candidates [young analysts in training and in analysis with them] should pattern their lives."[36] You feel that Masson is saying: These are analysts. They presume to judge and guide and understand individual human lives, and therefore they should be better human beings than others. But they aren't. Analysts, Masson argues, are dupes of their own theories, high-mindedly presenting a science of integrity that in fact is a parade of self-indulgent solipsism. They believe that they act in the best interests of their patients; in fact, they inevitably act out their own selfish fantasies. They are dull, ordinary people, and they are no better than the rest of us. "The only thing you can do with an illusion," Masson explains at the end of a chapter, "is to shatter it."[37]

The anger against Freud is not an anger against an outmoded intellectual theory. Some of the most vitriolic critics have trained or read deeply in psychoanalysis. Their anger is the dismay of betrayal and broken faith, of goodwill deceived and commitment abandoned. It has the same quality of visceral despair that one finds among the analysts who supervise young psychiatrists who no longer think that psychodynamic psychotherapy is important, and it has the same driven fury of the first generation of biomedically minded psychiatrists who wondered to their supervisors whether panic disorder was a brain disorder, were told that they feared intimacy, and then devoted their professional lives to proving that their supervisors had been wrong. I believe that the anger is a cry of moral outrage that became possible only after Prozac and its cousins created an alternate way of conceiving of emotional pain and acting as a moral agent with respect to it.

Therein lies the danger. The discoveries of psychiatric science are so exciting, the promise to manage mental illness so practical, the appeal of erasing our gloominess so enticing that it is tempting for Americans to adopt the ideas and generalize them wholeheartedly to a commonplace understanding of what it is to be human despite the fact that the real science is far more nuanced and complex. Because this new psychiatric science offers so much, it is tempting to ditch all of Freud's legacy because some of it has turned out to be wrong, misguided, or misused. That would be unfortunate. There is something of value in the approach to human suffering that emerged from Freud, for all the blindnesses and difficulties of the psychoanalytic enterprise and for all the power of the new psychiatric science. There is a sense of human complexity, of depth, an exigent demand to struggle against one's own refusals, and a respect for the difficulty of human life. Psychoanalysis teaches humility in the face of human pain. Its central concept is the unconscious, and its burden is that less of life happens by chance than we think and more of life is hidden from our awareness than we imagine. Our life contains more meaning from a psychoanalytic vantage point; we understand it less. Psychoanalysis also teaches that to respect someone is to acknowledge how much he has struggled, how great his difficulties have been, and to see that his own fears and insecurities have been his greatest obstacle. The idea of the unconscious carries with it the implication that life is harder than we realize, because we act not only in accord with visible circumstances but against fears and angers we find so alarming that we refuse even to acknowledge them. And so psychoanalysis also admires the courage to look with unflinching curiosity at oneself, to attempt not to be a turtle with its head pulled in. "A battle may be fought over Freud," the psychoanalyst and philosopher Jonathan Lear remarks, "but the war is over culture's image of the human soul. Are we to see humans as having depth—as complex psychological organisms who generate layers of meaning which lie beneath the surface of their understanding? Or are we to take ourselves as transparent to ourselves?"[38]

We desperately need to maintain (or, for the pessimists, to re-create) a culture of responsibility. As a well-known analyst, Hans Loewald, remarked about psychodynamic psychotherapy, "The movement from unconscious to conscious experience, from the instinctual life of the id to the reflective, purposeful life of the ego, means taking responsibility for one's own history, the history that has been lived and the history in the making."[39] The psychodynamic approach teaches that a sense of responsibility must accompany the recognition of the limitations of circumstance. Circumstances are obviously important. It matters enormously that you suffer from schizophrenia or bipolar disorder, that you were born with a vulnerability and that the vulnerability has become an illness, that you were traumatized by events outside your control. This is the context of suffering. Yet within those circumstances you must learn to see yourself as an intentional, effective, whole person and be so perceived by others. Those mutual commitments create the conditions for intentional, effective personhood. It may be neither helpful nor accurate to say that a person or his family is responsible for the fact that he hears voices or feels suicidal. But to leap from that insight to the sense that he is not capable of responsible choice is to deny him status as a fully moral person, and limit his capacity to behave like one. This does not mean that psychoanalysis should be the treatment of choice for schizophrenia. Far from it. It does suggest that the insights of the psychodynamic way of thinking may help psychiatric patients in a way that purely biomedical insights cannot.

It has become so easy for our society to use the medical model to deny responsibility. In 1998, a jury awarded a schizophrenic man damages against his psychiatrist after the schizophrenic shot another person, on the grounds that the psychiatrist hadn't told him how sick he really was.[40] This is not only absurd but counterproductive. It is counterproductive in two ways. First, a patient is better off and has a better prognosis if he learns that despite his illness, he must learn to become responsible for his actions in the world. That is what John Hood tries to teach his clients as a peer counselor; it is what psychotherapeutic intervention tries to teach, that we are responsible for much that happens in our life and that to acknowledge that responsibility is to be able to take charge of our life and change it for the better. Second, as a society, we are better off if we work within our culture with an understanding of all people as complex, conflicted persons who inevitably suffer but who must learn to live with that suffering and nonetheless choose to live good and productive lives. From the psychodynamic perspective, the mastery of bad circumstances is inherent to what a person is. Pain is not really divided into the kind a doctor can remove and the kind you are forced to live with. To know that sorrow is inevitable not merely because markets fail, floods rise, and loved creatures die but because men and women entangle their hopes with nameless dreads profoundly enriches our respect for what people do manage to accomplish, despite the demons clawing at their dreams. Psychodynamics teaches a great deal about human sadness and also about mastery and faith in human possibility.

"We are people, not diagnoses," a recently deceased client called Howie the Harp announced in a book on client-run self-help groups.[41] It is a common sentiment among those diagnosed with major mental illnesses. The

book (and others like it) is full of statistics that the mentally ill feel power-
less, stigmatized, out of control of their treatment and their lives. Client-
run groups focus on ways to help clients recognize their creativity and their
human capacity, their understanding of themselves as more than psychiatric patients. As John Hood remarked, "Take the Brady Bill. I bet he'd like
the dignity of being more than the guy who had his brain damaged. I think
he'd like to be remembered for doing something more constructive. When
it comes right down to it, NAMI or no NAMI, there's no greater stigma
than the client thinking his own brain's diseased. If I smoke and I come
down with lung cancer, no one in the city would be compassionate,
because I asked for it. But putting it in a medical model is like an excuse
for my behavior. When I talk to people, I have to say, 'I am a person with
schizophrenia,' and I don't like that. I'm not 'with' anything. I have severe
functional limitations when it comes to certain aspects of living. I'm not
'with' anything, I'm me. On the unit what I do is to teach people how to do
things. I do a public speaking group. Then I do a meeting skills group. It
teaches people things. I teach people to take responsibility for their
actions. That's good."

Once when I went on rounds in a city hospital, I saw a woman who had
been admitted to the psychiatric unit after seven hours of surgery to stitch
back together the wrist she had intentionally sliced to the bone. Her
wound was horrifying, but so was the cost in dollars and in physician
hours. Looking at her from the point of view of the little group of physicians huddled at the door, it was clear how helpful it was to see her as having an illness she couldn't control and that justified the surgery, because
otherwise who were we to abort such a determined suicide? To see her
despair as being only bodily, though, was not enough to help her. She was
depressed, but she was also homeless and alcoholic and had grown up bat-
ted from one foster home to another. She had good reason to be angry and
no reason to think that her circumstances would change. Giving her a
sense of possibility required that she be taught responsibility and choice:
to choose not to be alcoholic, not to be homeless. She also needed the
resources to be able to make those choices in the confidence that there
really were choices to make. She needed to know that if she gave up the
drink, she would have someplace to go and something to do. And for someone with her history, that process can take time and error and compromise
and flexibility. Our society needs to make a practical decision about how
much care we owe someone like her. As one psychiatric administrator
pointed out to me, you can handle schizophrenics by putting fifty of them
in a room with beds, a few nurses, and lots of Thorazine. We also need,
however, to make a moral decision, which is whether to understand such
people only as the detritus of a broken brain or also as people whose suffer-

ing implicates us, whose struggles are resonant with our struggles, who are located in a particular culture, and whose complexity and depth demand that we see their suffering as engaged in the struggle to be decent, responsible people.

We are so tempted to see ourselves as fixable, perfectible brains. But the loss of our souls is a high price to pay.

TECHNICAL APPENDIX

CONDITIONS OF THE RESEARCH

This work was funded as an anthropological project by the National Institute of Mental Health, the Spencer Foundation, the Wenner Gren Foundation, and the University of California, San Diego. The fieldwork period stretched from August 1989 until September 1994, with some additional weeks in 1995 and 1996, and further interviews and interactions, primarily with patients, in 1998 and 1999. Funding agencies covered different portions of the project—different time periods, locations, and specific goals.

The work received Institutional Review Board (Human Subjects) clearance both at the specific hospitals where I worked and, as a general project, from the university at which I teach. With the exception of one hospital, oral consent was permitted. Patients were always asked specifically for permission to have me observe if my presence as an observer was unusual (for example, in case conferences there are usually a number of observers, and the patient is asked whether he or she is comfortable with being observed by the group as a whole). In particular, I observed admissions or intake interviews but not therapy sessions or, in most cases, medication visits in which the patient had a long-standing relationship with the doctor. Patients often gave permission for me to sit in on initial interviews, the aim of which was to diagnose the condition, but they also frequently refused. When I served as a therapist, my patients were explicitly told that I was in training, that I was not licensed, and that I was an anthropologist. The goal of that training was to learn to act like a therapist and to provide appropriate therapy, and in that capacity, I served as a volunteer therapist at a clinic and my patients were people who would have been unable to afford therapy with someone else. Though I was in some sense trained to prescibe medication, in that I sat in on the training lectures, and while I have the expertise to understand much about psychopharmacology prescription, I never prescribed medication.

I contacted John M. Hood III through a patient advocacy group, and Vernon (and others) through John Hood. They chose to speak with me, and we met often over the course of a year. They have read, edited, and approved the last chapter.

CONFIDENTIALITY

I have attempted to maintain the confidentiality of those who spoke with me, unless they agreed to be identified by name. To this end, some, but not all, of the individuals described are conflations of two or three individuals and are ascribed quotations spoken by those individuals.

I have also edited the taped conversations I had with individuals, in a way that preserves both sense and meaning but makes them easier to read. Readers read them as texts, not spoken dialogue, and the rules of those two media differ. It is not my intention to make individuals seem less fluent than they appear in person, and to quote verbatim without any editing would have done exactly that.

CONTEXT OF DATA COLLECTION

I was concerned to have representativeness both in the hospitals and in the programs I visited. I conducted research with several groups of residents. Most prominently, these were the residents at a public university on the West Coast and the residents at a private university on the East Coast in several different training programs. Both universities were distinguished by their teaching expertise in both the biomedical and psychodynamic domains, and both demanded, in accordance with standards established by the American Psychiatric Association, that residents be trained in both. The American Psychiatric Association, of course, has many more specific requirements, including training in neurology and the history of psychiatry. The West Coast university, however, clearly emphasized psychodynamic training as an outpatient practice. Its inpatient units included units for veterans and units attached to a busy city hospital. The East Coast university had a more diverse range of approaches. Some of its units were clearly biomedical and driven by a biomedical research paradigm; some were clearly psychodynamic, though those were changing rapidly; some were aiming to be integrative. Moreover, while some units catered to the inner city, others catered to the elite, although those too were changing rapidly. The university offered several different training programs for psychiatry.

In addition, to put that experience in context, I visited an elite eastern psychoanalytically oriented treatment center for two weeks; I spent a week with the patients in the day treatment center attached to an eastern state hospital, where the patients were poor and chronically ill; I spent a week in the inpatient unit of a western community hospital where the patients were again poor and chronically ill; I spent more than a week's worth of days talking to elite scientists in the research section of a major hospital; I spent a few days at a large private hospital in the Midwest not attached to a university, and a few days at a large public university hospital in the South. In addition, I interviewed and spoke informally with training directors and residents from other systems, some of which were old and established and others of which were not.

PLAN OF THE RESEARCH

My initial research premise was that some feature in the experience of residency training, in addition to individual residents' preferences, was powerfully implicated in residents' orientations toward biomedical and psychodynamic psychiatry. However, in the course of my work, psychiatry began to change dramatically at the sites I visited. For example, Medicaid and Medicare came under managed care between the period of my first intensive visit to the East Coast and my second, and the impact on the tasks demanded of the residents was significant. During this period, it became clear that the apparently bleak future of psychodynamic psychiatry had profoundly affected residents' perspectives on their future practice. As a result, I refocused the work to try to understand what different perspectives demanded of the residents and what kinds of skills they had developed in order to achieve those tasks. In particular, I focused on the tasks of diagnosis and psychopharmacology, on the one hand, and psychotherapy, on the other.

SOURCES OF DATA COLLECTION

Participant observation: I spent more than three years as a participant observer (initially, just as a student) in the western training program. Most of that period involved part-time participation—ten to twenty hours a week throughout the period—but around four months of it involved full-time immersion. I attempted to acquaint myself with the basic structure of each major unit: the admissions interview or intake interview; the team meeting; the emergency room; call; the daily life of the resident. During my periods of full-time observation, I attempted to spend two days a week at the outpatient clinic, two days a week at a unit for veterans, and one day a week at a city hospital unit. On those days I would attend lectures, staff meetings, case conferences, team meetings, and community meetings; I attempted to get to know residents, other staff, and patients.

In one eastern training program, where I spent about ten to twelve weeks, I spent most of my time in one of the units. However, I also spent about two weeks in the child psychiatry unit and regularly visited the psychiatry emergency room. In another, where I spent more than four months, I had a regular schedule that involved going to lectures, watching admissions, and spending time on a biomedical unit, but I also attempted to sit in on rounds in a number of different units, and I attempted to meet with and follow all of the residents around at different times. In each setting I took extensive daily notes.

Semistructured taped interviews: I systematically conducted semistructured interviews with two "years" of residents annually at the western program for three years. The interviews followed the flow of the conversation but were focused on what was being learned and how the resident felt about the learning process. At the eastern programs, where the duration of my stay was shorter, I conducted interviews with one class in their first months after arrival as PGYIIs (first-year residents) and then one year following. Again, I focused on the process of learning: how comfortable residents felt with diagnosis, with using *DSM*, with the different axes in *DSM*, with psychotherapy, and so forth. I asked residents to describe how they arrived at a diagnosis or an assessment of the patient and how they arrived at a plan for treatment.

At the eastern programs, I also selected certain residents to interview in depth on various topics. Again, I attempted to talk to a range of residents: the more research-oriented, the more clinical but psychopharmacological, the more psychotherapeutic, and so forth. My goal here was to find "stars" and ask them to explain to me what they felt they knew and how they knew it.

In addition, I selected senior psychiatrists for short- or long-term taped interviews. Again, my goal was to find acknowledged expert teachers and to try to have them explain to me what they felt they taught residents, how they taught it, and whether they felt they were successful. Closer to the end of my project, I also interviewed a number of senior adminstrators about the challenges facing psychiatry. I interviewed senior psychiatrists at every program I visited, although not all of them agreed to be tape-recorded, and in some cases, where tape recording would have been inappropriate, I chose not to do so.

I have approximately two hundred hours of taped semistructured interview material, most of which was transcribed and reviewed. It served as the source for most of the quotations from residents and from senior psychiatrists.

Educational participation: I attended lectures to different residency classes in different locations. At the western training program, I attended all the lectures for PGYII (first-year) residents, about a fifth of those for the PGYIIIs (second-years), and half of those for the PGYIVs (third-years). At one eastern training program, I attended lectures to PGYIIs for two months: this was their summer "crash course." I attended lectures to their class in the summer of the second year. In addition, I read the material assigned in these classes and other material that I knew they studied and used (the standard psychiatric handbooks) but that were not specifically assigned.

I also attended many (around fifteen) psychiatric conferences: the American Psychiatric Association meetings (at least three times), the Society for Biological Psychiatry meetings, the American Psychoanalytic Association meetings, and others.

Finally, but not least, to the extent that I could participate in the training, I did so. I participated in seminars and asked and answered questions. I was trained to some extent as a therapist. In order to begin the therapy, I was required to conduct an "intake" interview that closely resembled an admissions note and in that context learned to write a diagnostically driven admissions note. I conducted psychodynamic psychotherapy as a volunteer with eight patients, three of them twice a week for more than a year and a fourth once a week for somewhat less than a year. I was supervised by four trained supervisors for this work. I was also in twice-weekly psychodynamic psychotherapy with a senior analyst for about three years. I did this following the advice that to understand therapy, one must do therapy and be in therapy.

Drawing on the relevant literature in psychiatric and psychological anthropology: I read widely in the literature associated with fieldwork in this area and used that material to formulate questions, hypotheses, and research goals. Because not all readers of this ethnography will be anthropologists, that literature is largely cited in the notes, and even there I am unable to do justice to the depth and thoughtfulness of the literature. There is a rich literature in the culture and sociology of hospitals, psychiatric and otherwise; of medical and psychiatric training; of psychiatric patients; of diagnostic practice; of morality, the self, and expertise.

NOTES

INTRODUCTION

Note: Short forms of references are given here; for full references, please see the Bibliography.

1. Michel Foucault, *Madness and Civilization*, pp. 278, 247.
2. George Devereux, *Basic Problems in Ethnopsychiatry*, p. 15.
3. Peter Shaffer, *Equus and Shrivings*, pp. 63–64.
4. R. D. Laing, *The Divided Self*.
5. Susan Cheever, "A Designated Crazy." Review of *Girl, Interrupted*, p. 20.
6. Susanna Kaysen, *Girl, Interrupted*, p. 41.
7. Ibid., p. 75.
8. Irving Gottesman, *Schizophrenia Genesis: The Origins of Madness*.
9. William Styron, *Darkness Visible*, pp. 43–50.
10. Harold Kaplan and Benjamin Sadock, *Pocket Handbook of Clinical Psychiatry*, p. 97; Stephen Stahl, *Essential Psychopharmacology*, pp. 99ff.
11. The lifetime prevalence is reported at 10 percent of all men and 20 percent of all women; see Kaplan and Sadock, *Pocket Handbook of Clinical Psychiatry*, p. 102.
12. This is obviously a limited description; a fuller account of current thinking can be found in psychiatric manuals, such as Kaplan and Sadock, *Pocket Handbook of Clinical Psychiatry; Diagnostic and Statistical Manual of Mental Disorders IV*; and later in this book. Schizophrenics are often unable to screen out irrelevant noise, their eyes often track objects in an unusual manner, and their brain ventricles become larger than the average for their skulls; see Philip Holzman et al., "A Single Dominant Gene Can Account for Eye Tracking Dysfunctions and Schizophrenia in Offspring of Discordant Twins"; David Braff, Dennis Saccuzzo, and Mark Geyer, "Information Processing Dysfunction in Schizophrenia: Studies of Visual Backward Masking, Sensorimotor Gating, and Habituation"; Nancy Andreasen et al., "Thalamic Abnormalities in Schizophrenia Visualized Through Magnetic Resonance Imaging."
13. Kaplan and Sadock, *Pocket Handbook of Clinical Psychiatry*, p. 83.
14. Susan Sheehan, *Is There No Place on Earth for Me?* p. 3.
15. Kay Redfield Jamison, *An Unquiet Mind*, 1995, pp. 36–38; Kate Millett also wrote a gripping memoir, *The Loony-Bin Trip*.
16. Jamison, *An Unquiet Mind*, p. 107.

17. Ibid., p. 114.

18. Arthur Kleinman, *Rethinking Psychiatry*, p. 16. Kleinman also summarizes the literature to date in the same book, pp. 18ff.

19. See Kay Redfield Jamison's study of the relationship between creativity and bipolar
disorder, particularly in poets, *Touched with Fire*. This connection is controversial:
Hagop Akiskal's somewhat different analysis is reported in Winifred Gallagher, *I.D.*

20. Sue Estroff, *Making It Crazy*, p. 255.

21. Erving Goffman, *Asylums*, p. 35. There is also good evidence that the prognosis of
schizophrenia is worse in industrial societies than in tribal villages. Some argue that
this difference may be an artifact of diagnostic process rather than disease, but it
seems fairly evident that social structure makes a difference to the prognosis of illness. See also Kleinman, *Rethinking Psychiatry*; Richard Warner, *Recovery from Schizophrenia: Psychiatry and Political Economy*; Kim Hopper et al., *Prospects for Recovery
from Schizophrenia—An International Investigation: Report from the WHO—Collaborative Project, The International Study of Schizophrenia.*

22. Allan Young, *The Harmony of Illusions*. Other notable psychiatric anthropologists
include Arthur Kleinman, Nancy Scheper-Hughes, Lorna Rhodes, Richard Warner,
Kim Hopper, and others.

23. See Joan Acocella, "The Politics of Hysteria."

24. Robert Desjarlais et al., *World Mental Health.*

25. Robert Wright, "The Evolution of Despair."

26. Kaplan and Sadock, *Pocket Handbook of Clinical Psychiatry*, p. 207.

27. This distinction is made in many places, but it is paraphrased here from Arthur Kleinman, Leon Eisenberg, and Byron Good, "Culture, Illness and Care: Lessons from
Anthropologic and Cross-Cultural Research."

28. Ibid., p. 252.

29. These data are reported and discussed in Margaret Lock, *Encounters with Aging:
Mythologies of Menopause in Japan and North America.*

30. George Engel, "The Clinical Application of the Biopsychosocial Model."

31. Hugh Gusterson, *Nuclear Rites*. For other examples, see Sharon Trawick, *Beamtimes
and Lifetimes: The World of High Energy Physics*; and Paul Rabinow, *Making PCR: A
Story of Biotechnology.*

32. Serious discussions of empathy can be found in Elaine Hatfield, John Cacioppo, and
Richard Rapson, *Emotional Contagion*; Nancy Eisenberg and Janet Strayer, *Empathy
and Its Development*; Virginia Demos, "Empathy and Affect: Reflections on Infant
Experience"; and Kenneth Clark, "Empathy: A Neglected Topic in Psychological
Research." Joseph Campos et al., "A Functionalist Perspective on the Nature of Emotion," and Joseph Campos, "A Reconceptualization of the Nature of Affect," provide a
model of emotion that helps refocus on the idealistic model of affect contagion. Most
of this work focuses on the use of empathy to understand distress; certainly, colloqui-
ally, people who are described as "empathic" are usually seen as people who understand other people's pain. For this reason, perhaps, one eminent emotion researcher,
Richard Lazarus, in *Emotion and Adaptation*, argues for the use of the word "compassion" in place of "empathy," as implicitly so does James Q. Wilson in *The Moral Sense*,
where he discusses sympathy in his analysis of what he calls the moral sense. Academic psychologists seem more often to argue that empathy is a process, *not* an emotion,
but the process they describe is certainly close to what is meant by compassion and
sympathy. As two emotion researchers remark, empathy is "an emotional response that
stems from another's emotional state or condition and that is congruent with the
other's emotional state or situation" (see Eisenberg and Strayer, *Empathy and Its*

Development, p. 5). My sense is that those who emphasize compassion or sympathy point to behavior that depends on the recognition of the other's experience; those who emphasize empathy focus on the process of recognizing the other's experience. Researchers identify as among the cognitive features involved: the capacity to differentiate between self and other; a direct association between cues of another's emotional state and the potential empathizer's past experiences of a similar emotion; symbolic associations between cues that symbolically indicate another's feelings and the empathizer's own past distresses; and the ability to role-take if the empathizer has no relevant past experience.

CHAPTER ONE: WHAT'S WRONG WITH THE PATIENT?

1. This is adapted with more user-friendly (but less precise) language from American Psychiatric Association, *Diagnostic and Statistical Manual of Mental Disorders IV [DSM IV],* p. 423.
2. Nancy Andreasen and Donald Black, *Introductory Textbook of Psychiatry,* pp. 324 325.
3. American Psychiatric Association, *DSM IV,* p. 327. Again, this is a less precise wording than that found in the *DSM IV,* but it is more user-friendly.
4. Eleanor Rosch (e.g., 1973, 1978) did the classic work in this area by demonstrating that commonly used categories had a definable structure: that they are built around a central member that has many features of other members of the category and is judged representative of it (this is the prototype) and that there is a level in the descriptive hierarchy of categories (man-made objects, furniture, chairs, rocking chairs) at which people learn the categories most easily, remember their names, and so forth. This level she called "basic level" categories: dogs, birds, tables, and chairs are examples of basic level categories but animals and secretary desks are not. The point is that categories are "motivated": they reflect, as Howard Gardner points out in *Frames of Mind,* "the perceptual structure of the perceived, the kinds of actions one can carry out, the physical structure of the world" (p. 346). This work has been considerably refined—Lakoff's account of idealized cognitive models, in which some kind of implicit theory is inherent in category use, is one example—but the claim that people cluster or chunk information together and then interpret later experience according to prior patterns of clustering seems undeniable. Some helpful literature on the topic includes Howard Gardner, *Frames of Mind;* George Lakoff, *Women, Fire and Dangerous Things;* Ulric Neisser, *Concepts and Conceptual Development;* Roy D'Andrade, *The Development of Cognitive Anthropology.*
5. A classic example of a somewhat more general effect is that when we have a cognitive model relating two features it affects our judgment on the probability of both occurring. For example, Amos Tversky and Daniel Kahneman asked a group of subjects (prior to 1983) to rate the probability of the following two sentences:

    a. A massive flood in California in 1983 causes more than a thousand people to drown.

    b. An earthquake in California in 1983 causes a flood in which more than one thousand people die.

The second sentence is usually judged more probable than the first, even though—since it requires two events and the first only one—it is less probable. However, people have models of California as a place where earthquakes happen and cause terrible damage (Lakoff, *Women, Fire and Dangerous Things,* p. 90). When psychiatrists have cognitive models for different illnesses, they are more likely to anticipate symptoms that are congruent with the model.

6. This was Charles Nuckolls from the University of Alabama, who has done extensive work with psychiatric residents and with psychiatry.

7. The philosophers perhaps most responsible for this discussion are Saul Kripke *(Naming and Necessity)* and Hilary Putnam *(Reason, Truth and History)*. The psychologist Frank Keil uses experimental data to point out that while people judge that the experimenter can change the defining characteristic of an artifact and thus change the artifact, they resist the idea that the experimenter can change the defining features of a natural object and thus change it: "If one takes a chair and carefully gives it leg extensions and saws off the back, most adults say that you have now turned it into a stool. By contrast, if one takes a raccoon, dyes its fur appropriately, fluffs its tail, sews a smelly sack inside, and even trains it to secrete its contents when alarmed, most adults will say that you still have a raccoon, albeit a strange one that looks and acts just like a skunk" (Keil, in Neisser, *Concepts and Conceptual Development,* p. 187). Keil argues that the distinction between cultural artifact and natural kind emerges very early, that it is present even in preschoolers, and that accounts of an object's origin are crucial to the distinction.

8. There are many diagnoses that can be codiagnosed: they are then called "comorbid." However, the "big three"—schizophrenia, manic-depressive disorder or bipolar disorder, and major depression—tend to be treated as mutually exclusive.

9. The example was provided by the psychologist Ellen Winner, who did not have Lyme disease.

10. This paragraph has been paraphrased from Andreasen and Black, *Introductory Textbook of Psychiatry,* pp. 154–160.

11. Stephen Stahl, *Essential Psychopharmacology,* p. 119.

12. These figures were reported in the *New England Journal of Medicine* by two of the leaders in the field; see R. Michels and P. M. Marzuk, "Progress in Psychiatry."

13. There was a great deal of discussion about the unconscious by those preceding Freud. The classic discussion of this history can be found in Henri Ellenberger, *The Discovery of the Unconscious.*

14. Heinz Kohut is an obvious psychoanalyst to include in discussions about empathy. I have not included him here not only because his work is controversial in the programs I visited—Ralph Greenson, certainly, but also Roy Schafer were treated as mainstream—but also because empathy plays a role in his theory not only in describing the analyst's technique but also in narcissistic psychopathology (see Kohut, *The Analysis of the Self* and "Introspection, Sympathy and Psychoanalysis"). A review of some of the psychoanalytic work on empathy, including Kohut's contribution, can be found in an article by Stephen Levy, "Empathy and Psychoanalytic Technique."

15. The classic, famous article is "Skill in Chess" by Herbert Simon and William Case.

16. One of the easiest ways to describe this process is by describing the difference between trying to remember a random string of numbers—53268127—which is hard to do unless you work at it—and trying to remember 19951996. The latter is easy because you "chunk" the numbers together so that you really have to remember only two items, not eight. One of the experts in the field of expertise (K. Anders Ericsson) argues that deliberate practice—not talent—is responsible for expert performance in a knowledge-based field and that the practice mostly consists of mastering information in an organized way. A decade is assumed to be required for mastery by nearly all expertise experts. Salient literature includes K. A. Ericsson and N. Charness, "Expert Performance," and K. A. Ericsson, R. Krampe, and C. Tesch-Romer, "The Role of Deliberate Practice in the Acquisition of Expert Performance." Also see Michele Chi,

Robert Glaser, and M. J. Farr, *The Nature of Expertise.* Howard Gardner presents a perspective that is more brain-based but still describes expertise as the perception of meaningful patterns; see Gardner, *Frames of Mind.*

17. See Lakoff, *Women, Fire and Dangerous Things,* on spatial metaphors: they are very common when talking about abstractions, so there is nothing particularly special here except the abstractness.

18. There is some experimental evidence that suggests that some people are indeed able to improve their capacity to identify emotions in other people. Some of this research is reported in Elaine Hatfield, John Cacioppo, and Richard Rapson, *Emotional Contagion.*

CHAPTER TWO: THE ARROW OF HARM

1. Byron Good, *Medicine, Rationality, and Experience,* p. 71.

2. Renee Fox, "Training for Uncertainty."

3. This impossibility is the insistent theme of the early ethnography of medicine. Renee Fox was among the first of these ethnographers, and her writings—*Experiment Perilous* and others—center on the experience of facing suffering with uncertainty. Howard Becker and his coauthors, in a famous study entitled *Boys in White,* emphasized the deep transformation of the young doctor in medical training. More recently, Mary-Jo Delvecchio Good's study of Harvard medical students, *American Medicine: The Quest for Competence,* underscores how impossible the task of learning to practice medicine has become. She argues that students are expected to develop both competency and caring and that the latter sometimes suffers in pursuit of the former.

4. Frederic Hafferty, *Into the Valley,* p. 62.

5. B. Good, *Medicine, Rationality, and Experience,* p. 73.

6. This clear separation of mind and body is, of course, one of the striking features of Western medicine in contrast to non-Western systems.

7. Samuel Shem, *The House of God,* p. 79.

8. Ibid., p. 97.

9. Charles Bosk, *Forgive and Remember.*

10. This was one of the more striking results of Sue Estroff's remarkable participant-observer study of poor mentally ill patients. One of the reasons deinstitutionalization didn't work, she pointed out, is that patients don't always like their antipsychotics because of the side effects; thus they don't take them outside the hospital, and the good effects produced by the medication do not materialize. One patient, for instance, said, "That damn Prolixin. I couldn't think clearly on it. I wasn't myself when I had so much of that. [The staff] wouldn't listen to me when I told them how I felt. They'd say, 'You look natural to us.' My back hurt. I couldn't sit still. Hell! I couldn't do nothing. My legs half up in the air. They're too heavy with that medication. I think you should be able to change doctors if you want to. I didn't like that. You should be able to have another opinion about medications. It didn't help me a bit." ("Martin" in Estroff, *Making It Crazy,* p. 99). Admittedly, Martin spoke at a time when the dosages were far heavier than what is normally given now, but nonetheless I have heard similar complaints. Some patients, it should be said, are not troubled by side effects, but many are sufficiently troubled to ditch the medication even though they admit that it makes them feel less crazy and better in that way.

11. Janet Malcolm uses this metaphor somewhere in her wonderful accounts of psychoanalysis. Other compelling accounts of psychoanalytic psychotherapy include Robert

Lindner, *The Fifty Minute Hour;* Samuel Shem, *Fine;* Irving Yalom, *Love's Executioner.* There are many classic accounts of how to teach psychotherapy. Among them are Rosemary Balsam and Alan Balsam, *Becoming a Psychotherapist: A Clinical Primer;* Michael Franz Basch, *Doing Psychotherapy;* Anthony Storr, *The Art of Psychotherapy:* and, in a broader context, Jerome Frank, *Psychotherapy and the Human Predicament.* See also an interesting book entitled *A Curious Calling: Unconscious Motivations for Practicing Psychotherapy* by Michael Sussman.

12. Perhaps the classic statement on contemporary, mainstream psychoanalytic thinking about transference is by Hans Loewald in *Psychoanalysis and the History of the Individual* and *Papers in Psychoanalysis.*

13. The criteria of the ASPD category have been extensively debated in part for this reason. Many people would prefer to see a more psychological account of conscienceless behavior, as for instance outlined by Hervey Cleckley in a classic called *The Mask of Sanity* (and indeed, some of the criteria of the most recent *DSMs* have been modified in this direction).

CHAPTER THREE: THE CULTURE AND ITS CONTRADICTIONS

1. Lorna Rhodes, *Emptying Beds.*

2. I am focusing on one particular unit here, but I have incorporated some anecdotes from another, very similar unit.

3. The classic anthropological discussion here is A. R. Radcliffe-Brown's account, in *Structure and Function in Primitive Society,* of what is called the "joking relationship." In matrilineal societies, where inheritance flows through the mother's line, sons often live with fathers but inherit from their mother's brothers, or (in our terms) their uncles. A nephew then often expects goods from his uncle that the uncle might prefer to give to his own son, with whom he has a greater emotional tie. The uncle-nephew relationship is often protected from the tension of that relationship through a socially mandated joking relationship in which the two men are expected to tease and harass each other. The general argument is that laughter rules along the lines of social tension.

CHAPTER FOUR: THE PSYCHIATRIC SCIENTIST
AND THE PSYCHOANALYST

1. See, e.g., R. L. Gellman [Gollub] and G. K. Aghajanian, "Serotonin 2 Receptor–Mediated Excitation of Interneurons in Piriform Cortex: Antagonism by Atypical Antipsychotic Drugs."

2. This work was reported in Daniel Goleman, "Provoking a Patient's Worst Fears to Determine the Brain's Role"; the more technical study appeared as S. L. Rauch, et al., "A PET Study of Simple Phobic Provocation."

3. For a more technical review of this area, see Randy Gollub and Scott L. Rauch, "Neuroimaging: Issues of Design, Resolution and Interpretation," and Scott Rauch, "Advances in Neuroimaging: How Might They Influence Our Diagnostic Classification Scheme?"

4. Hagop Akiskal, "Mood Disorders: Clinical Features"; see also Akiskal, "Cyclothymic Temperamental Disorders," "Borderline: An Adjective in Search of a Noun," and "The Temperamental Foundations of Affective Disorders."

5. Akiskal, "Borderline: An Adjective in Search of a Noun," p. 529.

6. A survey from the 1980s (J. A. Bodkin, R. L. Klitzman, and H. G. Pope, "Distinction Between Biological Psychiatrists and Psychotherapists") of psychiatrists associated with leading medical schools suggests that the common age-adjusted differences that distinguish biologically oriented psychiatrists from psychodynamically oriented ones were these: the biologically oriented were less likely to be "very satisfied" with their work, more likely to be male, more likely to do research, less likely to be divorced, and less likely to have, or at least to say that they have, first-degree relatives who were psychiatrically ill. Biological psychiatrists and psychotherapists were not distinguished by religious ethnicity, although lore suggests that Jewish psychiatrists are more likely to become psychodynamic psychotherapists and Christian psychiatrists to become scientists. The finding that they are less likely to be "very satisfied" with their work is surprising until one realizes that most of the survey respondents are not scientists but psychopharmacologists, and pill prescription palls after a while, particularly when compared to the intense emotional engagement of psychotherapy. A final significant difference is that more of the psychodynamically oriented psychiatrists had experimented with illicit drugs. LSD may have sent some psychiatrists into research on the brain and buttressed their beliefs in organic causes; others seem to have been drawn to the drugs for other reasons and no doubt explained their use as a symptom of their early dependency or rebellious needs. Obviously this last remark seems odd in the context of the enthusiasm I heard from the scientists for their experiences with illicit drugs—but it is true that while only scientists talked to me about the career-altering impact of recreational drugs, many more analysts seem actually to have used them.

7. Steven Shapin, *A Social History of Truth*, p. 417.

8. Hermann Hesse, *The Glass Bead Game (Magister Ludi)*, p. 154.

9. Lee David Brauer, "Basic Report about Members Who Are Graduates of Institutes. Survey of Psychoanalytic Practice."

10. Ibid., p. 18.

11. Ralph Greenson, *The Technique and Practice of Psychotherapy*, p. 279.

12. Paul Ekman is the psychologist most associated with research on the facial communication of emotion. In 1975, Ekman and his colleagues published a study demonstrating high cross-cultural agreement (especially in literate societies) on the interpretation of emotional meaning of certain facial expressions. Some theorists argue that emotions are primarily facial responses, although this position is not widely shared. General surveys of emotion can be found in Robert Plutchik, *Emotion: A Psycho-evolutionary Synthesis,* and Paul Ekman and Richard Davidson, eds., *The Nature of Emotion.*

13. Hans Loewald, *Papers on Psychoanalysis*, p. 308.

14. One of the more recent approaches to emotion has been the functional theory of emotion, argued for by Nico Frijda and Joseph Campos, among others. There the emphasis is upon the way in which emotions are not simple expressions, but regulate individual relationship to their environment and their goals. A more evolutionary approach emphasizes the communicative role of emotions; this is perhaps the ultimate thrust of Darwin's work and plays a powerful role in later evolutionary theories. The interesting piece of psychoanalysis for this discussion is that I suspect that the strangely deprived nature of the analytic relationship forces the analysand to become more emotional than he or she ordinarily would, simply as a means of communicating. In the psychoanalytic situation, emotions function as intensifiers of communication. This aspect of emotion is perhaps most strongly identified in the work of Silvan Tompkins; see Tompkins, *Exploring Affect*; Nico Frijda, *The Emotions*; and Ekman and Davidson, *Nature of Emotion.*

15. Anne Sexton's therapist made available tapes of their sessions to her biographer after her death. Although he did so after consideration and with a sense that she would have wanted him to do so, his action was harshly condemned by the psychoanalytic community.
16. Sigmund Freud, "Therapy and Technique," pp. 278, 236.
17. The phrase "wild analysis" was coined by Freud to indicate that there could be misuses of psychoanalytic practice and theory that did not serve patients.
18. Charles Brenner, *An Elementary Textbook of Psychoanalysis*, p. 120.
19. Sigmund Freud, *Dora: An Analysis of a Case of Hysteria.* Janet Malcolm wrote a marvelous essay on the Dora case, reprinted in Malcolm, *The Purloined Clinic.*
20. Philip Rieff, *Freud: The Mind of a Moralist*, p. 322.
21. Jonathan Lear, *Love and Its Place in Nature*, p. 187.
22. Elvin Semrad in Susan Rako and Harvey Maze, *Semrad: The Heart of a Therapist*, p. 119. Semrad also remarked that "love is love, no matter how you slice it. A touch of love is like a touch of pregnancy" (ibid., p. 33).

CHAPTER FIVE: WHERE THE SPLIT CAME FROM

1. For adult patients with major depressive disorder, the guidelines state, "Some patients with depression of mild severity can be treated with psychotherapeutic management or with psychotherapy alone. . . . Optimal treatment of major depression that is chronic or is moderate to severe generally requires some form of somatic intervention, in the form of medication or electroconvulsive therapy, coupled with psychotherapeutic management or psychotherapy"; see American Psychiatric Association, "Practice Guidelines for Major Depressive Disorder in Adults," p. 6. For bipolar patients, psychotherapy is less well researched and less emphasized but nonetheless treated as important: "Psychiatric management and psychopharmacologic therapy are essential components of treatment for acute episodes and for prevention of future episodes in patients with bipolar disorder. In addition, other specific psychotherapeutic treatments may be critical components of the treatment plan for some patients"; see American Psychiatric Association, "Practice Guidelines for Bipolar Disorder in Adults," p. 15. For patients with eating disorders, "[A]t the present time the best results appear to be linked to weight restoration accompanied by individual and family psychotherapies when the patient is ready to participate"; see American Psyciatric Association, "Practice Guidelines for Eating Disorders," p. 214.
2. Harold Kaplan and Benjamin Sadock, *Pocket Handbook of Clinical Psychiatry*, pp. 109, 111, 85.
3. L. Luborsky, L. B. Singer, and L. Luborsky, "Comparative Studies of Psychotherapies"; M. W. Lipsey and D. B. Wilson, "The Efficacy of Psychological, Educational and Behavioral Treatment: Confirmation from Meta-analysis." A study of six hundred psychoanalytic patients, begun in the 1950s and reported in the *Journal of the American Psychoanalytic Association* (H. Bachrach et al., "On the Efficacy of Psychoanalysis") concluded that 60 to 90 percent of patients had seen "significant" improvement as a result of psychoanalysis. See also D. H. Barlow, "Cognitive-Behavioral Therapy for Panic Disorder: Current Status" (an overview); D. H. Barlow and C. Lehman, "Advances in the Psychosocial Treatment of Anxiety Disorders" (on anxiety disorders); C. Spanier et al., "The Prophylaxis of Depression Episodes in Recurrent Depression Following Discontinuation of Drug Therapy: Integrating Psychological and Biological Factors" (on depression); E. Frank et al., "Efficacy of Interpersonal Psychotherapy as a

Maintenance Treatment of Recurrent Depression" (on depression); C. Fairburn et al., "Psychotherapy and Bulimia Nervosa: Longer-Term Effects of Interpersonal Psychotherapy, Behavior Therapy, and Cognitive Behavior Therapy" (on bulimia); D. Miklowitz, "Psychotherapy in Combination with Drug Treatment for Bipolar Disorder" (on bipolar disorder); I. Falloon, "Family Management in the Prevention of Morbidity of Schizophrenia" (on schizophrenia); M. Linehan et al., "Cognitive-Behavioral Treatment of Chronically Parasuicidal Borderline Patients" (on borderline personality disorder); Robert Waldinger and John Gunderson, *Effective Psychotherapy with Borderline Patients: Case Studies* (on borderline personality disorder); "Mental Health: Does Therapy Help?" (original research for an overview), and John Horgan, "Why Freud Isn't Dead" (an overview); M. Weissman and J. Markowitz, "Interpersonal Psychotherapy" (on interpersonal psychotherapy for depression); J. Persons et al., "The Role of Psychotherapy in the Treatment of Depression: Review of Two Practice Guidelines" (on depression); C. S. Gelernter et al., "Cognitive Behavioral and Pharmacological Treatments of Social Phobia" (on social phobia); and R. Ursano and E. K. Silberman, "Psychoanalysis, Psychoanalytic Psychotherapy and Supportive Psychotherapy" (an overview). Recent weaknesses of psychotherapy, along with a defense of it, can be found in a thick issue of *The Family Therapy Networker* (March–April 1995). My purpose is not to provide an exhaustive account of these studies but to indicate the tenor of their results. I have relied in part upon a recent issue of *Psychoanalytic Inquiry* (1997, suppl.) and two documents posted on the Internet: Susan Lazar, Elizabeth Hersh, and Sandra Hershberg, "The Psychotherapy Needs of Patients with Mental Disorders," and Glen Gabbard and Susan Lazar, "Efficacy and Cost-effectiveness of Psychotherapy."

4. E. Frank et al., "Efficacy of Interpersonal Psychotherapy as a Maintenance Treatment of Recurrent Depression"; see also D. Kupfer et al., "Five-Year Outcome for Maintenance Therapies in Recurrent Depression."

5. M. J. Lambert and A. E. Bergin, "The Effectiveness of Psychotherapy."

6. Some remain skeptical because of earlier, critical work. Possibly the most famous early critique is a 1952 paper by Hans Eysenck, "The Effects of Psychotherapy: An Evaluation." He argued there that the neurotic complaints that brought people into psychoanalysis would resolve after a certain length of time anyway and that there was no evidence that psychoanalytic treatment had anything to do with it. He continued his crusade through many books. Practicing psychotherapists had initially made relatively little attempt to refute his skepticism. Under the pressures of managed care reimbursement, far more studies have been done.

7. Irene Waskow and Morris Parloff, "Psychotherapy Change Measures: Introduction," p. 1.

8. "Mental Health: Does Therapy Help?," p. 734.

9. Ibid., p. 735.

10. Ibid., p. 739.

11. See, e.g., D. Spiegel et al., "Effect of Psychosocial Treatment on Survival of Patients with Metastatic Breast Cancer"; M. Linehan et al., "Cognitive-Behavioral Treatment of Chronically Parasuicidal Borderline Patients"; M. Linehan et al., "Naturalistic Follow-up of a Behavioral Treatment for Chronically Parasuicidal Borderline Patients"; J. Stevenson and R. Meares, "An Outcome Study of Psychotherapy for Patients with Borderline Personality Disorder"; Lizbeth Hoke, "Longitudinal Patterns of Behavior in Borderline Personality Disorder"; Richard Kluft, "The Post-unification Treatment of Multiple Personality Disorder: First Findings"; Richard Kluft, "The Natural History of Multiple Personality Disorder"; M. Strober, "Report Prepared for the

Use of the Mental Health Work Group, White House Task Force for National Health Care Reform"; A. Crisp et al., "Long-Term Psychotherapy Mortality in Anorexia Nervosa"; S. Blatt et al., "Impact of Perfectionism and Need for Approval on the Brief Treatment of Depression: The NIMH Treatment of Depression Collaborative Research Program"; M. Target and P. Fonagy, "Efficacy of Psychoanalysis for Children with Emotional Disorders."

12. R. Dossman et al., "The Long-Term Benefits of Intensive Psychotherapy: A View from Germany."

13. See, for example, Timothy Brock et al., "New Evidence of Flaws in the *Consumer Reports* Study of Psychotherapy"; Daniel Kriegman, "The Effectiveness of Medication: The *Consumer Reports* Study"; Jim Mintz, Robert Drake, Paul Crits-Christoph, "The Efficacy and Effectiveness of Psychotherapy: Two Paradigms, One Science"; Timothy Brock et al., "The *Consumer Reports* Study of Psychotherapy: Invalid Is Invalid"; Earl Hunt, "Errors in Seligman's 'The Effectiveness of Psychotherapy: The *Consumer Reports* Study' "; Mark Kotkin, Charles Daviet, and Joel Gurin, "The *Consumer Reports* Mental Health Survey." I am grateful to Richard Hermann for these references.

14. This is Lester Luborsky's argument. It is summarized in John Horgan, "Why Freud Isn't Dead," but was reported in L. Luborsky, "Comparative Studies of Psychotherapies."

15. For example, M. K. Shear et al., in "Cognitive Behavioral Treatment Compared with Nonprescriptive Treatment of Panic Disorder," claimed that "reflective listening" was as helpful as cognitive behavioral therapy in a controlled study of panic disorder.

16. The figure one third crops up fairly often. I have heard it presented by scientific panels at the American Psychiatric Association meetings; senior psychiatrists, for example Mardi Horowitz, confirm it (personal communication). Research presentations on drug efficacy tend to have numbers that break down in this way. Similar breakdowns in psychotherapy research can be seen in the Menninger Foundation Psychotherapy Research Project reported in Robert Wallerstein, *Forty-two Lives in Treatment: A Study of Psychoanalysis and Psychotherapy,* and "The Psychotherapy Research Project of the Menninger Foundation: An Overview"; see also H. Bachrach et al., "On the Efficacy of Psychoanalysis." Of course, there are differences among particular therapies, particular illnesses, and individuals: someone who responds well to antipsychotics may or may not respond well to supportive psychotherapy.

17. Steven Stahl, *Essential Psychopharmacology,* p. 110; see also D. Antonuccio et al., "Psychotherapy vs. Medication for Depression: Challenging the Conventional Wisdom with Data" and "Raising Questions About Antidepressants"; I. Elkin, "The NIMH Treatment of Depression Collaborative Research Program: Where We Began and Where We Are."

18. Harold Kaplan and Benjamin Sadock, *Pocket Handbook of Clinical Psychiatry,* p. 110.

19. Ibid., p. 84.

20. M. Weissman et al., "Sex Differences in Rates of Depression: Cross-National Differences."

21. G. E. Hogarty et al., "The Environmental-Personal Indicators in the Course of Schizophrenia (EPICS) Research Group: Family Psychoeducation, Social Skills Training and Maintenance Chemotherapy in the Aftercare Treatment of Schizophrenia. II: Two-Year Effects of a Controlled Study on Relapse and Adjustment."

22. G. Klerman et al., "Treatment of Depression by Drugs and Psychotherapy." This was an early study but an important one. There was no difference in outcome between the use of medication alone and medication and psychotherapy, but because it was clear

that medication and psychotherapy targeted somewhat different problems (psychotherapy addressed social functioning), it was concluded that the combination had produced the best outcome.

23. J. M. Schwartz et al., "Systematic Changes in Cerebral Glucose Metabolic Rate After Successful Behavior Modification Treatment of Obsessions and Compulsive Disorder"; L. Baxter et al., "Caudate Glucose Metabolic Rate Changes with Both Drug and Behavior Therapy for Obsessive-Compulsive Disorder."

24. E. Kandel, "Psychotherapy and the Single Synapse: The Impact of Psychiatric Thought on Neurobiologic Research."

25. H. Horgan, "Why Freud Isn't Dead," p. 106.

26. Attributed to Martin Seligman, an authority on efficacy research; see John Horgan, "Why Freud Isn't Dead," p. 110; another group of psychologists, whose meta-analysis of recent outcome research was reported in the December 1995 issue of *Professional Psychology*, concluded that "psychological interventions, particularly cognitive-behavioral, are at least as effective as medication in the treatment of depression, even if severe" (D. Antonuccio et al., "Psychotherapy vs. Medication for Depression: Challenging the Conventional Wisdom with Data," p. 109). (Most studies of psychotherapy actually seem to argue that one type is as good on average as any other but that longer treatment is better.)

27. See E. Frank et al., "Efficacy of Interpersonal Psychotherapy as a Maintenance Treatment of Recurrent Depression."

28. Recent work in the area, more specifically targeted than previous work and more focused to compare psychotherapy with outcome measures of other interventions, has been summarized in "Psychotherapy, Cost-Effectiveness and Cost Offset: A Review of the Literature," by Glen Gabbard et al. (unpublished manuscript), and less comprehensively in Gabbard et al., "The Economic Impact of Psychotherapy: A Review." They list a long series of studies on a variety of specific conditions. For example: A 1983 British study of patients with severe chronic obstructive airway disease randomly located patients in one of three kinds of therapy or to an untreated control group. At the six-month follow-up, only 31 percent of the patients in the therapeutic groups required hospitalization, while 77 percent of the no-therapy group were readmitted. The authors calculated that the use of therapy had resulted in substantial savings; see R. Rosser et al., "Breathlessness and Psychiatric Morbidity in Chronic Bronchitis and Emphysema: A Study of Psychotherapeutic Management." See also S. Lazar and G. Gabbard, "The Cost-effectiveness of Psychotherapy."

29. G. Gabbard et al., "The Economic Impact of Psychotherapy: A Review."

30. A. Zients, "A Presentation to the Mental Health Work Group, White House Task Force for National Health Care Reform."

31. N. Schooler and S. Keith, "The Role of Medication in Psychosocial Treatment"; N. Schooler and S. Keith, "The Clinical Research Base for the Treatment of Schizophrenia."

32. M. Linehan et al., "A Cognitive-Behavioral Treatment of Chronically Parasuicidal Borderline Patients"; J. Stevenson and R. Meares, "An Outcome Study of Psychotherapy for Patients with Borderline Personality Disorder."

33. C. Hellman et al., "A Study of the Effectiveness of Two Group Behavioral Medicine Interventions for Patients with Psychosomatic Complaints."

34. J. Strain et al., "Cost Offset from Psychiatric Consultation–Liaison Intervention with Elderly Hip Fracture Patients."

35. D. Spiegel et al., "Effect of Psychosocial Treatment on Survival of Patients with Metastatic Breast Cancer."

36. F. I. Fawzy et al., "Malignant Melanomas: Effects of an Early Structured Psychiatric Intervention, Coping and Affective State on Recurrence and Survival Six Years Later."

37. See Lazar and Gabbard, "The Cost-effectiveness of Psychotherapy."

38. I learned this term from Kim Hopper of the Nathan Kline Psychiatric Institute.

39. *The Question of Lay Analysis* (1950); see the discussions in Peter Gay, *Freud*, pp. 489ff., and Nathan Hale, *The Rise and Crisis of Psychoanalysis in the United States*, pp. 214ff. It was possible for a non-M.D. to get an exemption or to train for research purposes, as many social scientists did.

40. M. Sabshin, "Turning Points in Twentieth-Century Psychiatry," p. 1269.

41. The struggle between neurologists and psychiatrists over these potential patients is well told in Andrew Abbott, *The System of Professions*.

42. Elizabeth Lunbeck, *The Psychiatric Profession*; see also Abbott, *System of Professions*; Nancy Tomes, *The Art of Asylum-Keeping*.

43. Lunbeck, *Psychiatric Profession*; see also William Caudill, *The Psychiatric Hospital as a Small Society*; Alfred Stanton and Morris Schwartz, *The Mental Hospital*.

44. Laurence Friedman, *Menninger*, p. 197; also see a wonderful trilogy of novels on psychiatry and the First World War by Pat Barker: *Regeneration*, *The Eye in the Door*, and *Ghost Road*.

45. Judd Marmor, quoted in Hale, *The Rise and Crisis of Psychoanalysis in the United States*, p. 205.

46. Ibid., p. 188; also see pp. 187–210ff. Paul Starr, in *The Social Transformation of American Medicine*, cites figures of more than a million men rejected for military service based on mental illness, and 850,000 hospitalized during the war for psychoneuroses.

47. John Talbott, *The Death of the Asylum: A Critical Study of State Hospital Management*, pp. 24ff.; Sabshin, "Turning Points in Twentieth Century Psychiatry"; J. Romano, "Reminiscences: 1938 and Since."

48. See, e.g., Sherry Turkle, *Psychoanalytic Politics*, on the differences between psychoanalysis in the United States and France; see also Hale, *The Rise and Crisis of Psychoanalysis in the United States*; Lunbeck, *The Psychiatric Profession*.

49. *The Atlantic*, Special Supplement: "Psychiatry," p. 62.

50. N. Zinberg, "Psychiatry: A Professional Dilemma," p. 10.

51. *The Atlantic*, Special Supplement: "Psychiatry," p. 72.

52. This is the arena in which Adolf Grunbaum's scrutiny of psychoanalysis, *The Foundations of Psychoanalysis: A Philosophical Critique*, was based. Freud argued that an analyst's interpretations were confirmed by a patient's ultimate (if not immediate) support of them. This (bluntly summarized) is the "tally" theory. Grunbaum rightly dismisses the tally theory as grounds for the sciencelike nature of psychoanalysis on the basis of a psychoanalyst's influence over a patient. However, psychoanalysis has not been affected much by the arguments that soared in the philosphical journals. Contemporary analysts tend to treat interpretation and insight as only one piece of the process of therapeutic change, and not necessarily as the most important one.

53. Roy Schafer, *Aspects of Internalization*, p. xx.

54. Bertram Lewin, *The Psychoanalysis of Elation*, p. 54.

55. Susan Rako and Harvey Mazer, *Semrad: The Heart of a Therapist*, p. 179.

56. Ibid., p. 36.

57. Ibid., p. 105.

58. Gregory Bateson, *Steps to an Ecology of Mind*, p. 217.

59. Donald Light, *Becoming Psychiatrists*, p. 7.

60. Quoted in E. Kandel, "A New Intellectual Framework for Psychiatry," p. 459. Kandel is a famous psychiatric researcher, one of Semrad's former residents.

61. Arnold Rogow, *The Psychiatrists*, p. 10.
62. Leo Srole et al., *Mental Health in the Metropolis: The Midtown Manhattan Study*, p. 230. One of the more remarkable things about the study is that *all* the Puerto Ricans were assessed as "ill." Psychiatric anthropologists and anthropological psychiatrists interpret data like these as a powerful indication that the American diagnostic system is culturally biased.
63. American Psychiatric Association, *Careers in Psychiatry*, pp. 10, 85.
64. R. Waggoner, "The Presidential Address: Cultural Dissonance and Psychiatry," p. 42.
65. *Statistical Abstract of the United States*, Table 360.
66. Charles Kadushin, *Why People Go to Psychiatrists*, p. 4. The quotation continues, "The opinion leaders of the nation's culture . . . form at least one third of those who have been in analytic office treatment." This is quite a peculiar book. It reports a study of 1,452 applicants to ten New York City psychiatric clinics and emphasizes the culturally sophisticated network that made up more than half of the sample. The author refers to this social stratum as the "Friends and Supporters of Psychotherapy" and remarks that they are "the heroes of this book" (p. 58).
67. The address was galvanized by the Joint Commission on Mental Illness and Health, which published its report in 1961 under the direction of the director of Massachusetts Mental Hospital, Jack Ewalt. Quoted in Horace Whittington, *Psychiatry in the American Community*, p. 13.
68. The sociologist Andrew Scull argues that altruism and humanism had never driven the federal and state decisions in the community mental health movement anyway; it was the sheer enticement of saving money at the local level that made the program appealing; see Scull, *Decarceration*.
69. See Kim Hopper, "More Than Passing Strange: Homelessness and Mental Illness in New York City."
70. Thomas Scheff's book *Being Mentally Ill*, first published in 1966, was reissued in a new edition in 1984 with a stilted preface that revealed how deeply psychiatry had changed: "These are heady times for somatic theories of mental illness. I must point out that although their hypothesis is credible, it remains a hypothesis. To date, there has been no demonstrable link between neurotransmission and mental illness . . . [it] is just a theory. . . . Since the connection is still hypothetical, it is premature to discard the labeling theory of mental illness" (p. x).
71. David Rosenhan, "On Being Sane in Insane Places," p. 253.
72. Ibid.
73. R. Kendell, J. Cooper, and A. Gourley, "Diagnostic Criteria of American and British Psychiatrists"; see also S. R. Goldsmith and A. J. Mandell, "The Dynamic Formulation—A Critique of a Psychiatric Ritual"; and Donald Light, *Becoming Psychiatrists*.
74. President's Commission on Mental Health, vol. 2, p. 15. They did know that 3 percent of the American population, 6.7 million people, had been seen in the specialized mental health sector in 1975, that 1.5 million had been hospitalized, and that 12 percent of the nation's general health care expenditure was for mental health, a figure that has remained constant; see vols. 8, 9.
75. The Vice President of Blue Cross, Robert Laur, in Mitchell Wilson, "*DSM III* and the Transformation of Psychiatry: A History," p. 403.
76. Abbott, *The System of Professions*, p. 312.
77. Smith Kline and French Laboratories, *Ten Years of Experience with Thorazine*.
78. Tardive dyskinesia—involuntary muscle movement—is still a major risk of most of the antipsychotic medications, and it is not necessarily dose-related. Nevertheless, risk

increases with higher doses and longer courses. The "Thorazine shuffle," however, was a result of the high doses of medication given.

79. He had distinguished manic depression from schizophrenia out of a previously chaotic category of all forms of madness.

80. J. Feighner et al., "Diagnostic Criteria for Use in Psychiatric Research," p. 57. The information on Washington University can be found in R. W. Hudgens, "The Turning of American Psychiatry."

81. American Psychiatric Association, *DSM*, p. 24.

82. Ibid., p. 31.

83. Wilson, "*DSM III* and the Transformation of Psychiatry: A History," p. 405.

84. Ibid.

85. J. Endicott and R. Spitzer, "Use of the Research Diagnostic Criteria and the Schedule for Affective Disorders and Schizophrenia to Study Affective Disorders," p. 52.

86. Stuart Kirk and Herb Kutchins, *The Selling of DSM: The Rhetoric of Science in Psychiatry.*

87. American Psychiatric Association, "Schizophrenia, Simple Type," *DSM II,* p. 33; American Psychiatric Association, "Diagnostic Criteria for a Schizophrenia Disorder," *DSM III,* pp. 188–190.

88. G. Klerman et al., "Treatment of Depression by Drugs and Psychotherapy," p. 540.

89. Ibid., p. 544.

90. Details of the case are presented in G. Klerman et al., "The Psychiatric Patient's Right to Effective Treatment: Implications of *Osheroff vs. Chestnut Lodge.*" The case has been discussed both in the lay press and in professional journals without anonymity.

91. Klerman became a pivotal person in the field at this time in part because he was so well trained and respected by the psychoanalytic elite. Later in his life he produced a method of therapy called "interpersonal therapy," or IPT, which was intended to be a more demonstrably effective form of therapy than most eclectic psychoanalytically oriented therapies were.

92. Klerman, "The Psychiatric Patient's Right," p. 417.

93. There had, of course, been a number of studies of psychotherapy efficacy before this time—for example, Hans J. Eysenck, "The Effects of Psychotherapy: An Evaluation," and H. Strupp and S. Hadley, "Specific vs. Non-specific Factors in Psychotherapy: A Controlled Study of Outcome," in the latter of which researchers found no difference between experienced psychotherapists and college professors in handling depressed and anxious college students—but much of the more sophisticated work has been done more recently, and many people believe that there still has been no comprehensive study of intensive psychotherapy or psychoanalysis. The point, of course, is that psychoanalysts did not believe in the power of psychoanalysis because of randomized, controlled trials. They believed because they felt that it worked for them, their patients, or someone they knew.

94. A. Stone, "Law, Sciences and Psychiatric Malpractice: A Response to Klerman's Indictment of Psychoanalytic Psychiatry," p. 421.

95. Ibid., p. 424.

96. P. Kingsley, letter.

97. T. Pearlman, letter; R. Greenberg and S. Fisher, letter.

98. This is reported in S. Fisher and R. Greenberg, "Prescriptions for Happiness? (Effectiveness of Antidepressants)." The study described medication trials undertaken in 1958 to 1972. Fisher and Greenberg have more current work. See, for example, "How Sound Is the Double-blind Design for Evaluating Psychotropic Drugs?" They argue that a

meta-analysis of recent studies of new-generation antidepressants reveals that the reported efficacy of the old antidepressants falls markedly from earlier claims: "When researchers were evaluating the antidepressants in a context where they were no longer interested in proving its therapeutic power, there was a dramatic decrease in that apparent power, as compared to an earlier context when they were enthusiastically interested in demonstrating the drug's potency" (p. 37).

99. John Gedo, "A Psychoanalyst Reports at Mid-career."
100. John Horgan, "Why Freud Isn't Dead," p. 106.
101. Lewis Judd, "The Decade of the Brain in the United States."

CHAPTER SIX: THE CRISIS OF MANAGED CARE

1. Jennie. Kronenfeld, ed., *Changing Organizational Forms of Delivering Health Care*, p. xii.
2. Robert Schreter, Steven Sharfstein, and Carol Schreter, eds., *Managing Care, Not Dollars: The Continuum of Mental Health Services*, p. 1.
3. I owe some of the phrasing of this paragraph to Richard Hermann.
4. D. Kaiser, "Not by Chemicals Alone: A Hard Look at 'Psychiatric Medicine.'"
5. E. Marcus and S. Bradley, "Concurrence of Axis I and Axis II Treatment in Treatment-Resistant Hospitalized Patients."
6. Glen Gabbard, *Psychodynamic Psychiatry in Clinical Practice*, pp. 15–16.
7. Leon Eisenberg, "Mindlessness and Brainlessness in Psychiatry"; Phillip Slavney and Paul McHugh, *Psychiatric Polarities*; Gabbard, *Psychodynamic Psychiatry*.
8. Exemplary articles on the pressure that managed care can put upon doctors to judge their patients quickly but well include C. L. Caton et al., "The Impact of Discharge Planning on Chronic Schizophrenic Patients"; G. Gabbard et al., "A Psychodynamic Perspective on the Clinical Impact of Insurance Review"; S. Melnick and L. Lyter, "The Negative Impact of Increased Concurrent Review of Psychiatric Inpatient Care"; S. Scharfstein, "The Catastrophic Case"; N. Miller, "Managing McLean."
9. He was not at the meeting, although he knew the primary players. However, he expressed their sentiments neatly.
10. Wilfred Bion, *Experiences in Groups*, pp. 141–142.
11. Ibid., pp. 147–148.
12. Ibid., p. 146.
13. Alfred Stanton and Morris Schwartz, *The Mental Hospital*.

CHAPTER SEVEN: MADNESS AND MORAL RESPONSIBILITY

1. In antiquity, this was more of a problem for Christianity than for Judaism, for Christianity in particular elevates suffering as a means of growing close to God. In early Christian churches, Christ's face was sometimes modeled on that of Hippocrates (also, apparently, that of Aesculapius; see Immanuel Jakobovits, *Jewish Medical Ethics*, p. 296, n. 5). Still, Jews as well as Christians had strange small sects that refused, among other things, to subvert divine will through the use of human medicine (ibid. p. 303, ns. 5, 7; also p. 2).
2. Ibid., pp. 1ff.
3. Martin Luther, *Martin Luther: Selections from His Writings*, vol. 7, p. 113.

4. Ibid., p. 308.
5. Ibid., p. 113, Luther also says; "God does not want bodies to be killed; He wants them spared; indeed, He wants them to be nourished and fostered, in order that they might be fit for their calling and for the duties they owe their neighbor"; (ibid., vol. 2, p. 339).
6. Ibid., vol. 23, p. 203.
7. Nadine Gordimer, *Burger's Daughter.*
8. Midrash Samuel iv. 1., cited in Jakobovits, *Jewish Medical Ethics,* p. 304, n. 7.
9. Religion teaches us, as Clifford Geertz has remarked, not to avoid suffering but rather how to suffer, "how to make of physical pain, personal loss, worldly defeat, or the help-less contemplation of others' agony something bearable, supportable—something, as we say, sufferable" (Clifford Geertz, *The Interpretation of Cultures,* p. 104).
10. Mary Gordon, "George Eliot, Dorothea, and Me: Rereading (and Rereading) *Middle-march.*"
11. The actual source includes "not" before this sentence and defines which expenses will not be covered; the Supreme Court has suggested that the statute be interpreted to require all states to cover all medically necessary services for patients with Medicaid (Arthur Lazarus, ed., *Controversies in Managed Mental Health Care,* p. 161).
12. Joseph McManus, *The Fundamental Ideas of Medicine,* p. 11.
13. For instance, is it normal for a woman to have a baby, in which case infertility should be classified as an illness, an injury, or a malformed organ—or is it a privilege, like a beautiful nose? At the age of forty? At twenty-five?
14. Contrast "the stove is burning" with "the man is paying his gas bill," Elizabeth Anscombe explained in her classic account of intention, and then consider the "enor-mous apparent complexity of 'doing' in the latter case" (G.E.M. Anscombe, *Intention,* p. ix). The stove *is,* in the same way that the colon cancer is, and either it is burning or it is not. The stove has neither wants nor self-interests. The man paying his bills, how-ever, has many complicated desires, some of which are bound to be in conflict about writing checks and giving them away. Saying exactly in what way this has more "enor-mous apparent complexity" is, of course, a large question, but it catches up all the skeins of essential suffering, all the small decisions with unknown consequences that shape the way we feel, hope, and decide again.
15. As Lawrence Rosen points out in *Other Intentions,* the inference of intention is cul-turally shaped. We could, the volume reminds us, like Tibetan Sherpas, infer the pres-ence of malevolent unearthly beings from illness, accidents, and misfortunes and conduct rituals to exorcize the demons. Or, like the Kaqchikel Maya, living through army sweeps, disappearances, and threats of civil war, we could hesitate to infer inten-tion at all and wait with suspicious watchfulness for the worst to take place.
16. Charles Taylor, *Sources of the Self,* p. 15.
17. James Wilson, *The Moral Sense,* p. 32; see also Kenneth Clark, "Empathy: A Neglected Topic in Psychological Research"; Nancy Eisenberg and Janet Strayer, *Empathy and Its Development;* Virginia Demos, "Empathy and Affect: Reflections on Infant Experience."
18. See discussion by Martin Hoffman in Eisenberg and Strayer, *Empathy and Its Devel-opment,* pp. 47–80.
19. Shweder is perhaps the most important living anthropological student of morality. He sits between anthropology and psychology, enabling a fruitful interchange between the two. His work on morality is notable in part for its successful challenge of the dominant psychological paradigm of morality, Lawrence Kohlberg's developmental model. Kohlberg developed a scale he could use to score an individual's moral state

that he modeled on a Piagetian developmental scale. There were three main stages, with two substages each. In the first stage, the individual explained moral behavior as motivated by self-interest (I won't steal because if I did the policeman would punish me); in the second, as motivated by convention (I don't steal because we don't steal); and finally as motivated by abstract moral principles (I won't steal because it is wrong to steal). Carol Gilligan argued that women often score poorly on Kohlberg's test, but that this is because they reason in a different manner from men. They hear the voice of care, not of justice. They worry about who will be hurt by their decisions, not about the abstract principle involved. In short, they are often utilitarian, not Kantian. Elliot Turiel discovered that children of all ages distinguish the conventional—Kohlberg's second stage—from the moral and that their ideas about things conventional and things moral develop in parallel. Shweder pointed out that Hindus have a very clear sense of the difference between what is moral and what is conventional but are willing to say that what is moral for them might be a convention for others. It is a sin, for example, for a Brahmin to eat meat, but not for an American or a lower-caste Hindu. Shweder also discovered that to Hindus it is not obvious that the correct answer to the Heinz dilemma is to steal. (The Heinz dilemma asks what you would do if your spouse were dying and the only way to save him or her was to steal some medication.) Many of his informants stubbornly refused to countenance stealing, on the grounds that immoral behavior in this life would lead to punishment in the next—which was probably why the spouse had been unlucky in the first place. Some of this discussion, as well as an argument about the necessary and discretionary features of morality, can be found in two summary articles: Richard Shweder, M. Mahapatra, and J. Miller, "Culture and Moral Development," and Richard Shweder and Jonathan Haidt, "The Future of Moral Psychology: Truth, Intuition and the Pluralist Way."

20. "Of course," comments the anthropologist Wendy James in her wise study of a hunting people in Sudan, *The Listening Ebony,* "the Uduk have constructed what we could, in a conventional sense, identify as a 'morality,' that is, a set of publicly sanctioned principles governing personal and general social behavior." But that, she says, does not capture the way the Uduk actually live. What counts in the moral, she says, is "the store of reference points from which a people, as individuals or as a collectivity, judge their own predicament, their own condition, themselves as persons" (pp. 146–147).

21. There are contradictions in the use of such models, of course, because cultural models about the world confront the world's complexities. The philosopher Sara Ruddick, who turned to an anthropology of mothering to write what must be the first closely reasoned ethics text about play dates and changing diapers, argues that the way people solve those contradictions is what we should call their "morality." The goal of motherhood, she points out, is to protect, nurture, and to train. She asks, "If a child wants to walk to the store alone, do you worry about her safety or applaud her developing capacity to take care of herself?" (Ruddick, *Maternal Thinking,* p. 23.) The mother makes a choice based on what she thinks is right for her child and what she believes a good mother should do. Her moral decision-making process has more to do with local sensibilities about proper behavior than with abstract, universal values.

22. Unni Wikan, *Managing Turbulent Hearts,* p. 107.

23. Clyde Kluckhohn, the major influence of the group, did state a formal and uselessly broad definition in which values were concepts of the desirable that influence action: "A value is a conception, explicit or implicit, distinctive of an individual or characteristic of a group, of the desirable which influences the selection from available modes,

means and ends of action" (Evon Z. Vogt and Ethel Albert, eds., *The People of Rim-rock*, p. 6).

24. In fact, some anthropologists argue that emotions are not only imbued with moral attitudes but in some sense *are* those attitudes. "Emotional experience," writes Catherine Lutz, "is more aptly viewed as the outcome of social relations and their corollary worldviews than as universal psychobiological entities" (Lutz, *Unnatural Emotions*, p. 94.) Anthropologists as a group have more or less given up explicitly theorizing about morality in recent years. Exceptions include Richard Shweder, Catherine Lutz, Wendy James, Steve Parish, Unni Wikan, and others. They stand on the shoulders of Meyer Fortes and Kenneth Read.

25. I learned to look for this quality as a result of a discussion with Kim Hopper, a psychiatric anthropologist at the Nathan Kline Institute.

26. John Hood, "Commentary," p. 1.

27. See Kim Hopper et al., eds., *Prospects for Recovery from Schizophrenia—International Investigation.*

28. Sharon Begley, "Beyond Prozac," p. 37.

29. Harper's Index, July 1997, p. 13, from Sanofi Research, Great Valley, Pa.

30. These quotations and facts are taken from two excellent essays, Daniel Zalewski, "Fissures at an Exhibition," and Jonathan Lear "The Shrink Is In." Zalewski concludes his essay on the chaos by remarking, "Given what's happened, maybe being a museum curator is the *real* impossible profession" (p. 77).

31. Frederick Crews, "The Unknown Freud," p. 55.

32. Ibid.

33. Ibid., p. 65.

34. Ibid., p. 56.

35. Ibid.

36. Jeffrey Moussaieff Masson, *Final Analysis*, p. 85.

37. Ibid., p. 86.

38. Lear, "The Shrink Is In," p. 24.

39. Hans Loewald, *Psychoanalysis and the History of the Individual*, p. 11.

40. This was the case involving Myron Liptzin and Wendell Williamson. The latter killed two men after leaving the former's care. Williamson was awarded half a million dollars. Reported in *Psychiatric News*, cited at http://www.psych.org.

41. "Howie the Harp," in Zinman, S. "Howie the Harp," and S. Budd, eds., *Reaching Across*, p. 24.

BIBLIOGRAPHY

Abbott, Andrew. *The System of Professions*. Chicago: University of Chicago Press, 1988.

Acocella, Joan. "The Politics of Hysteria." *The New Yorker,* April 6, 1998, pp. 64–78.

Akiskal, Hagop. "Mood Disorders." In Harold Kaplan and Benjamin Sadock, eds., *Comprehensive Handbook of Psychiatry VI*. Baltimore: Williams & Wilkins, 1995, pp. 1067–1079.

———. "Mood Disorders: Clinical Features." In Harold Kaplan and Benjamin Sadock, eds., *Comprehensive Handbook of Psychiatry VI*. Baltimore: Williams & Wilkins, 1995, pp. 1123–1152.

———. "The Temperamental Foundations of Affective Disorders." In Christoph Mundt et al., eds., *Interpersonal Factors in the Origin and Course of Affective Disorders*. London: Gaskell, 1996.

Akiskal, Hagop, et al. "Borderline: An Adjective in Search of a Noun." *Journal of Clinical Psychiatry* 46: 41–48 (1985).

Akiskal, Hagop, and William McKinney. "Overview of Recent Work in Depression." *Archives of General Psychiatry* 32: 285–305 (1975).

American Psychiatric Association. *Careers in Psychiatry*. New York: Macmillan, 1968.

———. *Diagnostic and Statistical Manual of Mental Disorders*. DSM I: 1952; DSM II: 1968. DSM III: 1980. DSM IV: 1994. Washington, D.C.: American Psychiatric Press.

———. "Practice Guidelines for Eating Disorders." *American Journal of Psychiatry* 150: 212–228 (1993).

———. "Practice Guidelines for Major Depressive Disorder in Adults." *American Journal of Psychiatry* 150 (suppl.): 1a–26a (1993).

———. "Practice Guidelines for Bipolar Disorder in Adults." *American Journal of Psychiatry* 151 (suppl.): 1a–36a (1994).

Andreasen, Nancy, and Donald Black. *Introductory Textbook of Psychiatry*. Washington, D.C.: American Psychiatric Press, 1995.

Andreasen, Nancy, et al. "Thalamic Abnormalities in Schizophrenia Visualized Through Magnetic Resonance Imaging." *Science* 266: 294–298 (1994).

Anscombe, G. E. M. *Intention*. New York: Cornell University Press, 1963.

Antonuccio, David. "Psychotherapy for Depression: No Stronger Medicine." *American Psychologist* 50: 450–452 (1995).

Antonuccio, David, William Garland, and G. DeNelsky. "Psychotherapy vs. Medication

317

for Depression: Challenging the Conventional Wisdom with Data." *Professional Psychology* 26: 574–586 (1995).

Antonuccio, David, et al. "Raising Questions About Anti-depressants." *Psychotherapy and Psychosomatics* 68: 3–14 (1999).

The Atlantic. Special Supplement: "Psychiatry." 208 (1) (July 1961).

Axline, Virginia. *Dibs: in Search of Self*. New York: Ballantine, 1964.

Bachrach, H., et al. "On the Efficacy of Psychoanalysis." *Journal of the American Psychoanalytic Association* 39 (4): 871–916 (1991).

Balsam, Rosemary M., and Alan Balsam. *Becoming a Psychotherapist: A Clinical Primer*. Boston: Little, Brown, 1979.

Barker, Pat. *Regeneration*. New York: Penguin, 1991.

———. *The Eye in the Door*. New York: Penguin, 1993.

——— *The Ghost Road*. New York: Penguin, 1995.

Barlow, D. H. "Cognitive-Behavioral Therapy for Panic Disorder: Current Status." *Journal of Clinical Psychiatry*, 58 (suppl.): 32–37 (1997).

Barlow, D. H., and C. Lehman. "Advances in the Psychosocial Treatment of Anxiety Disorders." *Archives of General Psychiatry* 53: 727–735 (1996).

Basch, Michael F. *Doing Psychotherapy*. New York: Basic Books, 1980.

Bateson, Gregory. *Steps to an Ecology of Mind*. New York: Ballantine, 1972.

Baxter, L., et al. "Caudate Glucose Metabolic Rate Changes with Both Drug and Behavior Therapy for Obsessive-compulsive Disorder." *Archives of General Psychiatry* 49: 681–689 (1992).

Becker, Howard S., et al. *Boys in White*. Chicago: University of Chicago Press, 1961.

Begley, Sharon. "Beyond Prozac." *Newsweek*, February 7, 1994, pp. 37–42.

Bion, Wilfred. *Experiences in Groups*. New York: Basic Books, 1961.

Blatt, S., et al. "Impact of Perfectionism and Need for Approval on the Brief Treatment of Depression: The NIMH Treatment of Depression Collaborative Research Program Revisited." *Journal of Consulting and Clinical Psychology* 63: 125–132 (1995).

Bodkin, J. A., R. L. Klitzman, and H. G. Pope. "Distinction Between Biological Psychiatrists and Psychotherapists." Unpublished manuscript.

Bosk, Charles. *Forgive and Remember*. Chicago: University of Chicago Press, 1979.

Braff, David, Dennis Saccuzzo, and Mark Geyer. "Information Processing Dysfunction in Schizophrenia: Studies of Visual Backward Masking, Sensorimotor Gating and Habituation." In S. R. Steinhauer, J. H. Gruzelier, and J. Zubir, eds., *Handbook of Schizophrenia*, vol. 5: *Neuropsychology, Psychophysiology, and Information Processing*. New York: Elsevier Science Publishers, 1991.

Brauer, Lee David. "Basic Report About Members Who Are Graduates of Institutes. Survey of Psychoanalytic Practices." New York: American Psychoanalytic Association, 1990.

Brenner, Charles. *An Elementary Textbook of Psychoanalysis*. New York: International Universities Press, 1973 (first published 1955).

Campos, Joseph. "A Reconceptualization of the Nature of Affect." Review of Nico Frijda, *The Emotions*. *Contemporary Psychology* 34 (7): 633–635 (1989).

Campos, J., et al. "A Functionalist Perspective on the Nature of Emotion." *The Japanese Journal of Research on Emotions* 2 (1): 1–20 (1994).

Caton, C. L., et al. "The Impact of Discharge Planning on Chronic Schizophrenic Patients." *Hospital and Community Psychiatry* 35: 255–262 (1984).

Caudill, William. *The Psychiatric Hospital as a Small Society*. Cambridge, Mass.: Harvard University Press, 1958.

Bibliography

Cheever, Susan. "A Designated Crazy." Review of Susanna Kaysen, *Girl, Interrupted. New York Times Book Review,* June 20, 1993, p. 25.

Chi, M., R. Glaser, and M. Farr. *The Nature of Expertise.* Hillsdale, N.J.: Lawrence Erlbaum, 1988.

Clark, Kenneth. "Empathy: A Neglected Topic in Psychological Research." *American Psychologist* 35 (2): 187–190 (1980).

Cleckley, Hervey. *The Mask of Sanity.* St. Louis: Mosby, 1941.

Cooper, Arnold, and Robert Michels. "Review of *Diagnostic and Statistical Manual of Mental Disorders III.*"*American Journal of Psychiatry* 138 (1): 128–129 (1981).

Crews, Frederick. "The Unknown Freud." *The New York Review of Books,* November 18, 1993, pp. 55–66.

Crisp, A., et al. "Long-Term Mortality in Anorexia Nervosa." *British Journal of Psychiatry* 161: 104–107 (1992).

Crits-Christoph, P., A. Cooper, and L. Luborsky. "The Accuracy of Therapists' Interpretations and the Outcome of Dynamic Psychotherapy." *Journal of Consulting and Clinical Psychology* 56: 490–495 (1988).

D'Andrade, Roy. *The Development of Cognitive Anthropology.* Cambridge, England: Cambridge University Press, 1995.

Demos, Virginia. "Empathy and Affect: Reflections on Infant Experience." In Joseph Lichtenberg, Melvin Bornstein, and Donald Silver, eds., *Empathy.* Hillsdale, N.J.: Analytic Press, 1984.

Desjarlais, Robert, et al. *World Mental Health.* New York: Oxford University Press, 1995.

Detre, T., and M. McDonald. 1997. "Managed Care and the Future of Psychiatry." *Archives of General Psychiatry* 54: 201–204 (1997).

Devereux, George. *Basic Problems in Ethnopsychiatry.* Chicago: University of Chicago Press, 1980 (first published 1956).

Dossman, R., et al. "The Long-Term Benefits of Intensive Psychotherapy: A View from Germany." In Susan Lazar and James Bozzuto, eds., *The Journal of the American Academy of Psychoanalysis: Extended Dynamic Psychotherapy: Making the Case in an Era of Managed Care.,* 1997, pp. 74–86.

Dudley, Kathryn. *The End of the Line.* Chicago: University of Chicago Press, 1994.

Eisenberg, Leon. "Mindlessness and Brainlessness in Psychiatry." *British Journal of Psychiatry* 148: 497–508 (1986).

Eisenberg, Nancy, and Jane Strayer. *Empathy and Its Development.* Cambridge, England: Cambridge University Press, 1987.

Ekman, Paul, and Richard Davidson, eds. *The Nature of Emotion.* New York: Oxford University Press, 1994.

Ekman, Paul, and Wallace Friesen. *Unmasking the Face.* Englewood Cliffs, N.J.: Prentice Hall, 1975.

Elkin, Irene. "The NIMH Treatment of Depression Collaborative Research Program: Where We Began and Where We Are." In Allen Bergin and Sol Garfield, eds., *Handbook of Psychotherapy and Behavior Change,* 4th ed. New York: John Wiley and Sons, 1994.

Ellenberger, Henri.*The Discovery of the Unconscious.* New York: Basic Books, 1970.

Endicott, J., and R. Spitzer. "Use of the Research Diagnostic Criteria and the Schedule for Affective Disorders and Schizophrenia to Study Affective Disorders." *American Journal of Psychiatry* 136 (1): 52–56 (1979).

Engel, George. "The Clinical Application of the Biopsychosocial Model." *American Journal of Psychiatry* 137 (5): 535–544 (1980).

Bibliography

Ericsson, K. Anders, and Neil Charness. "Expert Performance." *American Psychologist* 49 (8): 725–747 (1994).

Ericsson, K. Anders, Ralf Krampe, and Clemens Tesch-Romer. "The Role of Deliberate Practice in the Acquisition of Expert Performance." *Psychological Review* 100: 363–406 (1993).

Estroff, Sue. *Making It Crazy.* Berkeley: University of California Press, 1981.

Eysenck, Hans J. "The Effects of Psychotherapy: An Evaluation." *Journal of Consulting Psychology* 16: 319–324 (1952).

Fairburn, C., et al. "Psychotherapy and Bulimia Nervosa: Longer-Term Effects of Inter-personal Psychotherapy, Behavior Therapy, and Cognitive Behavior Therapy." *Archives of General Psychiatry* 50: 419–428 (1993).

"Fallen from Grace: How Psychotherapy Can Redeem Its Tarnished Reputation." *Family Therapy Networker,* March–April 1995.

Falloon, I., et al. "Family Management in the Prevention of Morbidity of Schizophrenia." *Archives of General Psychiatry* 42: 887–896 (1985).

Fawzy, F. I., et al. "Malignant Melanoma: Effects of an Early Structured Psychiatric Intervention, Coping and Affective State on Recurrence and Survival Six Years Later." *Archives of General Psychiatry* 50: 681–689 (1993).

Feighner, J., et al. "Diagnostic Criteria for Use in Psychiatric Research." *Archives of General Psychiatry* 26 (1): 57–63 (1972).

Fisher, Seymour, and Roger P. Greenberg. "How Sound Is the Double-blind Design for Evaluating Psychotropic Drugs?" *Journal of Nervous and Mental Disease,* 181: 345–350 (1993).

———. "Prescriptions for Happiness? (Effectiveness of Antidepressants)." *Psychology Today* 28: 32–38 (1995).

Fonagy, P., and M. Target. "Predictors of Outcome in Child Psychoanalysis: A Retropec-tive Study of 763 Cases at the Anna Freud Centre." *Journal of the American Psychoan-alytic Association* 44: 27–77 (1996).

Foucault, Michel. *Madness and Civilization.* New York: Vintage, 1965.

Fox, Renee. *Essays in Medical Sociology.* New Brunswick, N.J.: Transaction Books, 1988.

———. *Experiment Perilous,* Philadelphia: University of Pennsylvania Press, 1959.

Frank, Ellen, et al. "Three-Year Outcomes for Maintenance Therapies in Recurrent Depression." *Archives of General Psychiatry* 47: 1093–1099 (1990).

———. "Efficacy of Interpersonal Psychotherapy as a Maintenance Treatment of Recur-rent Depression." *Archives of General Psychiatry* 48: 1053–1059 (1991).

Frank, Jerome. *Psychotherapy and the Human Predicament.* New York: Schocken, 1978.

Freud, Sigmund. *The Question of Lay Analysis.* New York: Norton, 1950.

———. *Therapy and Technique.* New York: Macmillan, 1963.

———. *Dora: An Analysis of a Case of Hysteria.* New York: Collier, 1963.

Friedman, Laurence. *Menninger.* New York: Knopf, 1990.

Frijda, Nico. *The Emotions.* Cambridge, England: Cambridge University Press, 1986.

Gabbard, Glen. *Psychodynamic Psychiatry in Clinical Practice.* Washington, D.C.: Ameri-can Psychiatric Press, 1990.

Gabbard, Glen, et al. "A Psychodynamic Perspective on the Clinical Impact of Insurance Review." *American Journal of Psychiatry* 148: 318–323 (1991).

———. 1997. "The Economic Impact of Psychotherapy: A Review." *American Journal of Psychiatry* 154: 147–155 (1997).

———. "Psychotherapy, Cost-Effectivenss and Cost Offset: A Review of the Literature." Unpublished manuscript.

Bibliography

Gallagher, Winifred, I.D. New York: Random House, 1996.

Gardner, Howard. Frames of Mind. New York: Basic Books, 1983.

———. The Mind's New Science: A History of the Cognitive Revolution. New York: Basic Books, 1987.

Gay, Peter. Freud. New York: Doubleday Anchor, 1988.

Gedo, John. "A Psychoanalyst Reports at Mid-career." American Journal of Psychiatry 136: 646–649 (1979).

Geertz, Clifford. The Interpretation of Cultures. New York: Basic Books, 1973.

Gelernter, C. S., et al. "Cognitive-Behavioral and Pharmacological Treatments of Social Phobia." Archives of General Psychiatry 48: 938–945 (1991).

Gellman [Gollub], R. L., and G. K. Aghajanian. "Serotonin 2 Receptor–Mediated Excitation of Interneurons in Piriform Cortex: Antagonism by Atypical Antipsychotic Drugs." Neuroscience 58: 515–525 (1994).

Goffman, Erving. Asylums. New York: Doubleday, 1961.

Goldsmith, S. R., and A. J. Mandell. 1969. "The Dynamic Formulation—A Critique of a Psychiatric Ritual." American Journal of Psychiatry. 125(12):123–130.

Goleman, Daniel. "Provoking a Patient's Worst Fears to Determine the Brain's Role." New York Times, June 13, 1995.

Gollub, Randy, and Scott Rauch. "Neuroimaging: Issues of Design, Resolution and Interpretation." Harvard Review of Psychiatry 3: 285–289 (1996).

Good, Byron. Medicine, Rationality and Experience. Cambridge, England: Cambridge University Press, 1994.

Good, Mary-Jo Delvecchio. American Medicine: The Quest for Competence. Berkeley: University of California Press, 1995.

Gordimer, Nadine. Burger's Daughter. New York: Viking, 1979.

Gordon, Mary. "George Eliot, Dorothea, and Me: Rereading (and Rereading) Middlemarch." New York Times, May 8, 1994.

Gottesman, Irving. Schizophrenia Genesis: The Origins of Madness. New York: Freeman, 1991.

Greenberg, Joanne. I Never Promised You a Rose Garden. New York: Holt, Rinehart and Winston, 1964.

Greenberg, Roger, and Seymour Fisher. Letter. American Journal of Psychiatry 148 (1): 141 (1991).

Greenson, Ralph. The Technique and Practice of Psychoanalysis. New York: International Universities Press, 1967.

Grob, Gerald. Mental Institutions in America. New York: Free Press, 1973.

———. "Origins of DSM-I: A study in Appearance and Reality." American Journal of Psychiatry 148: 421–431 (1991).

Grunbaum, Adolf. The Foundation of Psychoanalysis: A Philosophical Critique. Berkeley: University of California Press, 1984.

Gunderson, John, et al. "Effects of Psychotherapy in Schizophrenia. II: Comparative Outcome of Two Forms of Treatment." Schizophrenia Bulletin 10 (4): 564–598 (1984).

Gusterson, Hugh. Nuclear Rites. Berkeley: University of California Press, 1996.

Hafferty, Frederic. Into the Valley: Death and the Socialization of Medical Students. New Haven: Yale University Press, 1991.

Hale, Nathan. The Rise and Crisis of Psychoanalysis in the United States. New York: Oxford University Press, 1995.

Hatfield, Elaine, John Cacioppo, and Richard Rapson. Emotional Contagion. Cambridge, England: Cambridge University Press, 1994.

Bibliography

Hellman, C., et al. "A Study of the Effectiveness of Two Group Behavioral Medicine Interventions for Patients with Psychosomatic Complaints." *Behavioral Medicine* 16: 165–173 (1990).

Hesse, Hermann. *The Glass Bead Game (Magister Ludi).* New York: Henry Holt, 1969 (first published 1949).

Hogarty, G. E., et al. "Family Psychoeducation, Social Skills Training and Maintenance Chemotherapy in the Aftercare Treatment of Schizophrenia. II: Two-Year Effects of a Controlled Study on Relapse and Adjustment." *Archives of General Psychiatry* 48: 340–347 (1991).

Hoke, Lizbeth. "Longitudinal Patterns of Behavior in Borderline Personality Disorder." Ph.D. dissertation, Boston University, 1989.

Holzman, Philip, et al. "A Single Dominant Gene Can Account for Eye Tracking Dysfunctions and Schizophrenia in Offspring of Discordant Twins." *Archives of General Psychiatry* 45: 641–647 (1988).

Hood, John. "Commentary." *Corner Clubhouse Newsletter,* Winter 1996–97, p. 1.

Hopper, Kim, "More Than Passing Strange: Homelessness and Mental Illness in New York City." *American Ethnologist* 15 (1): 158–167 (1988).

Hopper, Kim, et al., eds. *Prospects for Recovery from Schizophrenia—An International Investigation: Report from the WHO—Collaborative Project, the International Study of Schizophrenia.* Westport: Psychosocial Press, in press.

Horgan, John. "Why Freud Isn't Dead." *Scientific American,* December 1996, pp. 106–111.

Hudgens, R. W. "The Turning of American Psychiatry." *Missouri Medicine,* June 1996, pp. 283–291.

Hyman, Steven, and Eric Nestler. *The Molecular Foundations of Psychiatry.* Washington, D.C.: American Psychiatric Press, 1993.

Jakobovits, Immanuel. *Jewish Medical Ethics.* New York: Bloch, 1975 (first published 1959).

James, Wendy. *The Listening Ebony.* Oxford: Clarendon, 1988.

Jamison, Kay Redfield. *Touched with Fire.* New York: Free Press, 1993.

———. *An Unquiet Mind.* New York: Knopf, 1995.

Jones, Thom. *Cold Snap.* Boston: Little, Brown, 1995.

Judd, Lewis. "The Decade of the Brain in the United States." Unpublished manuscript.

———. "The Decade of the Brain: Prospects and Challenges for NIMH." *Neuropsychopharmacology* 3: 309–310 (1990).

Kadushin, Charles. *Why People Go to Psychiatrists.* New York: Atherton, 1969.

Kaiser, D. "Not by Chemicals Alone: A Hard Look at 'Psychiatric Medicine.' " *Psychiatric Times,* December 1996, pp. 42–44.

Kandel, Eric. "Psychotherapy and the Single Synapse: The Impact of Psychiatric Thought on Neurobiologic Research." *New England Journal of Medicine* 301: 1028–1037 (1979).

———. "A New Intellectual Framework for Psychiatry." *American Journal of Psychiatry* 155: 457–469 (1993).

Kaplan, Harold, and Benjamin Sadock. *Pocket Handbook of Clinical Psychiatry.* Baltimore: Williams & Wilkins, 1996.

Kaysen, Susanna. *Girl, Interrupted.* New York: Random House, 1993.

Kendell, R., J. Cooper, and A. Gourley. "Diagnostic Criteria of American and British Psychiatrists." *Archives of General Psychiatry* 125 (12): 1738–1743 (1971).

Kingsley, P. Letter. *American Journal of Psychiatry* 148 (1): 139 (1991).

Kirk, Stuart, and Herb Kutchins. *The Selling of DSM: The Rhetoric of Science in Psychiatry.* New York: A. de Gruyter, 1992.

Kleinman, A. *Social Origins of Distress and Disease: Depression, Neurasthenia, and Pain in Modern China*. New Haven, Yale University Press, 1986.

————. *Rethinking Psychiatry*. New York: Free Press, 1988.

————. *Writing at the Margin*. Berkeley: University of California Press, 1995.

Kleinman, A., L. Eisenberg, and B. Good. "Culture, Illness and Care: Clinical Lessons from Anthropologic and Cross-Cultural Research." *Annals of Internal Medicine* 88 (2): 251–258 (1978).

Klerman, G. "The Psychiatric Patient's Right to Effective Treatment: Implications of *Osheroff vs. Chestnut Lodge*." *American Journal of Psychiatry*, 147 (4): 409–418 (1990).

Klerman, G., et al. "Treatment of Depression by Drugs and Psychotherapy." *American Journal of Psychiatry* 131: 186–191 (1974).

————, "A Debate on *DSM-III*." *American Journal of Psychiatry* 141 539–553 (1984).

Kluft, Richard P. "The Natural History of Multiple Personality Disorder." In Richard P. Kluft, ed., *Childhood Antecedents of Multiple Personality*. Washington, D. C.: American Psychiatric Press, 1985, pp. 197–238.

————. "The Post-unification Treatment of Multiple Personality Disorder: First Findings." *American Journal of Psychotherapy* 42: 212–228 (1988).

Kohut, H. "Introspection, Empathy and Psychoanalysis." *Journal of the American Psychoanalytic Association*, 7: 459–483 (1959).

————. *The Analysis of the Self*. New York: International Universities Press, 1971.

Kramer, Peter. *Listening to Prozac*. New York: Viking, 1993.

Kripke, Saul. *Naming and Necessity*. Cambridge, England: Cambridge University Press, 1980.

Kronenfeld, Jennie, et al. "Changing Health Practices: The Experience from a Worksite Health Promotion Project." *Social Science and Medicine* 26: 515–523 (1988).

Kronenfeld, Jennie, ed. *Changing Organizational Forms of Delivering Health Care: The Impact of Managed Care and Other Changes on Patients and Providers*. Greenwich, Conn.: JAI Press, 1998.

Kupfer, D., et al. "Five-Year Outcome for Maintenance Therapies in Recurrent Depression." *Archives of General Psychiatry* 49: 769–773 (1992).

Laing, R. D. *The Divided Self*. London: Tavistock, 1960.

Lakoff, George. *Women, Fire and Dangerous Things*. Chicago: University of Chicago Press, 1987.

Lambert, M. J., and A. E. Bergin. "The Effectiveness of Psychotherapy." In Allen E. Bergin and Sol Garfield, eds., *Handbook of Psychotherapy and Behavior Change*, 4th ed. New York: John Wiley and Sons, 1994, pp. 141–150.

Lazar, Susan, ed. *Supplement: Extended Dynamic Psychotherapy: Making the Case in an Era of Managed Care*. *Psychoanalytic Inquiry*. New York: Analytic, 1997.

Lazar, Susan, and Glen Gabbard. "The Cost-effectiveness of Psychotherapy." *Journal of Psychotherapy Practice and Research* 6 (4): 307–314 (1997).

Lazarus, Arthur, ed. *Controversies in Managed Mental Health Care*. Washington, D.C.: American Psychiatric Press, 1996.

Lazarus, Richard. *Emotion and Adaptation*. New York: Oxford University Press, 1991.

Lear, Jonathan. *Love and Its Place in Nature*. New York: Farrar, Straus and Giroux, 1990.

————. "The Shrink Is In." *The New Republic*, December 25, 1995, pp. 18–25.

Levy, Stephen. "Empathy and Psychoanalytic Technique." *Journal of the American Psychoanalytic Association* 33: 353–378 (1985).

Lewin, Bertram D. *The Psychoanalysis of Elation*. New York: Psychoanalytic Quarterly Press, 1961.

Light, Donald. *Becoming Psychiatrists*. New York: Norton, 1980.

Bibliography

Lindner, Robert. *The Fifty Minute Hour.* New York: Dell, 1954.

Linehan, M., et al. "Cognitive-Behavioral Treatment of Chronically Parasuicidal Border-line Patients." *Archives of General Psychiatry* 48: 1060–1064 (1991).

Linehan M., H. Heard, and H. Armstrong. "Naturalistic Follow-up of a Behavioral Treatment for Chronically Parasuicidal Borderline Patients." *Archives of General Psychiatry* 50: 971–974 (1993).

Lipsey, Mark, and David Wilson. "The Efficacy of Psychological, Educational and Behavioral Treatment Confirmation from Meta-analysis." *American Psychologist,* 48: 1181–1210 (1993).

Lock, Margaret. *Encounters with Aging: Mythologies of Menopause in Japan and North America.* Berkeley: University of California Press, 1993.

Loewald, Hans. *Psychoanalysis and the History of the Individual.* New Haven: Yale University Press, 1978.

———. *Papers on Psychoanalysis.* New Haven: Yale University Press, 1980.

Luborsky, L., et al. "Do Therapists Vary Much in Their Success? Findings from Four Outcome Studies." *American Journal of Orthopsychiatry* 56: 501–512 (1986).

Luborsky, L., B. Singer, and L. Luborsky. "Comparative Studies of Psychotherapies." *Archives of General Psychiatry* 32: 995–1008 (1975)

Lunbeck, Elizabeth. *The Psychiatric Profession.* Princeton, N.J.: Princeton University Press, 1994.

Luther, Martin. *Martin Luther: Selections from His Writings,* John Dillenberger, ed., Garden City, N.Y.: Doubleday, 1961.

Lutz, Catherine. *Unnatural Emotions.* Chicago: University of Chicago Press, 1988.

Malcolm, Janet. *Psychoanalysis: The Impossible Profession.* New York: Knopf, 1981.

———. *In the Freud Archives.* New York: Knopf, 1984.

———. *The Purloined Clinic.* New York: Knopf, 1992.

Marcus, E., and S. Bradley. "Concurrence of Axis I and Axis II Illness in Treatment-Resistant Hospitalized Patients." *Psychiatric Clinics of North America* 10: 177–184 (1987).

Markus, Hazel, and Shinobu Kitayama. "A Collective Fear of the Collective: Implications of Selves and Theories of Selves." *Personality and Social Psychology Bulletin* 20 (5): 568–579 (1994).

Masson, Jeffrey Moussaieff. *Final Analysis.* Reading, Mass.: Addison-Wesley, 1990.

McManus, Joseph. *The Fundamental Ideas of Medicine.* Springfield, Ill.: Charles C. Thomas, 1963.

Melnick, S., and L. Lyter. "The Negative Impact of Increased Concurrent Review of Psychiatric Inpatient Care." *Hospital and Community Psychiatry* 38: 300–303 (1997).

"Mental Health: Does Therapy Help?" *Consumer Reports,* November 1995, pp. 734–739.

Michels, R., and P. M. Marzuk. "Progress in Psychiatry," part I. *New England Journal of Medicine* 329 (8): 552–560; part II, 329 (9): 628–638 (1993).

Miklowitz, D. "Psychotherapy in Combination with Drug Treatment for Bipolar Disorder." *Journal of Clinical Psychopharmacology* 16: 56S–66S (1996).

Miller, Alice. *The Drama of the Gifted Child.* New York: Basic Books, 1981.

Miller, N. "Managing McLean." *The Boston Globe Magazine,* September 10, 1995.

Millett, Kate. *The Loony-Bin Trip.* New York: Simon and Schuster, 1990.

Neisser, Ulric, ed. *Concepts and Conceptual Development.* Cambridge, England: Cambridge University Press, 1987.

Pearlman, T. Letter. *American Journal of Psychiatry* 148 (1): 139 (1991).

Bibliography

Persons, L., M. Thase, and P. Crits-Christoph. "The Role of Psychotherapy in the Treatment of Depression: Review of Two Practice Guidelines." *Archives of General Psychiatry* 53: 283–290 (1996).

Plutchik, Robert. *Emotion: A Psychoevolutionary Synthesis.* New York: Harper and Row, 1980.

President's Commission on Mental Health, *Report to the President from the President's Commission on Mental Health,* vols. I–IV. Washington, D.C.: U.S. Government Printing Office, 1978.

Putnam, Hilary. *Reason, Truth and History.* Cambridge, England: Cambridge University Press, 1981.

Rabinow, Paul. *Making PCR: A Story of Biotechnology* Chicago: University of Chicago Press, 1996.

Radcliffe-Brown, Alfred Reginald. *Structure and Function in Primitive Society.* London: Cohen and West, 1952.

Rako, Susan, and Harvey Mazer. *Semrad: The Heart of a Therapist.* New York: Jason Aronson, 1980.

Rauch, Scott. "Advances in Neuroimaging: How Might They Influence Our Diagnostic Classification Scheme?" *Harvard Review of Psychiatry* 4: 159–162 (1996).

Rauch, Scott, et al. "A Positron Emission Tomographic Study of Simple Phobic Symptom Provocation." *Archives of General Psychiatry* 52: 20–28 (1995).

Read, Kenneth. *The High Valley.* New York: Scribner's, 1965.

Rhodes, Lorna. *Emptying Beds.* Berkeley: University of California Press, 1991.

Rieff, Philip. *Freud: The Mind of the Moralist.* New York: Viking Press, 1959.

Rogow, Arnold. *The Psychiatrists.* New York: Putnam, 1990.

Romano, J. "Reminiscences: 1938 and Since." *American Journal of Psychiatry* 147: 785–792 (1990).

Rosch, Eleanor. "Natural Categories." *Cognitive Psychology* 4: 328–50 (1973).

———. "Principles of Categorization." In Eleanor Rosch and Barbara Lloyd, eds., *Cognition and Categorization.* Hillsdale, N.J.: Lawrence Erlbaum Associates, 1978, pp. 27–48.

Rosen, Lawrence, ed. *Other Intentions.* Santa Fe, N.M.: School of American Research, 1995.

Rosenhan, David. "On Being Sane in Insane Places." *Science* 179: 250–258 (1973).

Rosser, R., et al. "Breathlessness and Psychiatric Morbidity in Chronic Bronchitis and Emphysema: A Study of Psychotherapeutic Management." *Psychological Medicine* 13: 93–110 (1983).

Rubin, Theodore. *Jordi: Lisa and David.* New York: Ballantine, 1962.

Ruddick, Sara. *Maternal Thinking.* Boston: Beacon Press, 1989.

Sabshin, M. "Turning Points in Twentieth-Century Psychiatry." *American Journal of Psychiatry* 149: 1267–1274 (1990).

Sargant, William. "Psychiatric Treatment Here and in England." *Atlantic Monthly* 214 (1): 88–95 (1964).

Schafer, Roy. *The Analytic Attitude.* New York: Basic Books, 1983.

———. *Aspects of Internalization.* Madison, Conn.: International Universities Press, 1990 (first published 1968).

———. *Retelling a Life.* New York: Basic Books, 1992.

Scharfstein, S. "The Catastrophic Case." *General Hospital Psychiatry* 11: 268–270 (1989).

Scheff, Thomas. *Being Mentally Ill,* 2nd ed. New York: Aldine, 1984.

Schooler, N., and S. Keith. "The Role of Medication in Psychosocial Treatment." In Marvin Herz, Samuel Keith, and John Docherty, eds., *Handbook of Schizophrenia:*

Psychosocial Treatment of Schizophrenia, vol. 4. New York: Elsevier Science Foundation, 1990, pp. 45–67.

———. "The Clinical Research Base for the Treatmen of Schizophrenia." *Psychopharmacology Bulletin* 29: 431–446 (1993).

Schreter, Robert, Steven Sharfstein, and Carol Schreter, eds. *Managing Care, Not Dollars: The Continuum of Mental Health Services.* Washington, D.C.: American Psychiatric Press, 1997.

Schwartz, J. M., et al. "Systematic Changes in Cerebral Glucose Metabolic Rate After Successful Behavior Modification Treatment of Obsessive-Compulsive Disorder." *Archives of General Psychiatry* 53: 109–113 (1996).

Scull, Andrew. *Decarceration.* Englewood Cliffs, N.J.: Prentice Hall, 1977.

Sechehaye, Marguerite. *The Autobiography of a Schizophrenic Girl.* New York: Grune and Stratton, 1951.

Shaffer, Peter. *Equus and Shrivings.* New York: Avon, 1975.

Shapin, Steven. *A Social History of Truth.* Chicago: University of Chicago Press, 1994.

Shapiro, David. *Neurotic Styles.* New York: Basic Books, 1965.

Shear, M. K., et al. "Cognitive Behaviorial Treatment Compared with Nonprescriptive Treatment of Panic Disorder." *Archives of General Psychiatry* 51: 395–401 (1994).

Sheehan, Susan. *Is There No Place on Earth for Me?* New York: Vintage, 1982.

Shem, Samuel. *The House of God.* New York: Dell, 1978.

———. *Fine.* New York: St. Martin's Press, 1985.

Shweder, Richard, and Jonathan Haidt. "The Future of Moral Psychology: Truth, Intuition and the Pluralist Way." *Psychological Science* 4(6): 360–365 (1993).

Shweder, R., M. Mahapatra, and J. Miller. "Culture and Moral Development." In Jerome Kagan and Sharon Lamb, eds. *The Emergence of Morality in Young Children.* Chicago: University of Chicago Press, 1987, pp. 1–79.

Simon, Herbert, and William Case. "Skill in Chess." *American Scientist* 61: 394–403 (1973).

Slavney, Phillip R., and Paul R. McHugh. *Psychiatric Polarities.* Baltimore: Johns Hopkins University Press, 1987.

Smith Kline and French Laboratories. *Ten Years of Experience with Thorazine 1954–1964.* Philadelphia: Smith, Kline and French Laboratories, 1964.

Spanier, C., et al. "The Prophylaxis of Depressive Episodes in Recurrent Depression Following Discontinuation of Drug Therapy: Integrating Psychological and Biological Factors." *Psychological Medicine* 26: 461–475 (1996).

Spiegel, D., et al. "Effect of Psychosocial Treatment on Survival of Patients with Metastatic Breast Cancer." *Lancet* 2: 888-891 (1989).

Srole, Leo, et al. *Mental Health in the Metropolis: The Midtown Manhattan Study.* New York: McGraw-Hill, 1962.

Stahl, Stephen. *Essential Psychopharmacology.* Cambridge, England: Cambridge University Press, 1996.

Stanton, Alfred, and Morris Schwartz. *The Mental Hospital.* New York: Basic Books, 1954.

Stanton, A., et al. "Effects of Psychotherapy in Schizophrenia. I: Design and Implementation of a Controlled Study." *Schizophrenia Bulletin* 10 (4): 520–563 (1984).

Starr, P. *The Social Transformation of American Medicine.* New York: Basic Books, 1982.

Statistical Abstract of the United States. Washington, D.C.: United States Dept. of Commerce, 1971.

Stevenson, J., and R. Meares. "An Outcome Study of Psychotherapy for Patients with Borderline Personality Disorder." *American Journal of Psychiatry* 149: 358–362 (1992).

Stone, A. "The New Paradox of Psychiatric Malpractice." *New England Journal of Medicine* 311: 1384–1387 (1984).

———. "Law, Sciences and Psychiatric Malpractice: A Response to Klerman's Indictment of Psychoanalytic Psychiatry." *American Journal of Psychiatry* 147: 419–427 (1990).

Storr, Anthony. *The Art of Psychotherapy.* New York: Methuen, 1980.

Strain, J., et al. "Cost Offset from Psychiatric Consultation-Liaison Intervention with Elderly Hip Fracture Patients." *American Journal of Psychiatry* 148: 1044–1049 (1991).

Strober, M. "Report Prepared for the Use of the Mental Health Working Group, White House Task Force for National Health Care Reform." 1993.

Strupp, H., and S. Hadley. "Specific vs. Nonspecific Factors in Psychotherapy: A Controlled Study of Outcome." *Archives of General Psychiatry* 36: 1125–1136 (1979).

Styron, William. *Darkness Visible.* New York: Vintage, 1990.

Sussman, Michael. *A Curious Calling: Unconscious Motivations for Practicing Psychotherapy.* Northvale, N.J.: Jason Aronson, 1992.

Szasz, Thomas. *The Myth of Mental Illness.* New York: Hoeber-Harper, 1961.

Talbott, John. *The Death of the Asylum: A Critical Study of State Hospital Management, Services and Care.* New York: Grune and Stratton, 1978.

Target, M., and P. Fonagy. "Efficacy of Psychoanalysis for Children with Emotional Disorders." *Journal of the American Academy of Child and Adolescent Psychiatry* 33: 361–371 (1994).

Taylor, Charles. *Sources of the Self.* Cambridge, Mass.: Harvard University Press, 1989.

Tomes, N. *The Art of Asylum-Keeping.* Philadelphia: University of Pennsylvania Press, 1994 (first published 1984).

Tompkins, Silvan. *Exploring Affect,* V. Demos, ed. Cambridge, England: Cambridge University Press, 1995.

Torrey, E. Fuller. *The Death of Psychiatry.* Radnor, Pa.: Chilton, 1974.

Traweek, Sharon. *Beamtimes and Lifetimes: The World of High Energy Physics.* Cambridge, Mass.: Harvard University Press, 1988.

Trilling, Lionel. *Sincerity and Authenticity.* Cambridge, Mass: Harvard University Press, 1972.

Turkle, Sherry. *Psychoanalytic Politics.* New York: Basic Books, 1978.

———. *Life on the Screen.* New York: Simon and Schuster, 1995.

Ursano, R., and E. K. Silberman. "Psychoanalysis, Psychoanalytic Psychotherapy and Supportive Psychotherapy." In Robert Hales, Stuart Yudofsky, and John Talbott, eds., *The American Psychiatric Press Textbook of Psychiatry,* 2nd ed. Washington, D.C.: American Psychiatric Press, 1994.

Vogt, Evon Z., and Ethel Albert, eds. *The People of Rimrock.* Cambridge, Mass.: Harvard University Press, 1966.

Waggoner, R. "The Presidential Address: Cultural Dissonance and Psychiatry." *American Journal of Psychiatry* 127: 41–48, 1970.

Waldinger, Robert C., and John G. Gunderson. *Effective Psychotherapy with Borderline Patients: Case Studies.* New York: Macmillan, 1987.

Wallerstein, Robert. *Forty-two Lives in Treatment: A Study of Psychoanalysis and Psychotherapy.* New York: Guilford, 1986.

———. "The Psychotherapy Research Project of the Menninger Foundation: An Overview." *Journal of Consulting and Clinical Psychology* 57: 195–205 (1989).

Warner, Richard. *Recovery from Schizophrenia: Psychiatry and Political Economy.* New York: Routledge and Kegan Paul, 1985.

Bibliography

Waskow, Irene E., and Morris B. Parloff, eds. "Psychotherapy Change Measures: Intro-
    duction." Outcome Measures Project, Clinical Research Branch. Rockville, Md.:
    National Institute of Mental Health, 1995.

Weissman, M., et al. "Sex Differences in Rates of Depression: Cross-National Differ-
    ences." *Journal of Affective Disorders* 29: 77–84 (1993).

Weissman, M., and J. Markowitz. "Interpersonal Psychotherapy." *Archives of General
    Psychiatry* 51: 599–606 (1994).

Whittington, Horace. *Psychiatry in the American Community.* New York: International
    Universities Press, 1966.

Wikan, Unni. *Managing Turbulent Hearts.* Chicago: University of Chicago Press, 1990.

Wilson, J. Q. *The Moral Sense.* New York: Free Press, 1993.

Wilson, Mitchell. *"DSM III* and the Transformation of Psychiatry: A History." *American
    Journal of Psychiatry* 150: 399–410 (1993).

Wright, Robert. "The Evolution of Despair." *Time,* August 28, 1995, pp. 50–57.

Yalom, Irvin. *Love's Executioner.* New York: Basic Books, 1989.

Young, Allan. *The Harmony of Illusions.* Princeton, N.J.: Princeton University Press, 1995.

Zalewski, D. "Fissures at an Exhibition." *Lingua Franca,* November–December, 1995, pp.
    74–77.

Zients, A. "A Presentation to the Mental Health Working Group, White House Task
    Force for National Health Care Reform," April 23, 1993.

Zinberg, N. "Psychiatry: A Professional Dilemma." *Daedalus,* 1963, pp. 808–823.

Zinman, S., "Howie the Harp," and S. Budd, eds. *Reaching Across.* Sacramento: Califor-
    nia Network of Mental Health Clients, 1987.

⊰⧉⊱

ACKNOWLEDGMENTS

Many people have contributed to this book along the long road of its creation. It gives me great pleasure to thank Hagop Akiskal, Daniel Bell (who came up with the title), Shelley Burtt, Lincoln Caplan, Jennifer Cole, Jonathan Cole, Michael Cole, Roy D'Andrade, Steven Frisch, Howard Gardner, Randy Gollub, Alice Graham-Brown, Leslie Greis, John Gunderson, Hugh Gusterson, Leston Havens, Richard Hermann, Anne Hoger, John M. Hood III, Kim Hopper, Mardi Horowitz, Carol Janeway (a wonderful editor), Jean Jackson, Kay Jamison, Lewis Judd, Arthur Kleinman, Jill Kneerim (a great agent), Jonathan Kolb, Donald Kripke, George and Winifred Luhrmann, Matthew McCubbins, Kathleen Much, Robert Nemiroff, Joel Robbins, Lisa Robinson, Simon Schama, Edward Shapiro, Bennett Simon, Neil Smelser, Melford Spiro, Carola Suarez-Orozco, Robert Tyson, Vernon, Ellen Winner, Sidney Zisook, and the psychiatrists and patients I have not named but who generously allowed me to spend time with them.

$$❀$$

INDEX

A NOTE ABOUT THE AUTHOR

Tanya Luhrmann is Professor of Anthropology at the University of California, San Diego. She is the author of two previous books, *Persuasions of the Witch's Craft* and *The Good Parsi*. She lives in Solana Beach, California.

A NOTE ON THE TYPE

This book was set in Fairfield, the first typeface from the hand of the distinguished American artist and engraver Rudolph Ruzicka (1883–1978). In its structure Fairfield displays the sober and sane qualities of the master craftsman whose talent has long been dedicated to clarity. It is this trait that accounts for the trim grace and vigor, the spirited design and sensitive balance, of this original typeface.

Rudolph Ruzicka was born in Bohemia and came to America in 1894. He set up his own shop, devoted to wood engraving and printing, in New York in 1913 after a varied career working as a wood engraver, in photoengraving and banknote printing plants, and as an art director and freelance artist. He designed and illustrated many books, and was the creator of a considerable list of individual prints: wood engravings, line engravings on copper, and aquatints.

COMPOSED BY DIX, SYRACUSE, NEW YORK
PRINTED AND BOUND BY R.R.DONNELLEY AND SONS,
HARRISONBURG, VIRGINIA
DESIGNED BY ROBERT C. OLSSON